Critical Heritage Studies and the Futures of Europe

Edited by
Rodney Harrison, Nélia Dias
and Kristian Kristiansen

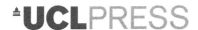

First published in 2023 by
UCL Press
University College London
Gower Street
London WC1E 6BT

Available to download free: www.uclpress.co.uk

Collection © Editors, 2023
Text © Contributors, 2023
Images © Contributors and copyright holders named in captions, 2023

The authors have asserted their rights under the Copyright, Designs and Patents Act 1988 to be identified as the authors of this work.

A CIP catalogue record for this book is available from The British Library.

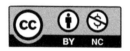

Any third-party material in this book is not covered by the book's Creative Commons licence. Details of the copyright ownership and permitted use of third-party material is given in the image (or extract) credit lines. If you would like to reuse any third-party material not covered by the book's Creative Commons licence, you will need to obtain permission directly from the copyright owner.

This book is published under a Creative Commons Attribution-Non-Commercial 4.0 International licence (CC BY-NC 4.0), https://creativecommons.org/licenses/by-nc/4.0/. This licence allows you to share and adapt the work for non-commercial use providing attribution is made to the author and publisher (but not in any way that suggests that they endorse you or your use of the work) and any changes are indicated. Attribution should include the following information:

Harrison, R., Dias, N. and Kristiansen, K. (eds). 2023. *Critical Heritage Studies and the Futures of Europe*. London: UCL Press. https://doi.org/10.14324/111.9781800083936

Further details about Creative Commons licences are available at https://creativecommons.org/licenses/

ISBN: 978-1-80008-395-0 (Hbk.)
ISBN: 978-1-80008-394-3 (Pbk.)
ISBN: 978-1-80008-393-6 (PDF)
ISBN: 978-1-80008-396-7 (epub)
DOI: https://doi.org/10.14324/111.9781800083936

Contents

List of figures		ix
List of tables		xiii
Contributors		xv
Preface and acknowledgements		xix

Introduction   1

Rodney Harrison, Nélia Dias and Kristian Kristiansen

Part I: Heritage and global challenges   13

1   Rethinking museums for the climate emergency   15

Rodney Harrison and Colin Sterling

2   From climate victim to climate action: heritage as agent
in climate change mitigation discourse   33

Janna oud Ammerveld

3   Syrian refugees' food in Lisbon: a heritage of food beyond
national borders   51

Marcela Jaramillo

4   Relations with objects: a longitudinal case study   67

Katie O'Donoghue

Part II: Curating the city: rethinking urban heritages   87

5   Erosion and preservation of the cultural and geological
heritage in megacity landscapes of the Global South:
a geo-aesthetic inquiry   91

Peter Krieger

6   Recognising urban heritage written in water:
mapping fluctuating articulations in time and space   107

Moniek Driesse

7   Participatory design in the context of heritage-development:
engaging with the past in the design space of historical
landscapes   125

Mela Zuljevic

8   The (over)touristification of European historic cities:
a relation between urban heritage and short-term rental
market demand   143

Łukasz Bugalski

9   Overtourism versus pandemic: the fragility of our
historic cities   157

Maria Pia Guermandi

Part III: Digital heritages and digital futures   173

10   Datafied landscapes: exploring digital maps as
(critical) heritage   177

Stuart Dunn

11   #Womenof1916 and the heritage of the Easter Rising
on Twitter   191

Hannah K. Smyth

12   The material and immaterial historic environment   209

William Illsley

13   Digitality as a cultural policy instrument: Europeana
and the Europeanisation of digital heritage   223

Carlotta Capurro

14 De-neutralising digital heritage infrastructures? Critical considerations on digital engagements with the past in the context of Europe 243

Gertjan Plets, Julianne Nyhan, Andrew Flinn, Alexandra Ortolja-Baird and Jaap Verheul

Part IV: Postcolonial legacies: 'European' heritages beyond Europe 263

15 Heritage pharmacology and 'moving heritage': making refugees, asylum seekers and Palestine part of the European conscience 265

Beverley Butler and Fatima Al-Nammari

16 How to tell the good guys from the bad guys … or not 289

Randall H. McGuire

17 Traumatic heritage: politics of visibility and the standardisation of plaques and memorials in the city of São Paulo, Brazil 309

Márcia Lika Hattori

18 Lampedusa here and there: activating memories of migration in Amsterdam's historic centre – a resource for whom? 329

Vittoria Caradonna

Afterword 347

Barbara Kirshenblatt-Gimblett

Index 357

List of figures

1.1   *Museum of Open Windows* exhibit as part of the Reimagining Museums for Climate Action exhibition at the Glasgow Science Centre for COP26.   20

1.2   *Existances* exhibit as part of the Reimagining Museums for Climate Action exhibition at the Glasgow Science Centre for COP26.   21

1.3   *Weathering With Us* exhibit as part of the Reimagining Museums for Climate Action exhibition at the Glasgow Science Centre for COP26.   22

1.4   Speaking with visitors to the Reimagining Museums for Climate Change exhibition during COP26.   24

1.5   Collecting responses to the question 'What if museums…?' from visitors to the Reimagining Museums for Climate Action exhibition during COP26.   24

2.1   Carbon emissions are reduced by 60 per cent in the Victorian terraced house case study as a result of energy efficiency interventions and by 62 per cent in the chapel conversion case study by 2050.   44

3.1   Store with Syrian products in Lisbon.   57

3.2   Syrian food advertising in Lisbon.   61

4.1   Patient information flyer. Research information flyer for the PhD project 'Relations with Objects'.   70

4.2   Object information card. Information card of a Palaeolithic stone tool outlining age and description of the object. UCL object-handling collection.   72

4.3   Portfolio artwork. Artworks created using photography and photoshop by a participant in the PhD research project 'Relations with Objects'.   74

4.4   Gunshot through wall. Artworks of a gunshot created using photography and photoshop by a participant in the PhD research project 'Relations with Objects'.   75

| 4.5 | Leaning Tower of Pisa and BT Tower. Artworks of buildings created using photography and photoshop by a participant in the PhD research project 'Relations with Objects'. | 76 |

4.5 Leaning Tower of Pisa and BT Tower. Artworks of buildings created using photography and photoshop by a participant in the PhD research project 'Relations with Objects'. 76

4.6 'Terminating the Tumour'. Artworks of a shell created using photography and photoshop by a participant in the PhD research project 'Relations with Objects'. 78

4.7 Untitled artworks for exhibition. Artworks of construction and buildings created using photography and photoshop by a participant in the PhD research project 'Relations with Objects'. 82

5.1 Mexico City, extended slum belts in the northeastern hills, 2015. 92

5.2 Scars I (2014). 96

5.3 Tuff exploitation, Volcano Yuhualixqui, Iztapalapa, Mexico City, 2017. 100

5.4 Informal housing on the outskirts of Pachuca, Hidalgo, Mexico, 2016. 102

6.1 Overlay of the borders of Mexico City, the hard-rock zone limit on the outside of the vanished Texcoco lake-bed zone and the crowdsourced map of the destruction after the 19 September 2017 earthquake, composed by Verificado19s. 110

6.2 *Journey to Atlan* map. Appendix of *This Morning, I Caught You in a Drop on My Finger* (Driesse 2019). 118

6.3 At the Cárcamo de Dolores (Waterworks of Dolores), Tláloc, the god of heavenly waters, is watching the skies and the engineering works in admiration as well as fear. Murals by Diego Rivera. 118

6.4 This *Santa Cruz Map* is a unique map of Mexico City as the capital of New Spain, from around 1550. Also known as the *Uppsala Map*, it currently resides in the map collection of the Uppsala University Library. 121

7.1 A hayfield with the Waterschei mine slagheap in the background. 129

7.2 A set of atlas drawings and the mapping notebook. 131

7.3 Houses and trees in Waterschei. 132

7.4 The 'garden city house' and 'rows of trees': using the atlas tool to trace how these 'things' became sites of tension between visions and practices through time. 132

8.1	Ashworth's three paradigms, supplemented by overtourism and resistance concepts, and juxtaposed with the rapid growth of international arrivals worldwide (UNWTO Tourism Barometer).	146
8.2	Crowded Via Pescherie Vecchie in Bologna – one of the most touristified streets in this city. Similar images are typical of a vast number of historic cities across Europe.	148
8.3	A bar chart showing the logarithmic distribution of active Airbnb listings in Europe. The series has been truncated to 42, presenting cities that exceeded 5,000 active listings on at least one occasion. For reasons of space, the remaining cities tend to average 1,000 active listings. Order by value for Q3 2019 is marked by a line on the top of the diagram.	152
8.4	The 185 European cities (with populations above 100,000) that exceeded 1,000 active listings in the 3rd quarter of 2019. It is the apogee of the Airbnb phenomenon – a moment of economic equilibrium for many of its vanguard cities.	153
9.1	Venice: a cruise ship in the San Marco basin, 2020.	161
9.2	Florence: the courtyard of the Uffizi Museum, 2019.	163
10.1	Screengrab from OpenStreetMap.	186
11.1	Word cloud of 'women of 1916' tweets.	191
11.2	Collocations of words or hashtags stemming from 'airbrush'.	201
11.3	Collocations of words or hashtags stemming from 'forgotten'.	202
12.1	The functions of a historic environment record as a simplified network.	214
13.1	The European Commission's investments in culture between 2000 and 2020.	227
13.2	Governance of the Europeana Foundation, as presented in the 2017 Business Plan.	235
14.1	Excerpt from Sir Hans Sloane's Catalogue of Fossils including Fishes, Birds, Eggs, Quadrupeds (Volume V).	251
14.2	Results of text mining analysis of territorial signifiers used in archaeological texts in conjunction with descriptions of archaeological phenomena.	253
15.1	'Talking Objects' case, 2019.	274
15.2	'Talking Turath/Heritage' theme, 2019.	274

15.3	'Exile/Nafy – Displacement and Repossession' theme, 2019.	276
15.4	'Home/Watan – Wholeness and Fragments of Place' theme, 2019.	279
15.5	'Promise/Wa'ad – Visions of Fulfilment' theme, 2019.	282
16.1	Equestrian statue of Juan de Oñate, Alcalde, New Mexico, 2006.	294
16.2	Statue of Junípero Serra in Golden Gate Park, San Francisco, 2015.	297
16.3	Decapitated statue of Father Junípero Serra, Monterey, California, 2015.	299
17.1	Graffiti on the front wall of a known collaborator's house. Organised by the social movement Levante Popular da Juventude as part of the *'escrachos populares'*.	315
17.2	Memorials and plaques in the city of São Paulo, 1985 to 2020.	318
17.3	Monument in honour of the disappeared people from the dictatorship of 1964–1985 at the Ibirapuera Park.	321
17.4	Pedestrian routes at the cemetery.	322
17.5	The location of each plaque and monument and the results of the 2018 Brazilian presidential elections (electoral data from Tribunal Superior Eleitoral).	324

List of tables

13.1	Projects for the creation of The European Library (TEL).	229
17.1	Plaques and monuments related to memories of repression and resistance in the city of São Paulo.	315

Contributors

Fatima Al-Nammari is Assistant Professor in the College of Architecture, Petra University, Jordan. Her research addresses integrated studies of the built environment, including disasters, heritage and development. She has rich and diverse experience spanning several countries with local, international and UN organizations. Her professional work has included projects in refugee camps, urban and refugee heritage management, and disaster preparedness.

Janna oud Ammerveld completed her PhD as a CHEurope Marie Skłodowska-Curie Trainee at the UCL Institute of Archaeology in 2022. Her PhD research, titled 'What Does Climate Change?', focused on the impact of climate change's presence as a hyperobject on the work of heritage policymakers in England and Sweden.

Łukasz Bugalski is Assistant Professor at the Faculty of Architecture, Gdańsk University of Technology. He has been trained in critical heritage studies (2017–2020) as part of the 'CHEurope' project (MSCA Innovative Training Network) conducted at IBC in Bologna. His research focuses on the intersection of urban studies and tourism economy studies.

Beverley Butler is Reader in Cultural Heritage at the UCL Institute of Archaeology. She directs the MA in Cultural Heritage Studies. Her key research interests include 'Heritage Wellbeing'; Cultural Memory; Heritage Syndromes and 'efficacies' – particularly in contexts of marginalization, displacement, conflict, illness and extremis. She conducts ongoing long-term fieldwork research in the Middle East – notably, in Egypt, Palestine and Jordan.

Carlotta Capurro is a postdoctoral researcher at Utrecht University and an associated researcher at the Netherlands Institute for Art History (RKD). Her main research interest lies in the ethics and politics of digital cultural heritage and data infrastructures.

Vittoria Caradonna obtained her PhD from the University of Amsterdam in 2023. Her dissertation tracks how cultural memory is mobilised by and across a variety of heritage projects, which are attempting to reckon with the afterlives of colonialism and slavery but also with the entrenched histories of postcolonial and contemporary migrations.

Nélia Dias is Associate Professor in the Department of Anthropology, University Institute of Lisbon, ISCTE-IUL (Portugal). She works in the fields of heritage, museum studies, and the history of anthropology and of human sciences from the early nineteenth century to the present. Her research has been supported by the Fondation de la Maison des Sciences de l'Homme, Max Planck Institute for the History of Science, Center for French History and Culture, Australian Research Council and the Fundação para a Ciência e Tecnologia.

Moniek Driesse is currently a PhD candidate at the University of Gothenburg's Department of Conservation. By conceptualising the term 'imaginary agency', and mobilising design research methods, she traces agencies of water in urban environments through time and space, to reimagine relationships of care between humans and the planet they inhabit.

Stuart Dunn is Professor of Spatial Humanities at King's College London, Visiting Professor at Riga Technical University and a Visiting Fellow of the Centre for Digital Humanities at the Australian National University. He is the author of *A History of Place in the Digital Age* (Routledge, 2019), coauthor of *Academic Crowdsourcing* (Chandos, 2017) and coeditor of Routledge's *International Handbook of Research Methods in Digital Humanities* (2020).

Andrew Flinn is Reader in Archival Studies and Oral History at University College London. He teaches and researches on critical archival studies and multimodal digital oral history. He is a trustee of the UK National Life Stories and vice-chair of the UK & Ireland Community Archives and Heritage Group.

Maria Pia Guermandi is Director of the Regional Museums System at Regione Emilia Romagna. Trained as an archaeologist specialising in classical and preventive archaeology, she has been project leader of many projects funded by the European Commission in the field of cultural heritage policies. Her current research interests focus on heritagisation processes, decolonisation, and cultural tourism as conflicted heritage.

Rodney Harrison is Professor of Heritage Studies at the UCL Institute of Archaeology, University College London, UK. He is (co)author or (co)editor of 20 books and guest-edited journal volumes and around 100 peer-reviewed journal articles and book chapters. Some of these have been translated into Chinese, Italian, Japanese, Polish and Portuguese language versions. In addition to the AHRC, his research has been funded by the UKRI/Global Challenges Research Fund, British Academy, Wenner-Gren Foundation, Australian Research Council, Australian Institute of Aboriginal and Torres Strait Islander Studies and the European Commission. He has conducted archaeological, anthropological and/or archival research in Australia, Southeast Asia, North America, South America, the Middle East, the UK and continental Europe.

Márcia Lika Hattori is a Brazilian archaeologist and forensic anthropologist. She completed her PhD, on the bureaucracy and the management of disappeared persons in São Paulo, Brazil, during the last dictatorship and the democratic period, at the Spanish National Research Council (CSIC) in 2022.

William Illsley works with humanities and heritage data as a research data advisor at the Swedish National Data Service. His research interests pertain to digital epistemologies in heritage, source critique and communication in virtual heritage, and social and spatial theory in studying historic environments. He undertook his PhD research at the University of Gothenburg as part of the cohort of students funded under the CHEurope Marie Curie ITN.

Marcela Jaramillo is a consultant for international organisations on cultural heritage and conflict-related issues. She is a PhD candidate in the Department of Anthropology at ISCTE – the University Institute of Lisbon, and holds MAs in world heritage and cultural projects, and in political science and philosophy.

Barbara Kirshenblatt-Gimblett is Distinguished Professor Emerita of Performance Studies, New York University, and Ronald S. Lauder Chief Curator of the Core Exhibition at POLIN Museum of the History of Polish Jews, in Warsaw.

Peter Krieger is Research Professor at the Institute of Aesthetic Research (Instituto de Investigaciones Estéticas) and Professor of Art History and Architecture at the National Autonomous University of Mexico (UNAM).

Kristian Kristiansen is Professor of Archaeology at the University of Gothenburg, and affiliated professor at Copenhagen University. His research spans from the prehistory of western Eurasia to critical heritage. He was one of the initiators of the European Association of Archaeologists, and is now working mainly within the new interdisciplinary field of archaeogenetic research, and its implications for both prehistory and the present. He has published 25 books, as author, coauthor and editor/coeditor, six of which are from Cambridge University Press, and more than 150 peer-reviewed papers.

Randall H. McGuire is SUNY Distinguished Professor at Binghamton University in Binghamton, New York. He received his BA from the University of Texas and his PhD from the University of Arizona. He has published extensively on Marxist theory and Indigenous archaeology. He does field work in Sonora, México.

Julianne Nyhan is Professor of Humanities Data Science and Methodology at TU Darmstadt, Professor of Digital Humanities in the Department of Information Studies and Director of the UCL Centre for Digital Humanities at University College London.

Katie O'Donoghue is a Marie Curie Early Career Researcher/PhD candidate at the Elizabeth Garrett Anderson Institute for Women's Health, University College London. She has an MA in Art Psychotherapy and many years of experience working in the health sector.

Alexandra Ortolja-Baird is Lecturer in Digital History and Culture at the University of Portsmouth. Her research intersects intellectual history, cultural heritage and digital humanities.

Gertjan Plets is Associate Professor in Heritage Studies and Archaeology in the Department of History and Art History at Utrecht University in the Netherlands.

Hannah K. Smyth is Lecturer in Archives and Records Management at University College London, Department of Information Studies. Her research engages commemoration, feminist uses of the past in social media, and the politics of digitisation.

Colin Sterling is Assistant Professor of Memory and Museums at the University of Amsterdam. His research investigates heritage and museums through the lens of art and ecology. He is the author of *Heritage, Photography, and the Affective Past* (Routledge, 2020) and coeditor of *Deterritorializing the Future: Heritage in, of and after the Anthropocene* (Open Humanities Press, 2020) and *Reimagining Museums for Climate Action* (Museums for Climate Action, 2021).

Jaap Verheul is Associate Professor of Cultural History at Utrecht University. He specialises in transnational, transatlantic and American cultural history. He applies digital humanities methods to analyse concepts, cultural perceptions, identity formation, and patterns of cultural transfer in large historical data sets.

Mela Zuljevic is a design researcher with a PhD in architecture (UHasselt, Belgium). She is currently a postdoctoral researcher at the Leibniz Institute for Regional Geography (Leibniz-Institut für Länderkunde – IfL), working at the intersection of design, cartography and landscape research.

Preface and acknowledgements

This book is an outcome of the project 'CHEurope: Critical Heritage Studies and the Futures of Europe: Towards an integrated, interdisciplinary and transnational training model in cultural heritage research and management'. The project was funded by the European Union's Horizon 2020 Research and Innovation programme under the Marie Skłodowska-Curie Actions (MSCA) – Innovative Training Networks (ITN) programme (Grant Agreement Nr – 722416). 'CHEurope' was a PhD training programme in cultural heritage studies and was the result of a collaboration between key European academic and non-academic organisations in Belgium, Italy, the Netherlands, Portugal, Spain, Sweden and the United Kingdom. The project ran for almost 5 years (November 2016 to August 2021), supporting the research and training of 15 Early-Stage Researchers (ESRs)/PhD students from Europe and other parts of the world.

The project was led by Kristian Kristiansen of the University of Gothenburg (UGOT), Sweden, with the assistance of project coordinator Gian Giuseppe Simeone (UGOT/Culture Lab, Belgium), without whom the project and this volume would not have been possible. The ESRs funded by the research programme were Khaled El-Samman Ahmed (UGOT), Anne Beeksma (Spanish National Research Council / Consejo Superior de Investigaciones Científicas (CSIC), Spain), Łukasz Bugalski (Istituto per I Beni Artistici, Culturali e Naturali of the Region Emilia Romagna (IBC), Italy), Vittoria Caradonna (University of Amsterdam (UvA), The Netherlands), Carlotta Capurro (Utrecht University (UU), The Netherlands), Moniek Driesse (UGOT), Nermin el-Sharif (UvA), William Illsley (UGOT), Marcela Jaramillo Contreras (ISCTE – University Institute of Lisbon, Portugal), Marcia Lika Hattori (CSIC), Nevena Markovic (CSIC), Katie O'Donoghue (University College London (UCL), United Kingdom), Janna Oud Ammerveld (UCL), Hannah K. Smyth (UCL) and Mela Zuljevic (Hasselt University (UHASSELT), Belgium). They were joined by named applicants, principal supervisors and work package leads Henric Benesch, Cecilia Lindhe, Ingrid Martins Holmberg,

Mats Malm and Ola Sigurdson (UGOT); Beverley Butler, Andrew Flinn, Rodney Harrison, Anne Lanceley, Michael Rowlands and Julianne Nyhan (UCL); Maria Pia Guermandi (IBC); Robin Boast, Chiara De Cesari and Rob van der Laarse (UvA); Liesbeth Huybrechts (UHASSELT); Gertjan Plets and Jaap Verheul (UU); Nélia Dias (ISCTE-IUL); and Felipe Criado Boado, Alfredo González-Ruibal, César Parcero-Oubiña and Cristina Sánchez-Carretero (CSIC), who each contributed to and participated in a range of activities over the 5 years of the project.

The project was also supported by a significant number of non-academic heritage and museum sector partner organisations. These included the National Museums of World Culture, Gothenburg, Sweden; KHM-Museumsverband / Weltmuseum Wien, Austria; Bohusläns Museum, Sweden; Göteborg City Museum, Sweden; Z33 – Huis voor Actuele Kunst, Belgium; National Museum of World Cultures, The Netherlands; Jewish Historical Museum, The Netherlands; Black Cultural Archives, UK; British Library, UK; Imaxin | Software S.L., Spain; Università Cattolica del Sacro Cuore, Italy; Netherlands Institute for Sound and Vision, The Netherlands; UCL Elizabeth Garrett Anderson Institute for Women's Health, UK; National Museum and Research Center of Altamira, Spain; Institut national de recherches archéologiques préventives (INRAP), France; Social Spaces, Inter-Actions, LUCA School of Arts, Belgium; Culture Lab SPRL/LTD, Belgium; Soprintendenza Archeologica di Roma, Italy; Stichting Imagine Identity and Culture, The Netherlands; Amsterdam Museum, The Netherlands; Swedish National Heritage Board, Sweden; Historic England, UK; CRESCER - Associação de Intervenção Comunitária, Portugal; Tropenmuseum, The Netherlands; Europeana Foundation, The Netherlands; University College London Hospitals NHS Foundation Trust, UK; Medelhavsmuseet, Sweden; Verhalenhuis Belvédère, The Netherlands; Asociación vecinal María Castaña, Spain; Cambridge Heritage Research Centre, UK; and Leibniz-Zentrum Moderner Orient, Germany.

The project organised six residential Joint Research Seminars and two Summer Schools. These were hosted by UCL (organised by Esther Breithoff and Rodney Harrison), UvA (organised by Robin Boast, Chiara De Cesari, Rob van der Laarse, Vittoria Caradonna and Nermin el-Sharif), UHasselt/Z33 (organised by Liesbeth Huybrechts and Mela Zuljevic), IBC (organised by Maria Pia Guermandi and Łukasz Bugalski), UU (organised by Gertjan Plets, Jaap Verheul and Carlotta Capurro), ISCTE-IUL (organised by Nélia Dias, Rodney Harrison, Janna Oud Ammerveld and Marcela Jaramillo Contreras), CSIC (organised by Felipe Criado Boado, César Parcero-Oubiña, Cristina Sánchez-Carretero, Alfredo González-Ruibal, Nevena Markovic, Anne

Beeksma and Marcia Lika Hattori) and UGOT (organised by Kristian Kristiansen, Khaled El-Samman Ahmed, Moniek Driesse and William Illsley), respectively. The project's final conference took place online on 15 and 16 October 2020 and was organised and hosted by UGOT. Many of the chapters in this volume were first presented at that conference. We thank the organisers, contributors and speakers at each of these events for their input to the research and training programme. The project was also supported by the joint UGOT–UCL Centre for Critical Heritage Studies.

We thank Matthew Leonard and Jillian Bowie for their careful and thorough copy-editorial work on the volume, and commissioning editors Chris Penfold and Pat Gordon-Smith at UCL Press for their work seeing the volume through to publication.

Further information about the project, and its online exhibition 'Yesterday is here. Exploring heritage futures across Europe and beyond', designed by curator and artist Nuno Coelho, is available at http://cheurope-project.eu/

Introduction

Rodney Harrison, Nélia Dias and Kristian Kristiansen

Cultural and natural heritage has been, and continues to be, central to 'Europe' and what might be more broadly termed 'the European project', in a number of important ways. As Benedict Anderson (1983) and others have noted, it was integrally bound up in the emergence of nation-states and in the imagination of (especially Western) Europe and its 'others' throughout the eighteenth and nineteenth centuries. As these states began to assume their modern form, it was increasingly used to identify and justify the sources of the differences over which their ideological, economic and spatial border conflicts were fought. After the Second World War, the idea of a 'common European heritage' provided a rationale for the emergence of the European Union, alongside a series of other regional and international organisations and initiatives. Despite widespread scholarly predictions during the 1990s of the death of the nation-state, the emergence of what have been termed 'new' populist nationalisms across Europe, perhaps most strongly signalled by the United Kingdom's withdrawal from the European Union but also by the rise of the Far Right across Europe, has shown how heritage and the imagined past continue to play a central role in practices of cultural and social governance. At the same time, the climate and extinction crises, along with the pandemic, are requiring a fundamental revision of all aspects of social, political and economic life. How are these phenomena changing the ways in which heritage operates? What new discourses and ontologies of heritage are emerging from these new social, political, economic and ecological contexts? In what ways must heritage be reconfigured to attend to the circumstances of the present and the uncertainties of the future?

Taking the present role of heritage in Europe and beyond as its starting point, this book presents a diverse range of case studies which explore key themes, including the role of heritage and museums in the migration and climate 'emergencies'; approaches to urban heritage conservation and practices of curating cities; digital and digitised heritage and heritagisation processes; the use of heritage as a therapeutic resource for improving psychological resilience and wellbeing; the interconnections between heritage, identity formation, citizenship, public policies, participation, planning, politics and tourism; and critical approaches to heritage and its management. The 18 essays in this volume draw on a range of disciplinary perspectives from across Europe and beyond to critically explore the multiple ontologies through which cultural and natural heritage have intervened and continue to intervene actively in redrawing the futures of Europe and the world. This chapter provides a brief introduction to the issues covered in the book and to its origins, scholarly framing and organisational logics.

Critical heritage studies and European nationalism

Critical heritage studies could be said to have emerged from observations of the ways in which heritage was used in the development and operation of what Benedict Anderson called 'Imagined Communities' (1983), through its function as a part of what Stuart Hall referred to as 'the educational apparatus of the nation-state' ([1999] 2008). This early work in critical heritage studies often focused very specifically on the role of heritage in a European (and/or Euro-American) context. As an officially sanctioned version of the monumental past, during the 1980s and 1990s, heritage began to be seen by scholars working across a number of different disciplinary contexts as functioning to delineate a nation's citizens from non-citizens by developing origin stories which justify contemporary norms by pushing them into an imagined past and hence moralise them, placing them outside of the realms of critical reflection. By delineating those who belonged to the nation-state, heritage also performed the opposite function, of identifying and explaining why certain individuals or groups of people should be seen as 'others' or non-citizens, and the limits that would thus be placed upon those persons as a result of this (Harrison 2013). This role of heritage in producing notions of difference was key to the colonial project, and to the justification of slavery and imperial expansion which was central to the development of modern European nation-states.

Much of the important work of critical heritage studies has thus been concerned with the ways in which heritage might be seen to operate, in the words of Tony Bennett, as a 'differencing machine' (2006), and the ways in which it is and has been operationalised for social governmental purposes in different contexts (e.g. see Tunbridge and Ashworth 1996; Sherman 2008; Ashworth, Graham and Tunbridge 2007). An obvious example of this is the ways in which differences between colonised and colonising populations have been treated in colonial museums, which have created scientific justification for illiberal forms of social governmental practices to be exercised upon these differentiated populations (e.g. see Bennett et al. 2017). Here we invoke an explicitly Foucauldian language of knowledge/power and the perspective of governmentality. In her influential book *Uses of Heritage*, Laurajane Smith (2006) draws on Foucauldian critical discourse analysis to chart the connection between power and the discourse of heritage, showing how the discourses of heritage both reflect and create a particular set of sociopolitical practices. She suggests we can use the structure and messages embodied in the language surrounding heritage to understand the dominant discourse of heritage 'and the way it both reflects and constitutes a range of social practices – not least the way it organises social relations and identities around nation, class, culture and ethnicity' (Smith 2006: 16). It is this dominant discourse that she terms the 'Authorised Heritage Discourse' (AHD). Smith's work has been very important in drawing attention to the knowledge/power effects of heritage and the concrete ways in which power is caught up and exercised through the exhibition and management of museums and heritage sites, a concern that has emerged as central to the interdisciplinary field of critical heritage studies.

Yet while early work on critical approaches to heritage was emerging in the 1980s and 1990s (see also Hobsbawm and Ranger 1983; Handler 1988; Lowenthal 1985, 1998; Nora 1984–1992; Samuel 1994), a number of scholars working in the fields of globalisation and cultural politics began to predict the demise of the nation-state as a social, cultural and political force. In *Modernity at Large* (1996), Arjun Appadurai, for example, pointed to the range of alternatives to the nation-state which had begun to be offered by new cultural forms emerging from the transnational circulation of images and ideas through the internet and new media. In doing so, he pointed to the growing tensions between the ideas of social, cultural and biological similarity and difference which had previously supported the idea of the nation-state, and the growing sense of homogeneity which the internet, mass migration and mass tourism often seemed to underline.

At the same time, other scholars have observed how a growing number of transnational non-governmental organisations, such as

INTRODUCTION 3

UNESCO, appeared to be assuming an increasingly important role in determining the governance of heritage as part of the neoliberalisation of the cultural sector, in a way which arguably supported this contention that the nation-state was losing its ability to control its own historical narratives (see further discussion in Meskell 2019 and de Cesari 2020). Nonetheless, it can also be argued that heritage continues to operate as a form of national 'soft power', deploying what Tim Winter calls forms of 'heritage diplomacy' (Winter 2014, 2015, 2016, 2019), thus complicating this view. Further, Meskell and colleagues have built a significant body of ethnographic work which shows how the role of state parties in the UNESCO World Heritage Committee tends to emphasise and revive national interests and competition, pitting one state against another (Meskell 2013, 2014, 2015, 2019; Meskell et al. 2015), while others have shown how heterogeneous UNESCO's World Heritage policies really are in their application 'on the ground' (e.g. see Bendix, Eggert and Perelmann 2013; Bondaz, Bideau, Isnart and Leblon 2014; Brumann and Berliner 2016).

This book thus sits among several recent scholarly works which aim to rethink the role of heritage in contemporary Europe, in the light of the problematic relationship between the idea of a unified 'European' heritage on the one hand (Lähdesmäki 2019) and the re-emergence of heritage as a significant social and political force as part of nationalist and populist projects within Europe on the other – albeit adopting a range of new forms in doing so. Significant here is Sharon Macdonald's book *Memorylands* (2013), in which she argues that heritage operates in a range of different ways and at different scales in European contexts which are more diverse and heterogeneous than had previously been acknowledged. Despite this, she argues that certain shared dispositions towards heritage, memory and the past occur across Europe today, themselves related to changing configurations of the nature of identities, joining the dots between Appadurai's arguments about the changing nature of identities with the proliferation of new media in the late twentieth century, to account for the persistence of local, regional and national expressions of identity. Nonetheless, she sees within these various forms of heritage performances and historical consciousness a broader shared European memory complex in which specific patterns of recollecting and remaking the past in the present might be determined.

Whitehead et al.'s (2019) edited volume *Dimensions of Heritage and Memory: Multiple Europes and the Politics of Crisis*, itself a product of a significant European Union (EU) Horizon 2020-funded project (CoHERE), similarly argues that the roles of heritage within Europe are significantly more complex and divergent than previously imagined. They analyse and explore a range of explicit policy instruments, projects and initiatives that emerged in the 2000s and 2010s precisely to address what was perceived to be a 'crisis' of European identity, and attempts to develop mechanisms by which national and European identity heritages might be reconciled with one another through interventions in the heritage sphere. One place where Macdonald's work (2013, see also 2009) and Whitehead et al.'s book converge is around an understanding that the disposition towards 'difficult' pasts does to some extent reflect a distinctive collective approach to the material traces of the twentieth century. Nonetheless, Whitehead et al. conclude that 'the European "heritage demos" can only ever fail as a project of total collectivisation, and indeed has the inherent liability to function as an object against which alternative collectivities are organised reactively and antagonistically' (2019: 23; but see Delanty 2018 for an alternative view). This has particularly been the case in discussions of the so-called 'Migration Crisis' in Europe (see an extended review of the literature on heritage, museums and the migration crisis in Harrison, Appelgren and Bohlin 2018).

Exploring this theme in more detail, several recent volumes focus on the role of heritage in nationalist and populist movements across Europe. *Classical Heritage and European Identities: The Imagined Geographies of Danish Classicism* (Funder, Kristensen and Nørskov 2019) shows how classical antiquity has been used to shape and reshape the concept of citizenship in Denmark since the eighteenth century. Reflecting arguments developed by Arjun Appadurai in *Fear of Small Numbers* (2006; see further discussion in Harrison 2013 in relation to heritage), *Populism and Heritage in Europe: Lost in Diversity and Unity* (Kaya 2020) and *European Memory in Populism: Representations of Self and Other* (de Cesari and Kaya 2020) provide comparative perspectives on the ways in which diverse but specific manifestations of heritage across Europe continue to be used in the construction of difference, to create majoritarian identities in opposition to minorities, for select political and social ends, points echoed by the work of Niklasson and Hølleland (2018; also see Galani, Mason and Arrigoni 2020; Herzfeld 2022; Lähdesmäki et al. 2020; Porciani 2020; Puzon, Macdonald and Shatanawi 2021). This is a theme developed by Bonacchi in *Heritage and Nationalism: Understanding Populism Through Big Data* (2022), in which she shows various ways in which individuals and collectives mobilise aspects of the Iron Age, Roman and medieval past of Britain and Europe to include or exclude 'others' through the study of social media.

Another body of work has been concerned with rethinking the colonial legacies of museums and heritage sites in Europe. Although this has been an active area of research and activism for decades, two recent events are emblematic of the acceleration of calls for action by sections of the public over the past few years. The first of these was the publication of the report on *The Restitution of African Cultural Heritage: Toward a New Relational Ethics*, written by Felwine Sarr and Bénédicte Savoy (2018) and published in French and English as a result of a commission by the French president, Emmanuel Macron. The report and its principles, although specific to French collections from sub-Saharan Africa, have stimulated significant discussion and debate across Europe on the topic of museums and their colonial legacies, and the case for repatriation of cultural items more generally.

Further discussion and debate emerged with urgency following the killing of George Floyd in May 2020, and the Black Lives Matter protests which focused on the issue of the removal of colonial and slavery-related statuary and the reinterpretation of heritage sites to acknowledge such legacies throughout the world. In the UK, the National Trust published its *Interim Report on the Connections between Colonialism and Properties now in the Care of the National Trust, Including Links with Historic Slavery* (National Trust 2020) at around this time; the report was met with much controversy, including claims of 'wokeness' and the government setting policies ('retain and explain') which specifically aimed to work against the removal of contested statues and objects from public display. These two sets of issues – the ongoing conflicts between European and national/regional/local identities, on the one hand, and ongoing discussions relating to the colonial legacies of European heritage in the context of renewed debates on migration and identity, on the other – act as key social and political contexts for the present book. These debates also trouble the idea of a singular 'Europe' and a singular 'European heritage' in important ways. Europe and its heritages are multiple, and what constitutes European heritages is contextual. Europe has always, as Edward Said has explained, been defined in opposition to its 'Other'. Accordingly, this volume includes perspectives and case studies from outside of 'Europe' to help frame and reflect on what constitutes 'Europe' and its heritages today, and the ways in which the idea of a European heritage is not fixed but always in flux.

Critical heritage studies and the futures of Europe

This book is an outcome of a significant international, interdisciplinary research project, funded by the European Union under the Marie

Skłodowska-Curie Actions (MSCA) – Innovative Training Networks (ITN) scheme. The project 'CHEurope: Critical Heritage Studies and the Futures of Europe: Towards an integrated, interdisciplinary and transnational training model in cultural heritage research and management', which ran from 2016 to 2021, involved collaboration between a number of European universities in Sweden, the United Kingdom, the Netherlands, Portugal, Spain, Belgium and Italy. The project supported the research and training of 15 Early-Stage PhD Researchers from Europe and other parts of the world and involved collaborations between around 50 senior and emerging academics and practitioners across these various institutions, in partnership with around 30 heritage partner organisations across ten different countries.[1] The book draws together researchers from the project, along with invited colleagues from outside the project, to explore its core themes of the role of critical heritage studies in understanding Europe's present and futures, and to present the findings of the project and affiliated initiatives (see further information at CHEurope 2022 and Bugalski and Guermandi 2019).

The diverse range of disciplines and perspectives presented in the book reflect the international nature of the project and the funder's insistence on *mobility* – in this case meaning that students funded as part of the project may not have resided or carried out their main activity (work, studies etc.) in the country of their subsequent host organisation for more than 12 months in the 36 months immediately before the call deadline. Thus, the Early-Stage Researchers came from a range of different countries inside and outside Europe, including Bosnia and Herzegovina, Brazil, Colombia, Egypt, Ireland, Italy, the Netherlands, Poland and the United Kingdom, each bringing with them a range of different disciplinary perspectives and experiences working and studying across a range of different regional and national contexts. This volume therefore reflects the project itself in presenting a diverse range of case studies, academic disciplines, conceptual approaches and national traditions of scholarship, organised across four parts, each of which represents a particular thematic focus. As in the cases discussed above (especially Macdonald 2013 and Whitehead et al. 2019), we see this diversity as a significant strength of the book, which resists attempts to neatly categorise and present European heritage – either within or outside Europe – as a coherent disciplinary field or a specific regional set of approaches and practices.

We began from the now well-developed truism that heritage should be understood to be as much about resourcing the future as it is about the past (see Harrison 2013, Harrison et al. 2020). An important dimension of the politics and the public sphere of our multicultural and increasingly globalised times, heritage involves working with the past to remake ourselves, our identities and the worlds we inhabit, to create a horizon of possibilities for the future (Koselleck 2004). We identified a set of challenges derived from the growing politicisation of heritage and its entanglement with some of the key sociopolitical issues of our times: urban conflicts, digitality, the future of welfare and public involvement. From these we developed five main themes for the project:

- Theorising heritage futures in Europe: heritage scenarios.
- Curating the city: trans-disciplinary inheritance/disinheritance processes in urban settings.
- Digital heritage: the future role of heritage and archive collections in a digital world.
- Heritage and wellbeing: migration and dislocation.
- Heritage management and citizen participation in a multicultural world.

The project's primary goal was therefore to reflect on the 'futurability' of heritage – by which we mean its capacity to practically and conceptually resource specific futures – and to train researchers to recognise in these novel demands new possibilities for using museums, cultural and natural heritage sites and archives in innovative ways. This perspective is developed in detail in Harrison et al.'s book *Heritage Futures: Comparative Approaches to Natural and Cultural Heritage Practices* (2020), which draws on the work of Italian Marxist theorist Franco Berardi (2017: 3), who uses this term to describe 'a layer of possibility which may or may not develop into actuality'. He suggests that futurability can be further broken down into a series of variables: possibility, potency and power. 'Possibility is content, potency is energy and power is form' (Berardi 2017: 1). Possibility is always plural, while potency is the energy with which possible futures are actualised. Power is the selection and enforcement of specific futures, which simultaneously excludes others from being actualised. This provides a means of connecting conventional analyses of power in heritage with an understanding of its future-making capacities.

The book is presented in four parts. These partially reflect the subthemes of the research project, but also represent key areas of contemporary concern relating to heritage in Europe and beyond and provide an organisational logic for the volume as a whole. Part 1, 'Heritage and global challenges', explores the ways in which heritage is reflected in contemporary discussions of the migration crisis and the climate emergency and related to discussions of health and wellbeing, and how the future is imagined through heritage discourses and practices in each of these areas. Part 2, 'Curating the city: rethinking urban heritages', considers the role of urban heritage in tourism, urban design and collective identity making in Europe and beyond. Part 3, 'Digital heritages and digital futures', explores the ways in which digitisation projects are refiguring heritage practices and identities, and uncoupling heritage from specific spaces, leading to new roles for heritage in both 'virtual' and 'real' life. Part 4, 'Postcolonial legacies: "European" heritages beyond Europe', explores the ways in which European approaches to heritage and heritage management have landed and been reworked in contexts outside Europe. Each of these parts is prefaced by a short introductory essay which explores the issues raised by the chapters in each section in comparative perspective. The book concludes with an afterword by Barbara Kirshenblatt-Gimblett, who contributed to the eighth and final joint research seminar of the project held in Lisbon in 2019, just before the shockwaves of the coronavirus pandemic began to be felt across the world.

Discussion and conclusion

This introduction has aimed to provide a contextual and conceptual framing for the case studies that follow, drawing attention to the ongoing contested relationship between European and national heritages and identities, and an understanding of heritage as a set of practices which aim to resource, and hence produce and control, specific imaginaries of the future. The diverse range of regional and disciplinary perspectives and case studies presented in the book undermines any sense that present approaches to the identification, preservation, representation, interpretation and management of heritage in Europe – and 'European' heritages outside Europe – are in any way homogeneous. Equally, they show how notions of a unified 'Europe' and 'European identity' remain in constant conflict with national, regional and local identities: identities which are actively shaped and reshaped in contrast with others. While it is perhaps true to say that heritage is always and inherently contested, emerging as it does within the context of a perception of endangerment or threat (Harrison 2013, Rico 2015, Vidal and Dias 2016), the widespread sense of crisis which has framed intra- and infra-European relations over the period in which the empirical materials presented in this book were gathered suggests that this has been particularly the case during this time.

Far from being remote from their fields of study, the chapters in this book also demonstrate the ways in which critical heritage studies has begun to engage more directly with those fields, with a view not simply to critique them from a distance, but instead to actively transform them. Critical studies of heritage have much to contribute to understanding and developing creative solutions to social, economic and ecological problems, which arise as a result of conflicts between different systems of value and their associated friction in contemporary societies. The chapters in this volume go some way towards showing how this might be done, in Europe and beyond.

Note

1. The heritage and museum sector partner organisations on the project were the National Museums of World Culture, Gothenburg, Sweden; KHM-Museumsverband / Weltmuseum Wien, Austria; Bohusläns Museum, Sweden; Göteborg City Museum, Sweden; Z33 – Huis voor Actuele Kunst, Belgium; National Museum of World Cultures, The Netherlands; Jewish Historical Museum, The Netherlands; Black Cultural Archives, UK; British Library, UK; Imaxin | Software S.L., Spain; Università Cattolica del Sacro Cuore, Italy; Netherlands Institute for Sound and Vision, The Netherlands; UCL Elizabeth Garrett Anderson Institute for Women's Health, UK; National Museum and Research Center of Altamira, Spain; Institut national de recherches archéologiques préventives (INRAP), France; Social Spaces, Inter-Actions, LUCA School of Arts, Belgium; Culture Lab SPRL/LTD, Belgium; Soprintendenza Archeologica di Roma, Italy; Stichting Imagine Identity and Culture, The Netherlands; Amsterdam Museum, The Netherlands; Swedish National Heritage Board, Sweden; Historic England, UK; CRESCER – Associação de Intervenção Comunitária, Portugal; Tropenmuseum, The Netherlands; Europeana Foundation, The Netherlands; University College London Hospitals NHS Foundation Trust, UK; Medelhavsmuseet, Sweden; Verhalenhuis Belvédère, The Netherlands; Asociación vecinal María Castaña, Spain; Cambridge Heritage Research Centre, UK; and Leibniz-Zentrum Moderner Orient, Germany.

References

Anderson, Benedict. 1983. *Imagined Communities: Reflections on the Origin and Spread of Nationalism*. London and New York: Verso.

Appadurai, Arjun. 1996. *Modernity at Large*. Minneapolis and New York: University of Minneapolis Press.

Appadurai, Arjun. 2006. *Fear of Small Numbers*. Durham and London: Duke University Press.

Ashworth, Gregory, Brian Graham and John Tunbridge. 2007. *Pluralising Pasts: Heritage, Identity and Place in Multicultural Societies*. London: Pluto Press.

Bendix, Regina, Aditya Eggert and Arnika Perelmann (eds). 2013. *Heritage Regimes and the State*. Göttingen: Göttingen University Press.

Bennett, Tony. 2006. Exhibition, Difference and the Logic of Culture. In Ivan Karp, Corinne Krantz, Lynn Szwaja and Tomas Ybarra-Frausto (eds), *Museum Frictions: Public Cultures/Global Transformations*. Durham and London: Duke University Press: 46–69.

Bennett, Tony, Fiona Cameron, Nélia Dias, Ben Dibley, Rodney Harrison, Ira Jacknis and Conal McCarthy. 2017. *Collecting, Ordering, Governing: Anthropology, Museums and Liberal Government*. Durham NC: Duke University Press.

Berardi, Franco. 2017. *Futurability: The Age of Impotence and the Horizon of Possibility*. London: Verso.

Bonacchi, Chiara. 2022. *Heritage and Nationalism: Understanding Populism Through Big Data*. London: UCL Press.

Bondaz, Julien, Florence Bideau, Cyril Isnart and Anaïs Leblon (eds). 2014. *Les Vocabulaires Locaux du 'Patrimoine'. Traductions, Négociations et Transformations*. Zurich and Berlin: Lit Verlag.

Brumann, Christoph and David Berliner (eds). 2016. *World Heritage on the Ground: Ethnographic Perspectives*. New York: Berghahn Books.

Bugalski, Łukasz and Maria Pia Guermandi (eds). 2019. *Heritage Explorations across Europe: CHEurope, Interdisciplinary Training Network in Critical Heritage Studies*. DOSSIER IBC 27(4). Online at http://cheurope-project.eu/wp-content/uploads/2020/03/IBC-dossier.pdf Accessed 11 March 2023.

de Cesari, Chiara. 2020. Heritage beyond the Nation-State? Nongovernmental Organisations, Changing Cultural Policies and the Discourse of Heritage as Development. *Current Anthropology* 61(1): 30–56.

de Cesari, Chiara and Ayhan Kaya (eds). 2020. *European Memory in Populism: Representations of Self and Other* (Critical Heritages of Europe). London: Routledge.

CHEurope (2022). *CHEurope: Critical Heritage Studies and the Futures of Europe*. Online at http://cheurope-project.eu/ Accessed 11 March 2023.

Delanty, Gerard. 2018. *The European Heritage: A Critical Re-interpretation*. London: Routledge.

Funder, Lærke Maria Andersen, Troels Myrup Kristensen and Vinnie Nørskov. 2019. *Classical Heritage and European Identities: The Imagined Geographies of Danish Classicism*. Abingdon and New York: Routledge.

Galani, Areti, Rhiannon Mason and Gabi Arrigoni (eds). 2020. *European Heritage, Dialogue and Digital Practices*. Abingdon and New York: Routledge.

Hall, Stuart. [1999] 2008. Whose Heritage? Un-settling 'The Heritage', Reimagining the Post-Nation. In Graham Fairclough, Rodney Harrison, John Jameson Jr and John Schofield (eds), *The Heritage Reader*. Abingdon and New York: Routledge: 219–228.

Handler, Richard. 1988. *Nationalism and the Politics of Culture in Quebec*. Madison: University of Wisconsin Press.

Harrison, Rodney. 2013. *Heritage: Critical Approaches*. Abingdon and New York: Routledge.

Harrison, Rodney, Staffan Appelgren and Anna Bohlin. 2018. Belonging and Belongings: On Migrant and Nomadic Heritages in and for the Anthropocene. In Yannis Hamilakis (ed.), *The New Nomadic Age: Archaeologies of Forced and Undocumented Migration*. Sheffield: Equinox: 209–220.

Harrison, Rodney, Caitlin DeSilvey, Cornelius Holtorf, Sharon Macdonald, Nadia Bartolini, Esther Breithoff, Harald Fredheim, Antony Lyons, Sarah May, Jennie Morgan and Sefryn Penrose. 2020. *Heritage Futures: Comparative Approaches to Natural and Cultural Heritage Practices*. London: UCL Press.

Herzfeld, Michael. 2022. *Subversive Archaism: Troubling Traditionalists and the Politics of National Heritage*. Durham NC: Duke University Press.

Hobsbawm, Eric and Terrance Ranger. 1983. *The Invention of Tradition*. Cambridge: Cambridge University Press.

Kaya, Ayhan. 2020. *Populism and Heritage in Europe: Lost in Diversity and Unity*. London: Routledge.

Koselleck, Reinhart. 2004. *Futures Past: On the Semantics of Historical Time*. New York: Columbia University Press.

Lähdesmäki, Tuuli. 2019. Founding Myths of European Union Europe and the Workings of Power in the European Union Heritage and History Initiatives. *European Journal of Cultural Studies* 22(5–6): 781–798.

Lähdesmäki, Tuuli, Viktorija Čeginskas, Sigrid Kaasik-Krogerus, Katja Mäkinen and Johanna Turunen. 2020. *Creating and Governing Cultural Heritage in the European Union: The European Heritage Label*. Abingdon and New York: Routledge.

Lowenthal, David. 1985. *The Past is a Foreign Country*. Cambridge: Cambridge University Press.

Lowenthal, David. 1998. *The Heritage Crusade and the Spoils of History*. Cambridge: Cambridge University Press.

Macdonald, Sharon. 2009. *Difficult Heritage: Negotiating the Nazi Past in Nuremberg and Beyond*. London: Routledge.

Macdonald, Sharon. 2013. *Memorylands: Heritage and Identity in Europe Today*. London: Routledge.

Meskell, Lynn. 2013. UNESCO's World Heritage Convention at 40: Challenging the Economic and Political Order of International Heritage Conservation. *Current Anthropology* 54(4): 483–494.

Meskell, Lynn. 2014. States of Conservation: Protection, Politics, and Pacting within UNESCO's World Heritage Committee. *Anthropological Quarterly* 87(1): 217–244.

Meskell, Lynn. 2015. Gridlock: UNESCO, Global Conflict and Failed Ambitions. *World Archaeology* 47(2): 225–238.

Meskell, Lynn. 2019. *A Future in Ruins: UNESCO, World Heritage and the Dream of Peace*. Oxford: Oxford University Press.

Meskell, Lynn, Claudia Liuzza, Enrico Bertacchini and Donatello Saccone. 2015. Multilateralism and UNESCO World Heritage: Decision-Making, States Parties and Political Processes. *International Journal of Heritage Studies* 21(5): 423–440.

National Trust. 2020. *Interim Report on the Connections between Colonialism and Properties now in the Care of the National Trust, Including Links with Historic Slavery*. Swindon: National Trust. Online at https://nt.global.ssl.fastly.net/binaries/content/assets/website/national/pdf/colonialism-and-historic-slavery-report.pdf Accessed 25 April 2023.

Niklasson, Elisabeth and Herdis Hølleland. 2018. The Scandinavian Far Right and the New Politicisation of Heritage. *Journal of Social Archaeology* 18(2): 121–148.

Nora, Pierre. 1984–1992. *Les Lieux de mémoire* (3 vols). Paris: Gallimard.

Porciani, Ilaria (ed.). 2020. *Food Heritage and Nationalism in Europe*. Abingdon and New York: Routledge.

Puzon, Katarzyna, Sharon Macdonald and Mirjam Shatanawi (eds). 2021. *Islam and Heritage in Europe: Pasts, Presents and Future Possibilities*. Abingdon and New York: Routledge.

Rico, Trinidad. 2015. Heritage at Risk: The Authority and Autonomy of a Dominant Preservation Framework. In Kathryn Lafrenz Samuels and Trinidad Rico (eds), *Heritage Keywords: Rhetoric and Redescription in Cultural Heritage*. Boulder: University Press of Colorado: 147–162.

Samuel, Raphael. 1994. *Theatres of Memory: Past and Present in Contemporary Culture*. London: Verso.

Sarr, Felwine and Bénédicte Savoy. 21 November 2018. *Rapport sur la restitution du patrimoine culturel africain. Vers une nouvelle éthique relationnelle* [The Restitution of African Cultural Heritage. Toward a New Relational Ethics] (pdf; report, in French and English). Paris. Online at https://www.about-africa.de/images/sonstiges/2018/sarr_savoy_en.pdf Accessed 25 April 2023.

Sherman, Daniel (ed.). 2008. *Museums and Difference*. Bloomington: Indiana University Press.

Smith, Laurajane. 2006. *Uses of Heritage*. London: Routledge.

Tunbridge, John and Gregory Ashworth. 1996. *Dissonant Heritage: The Management of the Past as a Resource in Conflict*. Chichester: Wiley.

Vidal, Fernando and Nélia Dias. 2016. Introduction: The Endangerment Sensibility. In Fernando Vidal and Nélia Dias (eds), *Endangerment, Biodiversity and Culture*. London: Routledge: 1–38.

Whitehead, Christopher, Susannah Eckersley, Mads Daugbjerg and Gönül Bozoğlu (eds). 2019. *Dimensions of Heritage and Memory: Multiple Europes and the Politics of Crisis*. Abingdon and New York: Routledge.

Winter, Tim. 2014. Beyond Eurocentrism? Heritage Conservation and the Politics of Difference. *International Journal of Heritage Studies* 20(2): 123–137.

Winter, Tim. 2015. Heritage Diplomacy. *International Journal of Heritage Studies* 21(10): 997–1015.

Winter, Tim. 2016. Heritage Diplomacy: Entangled Materialities of International Relations. *Future Anterior: Journal of Historic Preservation, History, Theory and Criticism* 13(1): 17–34.

Winter, Tim. 2019. *Geocultural Power: China's Quest to Revive the Silk Roads for the Twenty-First Century*. Chicago: University of Chicago Press.

Part I: Heritage and global challenges

The preservation of natural and cultural heritage cannot be separated from the social, political, historical, economic and ecological context in which it operates. The increasing recognition of the intersectionality of global sustainable development goals and global challenges of social and ecological justice has stimulated a focus within critical heritage studies on questions as to the relationship between heritage and individual and collective social and environmental health. The chapters in this part of the book are concerned with how heritage can respond and is responding to various social and ecological crises and is expanding and being transformed in the process.

Rodney Harrison and Colin Sterling (Chapter 1) explore the relationship between heritage and climate change. They describe the work of Reimagining Museums for Climate Action, a concepts competition, exhibition, research project and museums climate action 'toolkit' which invited people from outside museums to explore new ways in which museums might facilitate action for climate. They conclude that museums have a key role to play in facilitating action for climate, but that museums must change to realise this role.

Janna oud Ammerveld's chapter (Chapter 2) also explores the relationship between heritage and climate change, through an exploration of how climate change is impacting the work of a national heritage agency, Historic England. She shows how the conventional way of understanding the relationship between climate change and heritage is one in which climate change accelerates existing threats to heritage and creates new ones. She also documents the development of another discourse in which the historic built environment appears as an environmental champion and a key to climate mitigation. In this way of thinking, climate change emerges as another contributor both to heritage's endangerment sensibility (Vidal and Dias 2016) and as something which produces new forms of value for the historic environment.

Marcela Jaramillo's contribution (Chapter 3) takes as its framing the so-called 'European migration crisis' and explores the role of food and food practices in attempts by the Portuguese state and local communities to integrate Syrian refugees. She describes a general neglect of food and food heritages in official attempts to assimilate Syrian refugees by the state but observes the significant potential of food heritage to create affective bonds between newcomers, concluding that 'asylum policies should recognise the food practices of refugees as a form of heritage in their own right, as well as a means of integration', suggesting that this could lead to more inclusive integration 'in which the heritage of newcomers would be respected and validated', leading to more inclusive multicultural societies.

Finally, Katie O'Donoghue's chapter (Chapter 4) considers the role of heritage-based interventions for individuals undergoing curative treatment for cancer. Drawing on a longitudinal study of an individual patient's journey through treatment, she explores the role of objects and artworks in providing therapeutic support in aspects of patient experience in health-care settings. Her work supports other recent explorations of the potential contributions of natural and cultural heritage to mental and physical health and wellbeing.

In sum, these chapters document not only the changing role of heritage in relation to climate, migration and health, but also how these issues are themselves transforming heritage and heritage institutions across Europe and beyond. Each suggests important new trajectories for the futures of European heritage.

References

Vidal, Fernando and Nélia Dias. 2016. Introduction: The Endangerment Sensibility. In Fernando Vidal and Nélia Dias (eds), *Endangerment, Biodiversity and Culture*. London: Routledge: 1–38.

1
Rethinking museums for the climate emergency

Rodney Harrison and Colin Sterling

Introduction

Museums, galleries and collections are often seen as static and backwards-looking, more concerned with the past than with the present and the future. While this impression is slowly changing, they are perhaps not the most obvious subject to focus on when thinking about climate action. However, climate change is much more than simply an environmental or scientific concern. It impacts on all aspects of social, cultural, political and economic life, including museums. Questions of sponsorship, carbon emissions, waste, transport and the need for more sustainable buildings are currently being debated across the sector. At the same time, museums have an important role to play in communicating the climate emergency to the public. For many people, they remain a trusted source of information, with the capacity to inspire real change in individuals and society. Far from being relics of the past, museums are increasingly called upon to help shape a more just and sustainable future.

Museums are also deeply entrenched in broader histories of colonialism, globalisation and capitalism. As such, they are closely bound up with many of the forces that have led the planet to the brink of ecological collapse, including the separation of human and non-human life; the marginalisation and oppression of Black, Indigenous and minority ethnic peoples; and the celebration of progress narratives dependent on unlimited economic growth. Recent years have witnessed a profound shift in the way museums engage with such legacies, but their underlying logics of preservation, interpretation, curating, education and research remain largely unchallenged.

This chapter describes and reflects on an international collaborative research project, ideas competition, exhibition and series of activities – Reimagining Museums for Climate Action (RMCA) – which aimed for a significant intervention in contemporary thinking about museums, to inspire radical changes to address the climate emergency in the lead-up to the United Nations Framework Convention on Climate Change (UNFCCC) Conference – COP26[1] – held in Glasgow in November 2021 (Harrison and Sterling 2021; McGhie 2021; RMCA 2022). The chapter concludes with a discussion which draws on what we learned from the project and from our participation in various activities linked to COP26, and the implications for museums worldwide.

Why rethink museums? Museums and the climate emergency

A range of activities have emerged across the museum sector in recent years in response to the climate emergency. Across the globe, museums have mobilised to address the challenges of a warming world through curatorial work, collecting programmes, public engagement activities and new development strategies that do not shy away from the profound consequences of the climate emergency (e.g. Brophy and Wylie 2013; Cameron and Neilson 2014; Newell, Robin and Wehner 2016; L'Internationale 2016). At the same time, a broad range of initiatives have challenged the familiar idea of the museum in direct response to the climate emergency. These include activist-oriented climate museums in New York and the UK, but also the proposed Museum for the United Nations, whose first project – 'My Mark, My City' – aimed to galvanise climate action in communities around the world. Alongside these, we cannot fail to mention the urgent work of protest groups such as Culture Unstained and BP or Not BP, who seek to end fossil fuel sponsorship across the cultural sector (e.g. see Garrard 2021). There are important parallels here with broader initiatives that aim to address the ongoing role of museums and heritage in supporting systemic forms of racism and inequality. In the UK and the USA, campaign groups and forums such as Museum Detox, Museums Are Not Neutral, Museum as Muck and Decolonize This Place have drawn attention to the historical and contemporary injustices of the field in ways that often coalesce with the political dimensions of climate action. Such work helps to surface the dense entanglement of museums with destructive environmental forces, including colonialism and the extractivist methods of industrial capitalism. Museums have never been isolated from the injustices of the world, but their complicity in a range of oppressive and damaging structures is now being thrown into sharp focus on multiple fronts.

As the editors of *Ecologising Museums* note, 'the museum' is not just a 'technical operation but is also imbued with a certain (modern) mindset which itself raises questions of sustainability' (L'Internationale 2016: 5). Acknowledging the pervasiveness of this mindset leads to an important question, namely: 'To what degree are the core activities of collecting, preserving and presenting in fact attitudes that embody an unsustainable view of the world and the relationship between man [sic] and nature?' (L'Internationale 2016: 5). A growing subfield of climate-related publications in museum studies has begun to explore this line of enquiry in recent years, including three special issues of relevant academic journals on the subject in 2020 alone (Davis 2020; Sutton and Robinson 2020; Þórsson and Nørskov 2020). The breadth of case studies, creative interventions and conceptual approaches found across this literature provides a valuable overview of the manifold ways in which museums intersect with climate action. Some of the main dimensions of this work include the idea that museums are 'trusted spaces' in which different publics can engage with the science of climate change (Cameron, Hodge and Salazar 2013); the possibility for collections – especially natural history collections – to inform new approaches to biodiversity conservation (McGhie 2019a); the need for museums to promote alternative forms of consumption (Arfvidsson and Follin 2020); the opportunities for cross-cultural engagement that may emerge around specific objects and narratives related to climate change (Newell, Robin and Wehner 2016); and the potential to break down the boundaries between nature and culture through different modes of conservation and curating (Þórsson 2018). What such work highlights most clearly is the fact that there is no single pathway or theory of change for the sector in relation to climate issues – addressing this crisis involves new imaginaries, new practices, new concepts and new strategic alliances.

What we also find across much of this work is a recognition – sometimes explicit, sometimes implicit – that the emergence and spread of museums around the world tracks the rise of carbon emissions and environmental degradation in ways that can no longer be ignored. This realisation offers a useful corrective to an often optimistic reading of museums as a diverse global phenomenon. While the global museum 'franchise' described by Janes (2009) may be seen as a valuable tool in the fight against climate change on the one hand, it can also be read as an artefact of the Industrial Revolution, or of colonialism, or of the Great

Acceleration. Museums are being called into question in this moment of crisis precisely because they can be seen as both an instrument and a legacy of the processes that have led to this crisis. Even as they celebrate and promote their capacity to protect, conserve and 'care for' the planet, museums also embody and, in some cases, perpetuate the 'Great Derangement' (Ghosh 2016) that undergirds climate breakdown.

This brings us to an important point in understanding the roots of the RMCA project, which at its core aimed to inspire radical change in museums to address the climate emergency. The key point here is that, in many ways, this change is already upon us. As authors such as Timothy Morton (2013), David Wallace-Wells (2019) and Andreas Malm (2018) highlight, the climate emergency is more than simply a problem to be overcome so that we can get back to business as usual – it is, potentially, a knowledge system or condition as all-encompassing as modernity or postmodernity. Such a perspective recognises that the impacts of climate change are felt not just in rising temperatures, biodiversity loss and other environmental consequences, but in psychic experience, cultural responses, business, politics and our relationship to time and history (Wallace-Wells 2019: 155, Malm 2018: 11). This is the change that museums are currently navigating, just as much as they are confronting the damaging effects of a warming world. This vastly expands the scope of museological 'reimagining', which in our view can no longer be left to museologists alone.

A participatory thought experiment

How can we expand the dialogue around museums, and how might we move from speculating about what museums could be, to practically reimagining their role in the future? Prompted by the need for radical new thinking around museums and heritage in response to the climate emergency (and in direct contrast to previous work undertaken by one of us which focused more on engaging with heritage and museum practitioners and policymakers; see Harrison et al. 2020), RMCA began life as an international design and ideas competition, launched on 18 May 2020 for International Museums Day, that aimed to open up the discussion around this subject to new publics and new constituents. The competition specifically invited 'designers, architects, academics, artists, poets, philosophers, writers, museum professionals, Indigenous groups, community groups and the public at large to radically (re)imagine and (re)design the museum as an institution, to help bring about more equitable and sustainable futures in the climate change era'. Responding to the two main pillars of climate action, mitigation and adaptation (see also oud Ammerveld, this volume), the competition asked how museums could help society make the deep, transformative changes needed to achieve a net-zero or zero-carbon world. Rather than focus on a specific location or type of museum, the competition invited proposals that aimed to unsettle and subvert the very foundations of museological thinking in order to support and encourage meaningful climate action. It specifically asked for design and concept proposals that were radically different from the 'traditional' museum, or that explored new ways for traditional museums to operate. The responses, which could address any aspect of museum design and activity, ranged from the fantastical to the highly practical.

A number of different research trajectories came together in coauthoring the competition brief, including McGhie's policy-oriented work on museums and the United Nation's Sustainable Development Goals (e.g. McGhie 2019a, 2019b), Harrison's speculative approach to heritage as a future-making practice (Harrison 2013, 2015; Harrison et al. 2020; Harrison and Sterling 2021) and Sterling's interest in critical-creative design practices in heritage and museums (Sterling 2019). While these trajectories overlap in some ways, the gaps and tensions between research that is quite theoretical in outlook and work that is more concerned with policy and practice created a useful foundation for thinking holistically about museums and climate action. To this end, the brief encompassed issues of collecting, conservation and exhibition making, the links between decolonisation and decarbonisation, the need to challenge foundational principles, the desire for speculative ideas about what museums could be, and the relationship between museums and climate justice. As an activity linked to the UK's hosting of COP26 in Glasgow, the brief also paid particular attention to the various United Nations programmes connected to museums, including Action for Climate Empowerment.

The competition attracted over 500 expressions of interest, resulting in 264 submissions from 48 countries around the world. Working with an international panel of judges, and in partnership with the Glasgow Science Centre (GSC) as hosts, we selected eight winning entries to form the core of an exhibition to be hosted by the GSC in advance of COP26 and then during the event as part of the 'Green Zone'.[2] The exhibitors included established designers, curators, academics, sound artists, digital specialists, Indigenous film-makers, emerging architectural practices and museum managers – a good example of the transdisciplinary conversations and alliances required to 'reimagine' museums in any meaningful way. The international scope of the competition also underlined the fact that critical and creative thinking about museums often involves moving between different scales and contexts, from the hyper-local to the planetary, from city centres to forest ecosystems.

Reimagining museums for climate action: the exhibition

The exhibition was composed of an introduction and eight individual exhibits which were developed by eight competition-winning teams in consultation with the project team. These were as follows:

1. *Museum of Open Windows* (Livia Wang; Nico Alexandroff; RESOLVE Collective: Akil Scafe-Smith, Seth Scafe-Smith, Melissa Haniff; Studio MASH: Max Martin, Angus Smith, Conor Sheehan: UK), which aimed to repurpose the existing global infrastructure of museums to support inter-community collaboration and citizen research on climate change and climate action (see Figure 1.1).
2. *Existances* (Jairza Fernandes Rocha da Silva, Nayhara J. A. Pereira Thiers Vieira, João Francisco Vitório Rodrigues, Natalino Neves da Silva, Walter Francisco Figueiredo Lowande: Brazil), which aimed to show the power of collective knowledge in the fight against climate change, imagining a network of micro-museums embedded in and responding to the diverse lifeworlds of African and Amerindian communities in Brazil (see Figure 1.2).

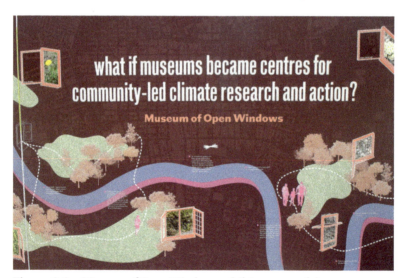

Figure 1.1 *Museum of Open Windows* exhibit as part of the Reimagining Museums for Climate Action exhibition at the Glasgow Science Centre for COP26. © Rodney Harrison.

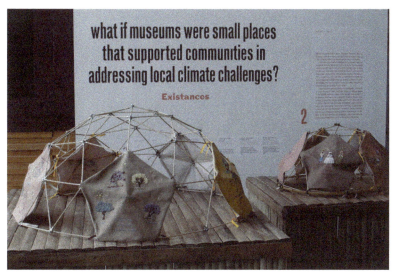

Figure 1.2 *Existances* exhibit as part of the Reimagining Museums for Climate Action exhibition at the Glasgow Science Centre for COP26. © Rodney Harrison.

3. *Natural Future Museums* (Takumã Kuikuro and Thiago Jesus: Brazil/UK), which asked what it would mean to confer museum status on existing Indigenous lands in forests and other places that play a key role in climate action, in doing so, questioning the very idea of the museum itself.
4. *Weathering With Us* (Isabella Ong and Tan Wen Jun: Singapore), which imagined a new kind of contemplative museum space where climate action is materialised in the very structure and experience of the building (see Figure 1.3).
5. *Dundee Museum of Transport* (Peter Webber, Alexander Goodger, Matthew Wong, Wendy Maltman and Katherine Southern: UK) which asked how a traditional museum might evolve to address the contemporary challenge of sustainable travel in an inclusive way.
6. *Elephant in the Room* (Design Earth: Rania Ghosn, El Hadi Jazairy, Monica Hutton and Anhong Li: USA), a short film, narrated by Donna Haraway, which offered a fantastical story in which a stuffed elephant comes to life and forces museums and wider society to confront their role in climate change.

7. *Story: Web* (The Great North Museum: Hancock, Open Lab: Simon Bowen, The Tyndall Centre/CAST: Sarah Mander, David de la Haye: UK), which mobilised existing museum collections to empower people to curate their own climate stories, experiences and networks on a global scale.

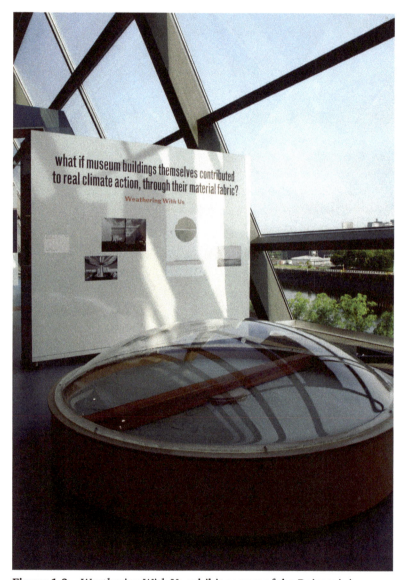

Figure 1.3 *Weathering With Us* exhibit as part of the Reimagining Museums for Climate Action exhibition at the Glasgow Science Centre for COP26. © Rodney Harrison.

8. *A Series of Collective, Non-Statistical Evidence* (pppooolll: Kamil Muhammad, Haidar El Haq, Amelia M. Djaja, Gregorius Jasson and Ken Fernanda: Indonesia), which applied familiar museum practices of collecting, display and participation to imagine spaces of dialogue, where different communities come together to share and articulate their personal experiences of climate change.

The exhibition also contained a selection of images from an additional 71 concepts and proposals from the competition which were featured on the Reimagining Museums for Climate Action website (RMCA 2022) to inspire radical change in museums to address the climate emergency. It was integrated within the existing Powering the Future display at the GSC to highlight the crucial role that cultural institutions must play in shaping the world of tomorrow. In addition to hosting this further long-list of proposals, a website was developed to provide virtual access to the exhibition for those who were unable to travel to Glasgow to visit in person, while a series of resources, events and activities to inspire new thinking both inside and outside of the sector on the role of museums in the climate emergency were also developed over this time.

Reimagining Museums for Climate Action at the UNFCCC COP26

The Reimagining Museums for Climate Action exhibition first opened at the GSC in June 2021, running through until mid-October 2021 and being seen by around 60,000 visitors. It reopened on 31 October 2021 as part of the official UNFCCC COP26 Green Zone over the two weeks of the conference from 31 October to 12 November, during which time it was seen by another 60,000 or so visitors (see Figure 1.4). The exhibition was also featured as one of 'Five incredible ideas from the COP26 Green Zone' as part of the COP26 Virtual Green Zone, hosted by Google Arts and Culture, which remains live as a virtual artefact of the exhibits and the activities which took place there.[3] RMCA team members participated in several events at the COP26 Blue and Green Zones, presenting a virtual plenary panel from COP26 for the Museums Association Conference and co-organising the panel 'Powering climate action through heritage policies, organisations, research and public programmes' which took place in the EU Pavilion.

During the two weeks of COP26, volunteers from a number of different organisations helped the RMCA team to engage with visitors by asking 'What if museums … ?' and collecting their ideas about how museums might change to empower them, and the groups they represented, to take their desired form of climate action (see Figure 1.5). These

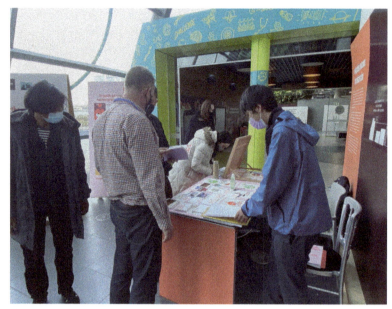

Figure 1.4 Speaking with visitors to the Reimagining Museums for Climate Change exhibition during COP26. © Rodney Harrison.

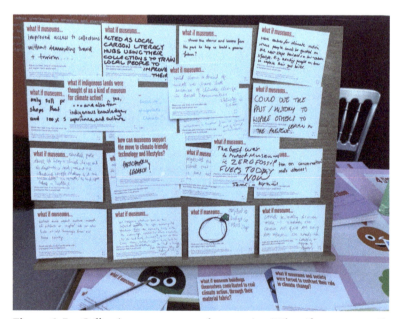

Figure 1.5 Collecting responses to the question 'What if museums…?' from visitors to the Reimagining Museums for Climate Action exhibition during COP26. © Rodney Harrison.

additional ideas, which we collected from visitors to the Green Zone during COP26, are also featured on the project website, and provide an additional set of concepts and ideas for museums to consider when taking radical action for climate.

Mobilising Museums for Climate Action: a toolbox of ideas

In addition to the ideas competition and exhibition, the project developed a series of open-access resources that aimed to explore how we can rethink the shape and purpose of museums, reimagine new forms of museum and mobilise the potential of museums – in current and new forms – to accelerate, amplify and transform climate action everywhere.

The Mobilising Museums for Climate Action 'toolbox' (McGhie 2021) is a collection of practical tools, frameworks, essential climate knowledge and opportunities that museums and their partners can adopt. The toolbox is organised into bite-size chunks to break through the complex and sometimes confusing nature of climate action work. The toolbox is available as a PDF and as a web-based version for automatic translation for accessibility in different languages.

Mobilising Museums for Climate Action is framed around a set of five ways for museums to contribute to climate action, which are addressed in different sections of the toolbox:

1. **Mitigation through museums.** Museums must support all of society to reduce its greenhouse gas emissions, rapidly, in line with Paris Agreement commitments, by encouraging and empowering people to understand the part they have to play in climate action, and to use less, waste less and make sure anything they do use is renewable. They can foster support, and sharing of resources, for nature conservation efforts that strengthen nature's ability to absorb greenhouse gas emissions.
2. **Mitigation in museums.** Museums must aggressively reduce greenhouse gas emissions across all aspects of their activity, in line with Paris Agreement commitments. They can ensure all staff and all people and organisations in the value chain understand the part they must play in climate action and are empowered to act through policies and resourcing so that every action is supporting climate action, in order to use less, waste less and make sure anything that is used is renewable. They can direct financial and other resources towards

nature conservation efforts that strengthen nature's ability to absorb greenhouse gas emissions, through their everyday decisions and procurement practices.

3. **Adaptation through museums.** Museums must support all of society and nature to face and cope with current and projected climate change impacts.
4. **Adaptation in museums.** Museums must understand how they will be impacted by climate change and adapt their practices, location, programmes and collections to be fit for the future.
5. **Climate action as part of sustainable development, climate justice and a just transition.** Museums must ensure that all climate change activity is undertaken in ways that do not themselves disenfranchise people or communities, locally or globally; and recognise that, in tackling climate change, other sustainable development challenges must be addressed at the same time.

In 2022, we received additional funding to run a series of workshops around the toolbox, in partnership with a number of key UK-based and international museum organisations and individual museums, showing how the principles developed as part of the project could be put into action in specific contexts. As a result of this additional funding, over 1,200 people participated in online and in-person events organised by the project team or to which project team members contributed, presenting the project and toolbox. In addition, over 30,000 people watched a recording of an event at the United Nations High-Level Political Forum for the Sustainable Development Goals, organised by Latvia, that included discussion of the project and its outcomes.

Reflections on the project and our involvement in COP26

Enabling, empowering and mobilising public action on climate will clearly be crucial to the goal of maintaining global heating at or below 1.5°C and to reimagining and recreating a net-zero or zero-carbon world. The Framework Convention on Climate Change and the Paris Agreement both recognise the crucial importance of involving the public in climate action. They both specify the importance of public education, training of key groups of staff, public awareness campaigns, public participation in climate change decision-making, public access to information on science and policy regarding climate change, and international cooperation. These six areas are known informally as Action for Climate Empowerment, or ACE.

The submissions we received from the ideas competition, the work we have done with and around the exhibition, and the discussions we had at COP26 itself show that museums have incredible potential not only to communicate but also, and perhaps more importantly, to become facilitators for real and radical climate action. Museums are specifically named as key institutions to facilitate public participation in climate action in the 10-year Glasgow Work Programme on Action for Climate Empowerment (and this is something we were particularly involved in following and contributing to at COP26 as a project team). Activities under the work programme are focused on four priority areas that aim to address gaps and challenges in implementing the six elements of ACE and to create opportunities to accelerate implementation. The four priority areas are as follows:

- Policy coherence, to strengthen coordination of ACE work at the international and national level.
- Coordinated action, to build partnerships that bring together different expertise, resources and knowledge to accelerate ACE implementation.
- Tools and support, to enhance access to tools and support for building capacity and raising awareness among various stakeholders regarding ACE.
- Monitoring, evaluating and reporting, to strengthen monitoring, evaluation and reporting of the implementation of all six ACE elements.

The Glasgow work programme reconfirms the key role that a broad range of stakeholders – such as national and subnational governments, educational and cultural institutions, the private sector, international and non-governmental organisations and the media – play in implementing ACE, and promotes cooperation, collaboration and partnerships among the diverse stakeholders.

But to do this, they need to do a number of things. The Mobilising Museums for Climate Action toolbox proposes five practical pathways to climate action for museums:

- Reducing emissions in museums, through a range of direct and indirect initiatives to rapidly shift away from fossil fuels in heating, energy and transport, and change working practices and standards that use these, or that are inefficient; as well as less direct ones, such as reducing employee business travel and commuting, reducing consumption of goods and services, and considering issues such as visitor travel to museums, investments and waste management (see McGhie 2021, Part d).

- Supporting society to reduce emissions.
- Ensuring museums are fit for the future to adapt to climate change.
- Supporting society's adaptation.
- Ensuring that climate action is fair and contributes to broader sustainable development goals (McGhie 2021).

But these practical goals can only be achieved by taking further action to rethink the roles of museums in society. To this end, there are another five ways in which we would suggest museums need to fundamentally change to reimagine themselves for future climate action.

First, and perhaps most fundamentally, they need to reckon with their histories, and how those histories continue to play out in the present. As shown by ongoing discussions about the restitution and repatriation of objects in museums, they need to take a critical look at their histories and the role played by the narratives they have produced – narratives of human exceptionalism, hierarchical understandings of human culture and an emphasis on 'progress' and 'civilisation' – in underpinning and helping to produce the current climate emergency.

Second, they need to rapidly decarbonise museum buildings and their operations (especially things like touring exhibitions which are incredibly carbon-intensive). This means benchmarking success differently – in terms not of numbers of visitors, but of how they interact with and facilitate social action. Third, they need to take a critical look at who they associate with and the sponsorship they receive – as emphasised by current protests at the Science Museum and British Museum and the work of activist groups like Culture Unstained and Fossil Free Culture.

Fourth, in addition to telling their own stories differently, they need to tell different stories. Any museum can be a 'climate museum', and some of the ideas in the exhibition and our various project outputs explore how this might be done. Finally, they need to see their role differently – as facilitators for individuals and communities, aiming to catalyse and support them in taking the climate action they wish to take, rather than as authorities.

Every part of society will need to make radical changes to address the climate emergency, and this includes museums and the cultural sector. Museums could, and in many cases are keen to, play a leading role in these transformations. But like all of society, they will only be able to do so if they make significant changes to the way they operate, the stories they tell and how they are told, the sponsorship they receive, and the ways in which they perceive their roles in relation to the publics they serve.

Conclusion

In *The Great Derangement*, Amitav Ghosh argues that 'the climate crisis is also a crisis of culture, and thus of the imagination' (Ghosh 2016: 9). Thus, there is an urgent need for new creative imaginaries to help confront the challenges of a warming world. Reimagining Museums for Climate Action has aimed to push forwards critical and creative thinking in a number of key areas. First, by recognising that museums are densely entangled with the problem of climate change, we sought to underline the need for an epistemic shift in museological thinking and practice to bring about meaningful climate action. Second, by highlighting the manifold ways in which museums are to some extent already embedded in the work of climate action, we hoped to draw together disparate strategies and approaches from across the sector. Third, by expanding the conversation around this problem to those outside the rather narrow field of 'museum studies', we sought to encourage transdisciplinary perspectives and imaginaries. Finally, by embracing speculative design as a creative methodology for the field, the project has aimed to challenge preconceptions about what a museum could or should be.

Taken collectively, the competition entries and suggestions collected from the public during COP26 suggest a number of important transformations which must take place in order for museums to become meaningful institutions in facilitating real climate action. The first relates to breaking down boundaries and moving away from authoritarian values of order and control. In an inevitably transforming future world, museums must accept and embrace the creative possibilities of uncertainty and change rather than work against these forces. This will mean reimagining the familiar structure of museums – the second major theme to emerge from the competition. Instead of centralised spaces and buildings, many of the submitted proposals called for non-hierarchical 'networks' enabling a decentralised approach to collecting, education and research. This would require a fundamental rethink of the way museums are typically governed – the third and perhaps most important theme to emerge across the competition entries.

Certain crises demand new forms of decision-making where experts and lay people can come together to imagine new futures.

As a participatory thought experiment, what the project perhaps demonstrates most clearly is the radical potential that still clings to the idea of the museum, taking us far beyond the walls of any single building or site to encompass community activism, digital infrastructures, citizen science and diverse forms of 'rewilding'. Such propositions do not simply imagine new purposes for 'the museum' as an apparatus of climate action; rather, they question and undermine the very substance of museological work and its role in the production of future worlds. We remain hopeful – despite the dire warnings for the future of the planet which have accompanied the Intergovernmental Panel on Climate Change (IPCC) Working Group I contribution to the Sixth Assessment Report – of the significant potential for museums to contribute to the broad social, ecological, economic and political transformations which will be required to address the climate emergency.

Acknowledgements

Reimagining Museums for Climate Action received funding from the Arts and Humanities Research Council (AHRC) as a joint initiative under Rodney Harrison's Heritage Priority Area Leadership Fellowship (AH/P009719/1) and Colin Sterling's Innovation Fellowship 'New Trajectories in Curatorial Experience Design' (AH/S00436X/1). It received further financial support from the joint University College London–University of Gothenburg Centre for Critical Heritage Studies (CCHS). The project was undertaken in partnership with Henry McGhie (Curating Tomorrow) and the Glasgow Science Centre. Rowan Ward was a postdoctoral researcher on the project, which was also assisted by Janna oud Ammerveld. See https://www.museumsforclimateaction.org for further information.

Parts of this essay reproduce passages also published in: Harrison, Rodney and Colin Sterling (in prep.), The Speculative and the Profane: Reimagining Heritage and Museums for Climate Action, in Nick Shepherd (ed.), *Resilient Heritage: Rethinking Heritage in Precarious Times* (London: Routledge); Harrison, Rodney and Colin Sterling (2021), Museums Otherwise: A Compendium of Possible Futures, in Rodney Harrison and Colin Sterling (eds), *Reimagining Museums for Climate Action* (London: Museums for Climate Action): 6–15; and the Reimagining Museums for Climate Action website (RMCA 2022).

Notes

1. In 1992, the world's governments committed to address the rapidly growing threat of global climate change by adopting the United Nations Framework Convention on Climate Change (UNFCCC), which aims to achieve the 'stabilisation of greenhouse gas concentrations in the atmosphere at a level that would prevent dangerous anthropogenic interference with the climate system'. The convention came into force in 1994. Since then, governments and their representatives have met twice a year to monitor progress, evaluate what action is needed to meet the convention's key goals, and agree programmes of activity that are then to be delivered in each country. Notably, the Kyoto Protocol of 1997 committed its signatories by setting internationally binding targets to reduce greenhouse gas emissions. The Paris Agreement of 2015 saw its signatories agree 'to strengthen the global response to the threat of climate change by keeping a global temperature rise this century well below 2 degrees Celsius above pre-industrial levels and to pursue efforts to limit the temperature increase even further to 1.5 degrees Celsius'. Each year, a meeting is held in Bonn, Germany, in the summer, to help set the direction for the larger, more important conference that is usually held in November or December. This larger meeting is often referred to as the COP, which means the 'Conference of the Parties'. COP26, the 26th Conference of the Parties to the UNFCCC, was originally scheduled to take place in November 2020, but was rescheduled for November 2021 on account of the global COVID-19 pandemic. This was the first year since 1984 that a COP had not been held.
2. The 'Green Zone' at any COP is the public-facing part of the conference. The 'Blue Zone' is the policy-facing part of the conference and is only accessible to official delegates.
3. https://artsandculture.google.com/story/reimagining-museums-for-climate-action-cabinet-office/tAWB_rRlcmpjkQ?hl=en

References

Arfvidsson, Helen and Ann Follin. 2020. Connectedness, Consumption and Climate Change: The Exhibition Human Nature. *Museum Management and Curatorship* 35(6): 684–696.

Brophy, Sarah and Elizabeth Wylie. 2013. *The Green Museum: A Primer on Environmental Practice*. Lanham: AltaMira Press.

Cameron, Fiona and Brett Neilson (eds). 2014. *Climate Change and Museum Futures*. New York: Routledge.

Cameron, Fiona, Bob Hodge and Juan Francisco Salazar. 2013. Representing Climate Change in Museum Spaces and Places. *WIREs Climate Change* 4(9): 9–21.

Davis, Joy (ed.). 2020. *Museums and Climate Action* [special issue]. *Museum Management and Curatorship* 35(6).

Garrard, Chris. 2021. Taking the Logos Down: From Oil Sponsorship to Fossil Free Culture. In Rodney Harrison and Colin Sterling (eds), *Reimagining Museums for Climate Action*. London: Museums for Climate Action: 52–59.

Ghosh, Amitav. 2016. *The Great Derangement: Climate Change and the Unthinkable*. Chicago and London: University of Chicago Press.

Harrison, Rodney. 2013. *Heritage: Critical Approaches*. Abingdon and New York: Routledge.

Harrison, Rodney. 2015. Beyond 'Natural' and 'Cultural' Heritage: Toward an Ontological Politics of Heritage in the Age of Anthropocene. *Heritage & Society* 8(1): 24–42.

Harrison, Rodney, Caitlin DeSilvey, Cornelius Holtorf, Sharon Macdonald, Nadia Bartolini, Esther Breithoff, Harald Fredheim, Antony Lyons, Sarah May, Jennie Morgan and Sefryn Penrose. 2020. *Heritage Futures: Comparative Approaches to Natural and Cultural Heritage Practices*. London: UCL Press.

Harrison, Rodney and Colin Sterling (eds). 2021. *Reimagining Museums for Climate Action*. London: Museums for Climate Action.

Janes, Robert. 2009. *Museums in a Troubled World: Renewal, Irrelevance or Collapse?* London and New York: Routledge.

L'Internationale (eds). 2016. *Ecologising Museums*. Paris: L'Internationale.

Malm, Andreas. 2018. *The Progress of This Storm: Nature and Society in a Warming World*. London: Verso.

McGhie, Henry. 2019a. *Museum collections and biodiversity conservation*. Curating Tomorrow. Online at http://www.curatingtomorrow.co.uk/wp-content/uploads/2020/01/museum-collections-and-biodiversity-conservation-2019.pdf Accessed 13 March 2023.

McGhie, Henry. 2019b. *Museums and the Sustainable Development Goals: A How-To Guide for Museums, Galleries, the Cultural Sector and their Partners*. Curating Tomorrow.

McGhie, Henry. 2021. *Mobilising Museums for Climate Action: Tools, Frameworks and Opportunities to Accelerate Climate Action in and with Museums*. London: Museums for Climate Action. Online at https://www.museumsforclimateaction.org/mobilise/toolbox Accessed 13 March 2023.

Morton, Timothy. 2013. *Hyperobjects: Philosophy and Ecology at the End of the World*. Minneapolis: Minnesota University Press.

Newell, Jennifer, Libby Robin and Kirsten Wehner. 2016. *Curating the Future: Museums, Communities and Climate Change*. London and New York: Routledge.

RMCA. 2022. Reimagining Museums for Climate Action website. Online at https://www.museumsforclimateaction.org/ Accessed 13 March 2023.

Sterling, Colin. 2019. Designing 'Critical' Heritage Experiences: Immersion, Enchantment and Autonomy. *Archaeology International* 22(1): 100–113. https://doi.org/10.5334/ai-401

Sutton, Sarah and Cynthia Robinson (eds). 2020. *Museums and Public Climate Action* [special issue]. *Journal of Museum Education* 45(1).

Þórsson, Bergsveinn. 2018. When Matter Becomes a Monster: Examining Anthropocenic Objects in Museums. *Museological Review* 22: 44–53.

Þórsson, Bergsveinn and Nørskov Vinnie (eds). 2020. *Curating Climate* [special issue]. *Nordisk Museologi* 30(3).

Wallace-Wells, David. 2019. *The Uninhabitable Earth: A Story of the Future*. London: Penguin.

2
From climate victim to climate action: heritage as agent in climate change mitigation discourse

Janna oud Ammerveld

Introduction

In the heritage discourse, climate change has become a major concern for the continued conservation of heritage places. Less attention has thus far been given to the role of heritage or the historic environment in the mitigation discourse. However, this is changing, as the heritage sector is looking for ways to reinterpret its work in the light of a changing climate. To reflect on the more recent endeavours taking place in the heritage sector, this chapter will focus on the work of Historic England (HE) in relation to climate mitigation. HE is the official heritage government authority and advisory body in England (Historic England, n.d.-a). For HE, climate change has predominantly been regarded as a risk to the historic environment and its conservation, as is common in the heritage sector (Historic England, n.d.-c, n.d.-g, 2016a). However, the organisation has increasingly engaged in the mitigation side of the climate change discourse as well. This work mainly focuses on representing the historic environment, especially the built historic environment, as an agent in the mitigation discourse. While the presentation of climate change as a threat to the historic environment and its conservation positions it as a 'victim' of the changing climate, their work focusing on mitigation aims to do the opposite and provides a proactive and positive role in a changing climate for the historic environment that HE champions.

The authorised climate discourse

In her book *Uses of Heritage*, Laurajane Smith (2006) introduced the concept of 'Authorised Heritage Discourse', which symbolises the overarching, globalised power narrative defining what official heritage is and who gets to determine that it be so. There is also a similar authorised discussion in the ways in which climate change is primarily presented in public discourse and policy (Morel and oud Ammerveld 2021). This discourse is based on quantitative scientific data, mostly consisting of calculations of greenhouse gas emissions, based on the Western scientific tradition, informing mitigation and adaptation responses.

This approach to climate change is symbolised by the work and the reports of the International Panel on Climate Change (IPCC). The IPCC has been described as the universally accepted authority on climate science and informant for policymaking (Mahony and Hulme 2018). Its reports inform many international and national climate change policies and practices, as well as the broader United Nations language directly linked to climate action, as used in the mitigation targets set in the Paris Agreement, the United Nations Framework Convention on Climate Change (UNFCCC) and Goal 13 of the Sustainable Development Goals on climate action. This discourse focuses on reducing CO_2 and greenhouse gas emissions as climate change action and has net-zero futures as the ultimate goal. According to the IPCC, mitigation 'involves actions that reduce the rate of climate change' and is achieved by 'limiting or preventing greenhouse gas emissions and by enhancing activities that remove these gases from the atmosphere' (IPCC, n.d.-b). On the other hand, adaptation is 'the process of adjustment to actual or expected climate and its effects. In human systems, adaptation seeks to moderate or avoid harm or exploit beneficial opportunities' (IPCC, n.d.-a). Adaptation practices focus on risk assessments and adaptation strategies meant to create disaster preparedness and the resilience to deal with the uncertainty related to future scenarios (Lei, Wang, Yue, Zhou and Yin 2014). So, where mitigation is about minimising future impact, adaptation is about preparing for such impacts.

However, there is also specific criticism of the strong emphasis on mitigation and the calculations behind these policies. For example, this framing excludes the humanities and the sociocultural dimensions and therefore leaves little engagement with the underlying social and economic drivers that fuel the parameters causing a changing climate (e.g. Castree et al. 2014; Goldman, Turner and Daly 2018; Pielke 1998; Swyngedouw 2020). Furthermore, while the IPCC reiterates its warnings for future climate scenarios and the urgency to act, its mitigation scenarios are also tied to the economic premise of growth in gross domestic product (GDP; Hickel and Kallis 2020). As a consequence, according to these critiques, it becomes impossible to radically question the current socioeconomic status quo, which a growing group of scholars points out as one of the most critical drivers of the climate crisis (Hickel 2020; Jackson 2009, 2021; Kallis et al. 2020; Raworth 2018; Soper 2020). Nightingale et al. (2020: 344) describe this as the 'externalisation' of climate change: 'the wider framing of climate change as an external threat to (separate) natural and human systems, coupled to adaptation policy decisions informed by best science, both of which cannot challenge existing political economic systems'.

Climate change and heritage: risk, threats and adaptation

In heritage practice and heritage studies, climate change has thus far mainly been approached as a threat and risk embedded in the above-described adaptation approaches. Likely, this is a direct result of the tangible impact that climate change has had on heritage sites across the world. As heritage work is still strongly influenced by its history within the conservation movement, heritage sites remain to be understood in terms of risk and threat and remain in need of protection to avoid damage or loss (DeSilvey and Harrison 2020; Harvey and Perry 2015). The consequences of a changing climate due to anthropogenic causes are now added to the list of potential threats.

As a result, the climate change–heritage relationship has mainly been discussed on the premise of risk (climate change to heritage) and vulnerability (heritage to climate change; see e.g. Bonazza et al. 2018; Cassar and Pender 2005; Fatorić and Seekamp 2017; Hollesen et al. 2018; Howard 2013; Kim 2011; Perez-Alvaro 2016; Perry 2015; Phillips 2015). Central to these studies is mapping change, vulnerability and risks at case study sites and developing tools, practices and methodologies to prepare for and adapt to the present and future risks caused by extreme weather events and a changing climate. Perez-Alvaro (2016), for example, discusses the impact of a changing climate on oceanic ecosystems and describes how this influences the in-situ preservation of underwater heritage. In addition, she discusses how some onshore heritage may turn into offshore sites in the future as sea levels rise. Howard (2013) and Phillips (2015) are other examples. Both turn to World Heritage Sites in Britain to discuss what changes may be needed in the management plans of these sites in light of climate change. Here, the heritage–climate change relationship has first and foremost been framed in terms of risk and vulnerability and as a threat to the certainty and linearity of conservation and heritage practices representing 'business as usual'. A concern for the conservation of heritage sites forms the central guidance in these responses. Thus, the primary response from the heritage sector follows the common framing of climate change as an environmental and external threat, in line with the 'authorised climate discourse' described above.

In contrast to the threat–victim relationship between heritage and climate change, this chapter addresses the work of HE in response to climate change focusing on mitigation. This work therefore starts from an understanding of climate change as a problem of greenhouse gas emissions, and of climate action as an effort to mitigate these emissions. In the context of this chapter, this work is limited to publicly available reports, webpages and documents, with a focus on the period between 2017 and 2020. Also included are reflections of staff on this work shared in (anonymised) interviews conducted between December 2019 and March 2020. Overall, this chapter aims to reflect on the ideas regarding heritage and climate change that underpin HE's responses based on mitigation and on what these responses mean for climate action.

'We need to be part of the solution, not the problem'

To the backdrop of the increasing presence of the climate change discourse in public opinion, individual concern and national and international politics, one of the main priorities for HE and the historic environment sector is to stay relevant within this new climate reality. As climate change is mainly approached as a problem based on carbon emissions and calculations, it is easy for outsiders to see old homes and buildings as inefficient in terms of energy usage and outdated in terms of insulation standards:

> I think often heritage people are seen as the bad guys in climate change in this country, because I've been in a number of places, in the kind of green building end of climate change issues, where the perception is old buildings are inefficient; therefore, you get rid of the old buildings, and you build new buildings which are energy efficient (Interview transcript, 31 January 2020, London).

And in the account of another member of staff:

> Well, we want the historic environment to be seen as a constructive part of the solution, and that is the main message … Rather than people who stand in the way of progress and want things to remain the same, that we are a constructive part of the future because we have useful knowledge, useful assets, and useful perspectives and expertise (Meeting transcript, 12 December 2019b, London).

HE's work on mitigation can be interpreted as part of this search and urge for relevance. While the impacts of climate change on heritage sites and their conservation may be its main concern, situating the historic environment – especially the built historic environment – as a positive agent in the climate change mitigation discourse is also essential to its work in response to climate change. The latter consists of a more proactive engagement, moving heritage from a 'victim' of the changing climate to an 'agent' in climate action. Essentially, it keeps its own work and purpose as an organisation relevant in a time where climate issues are finding their way to the top of political and public agendas: 'At Historic England, we recognise the urgent need for climate action and we believe that England's existing buildings have an essential role to play in fighting climate change' (Historic England, n.d.-e).

This mitigation-focused work can be divided into two parts: (1) energy efficiency and (2) embodied carbon in historic buildings. Each will be discussed separately in the following sections. These two strands have a significant overlap as both promote repair and conservation over replacing elements of (or entire) historic buildings. They represent two sides of the same coin, as they support an approach that claims historic buildings are inherently sustainable.

Mitigating climate change: energy efficiency in England's historic buildings

> What I tend to say when I'm lecturing to people who don't really know who we are or who have, I know, a preconception of what we do is to say that … I show them a picture of Lloyds[1] and say, this is a listed building. And I'll often put it up against a picture of St Paul's [cathedral]. And I'll say, I'll tell you which one's hard to deal with. It's not St Paul's that I lose sleep over.

> Because there's a tendency that the enlightenment rush towards measurement, models and theories has meant that we're quite sure that we're better at things than they were in the past. And I'm sorry, proof of the pudding is in the eating. We're clearly terrible at just about everything we do. In fact, we've just about trashed the planet in 200 years, which is really quite good going. It's a big planet (Interview transcript, 12 December 2019a, London).

The above is an anecdotal account shared in an interview to make the point that historic buildings have paid their dues to claim their place in the built environment. The interviewee used St Paul's Cathedral as an example because the sound architecture, durability and resilience to its local climate, and adaptability of this historic building make it likely to last for much longer. This contrasts with a contemporary building like the referenced Lloyds Banking Group headquarters in London, one of the youngest buildings to receive a Grade I listing from HE (Historic England n.d.-d). Notably, it is also a bank investing billions a year in the fossil fuel industry itself (Kirsch et al. 2021).

Part of HE's climate change work tries to oppose the idea that traditionally built houses and buildings are by definition outdated and obsolete, especially against the popularisation of low emissions innovations like passive houses and new technologies like triple-glazed windows. Instead, they provide homeowners with a rapidly expanding number of freely available reports and webpages advising on the adaptation of historic homes to increase their energy efficiency while also promoting traditional homes as highly adaptable to today's standards and resilient to the changeable and changing English weather. For example, 'thoughtful retrofitting' of traditional homes to increase their energy efficiency is the topic of an abundant set of resources available on HE's website, from a general 'how to' guide (Historic England 2018) to specific guidance on, for example, the insulation of pitched roofs (Historic England 2016c), flat roofs (Historic England 2016b), solid walls (Historic England 2012a) or timber floors (Historic England 2012b). Similarly, the webpage (Historic England n.d-e) that sets out HE's position on 'Modifying Historic Windows as Part of Retrofitting Energy-Saving Measures' promotes a 'repair not replace' approach as an act directed towards creating a sustainable society:

> It contributes to sustainability in its widest sense and has been the preferred solution of our predecessors. Proper maintenance and repair will ensure our old buildings continue to function effectively.

This approach is in the interest of owners, society more generally, the environment and future generations.

At the heart of HE's advice on improving the energy performance of buildings is the so-called 'whole building approach'. The 'How to Improve Energy Efficiency' guidance report (Historic England 2018: 9) defines this approach as:

> One that uses an understanding of a building in its context to find balanced solutions that save energy, sustain heritage significance, and maintain a comfortable and healthy indoor environment. A whole building approach also takes into account wider environmental, cultural, community and economic issues, including energy supply ... Most of all, it deals with specific situations as opposed to generalities.

Central to this approach is balancing the potential updating and retrofitting of a building's energy performance with the protection of its heritage values, in other words, balancing conservation and mitigation.

From costs to the homeowner to costs to the climate

The presentation of energy efficiency measures on HE's website has undergone changes through the years as public interest shifts. For several years, HE has framed adaptation measures meant to increase energy efficiency as economically beneficial to the homeowner (Interview transcript, 6 February 2020, London). However, this was not the original framing of this topic, as energy efficiency first became a primary point of concern between 2012 and 2015 as part of the UK government's failed Green Deal scheme.[2] A long-term staff member reflected on this as follows:

> If you look under the advice section under 'Your Home' (on the HE website), there is a whole section, for instance, on saving energy ... I think part of the issue is understanding how things are badged because, as I said, the driver that time was very much, yes, the reason why they were pushed from the government about the Green Deal and energy was being driven by climate change.
>
> But, from our consumer point of view, the reason why they were making changes or being interested in changes was about

saving money. It wasn't about saving the planet. And I think there has been a change, and it's happened very rapidly … I think about the last six months. I think it's very recent. I think it is very, very recent (Interview transcript, 6 February 2020, London).

On the HE website as of August 2021, the webpages on energy efficiency have direct hyperlinks to HE's designated climate change webpages (Historic England n.d-b). And where the previously referenced 'how to' guide from 2018 (Historic England 2018) for energy efficiency mentioned reducing carbon more tentatively as one of several reasons to pursue mitigation measures, the most recent report from 2020 titled *Energy Efficiency and Traditional Homes* (Historic England 2020a: 1) states in its introduction, 'The UK has declared a climate emergency which demands a new approach to managing change to the built environment. Taking a whole life approach to buildings means prioritising our existing buildings by making refurbishment and reuse worthwhile.'

So, initially supported by the government economic incentives of the 'Green Deal' to encourage homeowners to improve the energy performances of their homes, rooted in a climate change mitigation agenda, HE has adjusted to the expectations of their public (traditional homeowners). Only with the recent increase in public awareness and concern about climate change matters have mitigation measures been directly linked to climate action again. And with public awareness and the UK government's mitigation pledges, HE seems to feel more confident to frame their work increasingly as climate action: 'In terms of the government coming to net-zero, you're not going to be able to build your way out of this. You've got to deal with existing housing stock' (Interview transcript, 5 March 2020, London).

Mitigating climate change: embodied carbon in historic buildings

In addition to promoting the adaptability of historic homes to retrofitting and adjusting them to new energy standards, HE has conducted significant research on the so-called embodied carbon captured in the historic environment. Embodied carbon consists of the CO_2 emissions released during the whole lifetime of a building: from the mining of its materials until its demolition (Historic England on behalf of the Historic Environment Forum 2020). This information is relevant within the mitigation framework, as it allows making a comparison between the carbon sustainability of existing homes and new development projects. The energy necessary to build new buildings – from creating and processing materials to their transportation – and the emissions released during the process make up a significant part of the UK's total national emissions each year. In fact, 55 per cent of all the materials in the UK economy are used to make products for the construction industry – the construction of new buildings in England emits as much carbon dioxide as the whole of Scotland (Historic England on behalf of the Historic Environment Forum 2020). However, the embodied emissions of new developments (i.e. the emissions from the production and processing of the materials used) are often not included in the buildings' carbon footprint. Instead, new buildings are now often promoted as 'fossil-fuel free', but this only accounts for the energy they use (or do not use) once in use (Wainwright 2021). In a meeting of the Historic Environment Adaptation Working Group, a group coordinated by HE with the aim of sharing experiences on climate change work in the UK heritage sector, a member of the group reflected on this difference in standards:

> So, the existing historic buildings stock, you're looking at a lifespan of 300, 400 years, whereas what we're building, what we're delivering now, because the conditions on the developers aren't strict enough, in 30 years' time, we're going to have to be retrofitting them again.
> ... I think it is worth exploring how with a historic building, it's not just the embodied energy [i.e. carbon] since it's been built, but it's also the fact that you're not going to have to go back to that building. If you do it right, if you put in the right measures or do the right thing, you're not going to have to go back and revisit that again like you are going to with the stuff we're putting up now (HEAWG meeting, 16 January 2020, conference call).

HE's interest in the question of the amount of carbon involved in the lifetime of a traditional home is not entirely new. A long-term staff member pointed out that work on embodied carbon has been conducted before (Interview transcript, 31 January 2020, London). They shared that in the early 2000s, HE (then English Heritage) calculated the carbon stored in the materials used to build a Victorian house. However, soon after, the Brick Association commented on the study on economic grounds. It claimed the study did not make a fair comparison with today's building practices, as techniques to make bricks have become much more energy-efficient compared to Victorian times. Again, the profit-based marketplace caused friction here. Naturally, the Brick Association and its partners benefit more from the delivery of a set of new bricks than from the conservation of an existing set. However, HE accepted the critique, and according to the memory of that staff member, the conclusion was that for such detailed and specific calculations, the in-house expertise was not sufficient: 'So, I think on that side [energy efficiency, responsible retrofitting], we were comfortable. I think it was the big, embodied energy arguments we were not comfortable on, so we eased off on that (Interview transcript, 31 January 2020, London). Since the 2000s, this position has changed, as a change in the composition of teams and internal expertise, combined with new and more in-depth research on these same topics, has led to the publication of several reports on embodied carbon in the historic environment by HE (Interview transcript, 31 January 2020, London).

In 2019 and 2020, HE published two research reports and a themed 'Heritage Counts' issue on this topic (Duffy et al. 2019; Historic England 2020b; Historic England on behalf of the Historic Environment Forum 2020). Together, these produced quantitative evidence to argue in favour of the inherent sustainability of the historic environment. This allows HE to maintain its argument on embodied carbon and avoid the situation described in the above account from 20 years before.

The work on embodied carbon starts with a scoping study titled *Understanding Carbon in the Historic Environment*, a piece of research commissioned by HE and executed by Carrig Research (Duffy et al. 2019). This study aims to create a method and provide exemplary data to perform life-cycle analyses on built heritage. It does so by calculating the whole-life carbon of two case studies: a chapel refurbished for residential use and a refurbishment of an end-of-terrace Victorian house – a very common dwelling in English towns and cities. The study compares the energy performance and carbon sequestered in these two examples to those of a newly built project and includes the carbon costs of demolition and construction (see Figure 2.1). From this comparison, the authors (Duffy et al. 2019: 54) conclude as follows:

> The findings highlight that the energy-efficient refurbishment of historic buildings is necessary to achieve performances similar to new buildings. It was found that existing regulations, which consider operational emissions only, disadvantage historic building refurbishment in terms of carbon emissions assessment. In the case of the new-build, the omission of embodied carbon emissions would underestimate the total emissions by nearly 30 per cent.

The prioritisation of refurbishment over demolition is inherently sustainable, as the waste of many materials with carbon already embedded in them would be avoided.

This argument is supported by the research laid out in the publication titled *Valuing Carbon in pre-1919 Residential Buildings* produced by HE, which builds on the work done by Carrig Research (Historic England 2020b). It takes the carbon calculations from the latter and generalises them to apply to the full UK building stock dating from pre-1919. It uses these data to compare the carbon saved in three different scenarios, each representing a different scale of refurbishment projects over the next 10–25-year period. Together with the Carrig Research publication, this work shifts the focus from historic buildings as emitters of carbon to providing storage for carbon.

Both pieces of research described above form the basis for the 2019 'Heritage Counts' report (published in February 2020), titled *There's No Place Like Old Homes: Re-use and Recycle to Reduce Carbon* (Historic England on behalf of the Historic Environment Forum 2020). The target audience of Heritage Counts publications consists of the UK historic environment sector at large. The reports provide background research to show and support the value of the historic environment to society as a whole (Historic England n.d.-f). The 2019 report presents the work of both reports discussed above in a more user-friendly way for a larger audience by omitting the formulas from the methodologies and presenting the results in easily readable infographics (see Figure 2.1 for an example). Eventually, it concludes that 'traditional buildings are inherently sustainable' (Historic England on behalf of the Historic Environment Forum 2020: 45). Their baseline for this work is the comparison between the carbon needed for a newly built house and (refurbished) buildings from pre-1919 over the period until 2050. The focus on 2050 is a consequence of the UK Government policy goal to reach net-zero by then (Historic England on behalf of the Historic Environment Forum 2020: 8): 'If we are to meet the UK Parliament's legally binding commitment to become carbon neutral by 2050, then addressing the embodied carbon of the built environment must become a priority'.

The Heritage Counts research is framed as a direct response to the climate crisis, 'the biggest challenge facing us today', with the historic environment offering 'practical and effective solutions to the real and present danger posed by climate change' (Historic England on behalf of the Historic Environment Forum 2020: 4). These 'practical and effective solutions' are presented in terms of embodied carbon

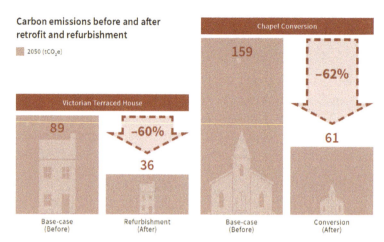

Figure 2.1 Carbon emissions are reduced by 60 per cent in the Victorian terraced house case study as a result of energy efficiency interventions and by 62 per cent in the chapel conversion case study by 2050. © Historic England, on behalf of the Historic Environment Forum 2020: 34. Reproduced under the Creative Commons licence CC BY-NC-ND 4.0.

and the understanding of sustainability in terms of carbon usage. Thus, the research is firmly grounded in a carbon understanding of the climate crisis. As a result, there is an identifiable 'solution' for the problem: mitigation. Moreover, this solution is simultaneously an argument in favour of the conservation and championing of the historic environment. For example, one of the main recommendations of the report links the results to a favourable context for conserving heritage sites at risk (2020: 48):

> Around the country there are so many examples of historic assets currently neglected, underused and even at risk of demolition. According to official estimates from the Historic England Heritage at Risk dataset there were over 4,612 designated heritage assets 'at risk' in 2019 … .
>
> On the other hand, there are also inspiring examples of 'at risk' historic buildings being brought into use, now providing much needed homes, working spaces, leisure and community spaces.

Supported by the detailed quantitative research, HE seems to find increasing strength to present itself as essential in moving forward to avert the consequences of the climate crisis. In the organisation's own slightly dramatic words, 'We must move towards a whole life carbon approach for buildings otherwise we may meet carbon targets without actually reducing carbon emissions and in the process *lose the war against climate change*' (Historic England on behalf of the Historic Environment Forum 2020: 9; my emphasis).

Conclusion and discussion

The ideas presented in this chapter show that a significant part of HE's climate change response, how they interpret their role in the climate change discourse and their contribution to climate action are based on an understanding of climate change as a carbon problem and climate action as a mitigation practice. This work underlines a new understanding of heritage conservation in the light of a changing climate as a practice suited to a circular or 'doughnut economy' (Raworth 2018) that understands resources as finite and stresses the importance of reusing and recycling as opposed to extracting materials from the earth for new products. The imagined future at the centre of this response is one of low carbon. These futures take place in the timeframes set by governments to reach net-zero (for the UK, 2050).

Through this understanding, HE has reframed the historic environment and its conservation as a resource in governments' mitigation agendas and the climate debate at large. Simultaneously, the arguments that it has built around the embodied carbon and life-cycle analysis of historic buildings and the guidance on improving energy efficiency standards are also arguments in favour of the conservation of the historic environment. In this way, it has created its own place and emphasised the relevance of the historic built environment and of itself as an organisation in a carbon age.

The architect Rem Koolhaas once wrote, 'We are living in an incredibly exciting and slightly absurd moment, namely that preservation is overtaking us' (Koolhaas and Otero-Pailos 2014: 3). However, the arguments presented in this chapter may actually argue the opposite: preservation should be taking over more in a marketplace where innovation and progress are often more economically rewarding (as Rem Koolhaas surely knows). This line of thinking is demonstrated by one member of HE staff in an answer to a question at their interview:

IV[3] Does, in a way, climate change almost offer you an extra argument to actually maintain these buildings?

IE Exactly. Quite so. I think that's an important thing, because that's when our resources get scarcer, it makes sense to use what you've got, really (Interview transcript, 26 February 2020, London).

Thus, the importance of mitigation has provided an additional framework to argue for the importance of the conservation of historic buildings in light of climate change. Just as the photosynthesis of plants is now reframed as carbon-capturing (Maris 2021), the conservation of historic buildings has become a climate mitigation measure that simultaneously leaves one with a feeling of doing good and being on the 'good side' of climate history.

However, according to the geographer Erik Swyngedouw (2020), a focus on mitigation, as well as the more common focus on adaptation present in the heritage sector, risks depoliticising the climate problem (see also Nightingale et al. 2020 for a similar critique). Swyngedouw argues that these measures do not question underlying socioeconomic relations that are part of the drivers of the climate change crisis on national and global scales. Instead, adaptation and mitigation are based on the belief that we can continue with life as usual as long as greenhouse gas emissions are reduced (Swyngedouw 2020).

Following Swyngedouw's critique, the framing of climate change as an issue of mitigation enables the continued treatment of climate change as an external impact and phenomenon (Nightingale et al. 2020) in the heritage discourse. As such, climate change does not need to be approached as a socio-material product of historical practices and ideas shaped by cultural ideologies (see Malm 2018 and Moore 2017, 2018, who argue that climate change is exactly this in their Capitalocene thesis); in other words, as the cumulative, negative outcome of *our* past, in the present and brought into the future – that is, *anthropogenic climate change as a form of our cultural heritage*. Instead, by focusing on the positive position the historic environment can take within net-zero futures, and on climate change as a carbon problem set in the present, HE can act on climate change without any radical rethinking or reinterpreting of what heritage represents and entails, or where its responsibility lies in the light of a changing climate.

Overall, the approach to climate change and climate change work discussed in this chapter works as an affirmative and amplifying agent to the conservation paradigm central to HE's work as a champion of England's historic environment. A focus on mitigation is safely contained within the area of their expertise, one might say their 'comfort zone': namely, the conservation and promotion of the historic environment. Within this framing, the organisation does not have to question any of the underlying drivers or consequences of the changing climate. In other words, climate change remains an external impact in the heritage discourse. However, the work shows the organisation's flexibility in adapting to the changing interests of society and the public they work for, in order to maintain their relevance in a changing environmental paradigm, representing the transactional alignment of the heritage sector to climate change opportunities.

Notes

1. Lloyds Banking Group London HQ building on Lime Street in the City of London, designed by Richard Rogers and opened in 1986.
2. The Green Deal was a government scheme that ran between 2013 and 2015, which provided homeowners and tenants with loans to use for improving the energy performance of their property. However, the deal failed and was used in very few cases.
3. IV = interviewer, IE = interviewee.

References

Bonazza, Alessandra, Ingval Maxwell, Milos Drdácký, Elizabeth Vintzileou and Christian Hanus. 2018. *Safeguarding Cultural Heritage from Natural and Man-Made Disasters: A comparative analysis of risk management in the EU*. Brussels. https://doi.org/10.2766/224310

Cassar, May and Robyn Pender. 2005. The Impact of Climate Change on Cultural Heritage: Evidence and Response. In *14th Triennial Meeting*, The Hague, 12–16 September 2005: preprints. London: James & James: 610–616.

Castree, Noel, William Adams, John Barry, Daniel Brockington, Esteve Corbera, David Demeritt, Rosaleen Duffy, Ulrike Felt, Katja Neves, Peter Newell, Luigi Pellizzoni, Kate Rigby, Paul Robbins, Libby Robin, Deborah Bird Rose, Andrew Ross, David Schlosberg, Sverker Sorlin, Paige West, Mark Whitehead and Brin Wynne. 2014. Changing the Intellectual Climate. *Nature Climate Change* 4: 763–768.

DeSilvey, Caitlin and Rodney Harrison. 2020. Anticipating Loss: Rethinking Endangerment in Heritage Futures. *International Journal of Heritage Studies* 26(1): 1–7. https://doi.org/10.1080/13527258.2019.1644530

Duffy, Aidan, Aneta Nerguti, Caroline Engel Purcell and Peter Cox. 2019. *Understanding Carbon in the Historic Environment: Scoping Study*. London: Historic England.

Fatorić, Sandra and Erin Seekamp. 2017. Securing the Future of Cultural Heritage by Identifying Barriers to and Strategising Solutions for Preservation under Changing Climate Conditions. *Sustainability* (Switzerland), 9(11): 2143. https://doi.org/10.3390/su9112143

Goldman, Mara, Matthew Turner and Meaghan Daly. 2018. A Critical Political Ecology of Human Dimensions of Climate Change: Epistemology, Ontology and Ethics. *WIREs Climate Change* 9(4): e526. https://doi.org/10.1002/wcc.526

Harvey, David and Jim Perry. 2015. Heritage and Climate Change: The Future is Not the Past. In David Harvey and Jim Perry (eds), *The Future of Heritage as Climates Change: Loss, Adaptation and Creativity*. London and New York: Routledge: 3–21.

Hickel, Jason. 2020. *Less is More: How Degrowth Will Save the World*. London: William Heinemann.

Hickel, Jason and Giorgos Kallis. 2020. Is Green Growth Possible? *New Political Economy* 25(4): 469–486.

Historic England. (n.d.-a). *About Us*. Online at https://www.historicengland.org.uk/about/ Accessed 5 February 2019.

Historic England. (n.d.-b). *Energy Efficiency and Older Houses*. Online at https://historicengland.org.uk/advice/your-home/saving-energy/energy-efficiency/ Accessed 12 December 2020.

Historic England. (n.d.-c). *Impacts of Climate Change*. Online at https://historicengland.org.uk/research/current/threats/heritage-climate-change-environment/impacts-climate-change/ Accessed 6 April 2022.

Historic England. (n.d.-d). *Lloyd's Building*. Online at https://historicengland.org.uk/listing/the-list/list-entry/1405493 Accessed 19 January 2022.

Historic England. (n.d.-e). *Modifying Historic Windows as Part of Retrofitting Energy-Saving Measures*. Online at https://historicengland.org.uk/whats-new/statements/modifying-historic-windows-as-part-of-retrofitting-saving-measures/ Accessed 12 December 2020.

Historic England. (n.d.-f). *On Behalf of the Historic Environment Forum: Heritage Counts*. Online at https://historicengland.org.uk/research/heritage-counts/ Accessed 12 December 2020.

Historic England. (n.d.-g). *What Are the Effects of Climate Change on the Historic Environment?* Online at https://historicengland.org.uk/research/current/threats/heritage-climate-change-environment/what-effects/ Accessed 6 April 2022.

Historic England. 2012a. *Energy Efficiency and Historic Buildings: Insulating Solid Walls (Guidance)* (Vol. HEAG081). Historic England. Online at https://historicengland.org.uk/images-books/publications/eehb-insulating-solid-walls/heag081-solid-walls Accessed 22 March 2023.

Historic England. 2012b. *Energy Efficiency and Historic Buildings: Insulation of Suspended Timber Floors (Guidance)* (Vol. HEAG086). Historic England.

Historic England. 2016a. *Climate Change Adaptation Report (Discovery, Innovation and Science in the Historic Environment)* (Vol. 28/2016). Historic England. Online at https://historicengland.org.uk/research/results/reports/6580/ClimateChangeAdaptationReport Accessed 22 March 2023.

Historic England. 2016b. *Energy Efficiency and Historic Buildings: Insulating Flat Roofs (Guidance)* (Vol. HEAG078). Historic England. Online at https://historicengland.org.uk/images-books/publications/eehb-insulating-flat-roofs/heag078-flat-roofs/ Accessed 22 March 2023.

Historic England. 2016c. *Energy Efficiency and Historic Buildings: Insulating Pitched Roofs at Ceiling Level (Guidance)* (Vol. HEAG077). Historic England. Online at https://historicengland.org.uk/images-books/publications/eehb-insulating-pitched-roofs-ceiling-level-cold-roofs/heag077-cold-roofs/ Accessed 22 March 2023.

Historic England. 2018. *Energy Efficiency and Historic Buildings: How to Improve Energy Efficiency (Guidance)* (Vol. HEAG094). Historic England. Online at https://historicengland.org.uk/images-books/publications/eehb-how-to-improve-energy-efficiency/heag094-how-to-improve-energy-efficiency/ Accessed 22 March 2023.

Historic England. 2020a. *Energy Efficiency and Traditional Homes (Historic England Advice Note)* (Vol. 14). Swindon: Historic England. Online at https://historicengland.org.uk/images-books/publications/energy-efficiency-and-traditional-homes-advice-note-14/heag295-energy-efficiency-traditional-homes/ Accessed 22 March 2023.

Historic England. 2020b. *Valuing Carbon in pre-1919 Residential Buildings*. London: Historic England. Online at https://historicengland.org.uk/content/docs/research/valuing-carbon-pre-1919-residential-buildings/ Accessed 22 March 2023.

Historic England on behalf of the Historic Environment Forum. 2020. *There's No Place Like Old Homes: Re-use and Recycle to Reduce Carbon* (Heritage Counts, 2019). Historic England. Online at https://historicengland.org.uk/content/heritage-counts/pub/2019/hc2019-re-use-recycle-to-reduce-carbon/ Accessed 14 March 2023.

Hollesen, Jorgen, Martin Callanan, Tom Dawson, Rasmus Fenger-Nielsen, Max Friesen, Anne Jensen and Marcy Rockman. 2018. Climate Change and the Deteriorating Archaeological and Environmental Archives of the Arctic. *Antiquity* 92(363): 573–586.

Howard, Andy. 2013. Managing Global Heritage in the Face of Future Climate Change: The Importance of Understanding Geological and Geomorphological Processes and Hazards. *International Journal of Heritage Studies* 19(7): 632–658. https://doi.org/10.1080/13527258.2012.681680

IPCC. (n.d.-a). *Working Group II Impacts, Adaptation and Vulnerability*. Online at https://www.ipcc.ch/working-group/wg2/ Accessed 21 June 2021.

IPCC. (n.d.-b). *Working Group III Mitigation of Climate Change*. Online at https://www.ipcc.ch/working-group/wg3/?idp=433 Accessed 5 February 2019.

Jackson, Tim. 2009. *Prosperity without Growth: Economics for a Finite Planet*. London: Earthscan.

Jackson, Tim. 2021. *Post Growth: Life after Capitalism*. Cambridge: Polity Press.

Kallis, Giorgos, Susan Paulson, Giacomo D'Alisa and Federico Demaria. 2020. *The Case for Degrowth*. Cambridge: Polity Press.

Kim, Hee-Eun. 2011. Changing Climate, Changing Culture: Adding the Climate Change Dimension to the Protection of Intangible Cultural Heritage. *International Journal of Cultural Property* 18(3):259–290.

Kirsch, Alison, Jason Opena Disterhoft, Grant Marr, Paddy McCully, Ruth Breech, Maaike Beenes and Colin Rees. 2021. *Banking on Climate Chaos: Fossil Fuel Finance Report 2021*. Rainforest Action Network, Banktrack, Indigenous Environmental Network, Oil Change International, Reclaim Finance and Sierra Club. Online at https://www.bankingonclimatechaos.org/wp-content/uploads/2021/10/Banking-on-Climate-Chaos-2021.pdf Accessed 14 March 2023.

Koolhaas, Rem and Jorge Otero-Pailos. 2014. *Preservation Is Overtaking Us* (ed, Jordan Carver). New York: Columbia Books on Architecture and the City.

Lei, Yongdeng, Jing'ai Wang, Yaojie Yue, Hongjian Zhou and Weixia Yin. 2014. Rethinking the Relationships of Vulnerability, Resilience and Adaptation from a Disaster Risk Perspective. *Natural Hazards* 70(1): 609–627. https://doi.org/10.1007/s11069-013-0831-7

Mahony, Martin and Mike Hulme. 2018. Epistemic Geographies of Climate Change: Science, Space and Politics. *Progress in Human Geography* 42(3): 395–424. https://doi.org/10.1177/0309132516681485

Malm, Andreas. 2018. *The Progress of this Storm*. London and New York: Verso.

Maris, Virginie. 2021. *Het Wilde Deel van de Wereld* (Dutch translation). Amsterdam: Boom uitgevers.

Moore, Jason. 2017. The Capitalocene, Part I: On the Nature and Origins of our Ecological Crisis. *Journal of Peasant Studies* 44(3): 594–630.

Moore, Jason. 2018. The Capitalocene Part II: Accumulation by Appropriation and the Centrality of Unpaid Work/Energy. *Journal of Peasant Studies* 45(2): 237–279.

Morel, Hana and Janna oud Ammerveld. 2021. From Climate Crisis to Climate Action: Exploring the Entanglement of Changing Heritage in the Anthropocene. *The Historic Environment: Policy & Practice* 12(3–4): 271–291. https://doi.org/10.1080/17567505.2021.1957261

Nightingale, Andrea Joslyn, Siri Eriksen, Marcus Taylor, Tomothy Forsyth, Mark Pelling, Andrew Newsham and Stephen Whitfield. 2020. Beyond Technical Fixes: Climate Solutions and the Great Derangement. *Climate and Development* 12(4): 343–352. https://doi.org/10.1080/17565529.2019.1624495

Perez-Alvaro, Elena. 2016. Climate Change and Underwater Cultural Heritage: Impacts and Challenges. *Journal of Cultural Heritage* 21: 842–848. https://doi.org/10.1016/j.culher.2016.03.006

Perry, Jim. 2015. Climate Change Adaptation in the World's Best Places: A Wicked Problem in Need of Immediate Attention. *Landscape and Urban Planning* 133: 1-11. https://doi.org/10.1016/j.landurbplan.2014.08.013

Phillips, Helen. 2015. The Capacity to Adapt to Climate Change at Heritage Sites: The Development of a Conceptual Framework. *Environmental Science and Policy* 47: 118–125. https://doi.org/10.1016/j.envsci.2014.11.003

Pielke, Roger. 1998. Rethinking the Role of Adaptation in Climate Policy. *Global Environmental Change* 8(2): 159–170.

Raworth, Kate. 2018. *Doughnut Economics: Seven Ways to Think Like a 21st Century Economist*. White River Junction: Chelsea Green Publishing.

Smith, Laurajane. 2006. *Uses of Heritage*. New York: Routledge.

Soper, Kate. 2020. *Post-Growth Living: For an Alternative Hedonism*. London and New York: Verso.

Swyngedouw, Eric. 2020. *Klimaatactie in gele hesjes: De postpolitieke impasse van de klimaatconsensus*. Brussels: VUBPRESS.

Wainwright, Oliver. 2021 (3 April). The Dirty Secret of So-Called 'Fossil-Fuel Free' Buildings. *The Guardian UK*.

3

Syrian refugees' food in Lisbon: a heritage of food beyond national borders

Marcela Jaramillo

Introduction

When people are forced to flee their country due to persecution, war or violence, they must leave behind not only most of the personal objects that have significant value in their lives, but also their territory constituted by material heritage – such as monuments, sites, buildings and cultural places, which provide them with a sense of belonging to a nation, region or community. However, they carry during their journey a suitcase full of memories that represent a refugee's 'basic human need' (Mire 2014), allowing them to recreate in a territory different from their own their practices, representations, expressions, knowledge and skills, while reminding them of who they are and where they belong.

Food practices are an important part of these memories and one that refugees often recreate outside their country. During their journey, and in the destination country, refugees try to reproduce their own food habits, adapting their recipes to the products they can find in the host country, using new cooking utensils and/or adjusting their food rituals to the cultural dynamics of their new context. Their aim is to continue to live as similarly as possible to the way they did at home, and eating practices are central to this. In this way, they can preserve and maintain their cultural identity in a country foreign to their own, but also develop it further through the sharing of food habits with other refugees and migrants, as well as with the locals themselves.

In the wake of the so-called 'European migrant crisis',[1] 2,402 people have so far sought refuge in Portugal, most of them Syrians (Reis Oliveira and Gomes 2019; Reis Oliveira 2021). For Syrians, food represents a fundamental element of their own cultural dynamics, as it not only brings the family together three times a day, after the mother, who has planned the day's menu in advance, has spent a considerable amount of time cooking, but it is also a form of hospitality towards guests, a way of doing business and celebrating a fraternal union together. In short, eating food is not only an act of nourishment for Syrians, but also represents the richness of being able to share a meal together around a table (Tahhan 2020). However, as a result of the civil war in Syria,[2] many Syrians have had to forcibly migrate in search of international humanitarian protection, making it difficult for them to carry out their usual food practices.

During their journey to Europe, refugees typically live in temporary camps, at borders, in the homes of acquaintances and strangers or in detention centres. In these spaces they have to adapt their habits to fit either the food they are offered or that which they can source. Finally, when they are relocated or resettled in one of the European member states, they are challenged by the way their food practices can differ from established European food heritage. The way in which this encounter between two food cultures is managed can have a direct impact on a refugee's chances of successful integration into the host country. One of the final recommendations provided by the book *Food & Migration: Understanding the Geopolitical Nexus in the Euro-Mediterranean*, launched in the wake of the so-called European migrant crisis, highlights how 'A research agenda on the "migration-food nexus" in countries of destination is needed. Food has a huge and unexplored potential for integration, by acting as a factor of inclusion' (Caracciolo, Aresu and Antonelli 2017: 109).

In this regard, Syrian asylum seekers rehomed in Portugal often face two opposing positions regarding how their food culture is conceived by the host country. This chapter explores these stances in the context of the integration of Syrian refugees into Portuguese society. On the one hand, there is the institutional position, which not only overlooks Syrian refugees' eating habits, but also contains dietary elements markedly different from their own. On the other hand, there is the perspective of civil society, which encourages refugees to use their food heritage as a mechanism to make their culture known in the country of destination, while weaving social ties with the locals. To carry out this research, I attended events related to food and refugees, visited refugee reception centres and conducted semi-structured interviews with staff from public institutions and non-governmental organisations (NGOs) and with Syrian refugees.

Syrian food practices overlooked by the Portuguese state

As stipulated by the Portuguese government, the integration process for asylum seekers, whether they are relocated or reintegrated, lasts 18 months.[3] This begins at the airport, when asylum seekers are received by a government official, who usually guides them to a reception centre[4] where they sometimes stay for days, perhaps weeks or months, while being assigned a place to live. Many asylum seekers initially spend time in such places, where they experience the initial stage of integration into Portuguese culture. Reception centres are where migrants sleep, complete daily activities and meet new people, but they are also places that cater for the central need of every human being – food consumption. Initially, when asylum seekers arrived at reception centres, food was provided directly by the facilities' canteens, and served at regular hours. The food available was varied and designed to provide the best nutrition. Nevertheless, the menus were typically based on what Portuguese people usually consumed.

Eventually, reception centres began to realise that Syrian asylum seekers did not usually eat in canteens, preferring to spend their limited monthly allowance[5] on ingredients, to cook and eat more in line with their cultural habits. Concerning this, 'Daniel', a former employee of a reception centre, said, 'Geralmente não gostam da comida que o JRS lhes dá e preferem cozinhar e gastar o dinheiro do seu saco para comprar comida' (They generally don't like the food that the JRS [Jesuit Refugee Service] gives them and prefer to cook and spend the money allocated to them on buying food; Interview, Lisbon, 1 November 2017). Food is an essential element in Syrian culture and not carrying out these practices leads to the forgetting of roots and undermines refugees' sense of identity and belonging. In this regard, 'Yara', from Damascus, Syria, who arrived in Lisbon in 2016 via a relocation programme, along with her four children, explained to me why she did not eat the food offered in the canteen at the reception centre: 'It is strange food, very different from the food in my country, I don't like it … my food reminds me of the beautiful things of my country' (Interview, Lisbon, 27 February 2020).

Another important issue that led Syrian refugees to refuse the food offered at reception centres was their uncertainty as to whether the food was prepared in accordance with Muslim requirements. Eighty-seven per cent of Syrians are Muslim (CIA, The World Factbook n.d.),[6] so their eating habits must follow the Koran's teaching, and food must be *halal*, or 'legal'. This includes fruit, vegetables and eggs. Meat must be from a halal slaughtered animal; milk must also be from a halal animal, while for cheese it depends on the ingredients. *Haram* foods, on the other hand, are prohibited foods, and include pork, crustaceans, blood, non-halal animal additives such as gelatine or tallow, alcohol and any food containing alcohol as an ingredient (Muslims in Britain n.d.). In this sense, the eating habits of Syrian refugees are very much determined by religion, so adapting to the food practices of non-Muslim countries is a culturally difficult process (Gurhan 2018).

In this regard, 'Daniel' said, 'De facto, em muitas ocasiões, eles ofereceram carne de porco aos recém-chegados' (In fact, on many occasions they [the reception centres] offered pork to the newcomers; Interview, Lisbon, 25 September 2019). Although pork is one of the most representative ingredients of Portuguese cuisine, its inclusion on the menus at reception centres, although certainly well-intentioned, threatened the basic principles of Muslim food culture. One of the refugees, interviewed for the study on the integration process led by the NGO ComParte, said:

> No Centro há muçulmanos e cristãos, mas a maioria de nós não come porco. E eles serviam muitas vezes porco. Nos primeiros dias nós passávamos fome. Porque é que eles estão a gastar dinheiro em algo que nós não vamos comer …? Nós sentimos que estávamos a ser forçados a ser como os portugueses. Nós viemos para cá, não para mudar a nossa cultura, mas para viver em segurança convosco. (There are Muslims and Christians at the Centre but most of them do not eat pork, and they [the reception centre] often served pork. In the first days we were hungry. Why are they spending money on something we will not eat …? We felt we were being forced to be like the Portuguese. We came here not to change our culture, but to live in safety with you.) (ComParte 2018: 23–24)

Syrian asylum seekers felt that by being offered food that did not follow Syrian food standards, they were being 'forced' to adapt to a culture different from their own. In this sense, feeding refugees in reception centres with typical Portuguese food could be understood as an assimilationist practice, as it forces refugees to follow the practices of the dominant culture.

Another challenge faced by Syrian refugees at reception centres was using the kitchen when they needed it. According to 'Daniel', 'A cozinha estava sempre fechada, era altura de pedir a chave, por isso tinham de cozinhar à vez, e não podiam cozinhar à noite, era proibido lá' (The kitchen was always closed, it was necessary to ask for the key, so they [asylum seekers] had to take turns cooking, and they could not cook at night, it was forbidden there) (Interview, Lisbon, 25 September 2019).

The fact that the use of the kitchen was restricted not only meant that Syrian mothers could not develop their cultural food practices in the way they were used to, but also that Syrian refugees could not adequately carry out one of the most important practices of the Muslim religion, Ramadan. In Syria, mothers spend most of their day in the kitchen, where they cook for their family. According to 'Yara', 'In our culture, when we get married, we take care of cooking for the family and children … In Syria women don't normally work so we spend more time cooking. It was frustrating when I could not cook for my children there [in the reception centre]' (Interview, Lisbon, 27 February 2020). For all the Syrian women I interviewed, cooking represented part of their 'cultural capital' (D'Sylva and Beagan 2011); it is important in their community for a woman to know how to cook well, so they play this role within their family with great pride.

Additionally, not allowing Syrian asylum seekers to use the kitchen in the evening limited their ability to follow the rules around breaking the fast that usually takes place during Ramadan, when special meals are shared with family and loved ones – in particular, the pre-dawn meal, called *suhur*, and the evening feast that breaks the fast, called *iftar*. Given the impossibility of using the kitchen at night, *suhur* and *iftar* were performed with many limitations. 'Fatima' from Aleppo, who left Syria in 2016 with her husband, son, sister and brother-in-law, said that 'In Ramadan, as it is a fast, we were hungry, and we could not cook for *suhur* because the kitchen was closed' (Interview, Lisbon, 7 May 2021). Although use of the kitchen is nowadays allowed in the evening during Ramadan, for 'Miguel', in charge of one of the reception centres, this remains a complex issue, as not only do refugees have to share the kitchen with many others at the same time, but also the kitchens are often too small, making it difficult to enjoy meals with loved ones:

> A questão da comida é mais forte e no Centro do Acolhimento é mais difícil para o Ramadão porque há pouco espaço para cozinhar, e normalmente é uma altura mais difícil para eles, porque têm que partilhar todos a cozinha, passam o dia com fome, portanto estão mais fragilizados pela fome, e é uma altura que fica mais tensa, que requer mas atenção. Nas famílias, na altura do Ramadão, do comer juntos, a comida ganha muita importância. (The issue of food is stronger and in the reception centre it is more difficult for Ramadan because there is little space to cook, and it is usually a more difficult

time for them, because they all have to share the kitchen. They spend the day hungry, so they are weaker with hunger, and it is a time that gets more tense, which requires more attention. In families, at the time of Ramadan, of eating together, food becomes very important.) (Interview, Lisbon, 11 July 2020)

Encouraging Syrian refugees to consume food that does not conform to their culture and religious practice causes numerous issues. Importantly, it limits a mother's main role in the family, namely cooking, but also affects the religious practice of Ramadan. Consequently, these top-down policies regarding food come close to taking for granted a unique body of cultural norms, the Portuguese ones. According to Harrison, 'assimilationist, integrationist or single core societies ... accept only a single core set of cultural values and norms. When immigration occurs, people assimilate forcibly and quickly' (2010: 171).

However, the promotion of assimilationist practices has arisen unintentionally in reception centres. The lack of experience of Portuguese governmental institutions in receiving so many people in need of humanitarian protection has caused them to overlook the variety of food customs with which asylum seekers arrive. Faced with these cultural clashes, reception centres have tried, as far as possible, to adapt progressively to the diversity of cultures. Today, for example, in one of the reception centres, refugees can cook within a set timetable, have a space in the kitchen to store their food and use the fridge. 'Inés', the coordinator of the resettlement unit in one of the reception centres, said:

We have facilities with a large fully equipped kitchen, where everyone can cook their own food. There is a timetable, which not only allows everyone the opportunity to cook, but also allows the cleaning staff access to clean up between meals. Everyone has the possibility of using the fridges and cooking whatever they want and prefer. This is better than having catering services because there are people who are vegetarians, or people who don't eat pork or meat (Interview, Lisbon, 17 March 2020).

Although the officials interviewed expressed their willingness to be more aware of the cultural diversity of newcomers in reception centres, asylum seekers are still facing many difficulties, such as inability to find adequate products to cook their food, to gather as a family during meals or to stay in the kitchen as long as they want, among others. Nevertheless, once asylum seekers are assigned a place to live, they begin to gain a measure of food autonomy that they did not have in the reception centres. Thus, the families make use of their monthly income by shopping mainly at Martin Moniz, a neighbourhood in Lisbon where most foreign food stores are located, where prices are affordable and where they can obtain those food products not readily available in local supermarkets (see Figure 3.1). However, given the reduced monthly income that many experience, they frequently have to request free food from the 'banco alimentar',[7] despite the fact that they often do not know what the products

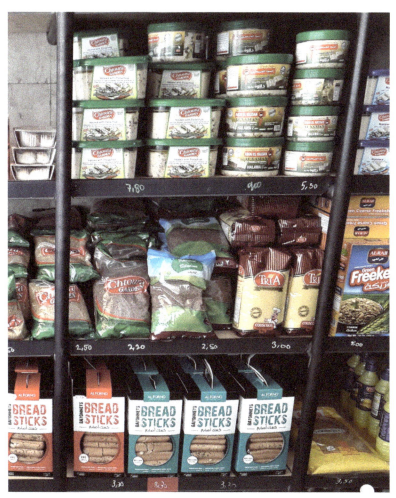

Figure 3.1 Store with Syrian products in Lisbon. © Marcela Jaramillo.

offered are for. 'Elisa', a NGO psychologist who supports refugees during their integration process, said, 'Muitas vezes não gostam dos produtos que lá oferecem, são muito exigentes com comida. E, por vezes, não compreendem para que servem certos produtos' (They often don't like the products they offer there; they are very demanding with food. And sometimes they don't understand what certain products are for; Interview, Lisbon, 3 March 2020).

Food is an essential factor in survival, and culinary practices are a distinctive element in the identities of individuals and communities (Parasecoli 2014; Ramli, Mohd Zahari and Isha 2014; Ramshaw 2016; Bertrán and Flores 2014; Matta, Suremain and Crenn 2020; Gurhan 2018; Brulotte and Di Giovine 2014; Timothy 2016). Offering food that does not conform to refugees' cultural norms makes refugees feel rejected and consequently limits their successful inclusion into the host country. 'João', who led the integration process for asylum seekers, notes:

> Não há formas mais fáceis de integração do que à mesa comer, para além de toda a teoria ... À mesa há sempre lugar para outra pessoa, à mesa há uma necessidade comum para todos, precisamos de nos alimentar. Da mesma forma na mesa podemos ser diferentes, posso usar talheres, ou paus, ou com a mão e partilhar os alimentos na mesma mesa. (There is no easier way to integrate than at the table eating, beyond all theories ... At the table there is always room for another person, at the table there is a common need for everyone, we need to feed each other. At the table we can also be different, I can use cutlery, or sticks, or with my hand and share the food at the same table.) (Interview, Lisbon, 20 March 2020)

Although it seems that 'João' is aware of the importance of including refugee food practices in the integration process, the diversity of refugees' food culture has so far not been discussed at the national level. Overlooking refugees' cultural characteristics, including their food practices, in the integration process leads to a perception among refugees that what identifies them culturally is rejected. Referring to food integration in Europe, Bartolomei states, 'Through it [food], we can manifest inclusiveness, belonging, attachment, in short being a symbolic expression of social bond. On the contrary, it can represent exclusivity, generate stereotypes and feelings of disgust that demarcate boundaries' (Bartolomei 2017: 86).

Food practices as an integration alternative promoted by civil society

Away from the institutionalised perspective, civil society organisations have suggested that food heritage is a major resource for refugee integration. When the European migrant crisis broke out, the sense of solidarity felt by many Portuguese with the Syrians began to be expressed through various demonstrations, in which they proved their philanthropic credentials in the face of this migratory phenomenon (Diário de Notícias 2015; Esquerda 2019; Observador 2020). In addition, there have been financial donations, participation in the Plataforma de Apoio aos Refugiados (PAR; Refugee Support Platform)[8] and the implementation of further cultural projects. The latter have employed the food practices of refugees as the main resource to integrate both the asylum seekers into Portuguese society and Portuguese society into the culture of the asylum seekers.

One of the most renowned projects managed by the Associação Pão a Pão (Bread to Bread Association) is the Mezze restaurant,[9] which was launched in 2017 through donations from individuals (PPL 2017). This restaurant, which offers Syrian food to diners, emerged from the desire to contribute to the integration of Syrian refugees in the community. In addition, this project carries out parallel activities related to Syrian culture such as workshops, conferences and talks, through which Portuguese society gets to know who these newcomers are. Francisca Gorjão, one of its founders, said:

> I think that this project is very important for people so that they don't give up their identity to be part of a community. This is the main focus of Mezze, *not only do people not give up their identity, but they also use it as a means to connect to the new community* [emphasis added]. So, they use the Syrian traditional food to make this connection between Syrian people and Portuguese people, or Lisbon residents (Interview, Lisbon, 7 July 2020).

This is not the only project to have employed food practices as a mechanism for integration of refugees. Make Food Not War, which began organising meals and lunches to promote the cuisine of Syrian refugees from 2015, today promotes refugee food practices in Lisbon during each of its events, using Facebook as a platform for dissemination. Its founder, Paulo Alexandre Mascarenhas Álvares, son of Mozambican immigrants, started the project with the idea of using food practices as a vehicle to promote dialogue between cultures and bring peoples closer together. According to him, 'Este projecto procura a inclusão social, onde todos nos podemos sentar à mesma mesa e partilhar e conhecer-nos uns aos outros' (This project seeks social inclusion, where we can all sit at the same table and share and get to know each other; Interview, Lisbon, 30 September 2020).

There is also the Marhaba[10] project, the name of which means 'welcome' in Arabic. This initiative, developed by the CRESCER association, seeks to integrate not only Syrian asylum seekers but also Eritreans and Iraqis through their food practices. The project began by inviting Portuguese society to be part of a Syrian communal meal, and today offers a catering service (CRESCER 2017). Additionally, the event Refugio Cultural, which was organised by the Associação para Onde?[11] [Association to Where?] on 28 October 2017, sought to make Portuguese society aware of the diversity of refugee cultural expressions, in particular the food practices of Syrian and Eritrean refugees (Dias Real 2017). Finally, Lisbon Project[12] is a Christian NGO that has conducted many evening events where the priority is to share traditional food and cultural expression. During these events, while the guests are eating, they enjoy music, poetry, dancing and other cultural practices of the refugee community. This project seeks not only to integrate refugees but also to make their culture known to the locals.

Other initiatives have been promoted by the Syrian refugees themselves. Tayybeh,[13] for example, has been run by a Syrian refugee couple, both from Damascus, who in their urgency to escape the bombings and associated terror of civil war, first migrated to the Arab Emirates before seeking asylum in Portugal, where they arrived in 2015 with their daughter and son. The project started in 2017 as a catering service and became a restaurant from 2019 (Cardoso 2019; Simão 2019; Onde vamos Jantar 2019). The same couple also founded the Quinta do Damasco[14] (Damascus' Farm), an initiative launched in January 2021 with the aim of producing organic Syrian food to be sold online. It also provided a space where people can go to meditate, learn to dance to traditional Syrian music, cook Syrian food or take part in other cultural activities.

Lara's Kitchen, promoted by Facebook since 2019, is another project that provides a Syrian food catering service, mainly for social events in Lisbon. Lara Alhalabi, the founder, is a young woman from Damascus who, after her eighth attempt to escape from Syria, was able to reach

Turkey, from where she was later resettled to a refugee camp in Greece before being transferred to Portugal in 2017. She said that despite the lack of support from the Portuguese state to carry out the project, she ventured to undertake it as a means of subsistence (Coutinho and Correia 2019). Similar is the case of the Baraa Syrian food initiative, managed by 'Fatima', who began working for the Marhaba project, but in 2019 launched her own catering service (see Figure 3.2). She advertises on Facebook too and offers Syrian food for diverse events in Lisbon (Interview, 28 February 2020).

The common denominator of the projects discussed in this section is that they have emerged through civil society initiatives, and their priority is to use refugee food practices to integrate Syrian refugees into Portuguese society and make locals aware of Syrian cultural heritage. In this sense, the bottom-up perspective affords an opportunity to integrate

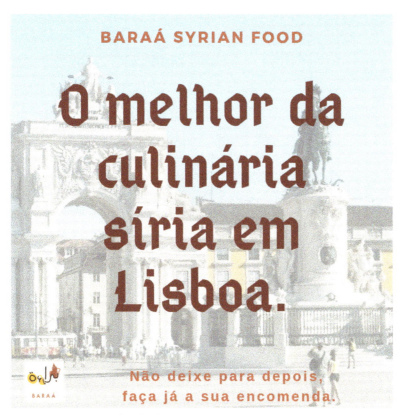

Figure 3.2 Syrian food advertising in Lisbon. © Baraa Alfetouri.

Syrian refugees through validation of their cultural identity, in particular their own food practices.

Conclusion

This chapter has considered official and unofficial responses to refugee food practices in Portugal as an example of the broader experience of refugees in what has been termed the European migrant crisis. For Syrian refugees, food practices have a special cultural value, and the ignorance of these practices by host countries can be read as a sign of hostility and a constraint to proper integration. In the context of Syrian refugees in Lisbon, Portugal, the top-down process has led to an assimilationist integration which, although unintentional, has been evidenced mainly in the refugee reception centres by the introduction of typical Portuguese foods into the refugees' diet. It is also seen through the ignoring of the 'culinary capital' that dignifies the role of Syrian women as feeders of the family, and of the need for refugee families to have access to meeting places to reunite with their loved ones during *iftar* and *suhur* during Ramadan.

Alternatively, a bottom-up dynamic has promoted events, restaurants, workshops and catering services where Syrian refugee food practices have been a key tool for two-way integration, as Syrian refugees adapt to the host society without giving up their own cultural identity, and as host communities meet the cultural needs of this diverse population while recognising and learning about their culture. Through this chapter I suggest that asylum policies should recognise the food practices of refugees as a form of heritage in their own right, as well as a means of integration. This proposal, largely unexplored in the context of the European migration crisis, would lead to inclusive integration in which the heritage of newcomers would be respected and validated, and therefore to the future enhancement of multicultural integration processes in Europe.

Acknowledgements

This chapter has emerged from a paper presented at the international conference Critical Heritage Studies and the Future of Europe, organised by the CHEurope project. I am grateful to the participants who kindly consented to be interviewed and to Professor Nélia Dias for reading an earlier draft of this chapter and giving me useful suggestions.

Notes

1. The 'European migrant crisis', also called the 'European migration crisis' or the 'European refugee crisis', is understood as the phenomenon in which Europe received an 'unprecedented' number of asylum applications, which reached 1.3 million in both 2015 and 2016 (Eurostat 2016).
2. For information about the civil war in Syria, see the book *Syria: The Fall of the House of Assad* (Yale University Press, 2013) by David Lesch.
3. According to Portuguese asylum policies, the asylum seekers should have access to health services, education, Portuguese language courses, labour market counselling, legalisation and permanent support during these 18 months. The state should also provide them with housing and a monthly allowance. At the end of this period, when the government support ends, asylum seekers are expected to be able to act autonomously without government support (Alto Comissariado para as Migrações 2017).
4. The national government, in partnership with Alto Comissariado para as Migrações (ACM) and the Jesuit Refugee Service (JRS), has four facilities in Lisbon to provide asylum seekers with temporary shelter: the Centro de Acolhimento Temporário para Refugiados (CATR), Centro de Acolhimento para Refugiados (CAR), Centro de Acolhimento para Refugiados (CAR II) and Casa De Acolhimento Para Crianças Refugiadas (CACR). In addition, there are the organisations belonging to the Plataforma de Apoio aos Refugiados (PAR), which was also given the responsibility of hosting new arrivals throughout the national territory.
5. The value is 150 euros for the first adult and 75 euros for a minor. In the case of households, the amount to be granted to the second adult or remaining adults in the household will be 107.50 euros (Alto Comissariado para as Migrações 2017).
6. Percentages for different religions are as follows: Muslim, 87 per cent (official; includes Sunni, 74 per cent, and Alawi, Ismaili and Shia, 13 per cent); Christian, 10 per cent (includes Orthodox, Uniate and Nestorian); Druze, 3 per cent; Jewish (few remaining in Damascus and Aleppo) (CIA, The World Factbook n.d.).
7. The 'banco alimentar' aims to provide food to those with limited financial resources. See https://www.bancoalimentar.pt/
8. https://www.refugiados.pt/
9. https://mezze.pt/
10. https://crescer.org/en/project/marhaba/
11. http://paraonde.org/
12. https://lisbonproject.org/
13. https://www.tayybeh.pt/
14. https://www.damasco.pt

References

Alto Comissariado para as Migrações. 2017. *Relatório de Avaliação Da Política Portuguesa de Acolhimento de Pessoas Refugiadas: Programa de Recolocação* [Evaluation Report on the Portuguese Refugee Reception Policy: Relocation Programme]. Lisbon: Alto Comissariado para as Migrações.

Bartolomei, Di Luca. 2017. Challenges of Food Integration in Europe. In Lucio Caracciolo, Alessandro Aresu and Marta Antonelli (eds), *Food & Migration: Understanding the Geopolitical Nexus in the Euro-Mediterranean*. Parma: Barilla Center for Food and Nutrition: 83–88.

Bertrán, Miriam and Nelly Flores. 2014. Identidad, Migración y Comida En La Globalización: Algunos Apuntes Desde La Ciudad de México [Identity, Migration and Food in Globalisation: Some Notes from Mexico City]. In Javier Medina (ed.), *Alimentación y Migraciones en Iberoamérica*. Barcelona: UOC: 53–58.

Brulotte, Ronda and Michael A. Di Giovine. 2014. Food and Foodways as Cultural Heritage. In Ronda Brulotte and Michael A. Di Giovine (eds), *Edible Identities: Food as Cultural Heritage*. Burlington: Ashgate: 1–28.

Caracciolo, Lucio, Alessandro Aresu and Marta Antonelli. 2017. *Food & Migration: Understanding the Geopolitical Nexus in the Euro-Mediterranean*. Parma: Barilla Center for Food and Nutrition.

Cardoso, Nuno. 2019. A Cozinha Típica Da Síria Pela Mão de Um Casal de Refugiados [The Typical Syrian Cuisine by the Hand of a Couple of Refugees]. *Evasoes*, 24 February 2019. Online at https://www.evasoes.pt/comer/tayybeh-a-cozinha-tipica-da-siria-pela-mao-de-um-casal-de-refugiados/ Accessed 15 March 2023.

CIA, The World Factbook. n.d. *Syria*. Washington, DC: Central Intelligence Agency. Online at https://www.cia.gov/the-world-factbook/countries/syria/#:~:text=According%20to%20a%20June%202022,humanitarian%20assistance%20across%20the%20country Accessed 15 June 2020.

ComParte. 2018. *Dos Prós Da Integração Para a Câmara Municipal de Lisboa: Todos Com Parte Na Decisão Acolhimento E Integração* [From the Pros of Integration to the Lisbon City Council: Everyone with a Part in the Reception and Integration Decision]. Lisbon: Comparte.

Coutinho, Ana Paula and Marta Correia. 2019. *Mesas Migrantes: Projetos de Alimentopia* [Migrant Tables: Alimentopia Projects]. Porto: UPorto Press.

CRESCER. 2017. Já Há Refugiados Em Lisboa! [There Are Already Refugees in Lisbon!]. Filmed December 2017 at YouTube, Smack, Portugal. Video, 3:35. Online at https://www.youtube.com/watch?v=9lW7SS14wK0 Accessed 15 March 2023.

Diário de Notícias. 2015. Manifestação de Apoio a Refugiados Junta Centenas e Termina Sem Incidentes [Demonstration of Support for Refugees Gathers Hundreds and Ends Without Incidents]. *Diário de Notícias*, 12 September 2015. Online at https://www.dn.pt/portugal/manifestacao-de-apoio-a-refugiados-junta-centenas-e-termina-sem-incidentes-4774992.html Accessed 15 March 2023.

D'Sylva, Andrea and Brenda Beagan. 2011. Food Is Culture, But It's Also Power: The Role of Food in Ethnic and Gender Identity Construction among Goan Canadian Women. *Journal of Gender Studies* 20(3): 279–89. https://doi.org/10.1080/09589236.2011.593326

Esquerda. 2019. Manifestação de Apoio a Refugiados Junta Centenas em Portugal [Demonstration in Support of Refugees Brings Together Hundreds in Portugal]. *Esquerda*, 8 November 2019. Online at https://www.esquerda.net/artigo/manifestacao-de-apoio-refugiados-junta-centenas-em-portugal/64330 Accessed 15 March 2023.

European Commission. 2015. *A European Agenda on Migration*. Brussels: European Commission.

European Commission. 2019. *Delivering on Resettlement*. Online at https://ec.europa.eu/home-affairs/sites/homeaffairs/files/what-we-do/policies/european-agenda-migration/201912_delivering-on-resettlement.pdf Accessed 15 March 2023.

Eurostat. 2016. *Asylum in the EU Member States: Record Number of over 1.2 Million First Time Asylum Seekers Registered in 2015*. Online at http://ec.europa.eu/eurostat/documents/2995521/7203832/3-04032016-AP-EN.pdf/790eba01-381c-4163-bcd2-a54959b99ed6 Accessed 15 March 2023.

Gurhan, Nazife. 2018. Migratory Kitchen: The Example of Syrians in Mardin. *Sosyoloji Araştırmaları Dergisi* 21(2): 86–113. https://doi.org/10.18490/sosars.476035

Harrison, Rodney. 2010. Multicultural and Minority Heritage. In Tim Benton (ed.), *Understanding Heritage and Memory*. Manchester: Manchester University Press: 164–201.

Matta, Raúl, Charles-Édouard de Suremain and Chantal Crenn. 2020. *Food Identities at Home and on the Move: Explorations at the Intersection of Food, Belonging and Dwelling*. London and New York: Routledge.

Mire, Sada. 2014. *Cultural Heritage: A Basic Human Need*. Filmed 18 February 2018 at TEDx Talks. Video, 19:03. Online at https://www.youtube.com/watch?v=V4UQYem6Dvc Accessed 15 March 2023.

Muslims in Britain. n.d. Work, Food, Drink and Social Etiquettes. In *Islam and Muslims in Britain: A Guide*. Online at http://guide.muslimsinbritain.org/guide8.html#8.2 Accessed 15 March 2023.

Observador. 2020. Manifestações Em Lisboa e Porto Pelo Acolhimento de 13.000 Refugiados de Moria Na UE [Demonstrations in Lisbon and Porto to Welcome 13,000 Refugees from Moria to the EU]. *Observador*, 13 September 2020. Online at https://observador.pt/2020/09/13/manifestacoes-em-lisboa-e-porto-pelo-acolhimento-de-13-000-refugiados-de-moria-na-ue/ Accessed 15 March 2023.

Onde vamos Jantar. 2019. Tayybeh: Ou Quando Um Restaurante é Uma História de Vida … [Tayybeh: Or When a Restaurant Is a Life Story …]. *Onde vamos Jantar*, 18 June 2019. Online at https://www.ondevamosjantar.com/tayybeh/ Accessed 15 March 2023.

Parasecoli, Fabio. 2014. Food, Identity and Cultural Reproduction in Immigrant Communities. *Social Research* 81(2): 415–40.

PPL. 2017. *Um Restaurante Do Médio Oriente Para a Integração de Refugiados* [A Middle East Restaurant for the Integration of Refugees]. Online at https://ppl.pt/fundacao-edp/restaurante-refugiados Accessed 15 March 2023.

Ramli, Adilah, Mohd Salehuddin Mohd Zahari and Noriza Isha. 2014. Food Heritage and Nation Food Identity Formation. In Norzuwana Sumarjan, Zahari Mohd Salehuddin Mohd, Radzi Salleh Mohd, Mohi Zurinawati, Hanafiah Mohd Hafiz Mohd, Bakhtiar Mohd Faeez Saiful, Zainal Artinah, Saiful Bakhtiar, Mohd Hafiz and Mohd Hanafiah (eds), *Hospitality and Tourism: Synergizing Creativity and Innovation in Research*. London: Taylor & Francis: 407–412.

Ramshaw, Gregory. 2016. Food, Heritage and Nationalism. In Dallen J. Timothy (ed.), *Heritage Cusines: Traditions, Identities and Tourism*. London and New York: Routledge: 53–64. https://doi.org/10.4324/9781315752525

Dias Real, Francisca. 2017. Refúgio Cultural: Vale a Pena Conhecer Os Projectos Destes Refugiados [Cultural Refuge: The Projects of These Refugees Are Worth Knowing]. *TimeOut*, 26 October 2017. Online at https://www.timeout.pt/lisboa/pt/blog/refugio-cultural-vale-a-pena-conhecer-os-projectos-destes-refugiados-102617 Accessed 15 March 2023.

Reis Oliveira, Catarina. 2021. *Requerentes e Beneficiários de Proteção Internacional En Portugal. Relatório Estatístico Do Asilo 2021* [Applicants and Beneficiaries of International Protection in Portugal. Asylum Statistics Report 2021]. Lisboa: Observatório das Migrações.

Reis Oliveira, Catarina and Natália Gomes. 2019. *Indicadores de Integração de Imigrantes. Relatório Estatístico Anual 2019* [Immigrant Integration Indicators. Annual Statistical Report 2019]. Lisbon: Observatório das Migrações.

Simão, Helena. 2019. Tayybeh: Este Restaurante Sírio Conta a História de Dois Refugiados Que Escolheram Portugal Para Recomeçar - Gastronomia [Tayybeh: This Syrian Restaurant Tells the Story of Two Refugees Who Chose Portugal to Start Again]. *SAPO Viagens*, 16 February 2019. Online at https://viagens.sapo.pt/saborear/gastronomia/artigos/tayybeh-este-restaurante-sirio-conta-a-historia-de-dois-refugiados-que-escolheram-portugal-para-recomecar Accessed 15 March 2023.

Tahhan, Antonio. 2020. *What Syrian Cuisine Can Teach Us About Humanity*. Filmed 5 February 2020 at TEDxMidAtlantic. Video, 14:19 Online at https://www.youtube.com/watch?v=MOErrBc9lss Accessed 15 March 2023.

Timothy, Dallen J.. 2016. Introduction: Heritage Cuisines, Foodways and Culinary Traditions. In Dallen J. Timothy (ed.), *Heritage Cuisines: Traditions, Identities and Tourism*: 1–24. London and New York: Routledge: 1–24. https://doi.org/10.4324/9781315752525

4

Relations with objects: a longitudinal case study

Katie O'Donoghue

Introduction

People with cancer who receive curative chemotherapy face many challenges, including quality of life while undergoing repeated cycles of treatment for symptomatic disease. These circumstances may dramatically alter support needs and personal relationships, threaten identity and psychological wellbeing, and present challenges for patients and families in navigating a complex health-care system (Diski 2016). Therapies that are feasible, acceptable and cost-effective are needed to help relieve the often profound emotional and psychosocial distress experienced during cancer treatment. This chapter outlines a longitudinal case study[1] concerned with exploring the interconnectedness of critical heritage and wellbeing and identifying the diverse object worlds encountered by patients undergoing cancer chemotherapy treatment.

Over the past few years, a body of research has explored how different types of cultural and/or natural heritage influence human wellbeing. Multiple studies have identified that meaningful engagement with different types of heritage can positively enhance a sense of wellbeing (Taçon and Baker 2019). This case study is part of the PhD project 'Relations with Objects', research which explored the interconnectedness of heritage and wellbeing through a series of qualitative studies with cancer patients. This case study explores the process and relations with objects of an individual undergoing chemotherapy treatment for colorectal cancer, in a London specialist hospital over an eight-month period. The project responds to the need for new approaches to support patients, approaches that may more fully utilise the skills and competencies of patients and health-care workers so that the provision of care and support keep pace with need. A strength of this study is that it is the first research to explore the impact of museum objects with cultural value longitudinally.

The interactions between the individual and the researcher (myself) took place within the hospital in different settings: the cancer clinic, the chemotherapy suite and the Macmillan support centre, all located in the same building. This case study is one of seven, each one highlighting a different treatment trajectory experience, meaning that, although each individual started on the same treatment, they had different experiences, changes to treatment or changes to prognoses. I believe it is important to present the different ways in which museum objects can be experienced in line with the uncertainty and differentiation between cancer experiences. This case study, for example, follows an individual who had no change to his chemotherapy treatment and was delivered a positive prognosis after treatment. The study explores how a museum object can sometimes become a transitional object, an object of meaning, a source of comfort for an individual (Winnicott 1951).

Placement setting, client's clinical presentation and referral process

For the purpose of this study, I will refer to the participant by the pseudonym 'Paul'. This case study focuses predominantly on three object-handling sessions that took place with Paul within the hospital. In each of the sessions, the UCL object loan box was available, containing age-value and replica objects such as an ancient Egyptian kohl pot, an ancient fossil of a brittle starfish, a Neolithic stone tool, an ancient brass coin from Alexandria, an abalone shell used in Native American cleansing and healing rituals and a replica Egyptian shabti (figurine). On each occasion, Paul had the option to engage and handle the objects contained in the box. The same objects were brought to each object-handling session so that their impact could be explored longitudinally. The case study also notes and explores the interactions with myself, the objects and the clinical environment, and interactions that took place outside of object-handling sessions.

The case of Paul

In his mid-fifties, Paul lives alone and was about to start his first-line treatment of chemotherapy when I first met him in the oncology clinic. I would describe Paul as an intelligent, engaged, polite and artistic individual with whom I enjoyed working. When I first met Paul, I was initially struck by how pallid, thin and unwell he looked, especially for someone still relatively young. His body language almost gave the impression that he was holding himself up tentatively and I perceived a real sense of fragility about him. I did note that when he was engaging in conversation, his eyes still seemed bright and clear, and he was interested in the creative and heritage aspects of the study. It is important to note that Paul's occupation was teaching, and this will be discussed in due course. Paul has a diagnosis of colorectal cancer and has had surgery to remove the tumour from his bowel, which means at the time of treatment he also had a stoma in situ. Paul also had surgery to remove two tumours in his liver before chemotherapy treatment commenced. Paul was identified by the clinical nurse specialists as about to commence first-line chemotherapy treatment, which made him eligible for engagement with the study.

First encounter

In line with my approved ethics proposal, I had presented my research project to the multidisciplinary team and handed out flyers for health-care professionals as first points of contact to give to eligible participants. During a clinic appointment, Paul's oncology consultant referred Paul to the research, gave him the information flyer (Figure 4.1) and told him that if he would like more information, I was in the clinic and could discuss the project further. Paul approached me and I answered his questions and gave more information regarding the project. I did this by talking through the participant information sheet and providing information regarding the longitudinal study. Paul wished to confirm consent there and then, but I explained that it was necessary to give him 24 hours to reflect on the study and that I would contact him the next day to see if he would like to confirm consent and we could then arrange the first session to coincide with his treatment. I rang Paul the next day, he confirmed his interest in participating and we booked in the first session.

First session

The first object-handling session took place in the chemotherapy suite. Paul was seated in the atrium at the back left of the room on a chair. Paul's interview was the first for the longitudinal participants and I remember thinking, 'I'm glad that I have facilitated a few sessions previously'. I felt

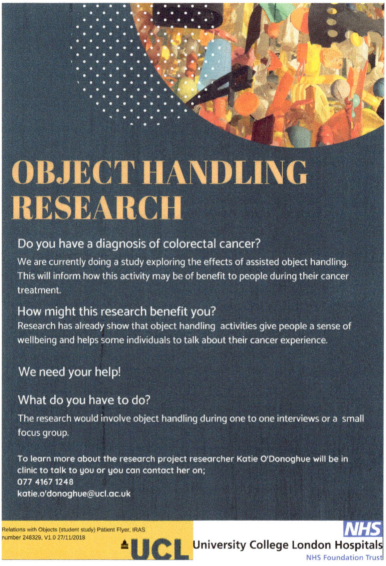

Figure 4.1 Patient information flyer. Research information flyer for the PhD project 'Relations with Objects'. © Katie O'Donoghue.

acutely aware that this was only the second session of chemotherapy for Paul and was wary in case the experience along with the sessions might be overwhelming.

I had brought with me the box of objects, the consent form and the interview questions sheet. As I greeted Paul, he smiled and seemed at ease. He informed me his drip had been set up. I checked in to see if he was happy for the session to go ahead and he nodded in agreement. I enquired as to how he felt today, and Paul shared that he was feeling good, and that it would be a few days until he would feel any side effects from the treatment. Paul talked about the architecture of the building and said he liked the urban feel of the interior produced by the concrete floors, walls and pillars. He also said he liked the repetition of colours and lines throughout. Interestingly, Paul also mentioned he preferred being in the space without people – people don't compliment the space as there is no 'uniformity'. I found this a fascinating comment and it made me wonder, could the reference to not liking people being in the space be a reminder of his own illness or lack of control in his current situation? This again made me think of psychological wellbeing. Paul commented on the glass roof of the atrium in the chemotherapy suite. He said he thought the roof was 'green and dirty' because of the mould or moss that stained the glass. Paul said the presence of this green, dirty roof really irritated him. I wondered, did the mould for him unconsciously parallel his own irritation and anger at his tumour and the feelings of lack of control relating to his cancer experience?

I believe this also relates to Ryff's concept of environmental mastery, which emphasises the ability to choose or change the surrounding context using physical or mental actions as well as being able to control events (Ryff 1989). As I got to know Paul more, I realised he was quite meticulous, tidy and, in his own words, 'a perfectionist'. The irritation regarding the mould on the roof I believe may have been symbolic in nature, representing his lack of environmental mastery, an aspect of psychological wellbeing, in that he may have felt he had no control over his own environment while in the clinical space and no autonomy (another facet of psychological wellbeing). Paul's narrative of how the mould 'irritated' him reminded me of how spaces become places when given meaning, and the construction of these places is aligned with the course of the individual's illness (Bates 2018). This place, the chemotherapy suite, can be experienced as a landscape of healthy and unhealthy spaces. This was a theme I noted through many of the interviews, with individuals describing different areas as healthy and others as sick.

On introducing the objects, a mat was laid on a table in front of Paul; I then carefully unboxed the objects and laid them on the table along with their information cards. The information cards gave a brief background for the objects, listing age, location and possible uses. An example can be seen in Figure 4.2.

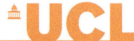

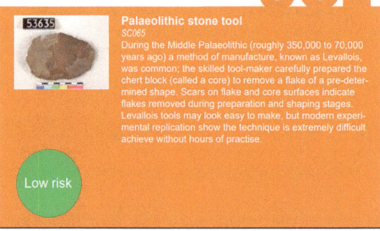

Figure 4.2 Object information card. Information card of a Palaeolithic stone tool outlining age and description of the object. UCL object-handling collection. Source: Katie O'Donoghue.

I then invited Paul to handle the objects. Paul was taken aback when handling the coin, using the word 'love' to describe his feelings towards it. He explained that the coin and fossil reminded him of his experience of living and working in Africa, a time in his life that he reflects on fondly. He commented as follows (R = respondent, I = interviewer):

R: These two are clearly my favourites.
I: The coin and the fossil?
R: Yes. If there was one I was to accidentally take home with me, it would be the coin.
R: The fossil, it is the age and the beauty of the fossil itself, and the period. I taught geography last year and a bit of the year before, and we talked about this particular geological period so that is interesting to me. Plus, I like the shape. And the coin is just … Maybe it is the weight and the age? They must be technologically advanced in coin making to get such good images. Those two I would love anyway.

When I enquired further about Africa, about whether he would like to return, Paul said,

Going back? I would love to go back, but I have been told that I can't, for the moment. And doctors aren't very keen actually because they want to keep me under close supervision. So, we will see.

I wondered about Paul's connection to his 'favourite objects' and how they reminded him of a time and place in his life on which he reflected fondly, and what they might represent with regards to his life pre-cancer.

Paul explained that it was on his return from teaching in Africa that he was diagnosed with cancer and now he is unsure if he will ever get to return. I later reflected on his connection to the coin, which in the session seemed to embody the memories and experiences of what he described as an enjoyable part of his life, while possibly also embodying a longing to return to the pre-morbid sense of self. Paul listed his three favourite objects after handling them: first the coin, then the brittle starfish fossil and finally the abalone shell. Towards the end of the session, Paul jokingly said he 'might accidently take it home'. He then asked to photograph the object he liked the most. Paul described the object-handling session as follows: 'To be able to pick up and explore something like this is very unusual and pleasing.'

Engagement in clinic

Prior to the second official object-handling session, Paul brought his portfolio of photographic artwork to his appointment at the oncology clinic. Paul approached me with his portfolio and explained that he wished to show me the images he had created. Due to the space constraints of the clinic, I suggested we go to the cancer support centre to view his art. On showing the pieces, Paul explained the inspiration behind each image. He shared that initially he was focused on and drawn to exploring the architecture of the centre and the spaces within, which is evident in Figure 4.3.

He also began to think about his time in Africa, where he was a teacher – a time in his life he described fondly. Paul was inspired to share an image from a memory in which he experienced friendly fire in his building. The event left bullet entry marks on his apartment walls. Using the photograph of the damaged wall, he manipulated the image (Figure 4.4), invoking questions in me about parallels between his experience of his home being attacked and damaged and the physical sense in which his body was not only 'attacked' by the cancer but also wounded,

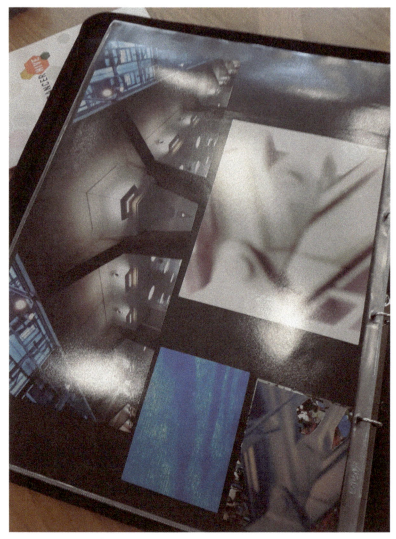

Figure 4.3 Portfolio artwork. Artworks created using photography and photoshop by a participant in the PhD research project 'Relations with Objects'. Reproduced with participant's permission.

marked by the necessary surgeries. Furthermore, it is interesting that it was this event that he chose to share in relation to his experience in the study, and it may be of note that it was in fact in Africa that his journey to his cancer diagnosis began.

However, Paul's focus on his artwork soon changed. He described how this new focus was inspired by his journey from the station to the

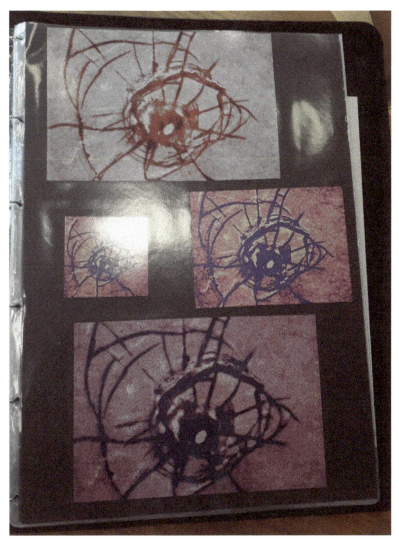

Figure 4.4 Gunshot through wall. Artworks of a gunshot created using photography and photoshop by a participant in the PhD research project 'Relations with Objects'. Reproduced with participant's permission.

hospital and how he had noticed the skyline filled with cranes and the famous BT Tower. This new direction and focus of his art can be seen in Figure 4.5. He said the BT Tower and cranes reminded him of the Leaning Tower of Pisa, which he visited when he was 21. He said this was a time in his life when he went travelling around Europe by himself for the first time. He remembered the time fondly and described it as a marker of his

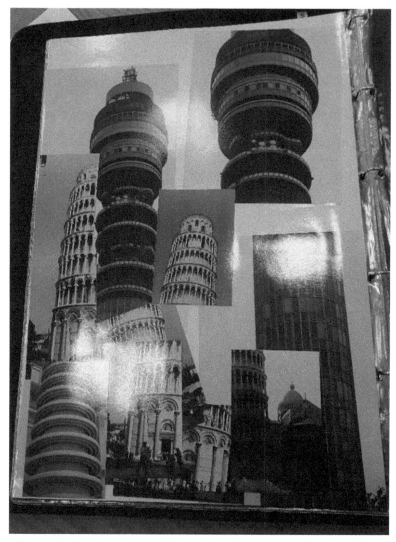

Figure 4.5 Leaning Tower of Pisa and BT Tower. Artworks of buildings created using photography and photoshop by a participant in the PhD research project 'Relations with Objects'. Reproduced with participant's permission.

transition from boyhood to manhood. It is interesting to reflect on the towers from a Freudian perspective, as a phallic symbol is meant to represent male generative powers. You can see that some of the tower images are spliced together and there is a real sense of rebuilding 'manhood' or maybe reintegrating aspects of his younger self into the person he is today.

Second session

When I arrived at the chemotherapy suite for the second session, Paul was already seated with his intravenous drip up and running. He was sitting on the right side of the chemotherapy suite, on the edge of the bays. It was quite cold considering it was the beginning of summer and I commented on the draught, enquiring if Paul was warm enough. Paul told me he was feeling good, particularly as he knew he only had a few more sessions of treatment left. When I asked how he felt compared to the last session, Paul replied that he felt 'much more positive, much more positive, I feel healthier'. Paul explained that he had been able to keep food down which had resulted in weight gain. He shared how his neighbour had also recently commented on how well he looked.

When I asked if any of the objects came to mind, he said, 'probably the coin'. He picked up the coin immediately once it was out of the box. He held the coin in his hands and turned it over with his fingers. I then asked if he had any different feelings or thoughts compared to the first time he handled the objects:

> R: Yes. I think although the coin is fascinating because of its age, I am more drawn to the shell now and the textures and the colours of the shell. Not the inside, but definitely the outside. It is more interesting visually. I am much more drawn to that and possibly this [the stone tool]. Not really that [the shabti replica]. It is fascinating that it is what it is, but this [the shell] is quite visually appealing and quite tactile.
>
> I: I do notice that both the objects you feel most drawn to are natural objects.
>
> R: Yes, which is strange because I quite like this man-made space.

Interestingly, Paul also described how, during his treatment, his plants and his garden became a major source of wellbeing for him, as he nurtured them and watched fruits and vegetables grow. Paul also shared a description of the artwork he was currently working on (see Figure 4.6), inspired by one of the objects:

> R: I did a piece using this. The shell, rotating it using Photoshop. There was one still and then using it, so it looks as though it is in motion.
>
> I: A bit like a video?
>
> R: But stills. It looks as if it has been slightly blurred and the blur increases with every shot. I have called it 'Terminating the Tumour'. We will have to see what it looks like when it is put together.

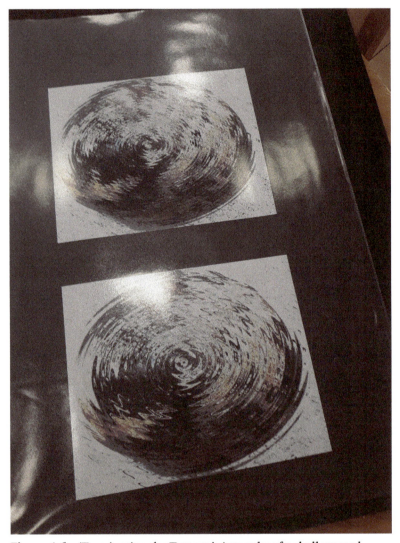

Figure 4.6 'Terminating the Tumour'. Artworks of a shell created using photography and photoshop by a participant in the PhD research project 'Relations with Objects'. Reproduced with participant's permission.

I: Can I ask what it was about the shell and the movement that made that title come to mind?
R: I think it was the way that particular shot came out. This did look quite dark and malevolent. Although I love this, it just looked, that particular shot …

I: When it moves in motion, is it then the underside comes up?

R: No, it was just this. It was a still of the shell as is and then the next one is looking as though it is in motion, so it is as if it is moving and I have taken a still, but it is slightly blurred. Then the next one is even more exaggerated and the next one is just lots of lines spinning round. I am not sure how to present it – whether to have it as a line or pieces in one photo. I will have to see.

I commented to Paul on the profound nature of his artwork and enquired if the history and use of the abalone shell had inspired his creative process, to which he replied, 'No'. I wondered whether perhaps, on an unconscious level, the history of the shell had had an impact, as the information card describes this abalone shell as being used in Native American cultures. This also links to Butler's (2011) paper on 'Heritage as Pharmakon', and the unpacking of how an object can be a composite of three meanings: remedy, poison and scapegoat. The history of this abalone shell was that it was used in cleansing and healing rituals as a smudge bowl, a bowl which would containing the burning embers of purifying and medicinal herbs, such as sage. The information card explained that Indigenous North Americans believed that abalone and sage together will carry their messages up to heaven. The abalone's meaning is one of solace, a connection to the ocean, the cycle of life, protection, ancient travel and journey. I find the fact that Paul chose the shell as the object for his art piece particularly interesting due to its perceived role in healing and cleansing rituals. It is possible that for Paul the shell became embodied unconsciously as a transitional object with the capacity and meaning to cure and heal, while also embodying the more 'dark and malevolent' side.

When I asked Paul to describe the relationship between his treatment experience and the objects, he said:

It has been a welcome diversion, absolutely. I wish I could have spent more time on the photographs. Maybe now I am feeling a bit perkier I will have another look.

That the objects were a welcome diversion from the clinical environment and indeed treatment was also evidenced in the 'Heritage in Hospitals' research project, an innovative three-year project which took museum objects to the bedsides of hospital patients and evidenced patients or clients demonstrating an increase in wellbeing, happiness and distraction from clinical surroundings after handling museum objects in the hospital setting (Ander et al. 2013).

Final session

The final session took place in the information support centre, which is laid out to resemble a living-room space, with tables and chairs and individual seating areas where people can relax or take some time out from the 'hospital environment' while also accessing further information from support services. This space, though quite welcoming aesthetically, had a sense of sadness, with those in the room always speaking in hushed tones. One might see individuals visibly upset, in crisis, sleeping, or resting because they were so unwell.

Although I was given permission to facilitate the session in the room, I did feel a contrast in Paul's presentation compared to those around him. He looked visibly healthier, his art portfolio occupying space on the table; there was a sense of wholeness in how he spoke and presented his work. The final session was in this space as Paul had completed his chemotherapy. When Paul arrived, I asked him to pick a place in the room where he felt comfortable to sit and talk. He chose a large table as he said he wished to lay out his bulky portfolio of work. When I asked Paul how he had been, he said he was feeling great and that he was booked in for his stoma reversal. Paul looked well, much different to the man I remember in the first session, having put on weight and no longer looking frail. I asked Paul if he wished to see the objects from the loan box, but he said, 'No, I don't want to see them, I feel moved on from that time in my life.'

I found this very interesting, considering his previous interest in the objects. As Paul did not wish to engage with them, I asked if he was happy to share his 'object of importance' in today's session and he took out his portfolio of artwork. Surprisingly, the previous artworks of the centre, the natural object and 'Terminating the Tumour' were gone. I enquired as to where these were, and was told, 'I actually framed it and gave it away to a friend, they loved it.' He was referring to 'Terminating the Tumour'. I asked if he intended to exhibit that piece, and he again replied, 'No. I feel I've moved on from there.' I asked in what way, and Paul replied, 'My artwork has moved on.' At the time I found this interesting; he had given away the piece and was not interested in exhibiting the artwork.

Paul then shared with me his new art pieces. He explained that as he felt better towards the end of treatment, he found himself looking upwards during his journey to the hospital from the station. He explained that he began to become interested in architecture in the skyline, and a particular structure he found fascinating was the BT Tower, a distinctive and iconic building located close to the hospital. This, as previously mentioned, gave him the idea of splicing the two monuments together, as shown in Figure 4.5.

The ascribed meaning-making, memories and temporality of splicing these two together are interesting and layered in that they suggest a creative expression of rebuilding. The leaning tower is imbued with the memory of being a young, healthy man, while the tower is also undeniably leaning, needing support to hold it up. The BT Tower, as Paul described it being in his view every treatment day, was a more contemporary, immovable and solid structure occupying the London skyline. The process of splicing the image to create something which is whole exudes a sense of autonomy, rebuilding of self, an amalgamation of past and present, combining old aspects of self with present experience, reflecting a sense of becoming whole and possible hopes for the future.

He talked about the process of his work and said he was very drawn to the 'space in between' captured in the photographed structures. When I asked him what he meant, Paul found he was unsure and recognised that he had spoken of this before. I wondered, was this space in between a possible unconscious parallel to his experience of treatment and illness? To reflect on the space in between, I refer to the construction of place and how the individual's experience of the hospital can be as a landscape of illness and wellness (Gesler 1992). This concept of healthy spaces refers to how certain environments seem to contribute to a healing sense of place. The space in between may represent the internal and external space that Paul's own being inhabits, recovering from cancer yet not completely in the clear – a reflection of his experience within the hospital and an extension of self and values. Could the space in between be a representation of Paul's experience and the reintegration of becoming 'whole' again?

Paul's art statement

As part of his participation in a patient art exhibition (see Figure 4.7), Paul shared an artist statement reflecting on his experience of treatment and his engagement with the objects:

> In the summer of 2018, I returned from teaching in Africa with persistent stomach pain and cramps and took myself to the Hospital for Tropical Diseases, thinking I had contracted an exotic and possibly unpleasant disease or parasite. Professional and committed staff were keen that I should not 'drop through

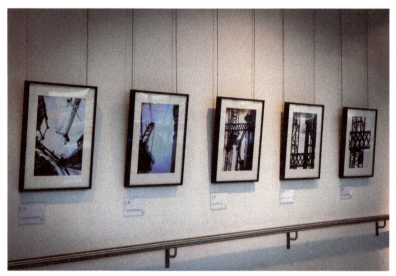

Figure 4.7 Untitled artworks for exhibition. Artworks of construction and buildings created using photography and photoshop by a participant in the PhD research project 'Relations with Objects'. Reproduced with participant's permission.

the net' and recommended further investigation. I was told immediately after the colonoscopy that I had cancer, the medical specialist who talked to me more distraught than I was, reassuring me that 'it' was 'eminently treatable'. As it turned out I also had three metastases in the liver as well, but by mid-December I had had two operations to remove the disease and was recovering at home.

I had already willingly agreed to different trials through my treatment journey when my oncology professor suggested another and introduced me to Katie, and I am so glad he did. Chemotherapy was often a depressing, demoralising and boring process. Just as I began to feel a little stronger and could face food willingly, the process would start again, but I found that the sessions offered to be not only a distraction from illness but rewarding and absorbing. I was shown a range of artefacts, asked to comment and think about a creative response. Significantly, despite the malaise that chemotherapy induces, I found I had an interest in developing a response and as the days grew warmer, I would photograph buildings and objects as I walked or tubed to Huntley Street from St Pancras station.

Initially, I had been sure that my work would grow and develop from an interest in the surface textures on some of the objects that I had been shown, and in the beautifully clean, stark lines of the internal architecture of the Macmillan centre. But as I spent more time in town, I noticed first the monolithic nature of the BT Tower/ Post Office Tower (as I shall always call it) and then as the weeks and months passed, the intricate mix of architectural structures around the redeveloped St Pancras site. Their elevation, combination of form and accompanying negative space an intriguing juxtaposition between the transient, the rigidity of steel and purposeful movement. The process that began with a range of unusual objects has encouraged, or perhaps given me permission to again express an interest in form, space, architecture and life.

Discussion and conclusion

This case study has explored how objects and creative works can sometimes become transitional objects – physical representations of experiences and relations with people associated with these experiences. The concept of 'transitional objects' provides an understanding of human development commencing with infancy and early childhood. The concept was first developed by Donald Winnicott in 1951 to describe the ways in which, as children procure and utilise transitional objects, this becomes indicative of how they will interact with and maintain human relationships. A child's transitional object may be, for example, a blanket or teddy bear – something that provides comfort during the transition of a child gaining and developing more independence from the caregiver (Winnicott 1953).

This case study is a compilation of Paul's experiences of object-handling sessions during his treatment trajectory. Paul attended three object-handling sessions over the course of his eight-month treatment, and in each session the object loan box was present with the option for Paul to engage with the objects or not. The final session also included Paul's chosen 'object(s) of importance'. During this process Paul also chose to document his experience of the cancer centre and engagement with objects through photography.

It was identified that the sessions seemed to coincide with some of the objects becoming transitional objects, and interestingly, just as Winnicott argued for children's transitional objects, Paul's attachment to certain objects decreased over time while also mirroring his temporal transitions of everyday life and cancer experience.

In the first session Paul was initially very taken with the coin, using the word 'love' to describe his feelings towards it and jokingly saying he'd like to keep it. He also shared that the coin reminded him of his experiences of living in Africa and that he would love to return but was unsure he would be able to, and this made him feel very connected to the object. In the second session he said he no longer felt attached to the coin and was drawn instead to the natural objects, particularly the shell. Throughout his treatment Paul had photographed the spaces and objects around him. He shared these works with me during visits to the clinic – one striking piece, as noted above, was the artwork 'Terminating the Tumour', which he gave away to a friend and did not wish to exhibit.

In the final object-handling session, Paul chose not to see or handle the objects, stating, 'I have moved on from that time,' and instead sharing with me the artworks that he later exhibited (Figure 4.7). It seems that the objects he has 'moved on from' embody the experience of treatment, and that, having transitioned from treatment to completion of treatment, he no longer wishes to handle them or see them, because those objects now embody the experience of treatment. According to Mark Brenner (2004), transitional objects continue through the course of our lives as objects that bring us back to a place and time and memory. And Paul did not want to revisit that place and time.

The object handling and creation of artworks also provided a space in which Paul created his own meanings, which we know is a key element in the promotion of patients' wellbeing during and after a traumatic event such as cancer (Martino and Freda 2016). I also refer to Hardy's (1988) reference to heritage as a 'value-loaded concept', meaning that in whatever form it appears, its very nature relates entirely to present circumstances. It is evident that the heritage objects provided a space for reflection and access to the temporality of being through a process of meaning-making. Paul ascribed value and meaning to the objects in how they related to his own present circumstances, the objects he had 'moved on from' possibly embodied with meaning related to illness and treatment experience. The heritage objects and artworks are ascribed meaning and value, and embody temporal markers for Paul. Schorch's (2014) research shows that certain meanings remain on an embodied level as an 'internal understanding' and resist any verbal 'expressibility'. This experience informs the processes of meaning-making during cross-cultural encounters within the material world. It is here that emotion encounters the realm of culture and thus the experience of heritage.

Moreover, this offers interesting insight into how heritage objects can provide a construction of narratives and support in the process of coping. Through the object-handling sessions and in the artist's statement, the reader can see that Paul has in his own way shared details of pivotal moments in his life (temporal markers) during his treatment. Paul has told his own story in a way of his choosing, and this may have supported him to make sense of and cope with the impact of cancer and treatment. It is posited by Brokerhof et al. (2020) that the creation of an illness narrative (a story the patient tells) can lend coherence to the distinctive events and long-term course of suffering, thus supporting the patient's self-awareness and wellbeing. In Paul's sessions and his artist statement, it does seem that through creating his own illness narrative he was able to re-engage with his sense of participation in everyday life. This evidence also implies that heritage may have the potential to provide therapeutic support in other aspects of health care and patient experience. To further understand and explore how heritage can be utilised as a therapeutic support, I would recommend more longitudinal studies that employ a mixed-methods approach.

Note

1. All the research and images presented in this case study received consent from the participant and full NHS research ethics approvals.

References

Ander, Erica, Linda Thomson, Guy Noble, Anne Lanceley, Usha Menon and Helen Chatterjee. 2013. Heritage, Health and Well-being: Assessing the Impact of a Heritage Focused Intervention on Health and Well-Being. *International Journal of Heritage Studies* 19(3): 229–242. https://doi.org/10.1080/13527258.2011.651740

Bates, Victoria. 2018. Sensing Space and Making Place: The Hospital and Therapeutic Landscapes in Two Cancer Narratives. *Medical Humanities* 45(1): 10–20. https://doi.org/10.1136/medhum-2017-011347

Brenner, Mark. 2004. *The Complete Guide to Transitional Objects*. New York: Simon & Schuster.

Brokerhof, Inge, Jan Fekke Ybema, Matthijs Bal and Andrew Soundy 2020. Illness Narratives and Chronic Patients' Sustainable Employability: The Impact of Positive Work Stories. *PLoS One* 15(2): e0228581. https://doi.org/10.1371/journal.pone.0228581

Butler, Beverley. 2011. Heritage as Pharmakon and the Muses as Deconstruction: Problematising Curative Museologies and Heritage Healing. In Sandra Dudley Amy Jane Barnes, Jennifer Binnie, Julia Petrov, and Jennifer Walklate (eds.), The Thing About Museums: Objects and Experience, Representation and Contestation. London: Routledge: 354–71.

Diski, Jenny. 2016. *In Gratitude*. New York: Bloomsbury.

Gesler, Wilbert. 1992. Therapeutic Landscapes: Medical Issues in Light of The New Cultural Geography. *Social Science & Medicine* 34(7): 735–746. https://doi.org/10.1016/0277-9536(92)90360-3

Hardy, Dennis. 1988. Historical Geography and Heritage Studies. *Area* 20(4): 333–338.

Martino, Maria and Maria Francesca Freda. 2016. Meaning-Making Process Related to Temporality During Breast Cancer Traumatic Experience: The Clinical Use of Narrative to Promote a New Continuity of Life. *Europe's Journal of Psychology* 12(4): 622–634. https://doi.org/10.5964/ejop.v12i4.1150

Ryff, Carol. 1989. Happiness is Everything, or Is It? Explorations on the Meaning of Psychological Well-Being. *Journal Of Personality and Social Psychology* 57(6): 1069–1081. https://doi.org/10.1037/0022-3514.57.6.1069

Schorch, Philipp. 2014. Cultural Feelings and The Making of Meaning. *International Journal of Heritage Studies* 20(1): 22–35. https://doi.org/10.1080/13527258.2012.709194

Taçon, Paul and Baker, Sarah. 2019. New and Emerging Challenges to Heritage and Well-Being: A Critical Review. *Heritage* 2(2):1300–1315. https://doi.org/10.3390/heritage2020084

Winnicott, Donald. 1953. Transitional Objects and Transitional Phenomena. *International Journal of Psychoanalysis* 34: 89.

Part II: Curating the city: rethinking urban heritages

In June 2022, a 3,400-year-old Mitanni Empire era city re-emerged, due to drought in Iraq, from the Tigris River. A couple of months earlier, in February 2022, a village named Aceredo, on the Spanish-Portuguese border, reappeared after 30 years underwater due to the construction of a reservoir. These and other examples demonstrate the need to consider, in urban heritage preservation and care, the geomorphology of the urban landscapes and their intrinsic instability and impermanence. Because such dynamic elements shape the relationships between urban past, present and future, innovative analytical frameworks and methodological tools are required to study them. The five chapters in this section explore the topic of curating the city in its double dimension: as a heritage management practice and as a relational approach in the sense of taking care of and for (see also Melhuish et al. 2022).

Peter Krieger's contribution (Chapter 5) provides an opportunity to reflect on these issues from outside of Europe, showing how the 'material heritage of Earth history' with its multilayered entangled temporalities provides 'a conceptual challenge for [managing] the cultural heritage of [Mexico] city'. Drawing on design research methods, Moniek Driesse's chapter (Chapter 6) similarly explores how new ways of understanding water as a 'carrier of cultural memory' might have an impact in terms of challenging and disrupting conventional ways of mapping. If water has given cities their shape, therefore urban heritage can be 'written in water'.

Mela Zuljevic (Chapter 7) explores the plurality of ways of caring for the present and the future of historic landscapes. Focused on a case study, the 'transition landscape' in Genk (Belgium), conceived for a UNESCO World Heritage Site nomination, Zuljevic analyses the value conflicts (preserving heritage value versus improving everyday life), the different heritage development agendas and the multiple uses of the past as a resource in future-making by the diverse actors involved in the process of curating garden cities. Drawing on participatory design, the chapter examines design both as a practice of 'future-making – by selecting specific pasts' and as a way of defuturing the pasts. In this case study, curating entails 'heritage protocols of care' and 'caring practices (that) challenge authorised protocols of care'; in other words, curating is a relational practice promoting participatory processes between institutional and non-institutional actors and fostering eco-sustainable living.

Focusing on historic cities, two complementary chapters by Lukasz Bugalski (Chapter 8) and Maria Pia Guermandi (Chapter 9) address the issue of over-tourism with its delicate balance between the management of urban heritage and conservation practices. To market sites as desirable destinations is intrinsic to the tourism industry; historic cities, such as Venice and Florence, became tourist destinations *par excellence*. Yet, the approach of 'destination management' does not entirely tackle the problem of over-tourism, as Maria Pia Guermandi highlights in her chapter. She explains how the pandemic has revealed the vulnerability of the conventional models of urban heritage management: underlining, on the one hand, the shortcomings of the 'tourism monoculture' in Venice and Florence, and on the other, the absence of a 'systemic response at the level of political decision-making and city administration'. As the tourism industry is recovering from the impact of the pandemic, and tourism is already, in some places, operating at higher levels than before the pandemic, the social, economic, cultural and environmental impact on the future of cities is a pressing matter not only in terms of intervention in planning but also regarding care of and concern for those who inhabit the spaces.

Each of the contributions to this section explores the relationships between urban past (in some cases even the 'deep past'), present and future and points out the ways in which curating the city requires cutting-edge ideas and original experiments in all spheres – from heritage research to policymaking to grassroot activism. By emphasising the 'unsustainability of conservation practices' in current urban heritage management, the contributions open the way, implicitly or explicitly, for curating as a practice 'of care to realise specific futures' (Harrison et al 2020: 42).

References

Harrison, Rodney, Caitlin DeSilvey, Cornelius Holtorf, Sharon Macdonald, Nadia Bartolini, Esther Breithoff, Harald Fredheim, Antony Lyons, Sarah May, Jennie Morgan and Sefryn Penrose. 2020. *Heritage Futures: Comparative Approaches to Natural and Cultural Heritage Practices*. London: UCL Press.

Melhuish, Clare, Henric Benesch, Dean Sully and Ingrid Martins Holmberg (eds). 2022. *Co-curating the City: Universities and Urban Heritage Past and Future*. London: UCL Press.

5

Erosion and preservation of the cultural and geological heritage in megacity landscapes of the Global South: a geo-aesthetic inquiry

Peter Krieger

Using geo-aesthetic research, this chapter reveals paradigmatic problems and solutions of natural heritage preservation. It focuses on a representative megalopolis of the Global South, Mexico City, and its surrounding landscapes – an extreme case of geomorphological alterations, which also contains conceptual lessons for the less endangered and better organised situation in Europe. Preserving the topographical identities of geo-landscapes is per se a global issue which stimulates transnational knowledge transfer. The conceptual origins of an aesthetic inquiry of landscape can be traced in the scientific and philosophical work of Alexander von Humboldt, a European who realised his decisive impetus on his travels to the Americas – a topographic transition of ideas, which to this day stimulates contemporary geo-conservation. Based on the conceptual extension of art historical methods towards a 'science' of the image, *Bildwissenschaft*, I shall explain how visual material, and photographs in particular, catalyse environmental knowledge and critique, as a requirement for preserving the endangered natural heritage on Earth, successfully applied in the United Nations Educational, Scientific and Cultural Organization (UNESCO) programme of Global Geoparks.

Conceptual challenges

Aerial views of contemporary megacities in the Global South reveal an accelerated process of structural and cultural erosion. The historical city centres persist as morphological markers, but in fact survive only as small remaining fragments in generic hyperurban extensions. In the case of Mexico City, a paradigmatic megalopolis of the twenty-first century (Krieger 2016: 257–277), the uncontrolled expansions, mainly informal housing, also conquer the natural heritage, the particular bio- and geo-diversity which awards an outstanding topographical identity to this volcanic mountain region. Figure 5.1 indicates how the traditional patterns of city and landscape dissolve – we see a structural dispersal and an advanced erosion of substance and values.

Erosion is a geological category which can be transferred to the understanding of city culture and landscape aesthetics: a dissolution and degradation of substance, coming to the extreme of complete denudation. Both the landscapes' profiles and the succinct cities' cultural configurations erode, but at the same time they generate new shapes of contemporary urbanised landscapes. On planet Earth's surface, processes of erosion are inevitable, but since the Anthropocene the human impact has accelerated this process of geomorphological reconfiguration. Hence it is necessary to tackle this problem in the debates of preserving, even 'curating' the city. What is more, research on critical heritage studies is not only relevant for the 'Future of Europe', but a question of global comparison.

In many cases, in urban research, and worse in tourist discourses, there is a reduction of the contemporary cities' complexity to a stereotype of historical centres. For example, many academic or popular

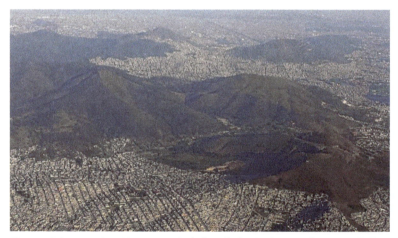

Figure 5.1 Mexico City, extended slum belts in the northeastern hills, 2015. © Peter Krieger.

tourist discourses on New York reduce this city to the central part of Manhattan, as an island with sharp contours, while the sprawling suburban areas, where more than 19 million people live, are faded out of collective consciousness. Land art practices of the 1960s, as realised by Robert Smithson (1979: 19; see also Linsley 2002: 38–55), and also critical landscape theory as presented by John Brinckerhoff Jackson (1984), have called for attention to these structural and cultural phenomena. In this chapter, I argue that such different artistic and aesthetic views on city and landscape should be taken into consideration when we revise the concepts and strategies of urban heritage protection.

Recent debates on the 'geological turn' (Ellsworth and Kruse 2013) have extended these conceptual revisions towards an inclusion of geo-heritage, which is not a static entity, but a dynamic element in the ongoing process of evolution. By definition, movement (of Earth's lithospheric plates) is opposed to any concept and strategy of static preservation. A vivid, metamorphic geo-heritage, which even generates destructive effects via earthquakes and volcanic eruptions, stands against the stiff, petrified cultural heritage of the cities. And we register an utmost gap of temporalities – geologic 'Deep Time'[1] differs extremely from the short cycles of cultural history. Thus, including the basic relevance of earth material and strata in the theoretical reflection on cultural heritage preservation is a conceptual challenge which requires changes to established routines of thinking and paradigms of acting.

Geo-aesthetics

This proposed conceptual change is based on the methods and contents of geo-aesthetics, which revives the common disciplinary roots of geology and art history in the nineteenth century. Both disciplines describe, classify and interpret objects. Both are historical sciences: geology analyses the history of planet Earth, and art history the cultural products from the first rock paintings of the Holocene to the digital image production of the Anthropocene. Of course, with disciplinary specialisation in the university system, and the division between the so-called 'two cultures' (Snow [1959] 2001), epistemic differences arose, which led to an increasing lack of communication, a characteristic estrangement of the natural sciences and the humanities. However, the conceptual extension of art history towards a *Bildwissenschaft* – a 'science'[2] of the image – opened the path for transdisciplinary coworking, inspired by the geological turn which defines geological events as cultural matters.

The idea of a 'science' of image was first introduced in the early twentieth century by the Hamburg art historian Aby Warburg (Diers 1995: 230),[3] who carried out a revolutionary conversion of traditional art history to *Kulturwissenschaft* ('science' of culture), extending the scope from artworks to all types of images, analysing their visual formulae, their epistemic and discursive functions – for instance, in the field of geosciences. Images work as catalysts for world views, knowledge production and politics. For geo-aesthetics, these parameters of *Bildwissenschaft* are decisive. And they are philosophically supported by the recent intellectual production of Bruno Latour, mainly his 'terrestrial manifesto', which profiles the complex and critical *earthbound* conditions as a political matter (Latour 2017a, 2017b). While Latour's writings remain on an abstract level, operating with words, Warburg's heritage has been developed further towards a political iconography – that is, a research which analyses how images operate in political processes, and in our case, how environmental problems such as erosion are represented in images, with their inherent iconographical patterns. The political iconography of hyperurban landscapes in the Anthropocene defines the transformation of earth material into a substance of civilisation as an archaic political matter since the first human settlements in the Holocene. Thus, the aerial view of an urbanised mountain landscape (Figure 5.1) is a political image; it shows how the organisation of the *polis*, the essential manifestation of politics, alters the Earth's crust.

Such a relationship between (geo)sciences and humanities, between scientific data, aesthetic appearance and political codifications, is based on the conceptual heritage of Alexander von Humboldt. His visionary understanding of landscapes, developed during his exploratory expeditions in the Americas around 1800, fell into oblivion with the disciplinary specialisation of the sciences in the nineteenth and twentieth centuries, but has been revived in contemporary transdisciplinary debates, for instance, on the geological turn.

Analysis of Figure 5.1 may explain how such transdisciplinary neo-Humboldtian research works. Stimulated by the visual shock effect of seeing a hyperurbanised landscape, questions arise: what concept of landscape do we have in mind? Do we confuse 'landscape' with 'nature', and thus become shocked about the factual environmental conditions which human beings generate? Do we recognise the destructive effects of human settlements?

Landscape is a human construction comprehensible in different visual modes, such as aerial photography (Krieger 2012; Brownlee, Piccoli and Uhlyarik 2015). Its visual conceptualisation – at least in Western thinking (Jullien 2016)[4] – operates through a neuronal process of sensorial cognition, which is, indeed, the basic definition of aesthetics.[5] Figure 5.1 catalyses knowledge on a 'geology of mankind', as defined by scientist Paul Crutzen in his epoch-making article of 2002 in the journal *Nature* (Crutzen 2002). Crutzen introduced a new name for the contemporary geological epoch: the Anthropocene. This term is still not officially recognised by the International Commission on Stratigraphy, but it has stimulated a controversial and critical debate on the non-sustainable management of planet Earth. The first indicators of human-made alterations in the Neolithic Revolution 11,000 years ago relate the Anthropocene to the act of dwelling. Of course, there is considerable variety and complexity involved in defining the Anthropocene (Scherer and Renn 2015; Davis and Turpin 2015), but one of its key notions is the exponential development of early housing to contemporary hyper-urbanisation. Such extended informal settlements on the outskirts of Mexico City, and many other megacities in the Global South, illustrate how humankind became a geological force. The construction of habitat is a creative act of civilisation but it is also an act of environmental destruction. And with the exponential growth of cities since the Industrial Revolution of the eighteenth century, this human ecological footprint became significant, leading from the suburban extensions of the Great Acceleration in the 1950s to the extreme of dystopic hyperurban settlements which erode and erase consequential natural areas, such as outstanding mountain morphologies. Urban expansion in the Anthropocene has conquered natural areas – recent scientific calculation estimates that nowadays only a quarter of the planet is covered by wilderness, free from human exploitation (Crutzen 2002).

While geologists trace the specific strata of the Anthropocene (Zalasiewicz et al. 2019; Zalasiewicz 2009), such as sedimented radionuclides, plastic waste and other toxic material merged with the soil, even with rocks (Robertson 2016), the image 'scientists' (*Bildwissenschaftler*) detect visual proofs of the destructive human impact on planet Earth. One of the most significant geological signatures of the Anthropocene is the use of cement, processed into reinforced concrete. Each square metre of the planet's surface is covered by an average of one kilogram of concrete.[6]

Figure 5.1 illustrates such abstract mathematical calculations: a dense carpet of informal concrete construction covers a huge part of the mountain landscape. Although cities only cover 2.5 per cent of the planet's surface, they contain about 40 per cent of the so-called 'technosphere', which is a self-referential entity of human-made mass – cities, infrastructures and industries – which at present weighs more than the biomass on our planet (Zalasiewicz et al. 2017; Zalasiewicz and Williams 2020). Thus, the natural heritage of Earth is reduced to a substance for human exploitation (Elhacham et al. 2020: 442–444).[7] And the city, as an essential product of the dominating species, the human being, even affects faraway landscapes and natural areas.

City and landscape

The energy concept of the cities in the Anthropocene is a major factor in environmental destruction, and as Figure 5.2 shows, a driving force of erosion. This artistic photography, produced in high-quality analogue by the well-regarded contemporary Mexican photographer Fernando Cordero in 2014, exposes the 'scars' inscribed in a rainforest with a high level of geo- and biodiversity. In this image taken from a helicopter, the artist–photographer reveals the geomorphological effects of the construction of a gas pipeline in the highlands of the Sierra de Hidalgo, 112 kilometres northeast of Mexico City (Palacios and Valle 2014; Krieger 2019b).[8] The detail shows how the 25-metre-wide strip for the tubes is

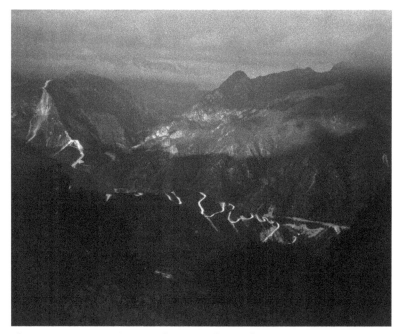

Figure 5.2   Scars I (2014). © Fernando Cordero.

excavated by Caterpillar D8 tractors, erasing part of the forest and accelerating the process of erosion.

Framed and aesthetically conceptualised, Cordero's instantaneous shot reveals different temporalities – the deep time inherent in the calcareous sedimentary formations from the Cretaceous period, and the presence of the Anthropocene, that is, the short cycles of human civilisation. This scarring infrastructural impact is for a structure which will only last for 25 years, because there is foreseeable deterioration due to the high pressure of flowing gas. After its expiry, the pipeline will not be dismantled, but abandoned, integrated in a process of secondary succession. However, the effects of erosion, which are captured in this and other more detailed photographs in the series, are destructive because the barren waste created to support the pipeline will remain arid, bare and infertile for a long period.

Such long-term effects, visible in the landscape, must be considered in relation to urban civilisation. Such 'scars' in natural areas result from the excessive and non-sustainable energy concepts of cities.[9] And this becomes evident in the eco-critical photography of Fernando Cordero. Images, in this case a work of art, serve as geo-aesthetic catalysts for rethinking cultural and natural, and especially geological, temporalities and thus for preserving the cultural and geological heritage of cities and landscapes.

When human beings exert geological force, which is the basic definition of the Anthropocene, erosion becomes a philosophical issue, reflecting on the environmental catastrophe which we witness. Considering the conceptual origin of 'catastrophe' in the eighteenth-century theatre, as an eye-catching event (Utz 2013: 10–12, 95), we may understand the function of images in the critical debates on natural and cultural heritage preservation. Perhaps the visual stocktaking of erosion is not as spectacular as documentary photography of earthquakes, but it can unfold similar epistemic effects. Also, the permanent process of erosion, in many cases accelerated by human intervention, is a geological issue which can stimulate multi-faceted collective consciousness of the dark side of the developed and preserved city culture. Furthermore, as expressed by Walter Benjamin, the notion of 'progress' (of city development, for instance) is based on the idea of the catastrophe, which is not what will come in the future, but what exists in the present (Benjamin 1972: 683),[10] if we continue the non-sustainable management of Earth's resources, including its geological heritage.

Playful self-destruction

Another mode of erosion is the opening of sinkholes, which in urban areas cause dissolution of the built heritage. Such collapses are sudden events resulting from long-term processes of sedimentation, but they are also caused by human interventions, such as non-sustainable water management and urban development on inadequate soils. A press photograph of a sinkhole in Iztapalapa, Mexico City, published on 24 May 2014 in *La Jornada*, exemplifies such human-made geophysical catastrophes, because large parts of this megacity have been developed on unstable former lake grounds. (See the press image on the second page at this link: https://www.jornada.com.mx/2014/05/24/0.) The over-pumping and extraction of groundwater reduces soil cohesion. and in the rainy season, when sudden cloudbursts fill these dried-out areas with enormous amounts of water, sinkholes occur. Such foreseeable catastrophes, which are a hazard to the lives and heritage of many inhabitants, are caused by corrupt and illegal real estate development on geophysically inappropriate sites.

Sinkholes expose the clashes between the natural conditions of the territory and its infrastructural impacts, involving, in the Mexican case, ignorance of the specific geological and water heritage (Krieger 2007, 2015a).[11] They also open insights into the complex stratification of the Earth's crust and unveil unexpected introspections of geological deep time. Lastly, they expose different geological and cultural temporalities.

Press photography reveals and frames the topic of sinkholes as basic problems of civilisation in the Anthropocene, and in the *La Jornada* image we do not only see accelerated geophysical erosion caused by human intervention, but also inherent cultural erosion. The image documents a sinkhole which occurred in 2014 in a zone of consolidated informal housing, where the originally illegal dwellers succeeded in converting their shacks into formal housing, including the application of ornamental apparatus, such as a balustrade and other neo-baroque design formulae (Krieger 2017b).

The neo-baroque dimension of this mega-urban scenery is expressed not only in ornamental detail, but also in philosophical and cultural notions. Neo-baroque principles, as imported from the world capital of entertainment, Las Vegas, to Mexico and many other countries, lead to an erosion of cultural values – 'fake' takes command as the replica gradually substitutes for the original, something seen in the historic baroque in Mexico. The photograph's detail reveals a cultural condition and revives the baroque notion of *vanitas*, the triumph of time over all human achievements. Ironically, from the balcony with the fake balustrade, the occupants of this consolidated house can observe their own decay, the sinking of a value which they created on unstable ground (a former lake in the Mexican basin). Thus, geological and cultural erosion of heritage are present in a contemporary visual interpretation of habitat in the Anthropocene. Non-sustainable urban development merges with what I call the neo-baroque notion of 'playful self-destruction' (Krieger 2017a; Debord 1967).[12] Here, the image fulfils epistemic functions; in geological terms, it compensates for the abstraction of physical models and diagrams (Carreón-Freyre, Cerca and Galloway 2010);[13] and in cultural terms, it opens up a critical view on the condition of cultural heritage in cities.

Material transformation

Indeed, the city is an instrument of transformation, of cultural reconfigurations and of material metamorphosis. Figure 5.3 exemplifies this, showing the Yuhualixqui volcano in Iztapalapa, an expanded zone of informal housing in the eastern parts of Mexico City. A transcontinental belt of more than 10,000 volcanoes crosses the country from the western to the eastern coast, continuing even in the highly urbanised areas such as Mexico City. The extinct volcano Yuhualixqui forms part of this belt, which generates topographical identity even amidst the megalopolis. Many of these volcanoes are protected natural areas. Since the early twentieth century, Mexican poets and artists, such as Dr Atl (Krieger 2015b) and Diego Rivera, have codified this geological morphology as a sublime expression of national (and nationalist) values. Volcanoes became objects of Mexican political iconography. Consequently, many preservation zones have been assigned around volcanoes, including at Yuhualixqui. Yet, such natural conservation is threatened by various factors. Probably the most archaic is the geophysical threat of active volcanoes, such as Popocatépetl, which may erupt in unexpected temporalities, cause destruction of nearby settlements and emit severe air pollution. Why should a destructive natural entity be protected? Furthermore, the 'conservation' of nature is a paradox, because nature is developing in a permanent metamorphous evolutionary process and is not a static element.

Another threat is the hyperurbanisation which erodes the characteristic mountain sceneries (Figure 5.1). The extended slum belt, for

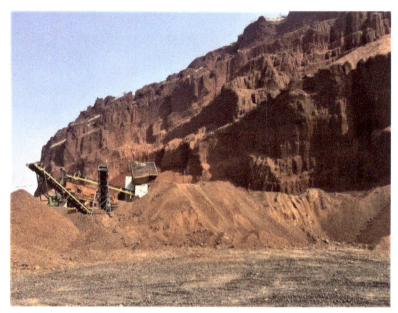

Figure 5.3 Tuff exploitation, Volcano Yuhualixqui, Iztapalapa, Mexico City, 2017. © Alejandra Trujillo.

example in Iztapalapa, is a power structure which questions the geological heritage of volcanoes. The outstanding monuments of geological deep time also suffer human-made erosion for economic reasons. As the case of Yuhualixqui shows, a volcanic landscape frequently serves as a resource for building material. The light volcanic tuff stone – known as *tezontle* in the native, pre-Columbian Nahuatl language – is employed in architecture and infrastructure projects.

Since colonial times, *tezontle* has been applied to façades to decorate monumental palaces. (In pre-Hispanic times, houses were mainly covered with plaster.) Thus, the local stone material was transformed into cultural substance, petrifying geological memory of these volcanic territories. The use of *tezontle* reduced its supply source, the volcanic mountains, but on a smaller scale compared to the contemporary exploitation of this material for infrastructural purposes, mainly for the foundations of landing strips in airports. The new megaproject – Mexico City's international airport (NAICM) – is built on the unstable 'gel'[14] soil of the former Texcoco lake and required huge amounts of *tezontle* in its construction. Until the cancellation of the project under the new government in 2018, an increasing number of protected volcanic sites were demolished to satisfy the huge demand for *tezontle*.

In this context, the photograph in Figure 5.3, taken despite violent threats from the owners of the Yuhualixqui *tezontle* quarry, is an image of an environmental crime scene. It shows how heavy machines dismantle the conical morphology of this extinct volcano. The plain zone in the foreground is the place where workers arrive each day in around 100 trucks, all to transport tuff to construction sites. Since the mid-1980s, when this volcanic site was sold by the city government to a private company, more than 60 per cent of the tuff has been removed – an act of human-made erosion which devalues geological heritage to a bare economic resource for unlimited exploitation.

Mountain ecology and aesthetics

Faced with such accelerated processes of erosion of natural and cultural substances in the megacities of the Anthropocene, initiatives of preservation quickly arose on a local, regional and international level, such as the UNESCO geopark Comarca Minera in Hidalgo, a Mexican state, northeast of Mexico City. Figure 5.4 shows how the problem of uncontrolled hyperurbanisation is manifest even in provincial parts of Mexico. The dense informal housing quarters are 'creeping' over the hills, erasing and eroding the outstanding geo-diversity of the area. Under these conditions, 'conservation' of nature makes sense. Yet, this is not only an issue of geological expertise, but also a challenge for transdisciplinary collaboration with the humanities, mainly with experts in geo-aesthetics.

The preparatory conceptual work for the UNESCO assignation of the Comarca Minera Geopark has introduced an innovative model of knowledge transfer between the geosciences and art history (*Bildwissenschaft)*, to elaborate sustainable models of research, preservation and education. The act of preservation cannot be based only on geological expertise; it also requires a complex understanding of landscapes as human constructs mediated through the image. The human intervention of 'conserving' geologically outstanding sites requires conceptual justification – it is not a scientific act per se. Human consciousness of the effects of accelerated erosion of natural values, catalysed in different types of images (such as Figures 5.1 to 5.4), is an act of sensorial cognition, which may produce a type of knowledge that offers conceptual and political orientation in environmental debates.

This type of aesthetic research on geo-landscapes is based on the conceptual heritage of Alexander von Humboldt, who related scientific measurement to an aesthetic understanding of the mountain landscapes

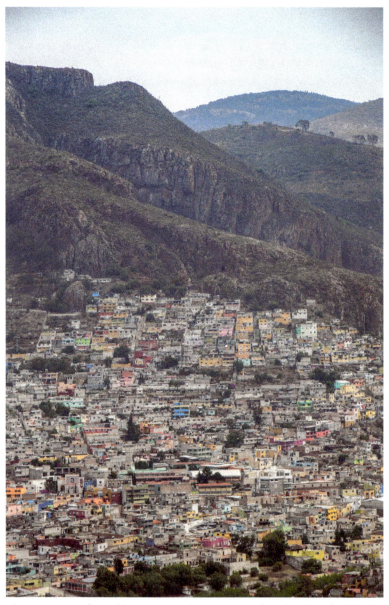

Figure 5.4 Informal housing on the outskirts of Pachuca, Hidalgo, Mexico, 2016. © Daniel Acosta.

which he described in his early nineteenth-century writing (von Humboldt 1986, 2004). Reviving this valuable intellectual heritage[15] in times of extreme disciplinary specialisation is a major challenge for research, and also for the practical work at a UNESCO geopark. Aesthetic research on mountain landscapes is necessarily a transdisciplinary enterprise, which relates hard facts and sensorial data. Images, as explained in this chapter, are not mere pleasant illustrations, but a source for critical knowledge production in the age of the Anthropocene.

A first result of such transdisciplinary geo-aesthetic research is the publication of the Comarca Minera Geopark's guidebook, which contains precise descriptions of selected sites, as well as essays from geologists, historians and art historians, presenting a wide thematical scope to readers (Canet Miquel 2018). The book, along with related educational and tourist offerings, promotes geo-diversity as a value and profiles alternatives to the non-sustainable development of cities and landscapes.

In conclusion, I postulate that critical heritage studies should include innovative research on geo-aesthetics, understanding the material evidence of Earth's history as a vivid, metamorphic heritage, with its own values opposed to the non-sustainable management of cities and landscapes in the Anthropocene. The visual representations of cultural and geological heritage in the megacity landscapes of the Global South, with their multi-layered entangled temporalities, reveal accelerated processes of erosion and high levels of devastation, and contain lessons for a global debate on 'curating' contemporary landscapes and cities. The suggested conceptual impact of *Bildwissenschaft* generates a productive, complementary and alternative view on critical heritage research and practice in general. Although the Mexican objects offered here may seem to be far away from Europe, they can suggest unexpected and critical revisions of established patterns of nature preservation, which is an urgent global enterprise in one of the most critical eras of planet Earth's history – the Anthropocene.

Notes

1. James Hutton, in his *Theory of Earth* of 1788, coined the term 'Deep Time'.
2. *Bildwissenschaft* is a German term for 'science' of the image, which cannot correctly be translated into English, because 'science' is monopolised by the natural sciences, while German *Wissenschaft* in Hegelian terms applies to all types of knowledge production.
3. Entry in Aby Warburg's diary for 12 February 1917, quoted in Diers.
4. The traditional Chinese conception of landscape is totally different.
5. In the Aristotelian sense of *aisthesis*.
6. Information from Professor Reinhard Leinfelder, Free University of Berlin, Germany.
7. The Earth's crust is a resource for building materials, such as cement, gravel, sand and asphalt.
8. It's the Tamazunchale-El Sauz Gas Pipeline (GTES).
9. A revealing date in these complex debates: the energy consumption of the last seven decades (i.e. since 1950) is 1.5 times higher than the total of the last 12,000 years. Information from Prof Leinfelder (see note 6).
10. Quotation in German: 'Der Begriff des Fortschritts ist in der Idee der Katastrophe zu fundieren. Dass es, so weiter geht, *ist* die Katastrophe. Sie ist nicht das jeweils Bevorstehende, sondern das

jeweils Gegebene. Strindbergs Gedanke: die Hölle ist nicht, was uns bevorstünde – *sondern dieses Leben hier*.'

11. Moniek Driesse, of the University of Gothenburg, is currently working on a doctoral thesis on the urban memory of water, entitled 'Mapping the City in Time and Space – and Water, that Runs Through it All'.
12. This interpretation is inspired by Guy [Ernest] Debord's (1967) analysis of the process of cultural erosion.
13. An example of the visual communication of the geosciences via diagrams is Carreón-Freyre, Cerca and Galloway (2010).
14. Geophysical explanation by the Mexican landscape architect Pedro Camarena.
15. International Colloquium Mountain Aesthetics and Ecology, 'The Conceptual Heritage of Alexander von Humboldt', realised in September 2019 in the context of the 250th birthday of Alexander von Humboldt (Mexico City, Instituto de Investigaciones Estéticas, UNAM, in collaboration with the Terra Foundation, Chicago; concept and organisation by Peter Krieger).

References

Benjamin, Walter. 1972. Zentralpark. In *Gesammelte Schriften*, Vol. I/2. Frankfurt/Main: Suhrkamp.

Brownlee, Peter John, Valeria Piccoli and Georgiana Uhlyarik (eds). 2015. *Picturing the Americas: Landscape Painting from Tierra Del Fuego to the Arctic*. New Haven: Yale University Press/Art Gallery of Ontario/Pinacoteca do Estado de Sao Paulo/Terra Foundation for American Art.

Canet Miquel, Carles (ed.). 2018. *Guía de campo del Geoparque de la Comarca Minera*. Mexico: UNAM.

Carreón-Freyre, Dora, Mariano Cerca and Devin Galloway (eds). 2010. *Land Subsistence, Associated Hazards and the Role of Natural Resources Development*. Mexico: IAHS Publication.

Crutzen, Paul. 2002. Geology of Mankind. *Nature* 415: 23.

Davis, Heather and Etienne Turpin (eds). 2015. *Art in the Anthropocene: Encounters Among Aesthetics, Politics, Environments and Epistemologies*. London: Open Humanities Press.

Debord, Guy. 1967. *La Société du Spectacle*. Paris: Éditions Buchet Chastel.

Diers, Michael. 1995. *Warburg aus Briefen*. Berlin: De Gruyter.

Elhacham, Emily, Liad Ben-Uri, Jonathan Grozovski, Yinon Bar-On and Ron Milo. 2020. Global Human-Made Mass Exceeds all Living Biomass. *Nature* 588: 442–444.

Ellsworth, Elizabeth and Jamie Kruse (eds). 2013. *Making the Geologic Now: Responses to Material Conditions of Contemporary Life*. Brooklyn, NY: Punctum Books.

Jackson, John Brinckerhoff. 1984. *Discovering the Vernacular Landscape*. New Haven and London: Yale University Press.

Jullien, François. 2016. *Von Landschaft leben oder Das Ungedachte der Vernunft*. Berlin: Matthes and Seitz.

Krieger, Peter (ed.). 2007. *Acuápolis*. México: Instituto de Investigaciones Estéticas, UNAM.

Krieger, Peter. 2012. *Transformaciones del paisaje urbano en México. Representación y registro visual (Transformations in Mexico's Urban Landscape. Representation and Visual Record)*. Madrid: El Viso/México: MUNAL.

Krieger, Peter. 2015a. The Eco-Aesthetics and History of Water in Mexico City – Concepts and Topics. In Louise Noelle and David Wood (eds), *The Aesthetics of Landscape in the Americas*. Mexico: Instituto de Investigaciones Estéticas: UNAM: 395–412.

Krieger, Peter. 2015b. Las geo-grafías del Dr Atl Transformaciones estéticas de la energía telúrica y atmosférica (Dr Atl's Geo-graphies: Aesthetic Transformations of Telluric and Atmospheric Energy). In *Dr Atl, Rotación Cósmica. A cincuenta años de su muerte*. Guadalajara: Instituto Cultural Cabañas: 12–47.

Krieger, Peter. 2016. Ecohistoria y ecoestética de la megalópolis mexicana – conceptos, problemas y estrategias de investigación. In *El historiador frente a la ciudad de México. Perfiles de su historia*. México: IIH/UNAM: 257–277.

Krieger, Peter. 2017a. Symbolic Dimensions and Cultural Functions of the Neo-Baroque Balustrade in Contemporary Mexico City: An Alternative Learning from Las Vegas. In Walter Moser, Angela Ndalianis and Peter Krieger (eds), *Neo-Baroques: From Latin America to the Hollywood Blockbuster*. Boston: Brill Rodopi.

Krieger, Peter. 2017b. *Epidemias visuales: El Neobarroco de Las Vegas en la Ciudad de México. (Visual Epidemics. Las Vegas Neo-Baroque in Mexico City)*. México: Escotto editores.

Krieger, Peter. 2018. Imágenes de lo arcaico, lo sublime y la memoria telúrica frente al paisaje urbanizado de la Comarca Minera. In Carles Canet Miquel (ed.), *Guía de campo del Geoparque de la Comarca Minera*. Mexico: UNAM 2018: 130–145.

Krieger, Peter. 2019a. *Transparencies/Transitions/Tapias – The Photography of Fernando Cordero*. México: Producciones Santa Lucía.

Krieger, Peter. 2019b. Fotografía de arquitectura y paisaje del Antropoceno tardío: el espíritu humboldtiano en la obra de Fernando Cordero. *Bitácora Arquitectura* 41: 122–131.

Krieger, Peter. 2019c. Substanz und Bild der Landschaft. Ökokritische Impulse und geoästhetische Dimensionen im Werk des mexikanischen Gegenwartsfotografen Fernando Cordero, *Rundbrief Fotografie* (Deutsches Dokumentationszentrum für Kunstgeschichte – Bildarchiv Foto Marburg; http://www.rundbrief-fotografie.de), Vol. 26 No. 4, NF. 104: 21–29.

Latour, Bruno. 2017a. *Facing Gaia: Eight Lectures on the New Climatic Regime*. Cambridge: Cambridge University Press.

Latour, Bruno. 2017b. *Où atterir? Comment s'orienter en politique*. Paris: La Découverte.

Linsley, Robert. 2002. Minimalism and the City: Robert Smithson as a Social Critic. *RES: Anthropology and Aesthetics* 41: 38–55.

Palacios, Kaim and Brena Valle (texts) / Fernando Cordero (photographs). 2014. *Estratos de lo invisible*. Mexico: Producciones Santa Lucía/Grupo Desarrollo Infraestructura.

Robertson, Kirsty. 2016. Plastiglomerate, *e-flux* #78, December. Online at https://www.e-flux.com/journal/78/82878/plastiglomerate/ Accessed 23 March 2023.

Scherer, Bernd and Jürgen Renn (eds). 2015. *Das Anthropozän. Zum Stand der Dinge*. Berlin: Matthes and Seitz.

Smithson, Robert. 1979. The Crystal Land. In Nancy Holt (ed.), *The Writings of Robert Smithson*. New York: NYU Press.

Snow, Charles Percy. [1959] 2001. *The Two Cultures*. London: Cambridge University Press.

Utz, Peter. 2013. *Kultivierung der Katastrophe. Literarische Untergangsszenarien aus der Schweiz*. München: Wilhelm Fink Verlag.

von Humboldt, Alexander. 1986. *Ansichten der Natur, mit wissenschaftlichen Erläuterungen und sechs Farbtafeln, nach Skizzen des Autors*. Berlin: Die Andere Bibliothek.

von Humboldt, Alexander. 2004. *Kosmos. Entwurf einer physischen Weltbeschreibung*. Frankfurt am Main: Eichborn.

Zalasiewicz, Jan. 2009. *The Earth After Us: What Legacy Will Humans Leave in the Rocks?* Oxford: Oxford University Press.

Zalasiewicz, Jan et al. 2017. Scale and Diversity of the Physical Technosphere: A Geological Perspective. *The Anthropocene Review* 4(1): 9–22. http://doi.org/10.1177/2053019616677743

Zalasiewicz, Jan, Colin N. Waters, Mark Williams and Colin P. Summerhayes. 2019. *The Anthropocene as a Geological Time Unit: A Guide to the Scientific Evidence and Current Debate*. Cambridge: Cambridge University Press.

Zalasiewicz, Jan and Mark Williams. 2020. Anthropocene: Human-Made Materials Now Weigh as Much as all Living Biomass, Say Scientists. In *The Conversation*, 9 December. Online at https://theconversation.com/anthropocene-human-made-materials-now-weigh-as-much-as-all-living-biomass-say-scientists-151721 Accessed 23 March 2023.

6
Recognising urban heritage written in water: mapping fluctuating articulations in time and space

Moniek Driesse

We have left dry land

and the relative safety of our positions.
This is a change of speed
somewhere we can re-manage our weight in the world
re-balancing ourselves.
A place to move together
a break from role, time and gravity
– a new tidal time –
the equal necessity of all moments.

(Amy Sharrocks, 'Invitation to Drift', 2018)

Introduction

Mexico City is built on a lake and accordingly its inhabitants face severe structural hydrological challenges. The ground above its subterranean basins has dried out, leaving porous soil exposed to earthquakes and destruction. Rivers have disappeared into subterranean tubes and been replaced by highways. No longer is water freely tending to the thirst of citizens, as it is bottled and sold to the highest bidder. While supply relies on pipes carrying water over distances measuring hundreds of kilometres, rainstorms flood the former waterways. The modernist paradigm of 'dreaming of dry land' initiated the draining of the lake, as this was, according to the seventeenth-century viceroy Luis de Velasco the Younger, 'how things are done in Genoa, Venice and other cities in Italy and the states of Flanders for the conservation, provisioning and order of the republic' (Candiani 2014: 49–50). Due to the imposition of these early modern modes of thought onto the precolonial urban space, Mexico City changed its relationship with its aquasphere in dramatic ways. In this sense, the story of water in Mexico City narrates how the redeployment of particular European imaginaries and landscape modification practices in colonial contexts became embedded in heritage discourses. Over time, these practices created urban planning paradigms, in which bifurcation between nature and culture was central (Krieger 2015: 409) and exploitation of both was the result (Escobar 2018: 11; Shiva 2002).

This chapter mobilises design research methods as part of a methodology to imagine our way out of this paradigm, by framing its discussion in a way that acknowledges multiple subjectivities beyond the human and places it in the field of critical heritage studies. In the first section of this chapter, water comes to the fore as a cultural subject that draws maps of cities. Not maps as in pieces of paper with dots and lines, but maps understood as the phenomena that guide human orientations in time and space. In this conceptualisation, heritage becomes a navigational system that allows us to understand our positioning in time and space. The focus moves from the map as an object to mapping as a performative and, thus, subjective, cultural and political activity. In that sense, mapping is understood as an act of becoming rather than a fixed ontology.

These conceptual manoeuvres lead to the main contribution of this chapter, which is a methodological framework that promotes a fluid approach to disciplinary epistemes, that acts as a translation mechanism between different fields of knowledge production. Rooted in design research methods, this approach seeks to create direct encounters with material realities in the urban environment to, subsequently, flow through various entangled scales of urban spatiality and temporality. It is important to emphasise here that design research is not proposed as a universal fix of analytical methods, but rather as a catalyst for storytelling practices that enable the weaving together of moments of data gathering and analysis.

The final section shows how this methodological framework offers insights regarding ways in which water acts in what Gunnar Olsson designates as 'cartographic reasoning' (Olsson 2007: 109, 240–243; 2020: 50–51, 105) in Mexico City, where waters play a significant role in the cartographical narratives that draw lines of power. Herewith, this investigation is indebted to the work of feminist scholar Astrida Neimanis, who, in her rethinking of negotiating just relations with more-than-human worlds, explores watery elements beyond their passive role as a resource (see, for example, Neimanis 2014, 2017). Through this lens, water goes beyond its mere materiality, allowing it to become a cultural subject in real terms.

In studies of water within urban heritage studies, the focus is often on its management and the surrounding materialities, such as the waterfront, the riverbank or the seaside. In studies of water within natural heritage, there are certain approaches to water within larger frames of natural environments – however, more often than not these stay within the dichotomy of nature–culture (for examples of both urban and natural heritage studies, see Willems and van Schaik 2015; Hein 2020). Although water is a central matter of interest in this chapter, it mainly focuses on the epistemic problem that is introduced to those who intend to map the city, as water is involved in encounters between varying scales of spatiality and temporality – like the history of building the city and the 'deep time' (McPhee 1981) of the elemental configurations of basic geological conditions.[1]

The reconfiguration of water as a carrier of cultural memory challenges cartography as a fixed ontology. This ontological fixation happens as maps make claims about the positioning of things in the world and their interrelationality in imaginary constructions guided by power relations, and these dynamics of power play a fundamental role in creating an unbalanced distribution of resources and social privileges. These structures showed themselves as a devastating earthquake hit Mexico City on 19 September 2017. Following the devastation it caused, the collective mapping project Verificado19s began visualising damaged buildings and shelters (Pogrebinschi 2021). This project revealed the story of how neglected building regulations, unequal distribution of resources and extractive politics produced a 'ghost image' (Tsing et al. 2017) of the drained Tenochtitlan basin, where the poorest buildings were relegated to the most brittle terrain (Cruz-Atienza, Tago and Sanabria-Gómez 2016; see Figure 6.1).

Based on these premises, what follows is an argument for epistemological reorientations of approaches to heritage, using mapping as an optic and water as its lens. This aligns with my proposal of a fluid approach of disciplinary epistemes in the sense that water is reconfigured as an active agent, allowing us to see it participating in the cartographic reasoning of urban narratives. For us to comprehend and engage with these narratives, we need new storytelling apparatus that enables us to explore what can happen beyond conventional subject–object divisions and linear time perspectives of development and decay. The methodology framed within this chapter is an exploration of just such an apparatus.

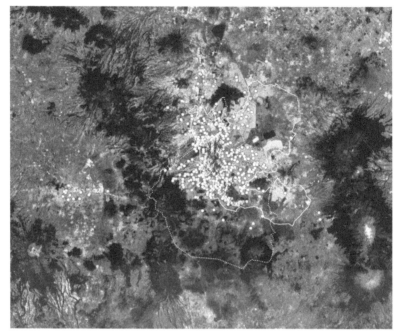

Figure 6.1 Overlay of the borders of Mexico City, the hard-rock zone limit on the outside of the vanished Texcoco lake-bed zone and the crowdsourced map of the destruction after the 19 September 2017 earthquake, composed by Verificado19s. © Moniek Driesse.

Working with change and instability – or when all knowledge becomes fluid

In her re-evaluation of the concepts of history and memory, Aleida Assmann argues as follows:

> While until fairly recently people were convinced that the past was closed and fixed and the future was open to change, we are now experiencing that the past is constantly changing and the future proves to be heavily determined by the past. The past appears to be no longer written in granite but rather in water; new constructions of it are periodically arising and changing the course of politics and history (Assmann 2008: 57).

Although I am aware that Assmann is talking here about water in a figurative sense, when taken seriously and to its furthest conclusion, the exploration of water as a carrier of memory goes beyond the realm of abstraction and becomes a perspective on change and instability. This is especially relevant as a response to the tendency of an increased focus towards the future in the field of critical heritage studies, a tendency seen in the following frequently cited passage:

> … 'heritage' has very little to do with the past but actually involves practices which are fundamentally concerned with assembling and designing the future – heritage involves working with … traces of the past to … remake both ourselves and the world in the present, in anticipation of an outcome that will help constitute a specific (social, economic or ecological) resource in and for the future (Harrison 2015).

This passage tends to place the problem of heritage within a world view with too easily separable dimensions of time – the past has passed, the present is in focus, the future is central. In times of environmental and social injustice – issues that become amplified in cities especially – my research aligns with Winter's plea (2013) to study heritage as an enabling force for working on different scales, temporalities and, also, anxieties and hopes. That means studying heritage not as a problem of management, but rather as a problem of translation between epistemologies (Byrne 2008).

In that sense, the fluid translation between epistemologies of knowledge production through water takes Winter's suggestions to a more radical level, by drawing on a 'pluriversal' approach (Escobar 2018; for considerations on heritage as worldmaking and pluriversal approaches to heritage ontologies, see for example Harrison et al. 2020; Breithoff 2020), while also seeking to go beyond narrow 'human regimes' (Tsing 2015). This means that it is not only essential to join forces across disciplines, but also necessary to reconnect different places from different times from different perspectives through different ways of knowing, employing sensitivity and critical thought on knowledge production itself.

As a matter-in-transformation that shapeshifts its ways into everyday experiences in multiple ways and timescales, water challenges human projections, polarised positions and established categories. In that sense, it expands notions of material or human agency, or even the fluid relationships between humans and the non-human materiality of water, as illustrated by Astrida Neimanis:

> No agent – no person, no biological entity, no material artefact – controls the world, but all of these things enter into various relationships with one another: weather and landforms worlding

hurricanes; boats and tides, weapons and disease, states and racist ideologies worlding colonisation. In such intricate patterns of material relation, agency is dispersed through the material world. … In this sense, there is no a priori 'cut' between human and non-human, between culture and nature. Instead, there are variations within a broader more-than-human field (Neimanis 2014: 36).

In what follows, a metonymic understanding of water as a mapping agent leads to a conceptual framework that allows for a deeper understanding of how water traces changing and unstable articulations in time and space with its inherent fluctuating nature.

Mapping fluctuating articulations through metaphors

In many, now conventional, approaches to cartography, like 'wayfinding' (Lynch 1960) and 'cognitive mapping' (Jameson 1990), spatial phenomena are interpreted as maps of relations between things and people in space, leading to the conclusion that the representation of space can never be as complete as space itself. In this tradition, the map is a metaphor. Swedish geographer Gunnar Olsson turns this relationship upside down. In his thinking, the metaphor is the map (Olsson 2014). With this epistemological reversal, Olsson puts the spatial aspect of the human experience at the centre of any analysis. The metaphor refers here to any figure of speech, drawing, statue or signification that includes representation and needs interpretation. The mapping capacity inherent in any of these metaphors becomes apparent when we pay attention to how they communicate and thereby constitute real-world relations.

As every rhetorician knows, the easiest way to be believed is to tell a story. And as every cartographer knows, all stories are in essence travel stories, infinite chains of metonymies in which one wor(l)d slides into another, a postmodern narrative with multidimensional meanings (Olsson 2007: 67).

Although most of Olsson's writing is philosophical rather than practical, it does argue that looking at the world through a lens of cartographic reasoning makes it possible to see articulations in time and space that emerge from different power relations. In a personal conversation, he stated:

To have a map, the only traditional map, [there are] only three things you need. A set of points, lines between the points and the projection scheme. Now, to name the points is not so difficult. Each one you give a name ... When it comes to the lines, the relations between them, that is of course much more difficult, because that relation does not have a physical counterpar t... So these lines are steeped in power (excerpt from a personal conversation with Gunnar Olsson, April 2018; see also Olsson 2020: 50).

In this theoretical frame, any iteration of metaphorical significance should be perceived as a potential dot on the map, producing a narrative line that allows us to understand our place in time and space. In that sense, heritage can be understood as a navigational system that suggests how to read metaphorical maps, in which what is perceived as heritage relies on a metonymic relation between the dots and the articulating lines in time and space. Take, for example, Mexico City, where a drained lake initiates a semiosis of meaning in diachronic space, leading thoughts back to the days when a lake was present, and a future when it is completely absent, leaving the city without any sources of water. Paradoxically, when water falls as rain over Mexico City, long-gone rivers reappear in a collage of time in a forced superimposition over the asphalt of today, causing flooding. The history of drainage over the centuries from the basin to the current megalopolitan desert – with its fragile soil due to water extractions and little to no space for its replenishment – was also revealed with the earthquake in September 2017, when the contours of Lake Texcoco became visible in the mapping of collapses and debris on the streets (Figure 6.1). Cultural memories of the city and the landscape that water carries in its meandering flow have become those of instability. It can no longer steady the ground above its subterranean basins as they dry out, leaving porous soil exposed to earthquakes and destruction.

With this account of the metonymic relations that water instigates, it can be argued that water acquires a subjectivity of its own. If this is so, then water ceases to be the passive backdrop on which the narrative takes place and becomes an active agent in producing narratives; we move it from the level of the canvas to the dots on the map, placed in specific materialities and space-times. In other words, although water is not human, it can have an agency of its own in the narration of the city. When the liquid space becomes centre stage and water a narrator of its own reality, relational narrative lines of power transform through the agency inherent in its fluctuating nature. However, Gunnar Olsson states that the relational lines between the dots on the map do not have physical counterparts that can be studied (personal communication, April 2018; see also Olsson 2020: 50). This means that the question remains how to move cartographic reasoning from the conceptual framework to a methodology that addresses the way in which we orient ourselves within these cartographies.

Watery points of orientation

Feminist and postcolonial scholar Sara Ahmed follows the concept of orientation through different spaces and temporalities. She argues that 'orientations shape not only how we inhabit space, but how we apprehend this world of shared inhabitancy, as well as "who" or "what" we direct our energy and attention toward' (Ahmed 2006: 3). In other words, orientations matter, both in the sense of something being a subject of consideration and as a material substance that occupies space. In that sense, waters and their continuing and multiform exchanges with other entities, places and times oblige us to consider multiple forces that give shape to the transforming lines between the dots on the map.

The following methodological framework employs Olsson's cartographic reasoning to create moments of orientation in time and space that explore metonymic articulations through focusing on watery dots on the city map of Mexico City. These dots, the iterations of signification that produce narratives, are the vantage points from which the orientations happen that Ahmed calls for. That is to say, the dots project narrative lines aimed in different directions, traced with diverse intentions, navigating through multiple dimensions of time and space. Therefore, narrative directionalities are conditioned by these points of orientation that can create, reinforce, challenge or disrupt articulations. Or, in Gunnar Olsson's words, 'these lines [between the dots on the map] are steeped in power. And that is where the trouble begins because when I baptise the lines, the lines begin to shake and they want to change form' (excerpt from a personal communication with Gunnar Olsson, April 2018).

Through its meetings with divergent ways of life and while it flows in multiple rhythms, scales and time trajectories, water forces us to constantly switch perceptions and conceptualisations. This means that Ahmed's moments of orientation, or rather, of reorientation, give shape to an inquiry that seeks to consciously direct attention towards water in order to reveal the relational narrative lines steeped in power that it traces and make them tremble. Following water not only allows for developing an understanding of its aesthetic values – in its cognitive sense – but also an understanding of the modes of worldmaking, in time and space, that it is capable of engaging as a sociopolitical subject. The following methods employed in this research allow for place-based sensory experiences of fluid cartographic reasoning that can create a metonymic ripple effect – direct encounters with water and interactions with the city that spin articulations in time and space.

From methodology to methods: navigating narrative lines

If we accept Assmann's assertion that a past is not so much set in stone but rather written in water, then our land-based cartographic vocabulary needs to be supplemented with fluid concepts. Although the methods used here find their inspiration in Olsson's cartographic reasoning and the narrative lines steeped in power that connect the dots on the map, they moreover seek to propose ways of expanding notions of – and ways of working with – fluctuating articulations in time and space. The model proposed here is informed by my practice as a design researcher, with a specific focus on a one-year process of inquiry into waters in Mexico City. The collection of material, creative process and analytical engagement emerge from movements back and forth between doing and learning, which designer Peter Gall Krogh and sociologist Ilpo Koskinen have described as a process characterised by 'drifting' (Krogh and Koskinen 2020). In the intention to build knowledge, the emergence of new insights during the process is received as an invitation to change cause and action. In that sense, acts of drifting can be perceived as particular efforts to instrumentalise a fluid methodology.

Given its focus on the role of water in the city, each of the stages of research in Mexico City has taken its name from a watery metaphor: permeation, drips and drops, a natural spring erupts, flows, floods, mist and evaporation, distillation. These designations were playful at first, merely labels in a research diary (Driesse 2019: 17–31), but as the project progressed, they evolved into a modus operandi: a methodological framework that invites the researcher to leave dry land and cast aside land-based perceptions of stability and fixedness in cartography. Envisioning research through this watery lens means that it flows through disciplines and across boundaries – but never aimlessly. In the following, I will present the seven stages through which the fluid methodology took shape. Whether these stages are understood metaphorically or propositionally does not matter in the end, as, to paraphrase Assmann, it is the state of fluid thinking and acting, offering new perspectives on the past, that reconfigures visions of the future.

1. The first stage of this watery research is Permeation. Before the eruption of any natural spring, underground basins need replenishment from the waters that permeate the grounds. The process of this fluid methodology starts with a phase in which orientations on water are directed through a specific occasion for action that emerges from a convergence of circumstances.
2. Drips and drops of information leak in through one-on-one conversations with local collaborators from different fields of study and backgrounds. The complexity and murkiness of the matter becomes apparent.
3. A natural spring erupts. Curated encounters between different communities of thought and practice tease out overlapping matters of concern.

In these first three phases, directing attention towards water matters in the sense that it comes to the fore as an ever-present material substance giving shape to the city which becomes a matter of consideration in varying ways. In Mexico City, this part of the process gave shape to moments of orientation which then defined specific watery dots on the map, with the changing narratives surrounding these places, to bring to the next stages of the project.

In 2016, the Rotterdam-based urban design office De Urbanisten published a report on rainwater management strategies for Mexico City (De Urbanisten 2016). Reading the report, I began to wonder if rainwater is manageable at all. This defined my mission to chart relations between water and the residents of Mexico City – to go beyond water as a problem of management. In the first three months of 2017, I asked inhabitants, considered as local experts, to show me the dots on the map representing specific places that could illustrate different relationships with water. In this way, I learned of the geographical location of watery points of orientation. These experts, each from a different field of knowledge production, were brought into conversation during three movie nights, showing films in which water was the protagonist, allowing me to assess the narratives that floated around these locations from the positions of different paradigms and to define common denominators.[2] From introductions to water and its meanderings in the city, the meetings became dialogues focused on three general themes: the human right to water, the multiplicity of water worlds, and water economies and hierarchies.

Building on these foundations, the next three phases of the research process aim to give shape to possible understandings of fluid articulations in time and space between the dots on the map. To go beyond linear connections, storytelling is employed as a method[3] in which attention becomes a relational matter between the observer and the observed, the listener and the storyteller, creating metonymic interpretations of hydro-cartographies.

4. In the Flows stage, water guides a place-based sensory experience, by walking its visible and invisible lines between dots on the map (inspired by Lucius Burckhardt's concept of 'strollology' and Richard Long's artwork *A Line Made by Walking*; see Burckhardt 1980).
5. Floods. A transposition of stories and experiences from one local context to a different environment is translated into a platform for storytelling presented publicly to a broad audience. Hereby, the methodology explores how places can resonate with each other by making articulations in time and space on various scales.
6. Mist and evaporation. These actions then open up space for creating narrative apparatuses to question conventional subject–object divisions and linear time perspectives.

In Mexico City, I walked a line connecting previously defined dots on the map to experience articulating narrative threads by myself and to explore what kinds of other stories and places would emerge from this meandering action. The 73-kilometre trail is depicted in the map *Journey to Atlan* (Figure 6.2) and stretches between Santa Catarina del Monte on Mount Tlaloc and the waterworks of the Cárcamo de Dolores.

Whereas Santa Catarina del Monte, like other villages on Mount Tlaloc, still relies on its own well, which it vehemently protects against interference from multinational corporations and pollution (Calle, Alberti Manzanares and Martínez Corona 2015), the Cárcamo de Dolores relies on the Cutzamala System, which provides approximately 30 per cent of Mexico City's water. While the murals at the Cárcamo de Dolores, painted by Diego Rivera, celebrate the engineering works (Figure 6.3), the Cutzamala System enforces a regime of scarcity and relegates water to the realm of the irregular. The deficiencies of the system are on the one hand technical – such as dredging issues and the lack of sufficient pressure. As pressure is low, water does not reach the precarious eastern parts of the city. On the other hand, the effects of the deficiencies are sociocultural, as is the case with the pollution and the inability to provide communities along the pipeline with 'sufficient, safe, acceptable,

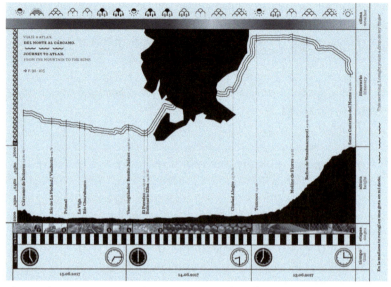

Figure 6.2 *Journey to Atlan* map. Appendix of *This Morning, I Caught You in a Drop on My Finger* (Driesse 2019). © Moniek Driesse.

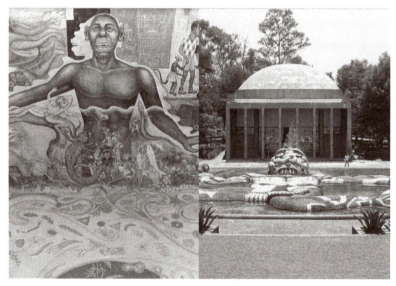

Figure 6.3 At the Cárcamo de Dolores (Waterworks of Dolores), Tláloc, the god of heavenly waters, is watching the skies and the engineering works in admiration as well as fear. Murals by Diego Rivera. © Sjamme van de Voort.

accessible and affordable water' (United Nations General Assembly 2010; Heller 2017).

In an effort to subvert this system, the journey took its point of departure from the side of the city opposite to the Cárcamo, to create an inverted map in its mirror image, letting water show its different ways. The three-day walk was an exercise in consciously paying attention to water – being attentive to how it moves, how it appears, what it does, what it is threatened by, how it organises itself and other bodies. In this embodied experience, in the repeated action of taking step after step, following the trails of water, affects and effects of its presence and absence could be felt and seen. It was during this walk, in the company of memory scholar Sjamme van de Voort, that the mnemonic dynamics embedded in water – processes of landscape and urban formation from visible and invisible geographical, physical and symbolic lines – became more apparent (Driesse and van de Voort 2019). The 'floods' are in fact not flooding but water remembering where it used to be. All water has a perfect memory and is forever trying to get back to where it was. It is an emotional memory – what the nerves and the skin remember. And a rush of imagination is our 'flooding'.

Through our walk, we gathered data in the form of photographs, commentaries from residents and observations on the socioeconomic differences that water creates in the megalopolis and the long memories that govern them. Passing on this data to collaborators from diverse disciplines – policymakers, philosophers, performance artists, craftspeople, culinary artists and others – transferred water from being the subject of the conversation to being an active agent in it. One of the results of this journey was an eco-fictional fable written by Mauricio Martinez, narrating the story of a thirsty city drowning in rainwater. Another result was a series of festival performances in Rotterdam, the Netherlands, in the summer of 2017. In collaboration with craftsman Sander Huijzer, a lifeboat came into being, and with performance artist Ilse Evers, there followed an interaction that modified the lifeboat into an installation that transformed water from nearby canals into potable water. This was mixed with a syrup that culinary artist Maidie van den Bos created from the plants and fruits that we collected along our trail in Mexico City, so that festival guests consumed our journey both literally and figuratively.

Allowing these metonymic interpretations of our map opened room for a wide range of possibilities for reimagination of the social and cultural values that it carries. In response to the performances in Rotterdam, Corinne Heyrman penned a letter addressed to 'Water'. Responses on

'Water's' behalf came from Henk Ovink, Lodewijk Abspoel and Feike de Jong, who took us a step closer to water in an attempt to change the perspective with which we approach it. Eva Pavlič Seifert's suggestion that we could have a relation to water defined by love rather than necessity takes us into a world where our needs are redefined, while Andre Dekker's account from the assembly of the *Parliament of Things* at the *Zandwacht* sculpture in Rotterdam takes the conversation to a level where it is apparent that our role as human beings is less significant than our ego imagines it to be. All of these contributions can be found in the book *This Morning, I Caught You in a Drop on My Finger* (Driesse 2019), in which my role as a cartographer came to the fore as I mapped this journey through watery worlds – documenting articulations in pictures and text, finding focus on fluidity.

7. Distillation. Through the previous interactions between different modes of knowledge production, water draws new maps, moving beyond discussions of whether an insignificant space becomes a place by adding meaning (see, for example, Tuan 1977, 1990; de Certeau 1984). It rather explores articulations, not only in time and space but also between the diversity in embedded meanings and perspectives on specific locations.

Water had drawn its map and had its say. During the distillation process, I therefore returned from the methodological part of my research to assume the analytical role. This included a visit to the archive of the University Library in Uppsala, Sweden, to see the *Santa Cruz Map* (Figure 6.4) of Mexico City from c.1550, as well as long conversations with geographer and philosopher Gunnar Olsson. The *Santa Cruz Map* clearly showed the present-day dried-up rivers tracing the line we had walked throughout the city. These acquired new meaning as relational narrative lines, steeped in power, started to tremble and seek new directions.

In the following phase, the process of publishing the book *This Morning, I Caught You in a Drop on My Finger* (Driesse 2019), various contributions to the project so far came together in what might be called a cartography of adjacent epistemes. In other words, subjective maps of water imaginaries came together, to be discussed with colleagues from academic disciplines adjacent to mine. In this mode of analysis, Mexico City ceased to be the main subject of the narratives wherein my research took place. By letting the metaphor be the map, this subject position

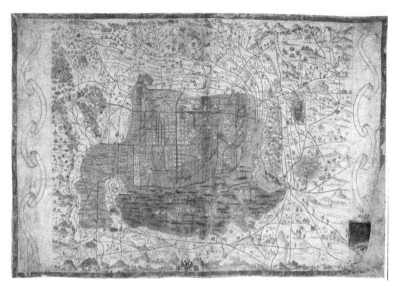

Figure 6.4 This *Santa Cruz Map* is a unique map of Mexico City as the capital of New Spain, from around 1550. Also known as the *Uppsala Map*, it currently resides in the map collection of the Uppsala University Library. Courtesy of Carolina Rediviva Library, Uppsala University, Sweden. Available in the public domain at http://www.alvin-portal.org/alvin/view.jsf?pid=alvin-record%3A85478&dswid=8531

had been allocated to the lake and the river. It is from the perspective of these water bodies that various dimensions and temporalities of space as a basic element of reasoning – cartographic reasoning – were explored with the intention to move away from Earth-bound ideas of space that create a false impression of stability and linear time.

Discussion

With the conceptual manoeuvre that allows for engagement with water in a way that promotes co-creation of the narratives that draw lines of power, I should declare that, of course, I am aware that water cannot actually speak. It does not have a voice in the human sense in that it has no lungs, vocal cords, tongue, lips to produce the words it needs to say. It is also safe to say that, *affectively*, water does not care about life in the city. However, while it may not be possible to build a dictionary, watery spaces might provide an alternative vocabulary that facilitates understanding of entangled materialities and space-times. To understand the agency of the non-human, the language of that which has no speech, the methodological framework set out in this chapter explores new forms of knowledge production, by searching for a confrontation with material relations in the urban environment that allow for aquatic imaginaries to flow through time and space. In that sense, the methodology reiterates the earlier mentioned statement by Neimanis (2014: 36) that agency is dispersed through these material relations.

The fluid approach resulting from this methodology has led us to accept Assmann's contention that the past is malleable and that our horizon of expectations changes with its fluctuations. With this realisation, the designation of heritage becomes a perspective on change in time and space that can be used as a tool to fluidly imagine urban realities in the past, present and future. In this conceptualisation, heritage is a navigational system, guiding human understanding of orientations in time and space.

From this perspective on heritage, the focus moves from the map as an object to mapping as a performative and, thus, cultural, social and political activity. This is where cartography ceases to be a fixed ontology and is rather understood as an act of becoming. When evaporated mists coalesce into drops of rain, distilled into new knowledge, water draws new maps. It enacts its agency, drawing lines of power through the imaginary of the city across time and space. The metaphor is turned around and the map has become the territory. Metonymic relations between places in time and space draw lines. This is a cartography of becoming, in which water is an active agent in the production of narratives, agency is imaginary, the imaginary has agency, heritage is a navigational system and mapping the city is a performative and thus cultural, social and political act. In that sense, this research responds to a need to examine and alter practices with which we articulate places in time and space so as to provide tools to (re-)imagine the past, present and future of living in the city.

Notes

1. The idea of 'deep time' was first described in 1788 by the Scottish geologist James Hutton, but it was American author John McPhee who coined the term almost 200 years later (see McPhee 1981).
2. All conversations were recorded. The names and backgrounds of invitees, as well as the full programme of the movie nights, can be found in the project diary in the publication resulting from the design research process (see Driesse 2019).
3. Anna Lowenhaupt Tsing promotes storytelling as a method and even claims to call it a science, an addition to knowledge (see Tsing 2015: 37).

References

Ahmed, Sara. 2006. *Queer Phenomenology: Orientations, Objects, Others*. Durham, North Carolina: Duke University Press.

Assmann, Aleida. 2008. Transformations between History and Memory. *Social Research: An International Quarterly* 75(1): 49–72.

Breithoff, Esther. 2020. *Conflict, Heritage and World-Making in the Chaco: War at the End of the Worlds?* London: UCL Press.

Burckhardt, Lucius. 1980. *Warum ist Landschaft schön? Die Spaziergangswischenschaft*. Kassel: Martin Schmitz Verlag.

Byrne, Denis. 2008. Heritage Conservation as Social Action. In Rodney Harrison, John Jameson and John Schofield (eds), *The Cultural Heritage Reader*. London: Routledge: 149–174.

Calle, Beatriz Elena Madrigal, Pilar Alberti Manzanares and Beatriz Martínez Corona. 2015. La Apantla: el agradecimiento para que no falte el agua. In *Cuicuilco*, 22(63): 29–61. Online at http://www.scielo.org.mx/scielo.php?script=sci_arttext&pid=S0185-16592015000200003&lng=es&nrm=iso Accessed 24 March 2023.

Candiani, Vera. 2014. *Dreaming of Dry Land: Environmental Transformation in Colonial Mexico City*. Stanford, CA: Stanford University Press.

Cruz-Atienza, Victor, Josue Tago and José David Sanabria-Gómez. 2016. Long Duration of Ground Motion in the Paradigmatic Valley of Mexico. In *Scientific Reports* 6, article 38807. https://doi.org/10.1038/srep38807

de Certeau, Michel. 1984. *The Practice of Everyday Life* (translated by Steven Rendall). Berkeley: University of California Press.

De Urbanisten. 2016. *Towards a Water Sensitive Mexico City: Public Space as a Rain Management Strategy*. Rotterdam. Online at http://www.urbanisten.nl/wp/wp-content/uploads/2016.07.21_Reporte_CAF_Urb-AEP_lr-2.pdf Accessed 17 December 2021.

Driesse, Moniek. 2019. *This Morning, I Caught You in a Drop on my Finger: About the City in Time and Space – and Water, That Runs Through it All*. Amsterdam: Idea Books.

Driesse, Moniek and Sjamme van de Voort. 2019. What is Hope in the Speech of the Rain? Imagining Water by Walking the Megalopolis. In Moniek Driesse (ed.), *This Morning, I Caught You in a Drop on my Finger: About the City in Time and Space – and Water, That Runs Through it All*. Amsterdam: Idea Books: 160–180.

Escobar, Arturo. 2018. *Design for the Pluriverse*. London: Duke University Press.

Harrison, Rodney. 2015. Beyond 'Natural' and 'Cultural' Heritage: Toward an Ontological Politics of Heritage in the Age of Anthropocene. *Heritage & Society*, 8(1): 24–42. https://doi.org/10.1179/2159032X15Z.00000000036

Harrison, Rodney, Caitlin DeSilvey, Cornelius Holtorf, Sharon Macdonald, Nadia Bartolini, Esther Breithoff, Harald Fredheim, Antony Lyons, Sarah May, Jennie Morgan and Sefryn Penrose. 2020. *Heritage Futures: Comparative Approaches to Natural and Cultural Heritage Practices*. London: UCL Press.

Hein, Carola (ed.). 2020. *Adaptive Strategies for Water Heritage: Past, Present and Future*. Cham: Springer Nature. https://doi.org/10.1007/978-3-030-00268-8

Heller, Léo. 2017. End of Mission Statement by the Special Rapporteur on Human Rights to Water and Sanitation Mr. Léo Heller, Mexico City, May 2017. United Nations, Office of the High Commissioner for Human Rights. Online at https://www.ohchr.org/en/NewsEvents/Pages/DisplayNews.aspx?NewsID=21608&LangID=E Accessed 24 March 2023.

Jameson, Fredric. 1990. Cognitive Mapping. In Cary Nelson and Lawrence Grossberg (eds), *Marxism and the Interpretation of Culture*. Chicago: University of Illinois Press: 347–360.

Krieger, Peter. 2015. The Eco-Aesthetics and History of Water in Mexico City – Concepts and Topics. In Louise Noelle and David Wood (eds), *Landscape Aesthetics in the Americas*. Mexico City: Instituto de Investigaciones Estéticas, UNAM: 397–413.

Krogh, Peter and Ilpo Koskinen. 2020. *Drifting by Intention: Four Epistemic Traditions from within Constructive Design Research*. New York: Springer.

Lynch, Kevin. 1960. *The Image of the City*. Cambridge, MA: MIT Press.

McPhee, John. 1981. *Basin and Range (Annals of the Former World Book 1)*. New York: Farrar, Straus and Giroux.

Neimanis, Astrida. 2014. Natural Others? On Nature, Culture and Knowledge. In Mary Evans, Clare Hemmings, Marsha Henry, Hazel Johnstone, Sumi Madhok, Ania Plomien and Sadie Wearing (eds), *SAGE Handbook of Feminist Theory*. Thousand Oaks, CA: SAGE: 26–45. https://www.doi.org/10.4135/9781473909502

Neimanis, Astrida. 2017. *Bodies of Water: Posthuman Feminist Phenomenology*. London: Bloomsbury.

Olsson, Gunnar. 2007. *Abysmal: A Critique of Cartographic Reason*. Chicago: The University of Chicago Press.

Olsson, Gunnar. 2014. Gunnar Olsson och det Kartografiska Tänkandet. Interview by Lars Mogensen. *Filosofiska rummet,* Sveriges Radio, 31 August 2014. Online at https://sverigesradio.se/avsnitt/420714 Accessed 24 March 2023.

Olsson, Gunnar. 2020. *Arkography*. Lincoln, NE: University of Nebraska Press.

Pogrebinschi, Thamy. 2021. LATINNO Dataset on Democratic Innovations in Latin America. WZB - Berlin Social Science Center. Data File Version 1.0.0. Online at https://doi.org/10.7802/2278 Accessed 26 April 2023.

Sharrocks, Amy. 2018. Invitation to Drift. *Performance Research* 23(7): 103–104.

Shiva, Vandana. 2002. *Water Wars: Privatisation, Pollution and Profit*. Boston: South End Press.

Tsing, Anna Lowenhaupt. 2015. *The Mushroom at the End of the World: On the Possibility of Life in Capitalist Ruins*. Princeton: Princeton University Press.

Tsing, Anna Lowenhaupt, Heather Swanson, Elaine Gan and Nils Bubandt (eds). 2017. *Arts of Living on a Damaged Planet: Ghosts and Monsters of the Anthropocene*. Chicago: University of Minnesota Press.

Tuan, Yi-Fu. 1977 (8th ed. 2001). *Space and Place*. Minneapolis: University of Minnesota Press.

Tuan, Yi-Fu. 1990. *Topophilia*. New York: Columbia University Press.

United Nations General Assembly. 2010 (July). Resolution A/RES/64/292. General Comment No. 15. The Right to Water. *UN Committee on Economic, Social and Cultural Rights*, November 2002. Online at https://digitallibrary.un.org/record/687002 Accessed 30 March 2023.

Willems, Willem and Henk van Schaik (eds). 2015. *Water & Heritage: Material, Conceptual and Spiritual Connections*. Leiden: Sidestone Press.

Winter, Tim. 2013. Clarifying the Critical in Critical Heritage Studies. *International Journal of Heritage Studies* 19: 532–545.

7
Participatory design in the context of heritage-development: engaging with the past in the design space of historical landscapes

Mela Zuljevic

Introduction

By engaging with a case study in the context of heritage-development, this chapter traces connections between participatory design (PD) and critical heritage studies (CHS) to explore a situated approach to designing the future of historical landscapes. In using heritage as a resource in spatial development, the conjunction of authorised heritage discourse (Smith 2006) with universalising development frameworks can defuture[1] (Fry 2019) the plurality of ways of caring for the historical landscape. This chapter starts from the assumption that a critical engagement with the past helps to contextualise and support PD approaches that can challenge such defuturing instigated by heritage-development. It foregrounds the concept of the design space – an imaginary landscape that emerges in the design process (Binder et al. 2011: 111–155), where different actors use the past to engage in future-making. Here I explore how the design space of historical landscapes is determined through heritage-development visions, but also configured by the existing practices and things in the landscape.

The chapter engages with these relations via a case study of a 'transition landscape' vision in Genk (a city in Belgium), designed within a nomination for a UNESCO World Heritage Site (WHS) and intertwined with a broader debate on the balance between historical preservation and sustainable spatial development. The research was undertaken through the participatory mapping and making of a *Transition Landscape Atlas* which involved multiple actors – residents and activists as well as experts in heritage and spatial development. By reflecting on the findings, the chapter outlines some directions for a situated PD approach that can critically engage with heritage-development in the design space of historical landscapes.

Heritage-development as a context for participatory design

This research began from an interest in how participatory approaches to designing the future of historical landscapes can learn from critical discussions on heritage as 'contemporary uses of the past' (Graham, Ashworth and Tunbridge 2000: 2). In the context of spatial development, these uses do not necessarily stand in opposition to change and transformation (Ashworth 2014), as is commonly assumed in aligning heritage with the goals of preservation or conservation. Rather, heritage is compatible with development as it 'has an inherent economic dimension' that competes with its social, political and cultural uses (Ashworth 2014: 7). In particular, the past can often be used as a resource in development visions favouring economic growth over other values, such as those of sociocultural plurality (Hayden 1995; Nasser 2014; De Cesari and Dimova 2018). In designing for the future of historical landscapes, experts increasingly see the need to negotiate between the interests of preserving heritage value and improving everyday life, with the urgency of sustainable transition (Labadi and Logan 2015). When these interests collide in complex settings, such as post-industrial landscapes with histories of migration, universalising frameworks of development can inhibit the sociocultural plurality of inhabitants and corresponding ways of caring for the landscape.

The work of Arturo Escobar (1995, 2018) explores the implications of design in both sustaining and challenging universalising frameworks of development. He critiques the Eurocentric model of development as a 'grand design gone sour' (Escobar 2018: xiii) that defutured plural ways of being in the South through a universalising vision with economic growth at its core. Escobar (2018: 15) emphasises the need to engage with the past and the 'historicity of the worlds and things of human creation' in order for design to acknowledge its participation in the temporal trajectories of universalising worldmaking. In design studies, different scholars (Fry 2019; Tonkinwise 2019; Tlostanova 2017) take these insights further to argue how stronger critical reflections on development as a universalising discourse of progress are crucial in designing for more diverse and sustainable ways of being. This chapter looks at how these discussions, concerned with the defuturing of indigenous and plural ways of being in the Global South, can become relevant also for the context of heritage-development in the Global North. This seems especially important in multicultural historical landscapes in Western Europe, such as the one in this research, where the diversity of ways of caring for the landscape can be hindered by mobilising heritage in development. I take up the nexus of heritage-development to designate this mobilisation as a specific research problem that can be addressed by PD in the context of historical landscapes.

The design space of historical landscapes as a site of defuturing

Participatory design (PD) is a research field focused on creating settings, methods and tools to enable people to take part in the process of developing a design that will affect them. It foregrounds plurality with its principle of focusing on how 'those affected by a design, should have a say in the design process' (Ehn 2008: 94). A key concept in PD is the design space, as a site of collective problem-framing and future-making, where different actors discuss conditions and visions for the future design object. Within this space, as different expectations and proposals are confronted, designers and participants (ideally) search for a balance in addressing the needs and interests of actors affected by the design at stake.

In the context of heritage-development, it is important to account for how the design space is configured by the authorised heritage discourse (AHD), where valorisation and preservation of the past are determined by the interests of the 'nation and class on the one hand, and technical expertise and aesthetic judgement on the other' (Smith 2006: 11). Represented in the authority of institutions such as the United Nations Educational, Scientific and Cultural Organization (UNESCO), AHD foregrounds and legitimises universalising world views and dominant 'narratives of Western national and elite class experiences' (Smith 2006: 299). In its management approach to historical sites, AHD tends to require 'the maintenance of a consensual view of the past and its meanings for the present' (Smith 2006: 79). This implies that, in the context of historical landscapes, their historical production through negotiation of plural meanings and agencies can be overshadowed by a universalising, consensus-based approach.

While the field of design, especially in development contexts, is generally perceived as a practice of future-making, it inevitably entails also *defuturing* aspects. For Fry (2019), defuturing is an imposed process of worldmaking that effectively unmakes a world. In the design space of heritage-development, this means that future-making – by selecting specific pasts that will enter this space – is also accompanied by the defuturing of the pasts that are rendered incompatible with the specific vision. This research aimed to trace what these engagements with the past in the design space reveal about such defuturing by development: How is the past used in the selection of what enters the design space and what is left outside? How are these uses reflective of universalising frameworks in AHD and heritage-development, and can they be challenged in participatory ways? In addressing these questions, I propose that PD approaches should engage with the social and public history contained in landscapes, following the way Dolores Hayden (1995) writes about the historical landscape as a context for greater responsibility of designers. As public history storehouses that nurture social and public memory, these landscapes encompass 'shared time in the form of shared territories' (Hayden 1995: 8). By starting from a case study tied to a UNESCO WHS nomination, I explore how a critical engagement with the past in the design space can effectuate such a context for design responsibility in PD approaches.

The rural-industrial transition landscape

In Genk, spatial planning and heritage experts have been exploring the future development of the city's post-mining landscape in terms of both economic growth and sustainable transition. Recently, these efforts became intertwined with the Rural–Industrial Transition Landscape (RITL) vision, developed as a nomination of the Hoge Kempen[2] area for a UNESCO WHS label. The Transition Landscape[3] was proposed as a unique window in time representing an important phase in Western history: the radical turning point from a rural to an industrial economic system, which brings them together in a 'delicate mosaic' (Metalidis, Van Den Bosch and Hermans 2018: 48). These systems are represented in the remnants of preindustrial hayfields, forests and watermills, as well as the industrial heritage of former mines, slag heaps (Figure 7.1) and garden cities built to accommodate the guest workers. The heritage of mining is also in the intangible landscape – many miners came from the south and east of Europe, and the north of Africa, bringing with them

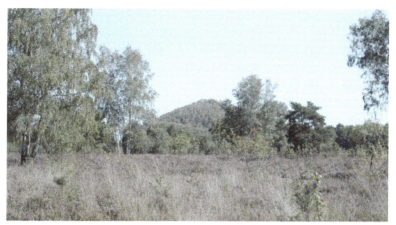

Figure 7.1 A hayfield with the Waterschei mine slagheap in the background. © Mela Zuljevic.

different ways of life and cultures. The mining sites closed by the 1980s and were eventually repurposed as a cultural centre, technology park and art museum, while the garden cities were designated as established architectural heritage.

Initiated in 2011 and coordinated by the Regionaal Landschap Kempen en Maasland (RLKM; a regional landscape organisation), the nomination was prepared together with several municipalities in the Hoge Kempen and the Flemish Heritage Agency. While the nomination was withdrawn in 2019 following advice from the International Council on Monuments and Sites not to inscribe, it also motivated collaborations between different actors in heritage, nature protection and spatial planning, as well as broader debates on the challenges of historical conservation in development. These debates eventually expanded to the concerns of sustainable transition, with these actors starting initiatives such as Tuinwijk 2.0,[4] which explores the sustainable future of the garden cities.

By following these debates and initiatives through participatory mapping, the research zoomed in on specific concerns in the garden city of Waterschei, one of the most diverse neighbourhoods in Genk (as well as Flanders), both in terms of the migration background of residents and their social status. Heritage and development experts whom I interviewed spoke about how the challenges of balancing between conservation and development were increasingly configured by the urgency of climate transition in planning the future of housing units, as well as shared green spaces. As sustainable transition becomes a mainstream concern of development, more insights are needed into how the negotiations between conservation and development agendas affect different people and communities in different ways. In the context of socially diverse neighbourhoods with migration history, such as Waterschei, these negotiations can also involve questions on the sense of belonging and awareness of heritage values, which are easily politicised to homogenise specific communities. By tracing how the design space of Waterschei was configured in the balancing between different development agendas, this chapter elucidates how uses of the past in this space reveal the defuturing aspects of these agendas.

Transition Landscape Atlas: a situated articulation of the design space

Design space in PD is defined as an imaginary space where different actors take part in the design process – but it is also a historical space (Zuljevic and Huybrechts 2021) where actors use the past as a resource in future-making. Hence, this space is shaped by historical development, as well as the previous and existing practices of people who engage with the landscape in their everyday lives. The research methodology was designed with the goal of grasping this complex design space, via participatory mapping and interviews with actors, while contextualising the insights with archival material and document analysis.

To contextualise the mapping, I reviewed archival material and literature on the historical development of the garden city – such as plans and amendments, evaluations in the Flemish Heritage Inventory, archived press material and photos. I continued with a document analysis focusing on uses of the past in the RITL nomination and adjacent projects and initiatives, such as Tuinwijk 2.0. I interviewed a group of experts who collaborated on these visions (representatives of the RLKM landscape management agency and the Spatial Development Department of the city of Genk). Finally, I spoke to different actors involved in community-based development (the Waterschei neighbourhood manager, a social development worker and a participation expert). Based on these steps and findings, I designed a participatory atlas toolkit composed of a notebook and a collection of drawings (Figure 7.2). This collection represented the transition landscape elements encountered in the archives, documents and interviews (such as things, actors and spaces). As such, it initially represented the

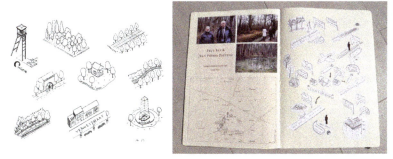

Figure 7.2 A set of atlas drawings and the mapping notebook. © Mela Zuljevic.

heritage-development visions and their relation to the frameworks of UNESCO and other institutions.

The next step was to expand and challenge this representation through participatory mapping with a group of 20 residents in Waterschei. Among these residents, there were also those who took up roles as activists in heritage-making (former miners who established a museum) or nature preservation (participants in the campaign to protect the plane trees in Waterschei). In this way, I expanded the atlas with bottom-up accounts, which helped to explore how the practices of residents and activists appropriated or challenged the heritage-development visions. To focus on entanglements and complexities between visions and practices, rather than their dichotomies, I traced how their relations revolved around specific things in the landscape. This approach emerged in the process of mapping and observing how focal statements in documents and interviews often engaged with two things: garden city houses and plane trees (Figure 7.3). Accordingly, the situated design space approach that I explored was based on the participatory mapping and historical contextualisation of three elements: visions, practices and things (Figure 7.4) in the design space.

As expressed by the experts, in Waterschei, the tensions between the interests of heritage and sustainable development surfaced in discussions over the maintenance and renovation of the garden city houses. As the management of houses became susceptible to both heritage and sustainability criteria, adherence to these criteria became difficult due to a lack of time or financial resources. For example, not all residents could access funds for sustainable renovation, or could equally perform the expected maintenance activities, such as cutting the hedges, due to their age. Similar

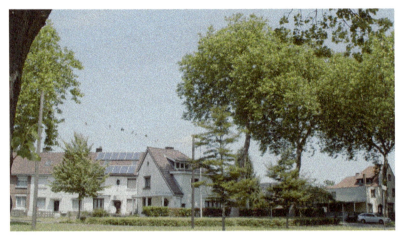

Figure 7.3 Houses and trees in Waterschei. © Mela Zuljevic.

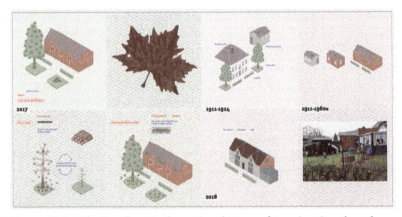

Figure 7.4 The 'garden city house' and 'rows of trees': using the atlas tool to trace how these 'things' became sites of tension between visions and practices through time. © Mela Zuljevic.

concerns were related to the preservation of plane trees in the shared green spaces, which were also valued as architectural heritage elements. Over time, these trees grew large, producing significant amounts of leafy waste that decomposes slowly due to its particular plasticity. This provoked groups of residents to organise calls for the trees to be removed, leading the city to approve their cutting down in 2016. Other residents and activists confronted this decision with petitions and protests to save the trees.

Things in visions: configuration of the design space through balancing between preservation and development

In the document analysis and interviews with experts, the expectations of change in visions for the future were tied to two ambitions: first, balancing between the interests of historical preservation and sustainable development; and second, raising awareness of heritage value among the residents. The UNESCO nomination file describes how the appearance of the garden city houses deteriorated after their ownership was transferred from the mining companies to the miners, because they started adapting them to their own needs and tastes. Eventually, the city decided to act 'against the encroachment of the harmonious image of the garden cities' (Metalidis, Van Den Bosch and Hermans 2018: 188) by establishing building directives and providing architectural expertise and subsidiary systems. The challenges of preservation are increasingly amplified today with the requirements for energy efficiency in the renovation of houses. This was described, by different experts I interviewed, as a difficult balancing act. Balancing was mentioned as a key ambition in the case of the plane trees as well. As Johan Van Den Bosch, a landscape expert who collaborated on the nomination file, said,

> The next important task is looking at how we can give those neighbourhoods a new future, without freezing the current situation, by giving people the opportunity to evolve in a living neighbourhood … How can you ensure this evolution, without compromising the heritage value? … The trees from 100 years ago are now enormous, so there is also understanding for those asking for them to be cut … On the other hand, they provide natural air conditioning, which is important in times of a warming climate. So, a certain balance has to be sought, but that is difficult (Johan Van Den Bosch, personal communication, 23 September 2020).

In achieving this balance, document analysis and interviews pointed to how the need to raise awareness of heritage value among the residents was considered crucial in the visions for the future. However, this heritage value was predefined in the documents and it was expected that the residents should preferably agree with it as such. This expectation is exemplified in the experts' view of participation as a way to tackle the lack of awareness in house renovations:

> Developing a participatory approach in the first step mostly implies awareness raising. Currently, there is no shared understanding of the property and its values by all stakeholders yet (Metalidis, Van Den Bosch and Hermans 2018: 225).

> Some inhabitants would prefer to cut down the trees ... Stepwise and strategically planned replacement programmes are included in the 'Garden City Tree Policy' developed by the municipalities ... But this aspect proves that awareness raising on the level of authenticity of the garden cities is not yet maximised (Metalidis, Van Den Bosch and Hermans 2018: 285).

In problematising this lack of awareness, some documents associate it with migration history, depicting multicultural neighbourhoods as challenging cases. For example, a publication distributed by a local development agency, which works on sustainable renovation programmes, describes the history of the neighbourhood transformation in the following way:[5]

> The rent was low or the houses, often in bad condition, were sold at low prices. The native population quickly became obsolete, and the vacant houses were occupied by migrants, who sought each other's proximity. Some working-class areas are now inhabited almost exclusively by these groups (Stebo 2010: 42).

> New rooms are being set up in attics, with skylight windows or chapels. Solar boilers and panels are becoming common. Satellite dishes adorn many *cité* houses, usually those of immigrant families who want to keep in touch with the home culture (Stebo 2010: 75).

The heritage value that the analysed documents propose taking into the future relies on the architectural qualities of housing ensembles, such as harmony and visual coherence between individual units. These qualities presumably stem from the intention of mining companies to provide pleasant working and living environments for the miners. Still, the nomination file acknowledges the contradictions in this evaluation, since the visual order was also a tool of social control for the mining companies:

> A very clear difference from Howards' model[6] was the fact that the idea of social equality was not adopted in the Hoge Kempen. It was

considered more important that the garden cities reflected the grandeur and identity of the mining companies ... Poor maintenance of the house (e.g. uncut hedge) or even children behaving badly were considered actions violating the image of the company and did not go unpunished (Metalidis, Van Den Bosch and Hermans 2018: 135).

Today, the efforts to conserve the heritage value are undertaken through combinations of measures and incentives such as subsidies for energy-efficient renovations which are conditioned with the obligation – to preserve or restore the house to be close to its original appearance. However, to apply for a subsidy, residents need to have renovation funding to start with. Waterschei is a socially diverse neighbourhood, where the property value is still lower than in other parts of Flanders, while some of the units also belong to social housing companies. In heritage-development visions (e.g. Tuinwijk 2.0), this is pinpointed as a challenge in terms of how some residents, due to their weak socioeconomic position, cannot afford to perform renovations in appropriate ways.

Things in practices: engaging with the houses and trees in the historical landscape

Conversations with residents in Waterschei[7] shed light on the challenges of living in the mining houses and reasons for their adaptation, from ensuring basic living standards to adjusting to family dynamics. The houses were outdated and often required significant renovation funding, as Azra, a young woman who recently bought a house with her family, told me: 'We did basic plastering and flooring work ... We had to spend about €10,000 before we could move in here … But we haven't done that much yet. We still need to install new heating, windows and doors' (Azra, personal communication, 19 November 2020).

Heritage values and the appearance of the neighbourhood were important to most of the respondents, although it was not something they paid much attention to. They would mainly encounter considerations of heritage in the process of asking for renovation permits, accessing subsidies or navigating renovation procedures. Mario, a retired resident, told me how roof adaptations, previously suggested by the city's advisors, were too expensive for him since he was the only one working in his family. His neighbour Frank, a young entrepreneur, added comments on how the renovation recommendations were complicated and not accessible enough: 'Basically, you should request adaptation rules and that's a very thick bundle. I think that's a bit absurd – a bit too much to just tile your own front yard' (Frank, personal communication, 26 November 2020).

When I asked the residents about what they saw as the values of living in the garden city, most of them spoke about strong community relations – living in Waterschei meant that they could stay close to their families and enjoy good relations with the neighbours. Many described it as a warm neighbourhood where strong social connections came from the history of mining that brought together people from many different cultures. Living with 'good neighbours' was addressed as a benefit that contributed to solidarity, as, for example, Asli experienced in doing renovation work: 'There are many buildings in the area that they are working on, so we could also contact each other for contacts and tips. That was a nice experience during the renovation, to get to know our neighbours' (Asli, personal communication, 26 November 2020).

Solidarity in care for the neighbourhood was important in the story of the plane trees as well. Luc Dirkx, the neighbourhood manager who got involved in the protests against the city's decision to cut down the trees, told me: 'Many neighbours help each other clean the leaves in the fall. This immense solidarity is sometimes forgotten in the debate about the trees' (Luc Dirkx, personal communication, 11 June 2020).

He was referring to how the tree debate was experienced as polarising for the neighbourhood. 'The trees lose all the leaves in autumn, which is a lot of work. The gutters get blocked, causing flooding' (Luc Dirkx, personal communication, 11 June 2020). Luc told me about the nuisance the residents experienced, adding how birds and mice find refuge in the greenery, contributing to these concerns. However, what started as an exhausting maintenance problem for some of the residents eventually evolved into a discussion which was at times politicised, especially through homogenising statements in social media debates related to the history of migration. For example, as some of my correspondents mentioned, certain positions in the debate were characterised as representative of Turkish or Italian communities.

In 2017, the city reversed its decision to cut down the trees and started a long-term participatory study to involve a larger number of residents in deciding their future. In this trajectory, resident-activists who opposed the cutting down argued that the trees were important for many different reasons: they retained water, cleaned the air, supported biodiversity and so on. However, once the city experts became more involved, they emphasised the heritage value of trees as a key argument for preservation. Katrien Colson, a designer who worked on the participatory trajectory, described how the focus on heritage sometimes amplified the polarisation:

136 CRITICAL HERITAGE STUDIES AND THE FUTURES OF EUROPE

I noticed that the people from outside the neighbourhood strongly pursued the heritage value while those who lived under the trees were not so much concerned with it … If you are constantly frustrated about the leaves, you will not wait for people who don't live in the neighbourhood to put it on the map, because they want to make the trees UNESCO heritage … The action committees stated that those outside of the neighbourhood had no right to speak, while people who lived outside felt that they had this right because they saw the issue and the value of the trees from a greater distance (Katrien Colson, personal communication, 3 July 2020).

As the debate progressed, other important roles of the trees were highlighted by different participants, making their full ecology more visible as a public concern. For example, some of the residents changed their opinion after acknowledging the importance of tree shade in reducing the effects of summer heat. Although conflict was present, Katrien and Luc agreed that the tree debate was not damaging for the neighbourhood on a long-term basis, because the participation process was handled with care. Katrien added that it was also necessary to undergo this conflict in order to move on to the next steps: 'A participation process should not avoid conflict, but you should be very careful with it … This way you really have the conversation that needs to be conducted … It taught me how a conflict can add value to a process, as long as you are caring enough' (Katrien Colson, personal communication, 3 July 2020).

Visions, things and practices: articulating the design space of the transition landscape

Mapping the entanglements of visions, things and practices, by starting from the houses and trees, helped articulate the plurality of positions in the design space, as well as tensions between heritage-development frameworks and the historical landscape. These tensions provide starting points for conceptualising a PD approach that can critically address how universalising mechanisms in heritage-development defuture landscape plurality. In the following paragraphs, I will focus on two tensions related to the garden city houses and trees, to propose how PD approaches could tackle them by engaging with caring practices and conflicts in a situated way.

The first tension I observed in the design space was between the ambitions of balancing and raising awareness in heritage-development visions, and the existing practices of residents related to the garden city houses. In the analysed documents, residents' adaptations of the houses were associated with a threatening impact on the heritage value of visual coherence. These adaptations were characterised as renovation errors associated with how the history of migration and the diversity of residents conditioned a lack of awareness of the prescribed heritage value. In contrast, the residents associated heritage regulations with obstacles in their everyday life and prioritised other values of the garden city, such as multiculturalism and solidarity. In this tension, I suggest that a certain continuity of social control, as a legacy of the mining companies, is present in how heritage-development visions configure the design space of the garden cities' future. This is enacted in the afterlife of the company image, initially imposed by the mining patrons, as a heritage value. In the conjunction of this value with development agendas, the control of the image shifted from the mining companies to the heritage-development experts. To enter the design space of the future garden cities, the residents are expected to foster attachments to their original company image as a shared heritage value. However, this value is determined through a predefined consensus which also creates expectations for appropriate protocols of care. In the design space, the continuity of social control through heritage protocols of care defutures plural ways of being in the house, neglecting how adaptations reflect the social history and cultural diversity of the garden city.

Thus, the valorisation of garden cities, based on the company image as a predefined object of value, can limit the attention to contemporary needs for adaptation, as well as the neighbourhood history after the mines were dismantled. Such an approach can also disregard existing practices of care in the neighbourhoods – for example, those emerging from the history of multicultural solidarity. A situated PD approach, in this context, could start by exploring how residents and activists care for the historical landscape, especially through practices of collective maintenance and repair work. In historical neighbourhoods, this is connected to considering them as sites of 'living heritage' (Poulios 2010). In such contexts, 'the core community cares about the material, but this caring is placed in a broad context and scope, that of the continuity of the community's association with heritage' (Poulios 2010: 178). PD approaches could help articulate how these caring practices reflect the social and public history of the landscape and, as such, provide the context for a greater responsibility in the design space. By acknowledging how caring practices challenge authorised protocols of care, we can tackle the detrimental effects that the universalising tendencies in consensus-based and Eurocentric heritage-development frameworks have for multicultural neighbourhoods and landscapes. In that sense, Escobar's critical approach to development based on Global South experiences can also become relevant for Western/Northern contexts where similar defuturing mechanisms are in place.

The second tension is related to the valorisation of trees as heritage elements in the rural–industrial transition landscape. Tricaud (2013) argues how little attention is given to gardens and greenery in the urban analysis of garden cities beyond valuing their role as an accessory to the urban form. This paradox was also relevant for the plane trees in Waterschei. I observed how their introduction to the design space was tied to their role as architectural heritage elements. The planting of different kinds of trees was a key design strategy in the original construction of the garden cities' company image, and this aesthetic role was valorised in heritage-development documents. The focus on trees as heritage elements modified the course of the neighbourhood debate by introducing additional tensions between the residents, the experts and the city. In particular, a distinction between insiders and outsiders in the tree debate was provoked by the emphasis placed on the heritage value of trees. The residents of the neighbourhood perceived this emphasis as an expert, elite and outsider interest, while the tension also triggered homogenising statements on cultural differences in perceiving the value of trees. In conversations with resident-activists who protested the decision to cut down the trees, they explained how their goal was also to challenge the polarising and homogenising statements in the debate by foregrounding nuance and solidarity among the residents. The polarisation also overshadowed the neighbourhood solidarity built around maintenance practices, as well as the complex ecological role of the trees. More attention was given to these aspects in the follow-up participatory trajectory. This revealed the tensions between the complex expectations of landscape maintenance and the simplistic perception of the landscape as an aesthetic image, where trees are reduced to heritage elements that contribute to this image.

In the participatory trajectory, conflict was present and inevitable – but it was also handled with care towards different perspectives. Conflict in PD is well studied, particularly in agonistic approaches (Björgvinsson, Ehn and Hillgren 2012; Keshavarz and Maze 2013) which argue that the goal of design participation should not be one of reaching a consensus. Rather, we should refrain from imagining design as a problem-solving practice and aim for articulating how confrontations between different positions are shaped or challenged by design. In this way, articulating conflict becomes a form of care in PD. This is particularly important when this articulation introduces complexity that can challenge the instrumentalisation of things in the landscape for polarising purposes. In Waterschei, the initially polarised positions of insiders and outsiders became nuanced over time, as the discussion progressed towards considering the trees as complex participants in climate ecologies and neighbourhood solidarity. A situated PD approach that articulates the conflicted perspectives on values of things in the historical landscape could help to rearticulate the polarised design space of insiders and outsiders, into a landscape produced in negotiating a plurality of positions.

Conclusion

In this chapter I have explored how a critical engagement with the past helps to support a PD approach that can tackle the defuturing in the design space of heritage-development, by understanding the historical landscape as a context for a greater responsibility. By making connections between the fields of CHS and PD, I looked at how participatory approaches to the design space can critically address the conjunction of authorised heritage discourses with universalising development frameworks. Such a PD approach, reflecting on the *Transition Landscape Atlas*, could start from mapping the design space as a historical space configured in the entanglements of things with heritage-development visions, as well as existing practices in the historical landscape. The participatory mapping focused on the garden city houses and plane trees as entry points into these entanglements, which helped reveal tensions between visions and practices and trace how the defuturing of plurality is driven by universalising heritage-development frameworks. By addressing how garden city adaptations reflect the social history and diversity of residents, I argued that universalising and Eurocentric visions can be challenged by articulating the caring potentials of existing practices in the design space. By tracing how the plane tree participatory trajectory responded to a polarising debate, I explored how conflict articulation in PD can take place by uncovering the complexity of the historical landscape. The articulation of the design space as a historical space of tensions between visions, things and practices could help advance the discussions in CHS on heritage as a discourse of future-making – while critically attending to its role in the defuturing of plurality in the historical landscapes.

Acknowledgements

The study has received ethical approval from SMEC Research Ethics Committee, under reference REC/SMEC/VRAI/190/105. I would like to thank Luc Dirkx, Katrien Colson and Johan Van Den Bosch for their participation and feedback on the text.

Notes

1. For Fry (2019: 295), 'defuturing' can be understood as an imposed process of worldmaking that effectively enviro-culturally unmakes a world, and in so doing displaces the prior temporal conditions of 'being-in-the-world'. He uses this term to explore how human actions, by design, actively reduce the future and how this is further enacted by designed things as agents that *design* our ways of being through time.
2. The Hoge Kempen is an area in the province of Limburg, covering the territory of several municipalities, with Genk as the largest one.
3. The site was nominated as a mixed, evolutionary cultural landscape (UNESCO n.d.).
4. 'Tuinwijk' is the Flemish translation of 'garden city'.
5. My translation from the original Dutch.
6. Ebenezer Howard was the founder of the garden city movements, whose ideas were appropriated by the mining companies.
7. Pseudonymised interviews with 20 residents in Waterschei in June–December 2020.

References

Ashworth, Gregory. 2014. Heritage and Economic Development: Selling the Unsellable. *Heritage & Society* 7(1): 3–17.

Binder, Thomas, Giorgio De Michelis, Pelle Ehn, Giulio Jacucci, Per Linde and Ina Wagner. 2011. *Design Things*. Cambridge: MIT Press.

Björgvinsson, Erling, Pelle Ehn and Per-Anders Hillgren. 2012. Design Things and Design Thinking: Contemporary Participatory Design Challenges. *Design Issues* 28(3): 101–116.

De Cesari, Chiara and Rosita Dimova. 2018. Heritage, Gentrification, Participation: Remaking Urban Landscapes in the Name of Culture and Historic Preservation. *International Journal of Heritage Studies* 25(9): 863–869.

Ehn, Pelle. 2008. Participation in Design Things. *Proceedings of the Tenth Conference on Participatory Design, PDC 2008*. Bloomington, USA.

Escobar, Arturo. 1995. *Encountering Development: The Making and Unmaking of the Third World*. Princeton: Princeton University Press.

Escobar, Arturo. 2018. *Designs for the Pluriverse: Radical Interdependence, Autonomy and the Making of Worlds*. Durham: Duke University Press.

Fry, Tony. 2019. Design Futuring in a Borderland of Postdevelopment. In Elise Klein and Carlos Eduardo Morreo (eds), *Postdevelopment in Practice: Alternatives, Economies, Ontologies*. New York: Routledge: 294–305.

Graham, Brian, Gregory Ashworth and John Tunbridge. 2000. *A Geography of Heritage: Power, Culture and Economy*. New York: Routledge.

Hayden, Dolores. 1995. *The Power of Place*. Cambridge, MA: MIT Press.

Keshavarz, Mahmoud and Ramia Maze. 2013. Design and Dissensus: Framing and Staging Participation in Design Research. *Design Philosophy Papers* 11(1): 7–29.

Labadi, Sophia and William Logan. 2015. Approaches to Urban Heritage, Development and Sustainability. In Sophia Labadi and William Logan (eds), *Urban Heritage, Development and Sustainability*. New York: Routledge: 1–20.

Metalidis, Ina, Johan Van Den Bosch and Klara Hermans. 2018. *World Heritage Nomination: Hoge Kempen Rural-Industrial Transition Landscape*. RLKM.

Nasser, Noha. 2014. Planning for Urban Heritage Places: Reconciling Conservation, Tourism and Sustainable Development. *Journal of Planning Literature*, 60(4): 467–479.

Poulios, Ioannis. 2010. Moving Beyond a Values-Based Approach to Heritage Conservation. *Conservation and Management of Architectural Sites* 12(2): 170–85.

Smith, Laurajane. 2006. *The Uses of Heritage*. London and New York: Routledge.

Stebo. 2010. *Mijncité: Met de mijncités naar de 21ste eeuw*. Stebo vzw.

Tlostanova, Madina. 2017. On Decolonizing Design. *Design Philosophy Papers* 15(1): 51–61.

Tonkinwise, Cameron. 2019. 'I Prefer Not To': Anti-progressive Designing. In Gretchen Coombs, Andrew McNamara and Gavin Sade (eds), *Undesign: Critical Practices at the Intersection of Art and Design*. New York: Routledge: 74–84.

Tricaud, Pierre-Marie. 2013. The Garden City, A Green City? In *Garden Cities, an Ideal to be Pursued* (Les Cahiers, Institut d'Aménagement et d'Urbanisme, no. 165). Île-de-France: IAU-idF: 56–59. Online at https://en.institutparisregion.fr/fileadmin/NewEtudes/Etude_986/Cahier_no_165_web.pdf Accessed 26 April 2023.

UNESCO. n.d. *Hoge Kempen Rural - Industrial Transition Landscape*. Online at https://whc.unesco.org/en/tentativelists/5623/ Accessed 24 March 2023.

Zuljevic, Mela and Liesbeth Huybrechts. 2021. Historicising Design Space: Uses of the Past in Participatory Prefiguring of Spatial Development. *Design Studies* 73: 100993. https://doi.org/10.1016/j.destud.2021.100993

8

The (over)touristification of European historic cities: a relation between urban heritage and short-term rental market demand

Łukasz Bugalski

Introduction

In this chapter, I wish to highlight the critical relationship between heritage management issues and building environment transformation. I argue that such a relationship is directly expressed through the tourism phenomenon, and it should be measured through the economic dimension of the short-term rental market, which introduces this rule of thumb: if there is a lack of demand, the brand of the city is weak; if there is too much demand, the city is endangered by over-tourism processes. The potential to measure this tourism phenomenon could become a crucial methodological asset for further research in heritage studies – especially in the context of the ongoing touristification of historic European cities.

The unexpected COVID-19 outbreak exposed the inherent problem of tourist-oriented overdevelopment. In just a few weeks, many popular and overcrowded tourist destinations became completely deserted. Consequently, according to an Economic Impact Report by the World Travel and Tourism Council (2021), almost 62 million jobs in tourism worldwide had disappeared during 2020 (representing a drop of 18.5 per cent). However, such a situation appears to be temporary in nature, and already the United Nations World Tourism Organization (UNWTO) has pledged 'a sustainable recovery' (World Tourism Organization 2021). Although it is unreasonable to expect a return to the pre-pandemic state, the UNWTO position fails to recognise the central issue related to pre-pandemic tourism-oriented economic deficiencies: *monoculture* (Agostini 2016). It appears that even a crisis on the scale of the COVID-19 pandemic may not be enough to trigger a paradigm shift in such deeply entrenched economic practice. Such a mechanism is known as 'path dependence' (Pierson 2000), which 'explains how the set of decisions one faces for any given circumstance is limited by the decisions one has made in the past or by the events that one has experienced, even though past circumstances may no longer be relevant' (Preager 2007).

Although the threat from homogeneous development based on a tourist economy has become clear, the main obstacle to any discourse on the impact of over-tourism on European cities is the lack of a proper 'toolkit' to adequately measure levels of touristification in relation to the spatial urban environment. It is essential to remedy this if we want to better understand this phenomenon. I argue, paradoxically, that one of the most serious outcomes of ongoing touristification – the change in the short-term rental market – could also be used as a specific way to index the process itself. Indeed, the economic origin of Airbnb data positions it at the intersection of tourism and urban studies, binding together a market dimension of the growth in tourism and community aspects of urban change caused by its impact (Bugalski 2020). Over recent years, a great deal of research has been devoted to this topic (e.g. Adamiak 2018; Picascia, Romano and Teobaldi 2017; Gutiérrez et al. 2017; Batista e Silva et al. 2018); however, most of it is case-study oriented and as such bereft of a more general view.

I have previously introduced a basic method rooted in the comparative potential of such data sets – reduced to their economic character – that would help assess and explain how touristification changes over time (Bugalski 2020). The simplicity of the method enables a basic comparison between multiple destinations from the beginning of this phenomenon (which flourished after 2014). Although the study presented here is limited to Europe (but not Russia and Turkey) and focused on cities with populations above 100,000, it is entirely possible to apply the method to other places (Bugalski 2020, 2021). Accordingly, this chapter examines the critical relationship between heritage management and the transformation of the built environment, which, as previously mentioned, is directly expressed through the tourism phenomenon. Consequently, the main argument of this chapter is that such a relationship should be measured according to the economic dimensions of the short-term rental market.

Although the management of urban heritage is crucial for the future of our cities, it is only one part of a more complex and ongoing urban process. Indeed, there are many diverse criteria involved in the constant changing of our cities, and it is useful here to mention several theories and concepts which relate directly to this chapter, for example that of 'the right to the city' (Harvey 2008), the struggle 'to secure the right to housing' (Farha and Schwan 2021), the need of cities to adopt 'pedestrianisation' (Forsyth 2015; Sim 2019) and 'the 15-minute city concept' (Moreno et al. 2021). Although many of the ideas presented in this chapter are introduced from an urban studies perspective, it should be emphasised that the relationship between the built environment and the tourism phenomenon, which is highly dependent on heritage management decisions, is crucial for all heritage workers.

The theoretical framework

It is difficult to adequately explain the relationship between heritage management and ongoing building environment transformation. The problematic gap between these disciplines has already been recognised (Ashworth 1989, 2003; Shoval 2018; Wells 2019; Ashworth and Page 2011), but nevertheless, it is not easy to fill the theoretical space. We could assume that such a relationship should originate in the theoretical framework appropriated for urban conservation studies. However, this is not always the case. According to Gregory Ashworth (2011), the current scientific discourse related to these issues is presented through three different paradigms (preservation, conservation and heritage planning; see Figure 8.1) existing in parallel, and 'this incomplete paradigm shift means that at least three quite different ways of treating the past in the present now coexist, often uncomfortably' (Ashworth 2013, relating to Graham, Ashworth and Tunbridge 2000). Such a situation blunts discussion, creating a cacophony of noise as opposed to scientific discourse, rooted in different (mis)understandings of words and meaning (Wells 2007). In most well-established scientific disciplines, this would not be possible.

The first paradigm – constructed at the beginning of the contemporary conservation movement in the late nineteenth century – concerns the need to maintain (to preserve) historic monuments, and as such is fully concentrated on the past. The second paradigm, which emerged in the 1960s after the fallout from the Second World War, is concerned with duration, 'keeping' something for future generations (to conserve),

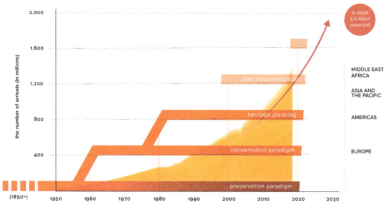

Figure 8.1 Ashworth's three paradigms, supplemented by overtourism and resistance concepts, and juxtaposed with the rapid growth of international arrivals worldwide (UNWTO Tourism Barometer).
© Łukasz Bugalski.

often by arbitrary decision-making around how older buildings function in current times. Finally, the third paradigm was shaped in the 1980s in relation to a postmodern understanding of the world and is concerned with how today's communities 'use' the past (heritage planning), and whether or not that heritage is tangible. Although the described differences between these three are perhaps an oversimplification, and ignore the many dependencies apparent between paradigms, they also demonstrate the difficulties inherently involved in such a process of incomplete paradigm shift. Moreover, we cannot assume that heritage planning is the ultimate aim of our current theoretical framework. The rapid growth of many tourism economies has produced several knock-on effects, perhaps the most interesting of which is the ongoing (over)touristification of cities and the reactions it produces – a rising resistance among citizens (Figure 8.1). Nevertheless, these concepts and ideas still await a proper explanation.

At the beginning of critical heritage studies, Lucas Lixinski (2015) simplified this theoretical framework, limiting it to a dichotomy of conservation theory – its 'orthodoxy' (the arbitrary – top-down – process of managing objects of the built heritage) and 'heterodoxy' (the discursive – bottom-up – process of managing the meanings of tangible and intangible heritage). Lixinski's concept relates to that of 'authorised heritage discourse', a term famously coined by Laurajane Smith (2006). At the same time, it acknowledges Ashworth's concerns that 'the result of this miscommunication [caused by the presented dichotomy] is that two bodies of knowledge that could (and should) be working together are growing apart' (Lixinski 2015: 211). Although Lixinski's concept is crucial for our study, and is further developed by Jeremy Wells (2019) in the context of built environment, it was nonetheless developed in isolation from contemporary circumstances. No theoretical approach to heritage studies can be adequately understood if the constant growth of the 'tourism phenomenon' is ignored.

The tourism phenomenon

The unparalleled scale of the recent growth in the tourism economy is largely down to the number of temporary visitors (Figure 8.1), and as such, its impact on other socioeconomic aspects must be acknowledged. The impact of the tourism phenomenon on the built environment was highlighted in the 1990s. Noha Nasser notably summarised it in 2003, briefly elaborating the main characteristics affecting historic European city centres (Nasser 2003). Such impacts are manifested through the diverse transformations of public space usage, housing market economics, the availability of services, the employment market, cultural heritage management and the everyday life of ordinary residents (Bock 2015; del Romero Renau 2018). This process can be identified as 'touristification' – a kind of gentrification caused by the needs of uncontrollable growth in the tourism economy (Cocola-Gant 2018), or more simply as 'gentrification through tourism'. Therefore, such a mechanism, deeply rooted in the relationship between the deindustrialisation and subsequent commercialisation of heritage (Harrison 2013: 79–81, 86–87), is not particular to the case of constantly ongoing urban change. An effective urban regeneration process – as well as effective urban conservation – often causes the simultaneous emergence of mass tourism threats.

In 2003, Noha Nasser pointed out that the tourism phenomenon has affected the built environment and local community culture, transforming urban heritage 'into a product for tourist consumption' (Figure 8.2). It was already clear that these practices were subject to global unrestrained growth resulting in a rising number of destinations competing for tourists' interest. Consequently, heritage sites are 'undergoing a redefinition and reinterpretation of their cultural heritage in order to be competitive and attractive' (Nasser 2003: 467). For urban heritage, this mainly leads to a 'commercial forces of consumer demand' response, replacing citizen-oriented policies with tourist-oriented ones, which in many cases

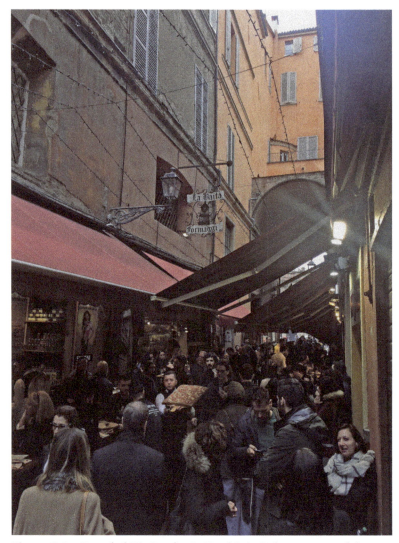

Figure 8.2 Crowded Via Pescherie Vecchie in Bologna – one of the most touristified streets in this city. Similar images are typical of a vast number of historic cities across Europe. © Łukasz Bugalski.

compromises conservation and cultural values. At the same time, mass tourism engages in a 'uniformity of global economy' with its standardised architecture, hotels, restaurant chains and so on, meaning 'local cultures are losing their local identities as the global "cultural industries" dominate'. In the end, this new, homogeneous kind of heritage usage, completely bereft of any sustainability, creates a monofunctional environment hostile to residents (Nasser 2003: 467).

As Rodney Harrison states, 'heritage has often been perceived to be compromised by its contingent relationship to other areas, tourism and the leisure industries in particular' (Harrison 2013: 7). However, such relationships only become possible due to understanding heritage as a resource used to fuel the tourism economy. Therefore, the fundamental perspective in understanding the tourism phenomenon – firmly setting the sociology of tourism – is found in John Urry's 'tourist gaze' (Urry 1990, 2002; Urry and Larsen 2011). Jonas Larsen (who coauthored the latest re-edition of Urry's work) describes this as evolving theory 'on the move' (Larsen 2014); 'tourism is about organising places as sights and gazing is about *consuming places* visually' (Larsen 2014: 306 in relation to Urry 1995).

At the same time, in the early 1990s, Gregory Ashworth and John Tunbridge presented their model of 'the tourist-historic city' – further developed and presented in the 2000 version of their book (Ashworth and Tunbridge 1990, 2000). This concept largely focused on several examples of exceptional historic city centres, mainly in smaller cities, such as Venice, Florence, Prague, Cracow or Dubrovnik, that qualify as examples of overtouristification. Those concepts perfectly correspond with the idea of the 'experience economy' introduced by Pine and Gilmore (1999), which – together with other terms such as mass tourism, Disneyfication/Disneyisation, McDonaldisation, museumification and theming – seems to be the best way to describe the process of heritage commercialisation through urban renewal and adaptive reuse (Harrison 2013: 84–88).

It is crucial to acknowledge that this problem is considered marginal when it comes to the rather sparse number of smaller cities. It is even possible that in some cases there has been a kind of acceptance of the death of selected cities (Settis 2016). However, when the threat is no longer limited to smaller cities and a few other exceptional cases, but starts to concern the most important European cities, like Rome, Barcelona, Amsterdam, Copenhagen or Berlin, the touristification process is becoming one of the fundamental drivers of the transformation of our urban environment. This is something clearly apparent in Europe, and is a phenomenon recognised by Sharon Macdonald as 'memorylands' (Macdonald 2013). Europe is a continent with a dense network of historic cities that should be recognised as the most vulnerable target of ongoing touristification.

Rapid touristification

According to UNWTO (2019; Figure 8.1), from the 1950s the number of international arrivals worldwide grew steadily, with an overall annual increase of more than 6 per cent (Becker 2013), becoming one of the most striking examples 'among the many growth curves pointing steeply upwards ... which have turned the twenty-first century world into a glowing hot planet' (Eriksen 2016: 62). In 2018, more than 1.8 billion people travelled internationally in a single year – twice as many as at the start of the twenty-first century. Until the recent COVID-19 outbreak, that number had been expected to grow to 2 billion by 2030 (UNWTO 2019).

Although this forecast is now likely to be significantly revised, tourism will probably remain one of the largest sectors of the world economy (Lew 2011; Du, Lew and Ng 2014). Therefore, it is still relevant to juxtapose the ongoing growth of the tourism phenomenon (in this case, the number of international arrivals) onto the emergence of new theoretical concepts and terms.

At this point, it is important to stress that just before the pandemic, overtourism was already a popular issue in mainstream media. Moreover, it has been continually present as an issue on the streets of (mainly southern) European cities in acts of demonstration, protest and even vandalism (as well as rising tourismphobia: Milano, Novelli and Cheer 2019a). Hence grassroots movements organise themselves in wider networks like SET (rete di città del Sud d'Europa di fronte alla Turistificazione), founded in 2018. Finally, a group of 22 municipalities – gathered in the Eurocities network – asked the EU commissaries for help in establishing 'a solid regulatory framework that can effectively help' them to manage the rapid growth of the short-term rental market (Halsema 2021). Nevertheless, the threats posed by ongoing (over) touristification still seem to remain ignored (according to 'path dependence'; Pierson 2000) as a major issue to be dealt with in the context of the urban environment. As the circumstances drastically change, the policy remains the same.

At the beginning of the century, Noha Nasser (2003) identified processes which seemed to further accelerate these problems (especially after the European debt-crisis of 2009–2014), such as changes in the housing market (rising prices, new players on the market and the new character of contemporary buildings), the decline of universities (lack of accommodation for students), and insufficient work in services (its seasonality and quality making it unsuitable for highly educated people). Consequently, such cities succumb to a state of saturation known as 'overtourism' (Koens, Postma and Papp 2018; Adie, Falk and Savioli 2020; Milano, Novelli and Cheer 2019b). Therefore, this ongoing touristification should be positioned at the very centre of urban studies, becoming a fundamental issue for the future of our cities.

I argue here that, paradoxically, one of the most serious outcomes of ongoing touristification – the change in the short-term rental market – could also be used as a specific way to index the process itself. It is crucial to highlight that the latest explosion in the short-term rental market is commonly identified with the foundation of the peer-to-peer platform Airbnb (Gutiérrez et al. 2017).

The short-term rental market

The economic origins of Airbnb data position it on an intersection of tourism and urban studies, bringing together a market dimension for the growth in tourism and the resulting community aspects of urban change caused by its impact. Data from AirDNA (a private venture specialising in providing complex data about the short-term rental market to property managers) has allowed for a comparative evaluation of the socioeconomic impact of ongoing touristification.

During my fellowship under the Marie Skłodowska-Curie Actions (MSCA) Innovative Training Networks (ITN) programme (Bugalski and Guermandi 2019), I conducted a study tracking the meteoric rise of Airbnb, focusing on the supply side of the phenomenon. For the most part, this took place during the mid-2010s, followed by a further period lasting until the COVID-19 outbreak at the beginning of 2020. This novel 'accommodation phenomenon' is subject to the laws of supply and demand, and the chaos caused by the pandemic disrupted things significantly (Bugalski 2020). Here, I discuss further a prototype case study prepared for Italian cities between 2016 and 2019 (Bugalski 2021).

The full study concerns a much wider range of 187 European cities with populations over 100,000 and more than 1,000 active Airbnb listings covering the six-year period from Q2 2014 to Q2 2020 (where 'Q2' indicates the 2nd quarter), although data for 2020 is additional and refers to the pandemic period. Forty-two cities had more than 5,000 active Airbnb listings (Figure 8.3), causing an enormous impact on their historic centres (Bugalski 2020). The summer of 2019, just before the COVID-19 outbreak, witnessed the highest rise in the European city short-term rental market to date. During this period, a record number of 185 cities also reached 1,000 active listings (Figure 8.4). Although such

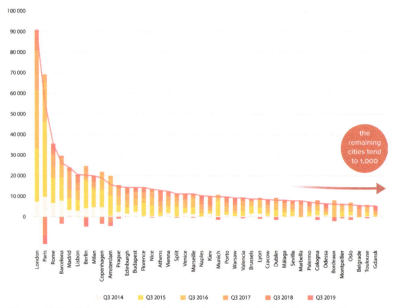

Figure 8.3 A bar chart showing the logarithmic distribution of active Airbnb listings in Europe. The series has been truncated to 42, presenting cities that exceeded 5,000 active listings on at least one occasion. For reasons of space, the remaining cities tend to average 1,000 active listings. Order by value for Q3 2019 is marked by a line on the top of the diagram. © Łukasz Bugalski.

an arbitrary set of values does not prejudge anything, it depicts the current state of our urban landscape (Bugalski 2020).

Indeed, the total number of active listings is not a perfect index, but it enables us to follow the growth of tourism economies (understood as the most extreme example of the 'service economy') through the urban change it causes. Although the tourism phenomenon is often positive in the urban context, the current tourism economy model is giving rise to homogeneous usage patterns that could be defined as a 'monoculture' (Agostini 2016).

An alternative future

The growth in the tourism phenomenon (unsustainable in its character and incomparable in its scale), manifested by an increase in temporary visitor numbers, will further affect many other socioeconomic aspects in

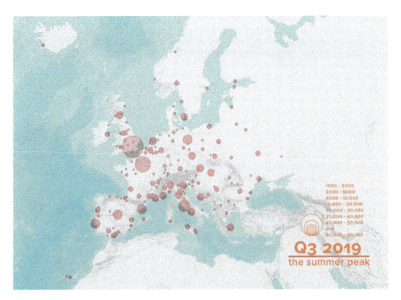

Figure 8.4 The 185 European cities (with populations above 100,000) that exceeded 1,000 active listings in the 3rd quarter of 2019. It is the apogee of the Airbnb phenomenon – a moment of economic equilibrium for many of its vanguard cities. © Łukasz Bugalski.

the destination cities. The COVID-19 outbreak has exposed these issues and forced us to seek solutions. Heritage management is not without influence on the ongoing (over)touristification of our cities. To achieve a sustainable urban environment, rules and regulations must be implemented to combat and cope with further growth in the tourism economy, particularly in the short-term rental market. However, it is also the responsibility of heritage workers to regulate the tourism economy through a wiser management of our heritage resources. It is crucial to adopt new policies such as the 'degrowth concept' (Hickel 2020; Kallis 2011), already considered an interesting solution to the issues caused by the booming tourism economy – success should no longer be solely measured through visitor numbers (Milano, Novelli and Cheer 2019b).

This issue is complex and in general it should be considered in a wider urban context. Cities such as Barcelona and Paris are already implementing measures to counter the ravages of overtouristification. These measures concern the liveability of a city, and spatial changes to the urban environment (cf. concepts such as 'superblocks', Mueller et al. 2020, and the '15-minute city', Moreno et al. 2021). These changes are crucial in understanding our relationship with tourism. Heritage and the built environment are closely connected, and further bound up with socioeconomic issues – characteristics that are central to discussions on urban studies and urbanism in general.

References

Adamiak, Czesław. 2018. Mapping Airbnb Supply in European Cities. *Annals of Tourism Research* 71 (February): 67–71. https://doi.org/10.1016/j.annals.2018.02.008

Adie, Bailey Ashton, Martin Falk and Marco Savioli. 2020. Overtourism as a Perceived Threat to Cultural Heritage in Europe. *Current Issues in Tourism* 23(14): 1737–1741. https://doi.org/10.1080/13683500.2019.1687661

Agostini, Ilaria (ed.). 2016. *Urbanistica Resistente Nella Firenze Neoliberista: Per Unaltracittà 2004-2014 e Firenze Fabbrica Del Turismo*. Firenze: Aión Edizioni.

Ashworth, Gregory. 1989. Urban Tourism: An Imbalance in Attention. In Chris Cooper (ed.), *Progress in Tourism, Recreation and Hospitality Research*. London: Belhaven: 33–54.

Ashworth, Gregory. 2003. Urban Tourism: Still an Imbalance in Attention? In Chris Cooper (ed.), *Classic Reviews in Tourism*. Clevedon, UK, and Buffalo, NY: Channel View Publication: 143–163.

Ashworth, Gregory. 2011. Preservation, Conservation and Heritage: Approaches to the Past in Present through the Built Environment. *Asian Anthropology* 10(1): 1–18. https://doi.org/10.1080/1683478X.2011.10552601

Ashworth, Gregory. 2013. Heritage in Planning: Using Pasts in Shaping Futures. In Greg Young and Deborah Stevenson (eds), *The Ashgate Research Companion to Planning and Culture*. Farnham, UK: Ashgate: 185–201. https://doi.org/10.4324/9781315613390-15

Ashworth, Gregory and Stephen Page. 2011. Urban Tourism Research: Recent Progress and Current Paradoxes. *Tourism Management* 32 (1): 1–15. https://doi.org/10.1016/j.tourman.2010.02.002

Ashworth, Gregory and John Tunbridge. 1990. *The Tourist-Historic City*. London and New York: Belhaven Press.

Ashworth, Gregory and John Tunbridge. 2000. *The Tourist-Historic City: Retrospect and Prospect of Managing the Heritage City*. Oxford: Pergamon.

Batista e Silva, Filipe, Mario Alberto Marín Herrera, Konštantín Rosina, Ricardo Ribeiro Barranco, Sérgio Freire and Marcello Schiavina. 2018. Analysing Spatiotemporal Patterns of Tourism in Europe at High-Resolution with Conventional and Big Data Sources. *Tourism Management* 68: 101–115. https://doi.org/10.1016/j.tourman.2018.02.020

Becker, Elizabeth. 2013. *Overbooked: The Exploding Business of Travel and Tourism*. New York and London: Simon & Schuster.

Bock, Kerstin. 2015. The Changing Nature of City Tourism and Its Possible Implications for the Future of Cities. *European Journal of Futures Research* 3: article 20. https://doi.org/10.1007/s40309-015-0078-5

Bugalski, Łukasz. 2020. The Undisrupted Growth of the Airbnb Phenomenon between 2014–2020: The Touristification of European Cities before the Covid-19 Outbreak. *Sustainability* 12(23): 1–20. https://doi.org/10.3390/su12239841

Bugalski, Łukasz. 2021. The Touristification of Italian Historic City Centres: The Lesson for Central Europe about the Airbnb Eruption. In *Heritage and Environment: The 5th Heritage Forum of Central Europe*. Kraków: International Cultural Centre: 281–293.

Bugalski, Łukasz and Maria Pia Guermandi (eds). 2019. Heritage Explorations across Europe: CHEurope, Interdisciplinary Training Network in Critical Heritage Studies. *Dossier IBC* 4 (27). Online at http://cheurope-project.eu/wp-content/uploads/2020/03/IBC-dossier.pdf Accessed 26 March 2023.

Cocola-Gant, Agustin. 2018. Tourism Gentrification. In Loretta Lees and Martin Phillips (eds), *Handbook of Gentrification Studies*. Cheltenham: Edward Elgar Publishing: 281–293.

Du, Ding, Alan Lew and Pin Ng. 2014. Tourism and Economic Growth. *Journal of Travel Research* 55(4): 454–464. https://doi.org/10.1177/0047287514563167

Eriksen, Thomas Hylland. 2016. *Overheating: An Anthropology of Accelerated Change*. London: Pluto Press.

Farha, Leilani and Kaitlin Schwan. 2021. The Human Right to Housing in the Age of Financialisation. In Martha Davis, Morten Kjaerum and Amanda Lyons (eds), *Research Handbook on Human Rights and Poverty*. Cheltenham: Edward Elgar Publishing: 385–400. https://doi.org/10.4337/9781788977517.00038

Forsyth, Ann. 2015. What Is a Walkable Place? The Walkability Debate in Urban Design. *URBAN DESIGN International* 20(4): 274–292. https://doi.org/10.1057/udi.2015.22

Graham, Brian, Gregory Ashworth and John Tunbridge. 2000. *A Geography of Heritage: Power, Culture and Economy*. London: Arnold.

Gutiérrez, Javier, Juan Carlos García-Palomares, Gustavo Romanillos and María Henar Salas-Olmedo. 2017. The Eruption of Airbnb in Tourist Cities: Comparing Spatial Patterns of Hotels and Peer-to-Peer Accommodation in Barcelona. *Tourism Management* 62: 278–291. https://doi.org/10.1016/j.tourman.2017.05.003

Halsema, Femke. 2021. Letter to The Portuguese EU Presidency from Eurocities on Draft of Digital Services Act. Online at https://eurocities.eu/wp-content/uploads/2021/03/Letter-to-EVP-Vestager-from-cities-on-DSA15032021.pdf Accessed 26 March 2023.

Harrison, Rodney. 2013. *Heritage: Critical Approaches*. London: Routledge.

Harvey, David. 2008. The Right to the City. *New Left Review* 53: 23–40. https://doi.org/10.4324/9780429261732-35

Hickel, Jason. 2020. *Less Is More: How Degrowth Will Save the World*. London: Penguin Random House.

Kallis, Giorgos. 2011. In Defence of Degrowth. *Ecological Economics* 70(5): 873–880. https://doi.org/10.1016/j.ecolecon.2010.12.007

Koens, Ko, Albert Postma and Bernadett Papp. 2018. Is Overtourism Overused? Understanding the Impact of Tourism in a City Context. *Sustainability (Switzerland)* 10(12): 1–15. https://doi.org/10.3390/su10124384

Larsen, Jonas. 2014. The Tourist Gaze 1.0, 2.0 and 3.0. In Alan Lew, Michael Hall and Allan Williams (eds), *The Wiley Blackwell Companion to Tourism*. London: Wiley Blackwell: 304–313.

Lew, Alan. 2011. Tourism's Role in the Global Economy. *Tourism Geographies* 13(1): 148–151. https://doi.org/10.1080/14616688.2010.531046

Lixinski, Lucas. 2015. Between Orthodoxy and Heterodoxy: The Troubled Relationships between Heritage Studies and Heritage Law. *International Journal of Heritage Studies* 21(3): 203–214. https://doi.org/10.1080/13527258.2014.922113

Macdonald, Sharon. 2013. *Memorylands: Heritage and Identity in Europe Today*. London and New York: Routledge.

Milano, Claudio, Marina Novelli and Joseph Cheer. 2019a. Overtourism and Tourismphobia: A Journey Through Four Decades of Tourism Development, Planning and Local Concerns. *Tourism Planning and Development* 16(4): 353–357. https://www.tandfonline.com/doi/full/10.1080/21568316.2019.1599604

Milano, Claudio, Marina Novelli and Joseph Cheer. 2019b. Overtourism and Degrowth: A Social Movements Perspective. *Journal of Sustainable Tourism* 27 (September): 1857–1875. https://doi.org/10.1080/09669582.2019.1650054

Moreno, Carlos, Zaheer Allam, Didier Chabaud, Catherine Gall and Florent Pratlong. 2021. Introducing the '15-Minute City': Sustainability, Resilience and Place Identity in Future Post-Pandemic Cities. *Smart Cities* 4(1): 93–111. https://doi.org/10.3390/smartcities4010006

Mueller, Natalie, David Rojas-Rueda, Haneen Khreis, Marta Cirach, David Andrés, Joan Ballester and Xavier Bartoll. 2020. Changing the Urban Design of Cities for Health: The Superblock Model. *Environment International* 134 (January): 1–13. https://doi.org/10.1016/j.envint.2019.105132

Nasser, Noha. 2003. Planning for Urban Heritage Places: Reconciling Conservation, Tourism, and Sustainable Development. *Journal of Planning Literature* 17(4): 467–479. https://doi.org/10.1177/0885412203017004001

Picascia, Stefano, Antonello Romano and Michela Teobaldi. 2017. The Airification of Cities: Making Sense of the Impact of Peer-to-Peer Short-Term Letting on Urban Functions and Economy. In *Proceedings of the Annual Congress of the Association of European Schools of Planning, Lisbon*. Online at: https://proceedings.aesop-planning.eu/index.php/aesopro/issue/view/5 Accessed 12 April 2023.

Pierson, Paul. 2000. Increasing Returns, Path Dependence and the Study of Politics. *American Political Science Review* 94(2): 251–267.

Pine, Joseph and James Gilmore. 1999. *The Experience Economy: Work Is Theatre and Every Business a Stage*. Boston: Harvard Business Review Press.

Praeger, Dave. 2007. Our Love of Sewers: A Lesson in Path Dependence. *Daily Kos*, 15 June 2007. Online at https://www.dailykos.com/stories/2007/06/15/346883/-Our-Love-Of-Sewers-A-Lesson-in-Path-Dependence Accessed 26 April 2023.

Romero Renau, Luis del. 2018. Touristification, Sharing Economies and the New Geography of Urban Conflicts. *Urban Science* 2(4): 104. https://doi.org/10.3390/urbansci2040104

Settis, Salvatore. 2016. *If Venice Dies*. New York: New Vessel Press.

Shoval, Noam. 2018. Urban Planning and Tourism in European Cities. *Tourism Geographies* 20(3): 371–376. https://doi.org/10.1080/14616688.2018.1457078

Sim, David. 2019. *Soft City: Building Density for Everyday Life*. Washington and London: Island Press.

Smith, Laurajane. 2006. *Uses of Heritage*. London and New York: Routledge. https://doi.org/10.4324/9780203602263

UNWTO. 2019. *World Tourism Barometer and Statistical Annex* 17(4).

Urry, John. 1990. *The Tourist Gaze: Leisure and Travel in Contemporary Societies*. London: Sage Publications.

Urry, John. 1995. *Consuming Places*. London and New York: Routledge.

Urry, John. 2002. *The Tourist Gaze*. 2nd ed. London: Sage Publications.

Urry, John and Jonas Larsen. 2011. *The Tourist Gaze 3.0*. 3rd ed. London: Sage Publications.

Wells, Jeremy C. 2007. The Plurality of Truth in Culture, Context and Heritage: A (Mostly) Post-Structuralist Analysis of Urban Conservation Charters. *City & Time* 3(2): 1–14.

Wells, Jeremy C. 2019. Bridging the Gap between Built Heritage Conservation Practice and Critical Heritage Studies. In Jeremy Wells and Barry Stiefel (eds), *Human-Centred Built Environment Heritage Preservation: Theory and Evidence-Based Practice*. New York: Routledge: 33–44. https://doi.org/10.4324/9780429506352-2

World Tourism Organization (UNWTO). 2021. *Recommendations for the Transition to a Green Travel and Tourism Economy*. Madrid, Spain: World Tourism Organization. Online at https://webunwto.s3.eu-west-1.amazonaws.com/s3fs-public/2021-05/210504-Recommendations-for-the-Transition-to-a-Green-Travel-and-Tourism-Economy.pdf?VersionId=wiwmhlGgXT4zwXles_Q8ycdITGIQfaMt Accessed 25 March 2023.

World Travel and Tourism Council (WTTC). 2021. *Travel & Tourism: Economic Impact 2021*. Online at https://wttc.org/Portals/0/Documents/Reports/2021/Global%20Economic%20Impact%20and%20Trends%202021.pdf Accessed 26 April 2023.

9
Overtourism versus pandemic: the fragility of our historic cities

Maria Pia Guermandi

Introduction

The pandemic and the lockdown measures that affected many European countries in 2020 and 2021 redesigned the face of our historic city centres in a matter of a few weeks.[1] As the images widely circulated in the media showed, entire neighbourhoods of our cities became deserted, not only because there were no more tourists, but because there have been no more resident citizens for some years.[2] The shock of COVID-19 highlighted the fragility of tourism monoculture from an economic point of view also and showed a wider audience the critical issues of a growth – that of cultural tourism – which took place in a framework of confused and still largely inadequate rules. Through the cross-fertilisation between knowledge regarding overtourism and the emerging COVID-19 literature (media as well as official statistical reports), this chapter aims to provide an initial assessment of the situation before and after the outbreak of the pandemic in Italy, starting with examples of some of the tourist cities par excellence (Venice and Florence).

The chapter underlines how a systemic response to the current crisis has not yet been developed at the level of political decision-making and city administration. The measures undertaken so far aim simply to restore the status quo ante, without corrective measures: the goal is therefore to recover tourist flows in the same qualitative and quantitative ways as in the pre-pandemic period. The coronavirus can be considered the other side of the coin of overtourism in terms of creating inequalities in access to cultural heritage.

Venice and Florence as Italian overtourism icons

Venice and Florence are among the most popular global tourism destinations, although they occupy only the 46th (Venice) and 51st (Florence) positions in the 100 most visited cities in the world (Yasmeen 2019).[3] Nevertheless, as reflected in the media and tourism studies, both cities, especially Venice, are notorious examples of 'overtourism'.

The term 'overtourism' entered into common language several years ago (it was added to the *Oxford English Dictionary* in 2018), reflecting how the phenomenon and its impacts at a social and urban level have multiplied since the start of the century (UNWTO, CELTH and ETFI 2018; Milano, Cheer and Novelli 2019).[4] Although there is no single definition of overtourism, the phenomenon, distinguishable from the more generic 'overcrowding', is linked to 'situations in which the impact of tourism, at certain times and in certain locations, exceeds physical, ecological, social, economic, psychological and/or political capacity thresholds' (Peeters et al. 2018: 22). It thus has negative implications for both residents and tourists, and gives rise to serious risks to nature and cultural heritage (D'Eramo 2017: 71). The damaging effects for tourists are temporary, but the impacts on living environments are long-lasting and result in a decline in quality of life, causing economic inequalities and social exclusion (Sequera and Nofre 2018).

A majority of studies on overtourism tend to blame the phenomenon and its negative consequences, not on the inexorable increase in tourist flows, but rather on poor management and, in particular, on a lack of adequate infrastructure. As a result, in recent years we have seen the emergence of a body of literature on 'destination management' as an approach to solving critical issues tied to overtourism (von Magius Møgelhøj 2021).

As is also demonstrated by the cases of Florence and Venice, however, the phenomenon cannot be managed 'downstream', and the destination management solutions conceived to date in various places around the world have proved to be ineffective,[5] starting with attempts to delocalise tourist flows. Tourism studies have focused on the impacts of overtourism on historic urban areas;[6] as reported by the United Nations World Tourism Organization (UNWTO), between 75 and 80 per cent of tourist flows are concentrated in cities (von Magius Møgelhøj 2021: 1).[7]

Before the pandemic broke out, overtourism saw progressive growth at a global level, and the problems caused by it became more acute as a result: between 2010, the year marking the recovery of tourism after the collapse triggered by the world economic crisis, and the outbreak of the pandemic in 2020, there were 10 consecutive years of sustained increase in tourist flows (UNWTO 2020). The new boom was aided by several factors, including the use of social media as a tool for relaunching various tourist destinations, with ratings and reviews given directly by tourists themselves, and the explosion of peer-to-peer platforms like Airbnb and TripAdvisor (Moreno-Gil and Coca-Stefaniak 2020; Bugalski 2021).

As Venice and Florence demonstrate, there has been a transformation in the urban character of the most affected cities, particularly as to how cultural heritage is appropriated and utilised, something seen most clearly in the examples of monuments and museums. The changes in social dynamics have been conspicuous during the pandemic. Dispossession, displacement and commodification have not abated; on the contrary, the pandemic has amplified the phenomena of marginalisation and inequality.[8]

The mechanisms employed by large real estate groups to buy property and progressively expand have been further developed: these conglomerates are capable of amassing and concentrating huge financial resources in the constant quest for investment opportunities. Living environments and cities with a rich artistic heritage are at the centre of these extractive processes whereby the production and wealth of local community assets are appropriated and the cities themselves turned into virtual museums and sanitised for the benefit of tourists or to cater for the international luxury market.

Florence and Venice represent two striking examples of the effects of overtourism, both because they are overwhelmed by tourist flows that well exceed the capacity of their historic city centres, and because of the impact on cultural heritage. Both have been included on the World Heritage List of the United Nations Educational, Scientific and Cultural Organization (UNESCO), Venice in 1980 and Florence in 1982; they have witnessed similar evolutions in urban dynamics and have also for some time been characterised as 'one-company towns', since the tourism industry is by far the most prevalent source of each city's economy.

The case of Venice

Venice has seen a progressive depopulation which has accelerated since the end of the Second World War (from 175,000 inhabitants in 1951 to fewer than 51,000 in August 2021).[9] The most reliable estimates speak of about 30,000,000 tourists per year in the last years before the pandemic, in an area of about 800 hectares (in reality, the area frequented by tourists is much smaller); hence, the tourist–resident ratio makes Venice a particularly significant case when it comes to overtourism (Seraphin, Sheeran and Pilato 2018; Visentin and Bertocchi 2019). The full conversion to a tourist economy, a process that has accelerated in the past 30 years, has led to a progressive selling-off of public buildings – in large part, monumental buildings of historical value – and their repurposing for tourism (Somma 2021).

Starting in the 1990s, the smaller islands in the Venetian lagoon – referred to as the 'health archipelago' of Venice, as they were once occupied by hospital facilities – were converted into seven-star oases (Bianchin 2008; Somma 2021: 41). The island of San Clemente, formerly home to a psychiatric hospital, was turned into the Palace Kempinski Hotel in 2016; the island of Sacca Sessola, formerly the site of a hospital for lung disease patients, now hosts the Marriott Venice Resort; and the island of Santa Maria delle Grazie, where there used to be an infectious disease hospital, will be converted into a luxury resort by the entrepreneur Giovanna Stefanel (Zorzi 2019). Thanks to the changes in building regulations facilitated by the local authority, the privatisation of public assets has thus also led to the dismantling of the public health-care system.

But even in Murano, the centre of glass production, starting from 2000, the foundries and 'conterie' (Venetian glass bead factories) have been turned into luxury hotels (Bertasi 2018; Lamberti 2021), while the areas around St Mark's Square, in the Rialto district and near to the railway station have been transformed into commercial strips connected by corridors patrolled by the local police. Moreover, for several decades the area extending from the Accademia Bridge to the Church of Santa Maria della Salute and the increasingly numerous locations occupied by the Venice Biennale have been diverted from residential use to so-called art tourism.

Finally, starting from 2010, in the spaces delimiting St Mark's Square, from the Procuratie Vecchie to the Royal Gardens, the religious and now tourist heart of the city, the municipal authority and the Italian Cultural Heritage Ministry have progressively removed all restrictions, granting the private owners – the insurance company Assicurazioni Generali – permission to renovate the interior spaces for their own activities, whether tourism-related or not (Somma 2021: 143). Venice has in fact become a laboratory researching the repurposing of an entire city.

From a cultural heritage viewpoint, UNESCO has invested in the city since the 1966 flood and the organisation's only field office in Italy is in Venice. Civil society organisations dedicated to safeguarding heritage and activist groups have been complaining to UNESCO for years about the damage caused to the city by overtourism, including the heavy environmental impact of the huge cruise ships allowed to enter the lagoon

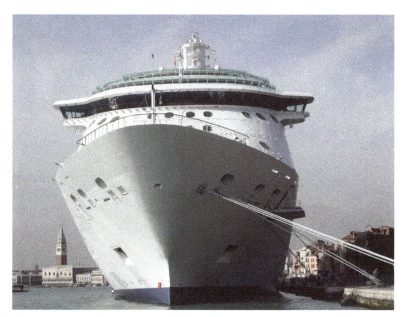

Figure 9.1 Venice: a cruise ship in the San Marco basin, 2020.
© Paola Somma.

(Figure 9.1). In particular, in 2014 the Associazione Italia Nostra submitted a request to have Venice included in the UNESCO red list of endangered world heritage sites. After many delays, the topic was discussed in 2021 in a special meeting of the UNESCO World Heritage Committee in Fuzhou, China. The Italian national media reported on the issue daily as the date of the World Heritage Committee meeting approached, framing inclusion in the list as a stain on the country's international prestige. Even the Italian prime minister stepped in to ward this off and on 13 July 2021 the government issued a decree banning cruise ships from entering the lagoon. Despite the requests of the World Heritage Centre and the International Council on Monuments and Sites (ICOMOS), which jointly drafted the most recent technical report on Venice in 2020, the UNESCO World Heritage Committee rejected the city's inclusion in the red list on 22 July 2021 (Ministero della Cultura 2021). Unanimous objections were raised by many national and international associations, which pointed out that a single decree could not solve the many systemic and critical issues that UNESCO observers had brought to the committee's attention (Italia Nostra Venezia 2021). In 2020, UNESCO included the art of Venetian glass beads on its List of Intangible Cultural Heritage of Humanity,[10] a decision that might be compared to including the Buddhas of Bamiyan on the World Heritage List, after they had been destroyed, as 'absent heritage' (Harrison 2013: 182), given that the workers who engaged in this art were expelled from Murano years ago.

The prevalence of tourism-related interests in the use of cultural heritage was further highlighted in 2020, when the Venetian civic museums – prestigious institutions that were transformed into a private foundation in 2008 (though the assets are public) and occupy some of the most monumental palaces in St Mark's Square and along the Grand Canal – remained closed well after lockdown restrictions were lifted because, according to the authorities, it was not economically feasible to keep them open in the absence of the normal tourist flows (Mi riconosci 2021).

An example of how urban dynamics have been subordinated to the logics of tourism was seen during the 'acqua grande' (the disastrous flooding of November 2019), when the City of Venice website offered tourists the chance to enjoy the 'esperienza originale di vedere la città allagata' ('the original experience of seeing the city flooded'; see Segre 2019: 40) as residents fought to save their livelihoods.

From a political standpoint, the emptying of the city, whose residents have fled to the mainland, to Mestre in particular, has facilitated these processes. The territory of the city of Venice encompasses all the municipalities of the Venetian mainland, with over 180,000 people, who thus represent a large majority of the population and of the electorate. The fate of Venice is decided not by people who actually live in Venice, but instead by a majority who engage in tourist-related activities there.

The case of Florence

In Florence the situation is similar. The historic city centre, a major cultural tourist attraction, is a very small area (500 hectares, or 5 per cent of the total municipal surface area) in proportion to the number of tourists passing through it (since 2016, about 20 million visitors per year according to the most up-to-date estimates: see Staglianò 2019; Agostini, Fiorentino and Vannetiello 2020: 6; see also Figure 9.2). Beginning in the first decade of the twenty-first century, the city has become increasingly specialised as an international tourist destination, thanks to promotional policies implemented by housing platforms and real estate multinationals with the aim of luring tourists.

Corporations have continued to take over public (and private) real estate properties, all inevitably turned into luxury hotels and resorts and no longer available for use by the community.

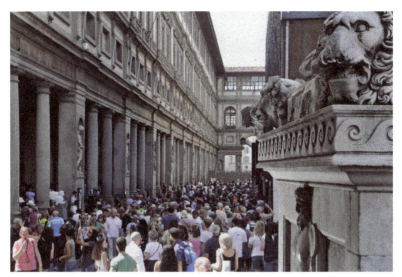

Figure 9.2 Florence: the courtyard of the Uffizi Museum, 2019.
© Ilaria Agostini.

The sale of convents, hospitals, pawnshops, theatres and so on, as in the case of Venice, was facilitated by increasingly less restrictive city planning rules conveniently adapted to meet the demands of investors. In just a few years, the former San Gallo military hospital, the former military health school of Costa San Giorgio, the former tobacco factory and the former municipal theatre were sold to large real estate holding companies, and the snatching up of property also extended to public housing ('case popolari', built in the city centre in the 1960s), Palazzo Minerbetti, an entire city block which was once the seat of the Cassa di Risparmio, the former Monte dei Pegni, the former National Theatre and Palazzo Portinari Salviati (Fiorentino 2019).

Since the beginning of the 2000s, the local authority has consistently favoured the conversion of residential units into bed and breakfasts (B&Bs) and other accommodation for tourists as a popular form of self-employment. In Florence, as in other southern European cities (Barcelona, Lisbon etc.), the number of B&Bs increased enormously in the years preceding the pandemic, as did the number of apartments rented out for short periods (Staglianò 2019; Bugalski 2021). Residents with Italian citizenship have been progressively replaced by foreign nationals: in 2017, foreigners represented 22.3 per cent of the city centre's population (Agostini 2020). The statistics tell us that every day of the year, before the pandemic, the number of city users (largely tourists) was about treble the number of residents (A. Montanari 2020: 289).

According to a 2018 study by the University of Siena, one out of four apartments in the historic centre of Florence is rented out to tourists via digital platforms, thus denying housing to residents: the highest ratio in Italy between homes offered online and the total number of dwellings (LADEST dell'Università di Siena 2018). In the meantime, the marginalised parts of the population have become a low-cost labour force in the tourism industry, with precarious contracts, if not off-the-books jobs: a characteristic of the labour market in the tourism industry that is unfortunately common nationwide and the result of obsolete regulations and a strongly fragmented labour supply.[11]

With regard to cultural heritage, in 2014 the Uffizi Museum and the Accademia Gallery, two of the most visited museums in Italy, were transformed by the Cultural Heritage Ministry into autonomous institutions with their own board of directors. After the change, some rooms in the Uffizi were reorganised to enable a quick visit to several selected artworks ('masterpieces').

The trend towards the progressive commodification of the city's cultural heritage was explicitly confirmed a couple of years ago when the drafting of regulations for the UNESCO centre was entrusted to the municipal Economic Development Department, not the Department of Culture.

The 'sanitisation' phenomenon, a prefectorial order issued on 9 April 2019, with the mayor's consent and the Italian government's approval, created a Red Zone of 17 areas in the centre of Florence where parking is prohibited and anyone who has been reported for violating the rules must leave the area (even if the violation has not yet been proved). This measure aims to 'protect the freedom of movement of residents' and of tourists. Not all tourists, however, because in 2017 the municipal authority had already adopted a measure whereby church steps are hosed down to prevent tourists from sitting on them and snacking, the objective being to protect 'urban decorum' (Operazione antibivacco 2017).

Commonalities between the cases

Despite the brevity of the above overviews of Venice and Florence, there are clearly many common mechanisms that in both cases have caused a change of approach to the city's management and the conservation of cultural heritage, which has become a resource to be exploited according to the rules of an extractive economy. Cities of art have thus been transformed into open-air mines and, in this context, tourism appears like a sort of colonialism – no longer imposed by states, but by multinational tourism and real estate conglomerates.[12]

Historic city centres have become places for up-market retail stores or globally standardised products, intended to appeal and cater to international tourism. At the same time, they are places of work, but work that is often insecure and underpaid. In these aseptic, separate, sectorised environments, tourism becomes a 'factory' – 'the' factory which replaces previous ones due to the crisis in industrial production and construction. The takeover of urban resources by large real estate investment and tourism industry groups has been labelled as 'city grabbing' (Agostini, Fiorentino and Vannetiello 2020: 8). It is a phenomenon that has progressively reduced the right to enjoy the historic city (Guermandi and D'Angelo 2019) by limiting access to housing and robbing the community of a collective use of large, monumental buildings and public spaces.

Venice and Florence have similarly seen a progressive process of expropriation of the most important public spaces – from Ponte Vecchio to the Pitti Palace (Poli and Vanni 2013; T. Montanari 2020) to St Mark's Square (Somma 2021: 143) – and their militarisation in order to make them 'safe' for tourist activities. Moreover, squares, bridges and monumental buildings, including those housing public institutions, are more and more frequently rented out for commercial or private events (fashion shows, gala dinners and weddings of magnates): paid-for stages to which the public is temporarily denied access, often with serious disruptions to urban mobility. The anthropological nature of residency has changed as thousands of city dwellers have abandoned the historic core, while the local business fabric, variety of goods sold and artisan workshops on offer have been replaced by things aimed directly at tourists.

Both cities have seen an increase in 'prohibitions', partitioning and limits, as epitomised by the 'DASPO urbano',[13] a national measure introduced in 2017 which restricts access in tourist areas (Law Decree 14/2017, Art. 5(2)(c)) and gives mayors the authority to erect 'fences' around monumental areas, making them out of bounds for certain categories of people and activities, such as begging. The urban DASPO is an additional security measure that limits the freedom of movement and access by using gates, poles, barriers, video cameras and so on, the result being a progressive expulsion of certain groups, which are increasingly excluded and marginalised.

These changes result from the lack of a general vision and planning strategy as an alternative to tourism, a lack which is due to the progressive reduction of room for action in public planning. Urban transformation has been decided by financial investment funds (Agostini and Bevilacqua 2016). In both cities, cultural heritage is at the centre of a pervasive commodification process that has by now taken over every space – cultural heritage is exploited solely for tourism purposes. A paradigmatic example of this process is paid admission to the main historic churches (and even those of less renown). Since the 1990s, churches that had always been used by the city's residents as 'covered public squares' have been converted into museums, becoming spaces accessible only by paying admission as though they were actual museums, without, however, fulfilling the research functions of the latter, while at the same time they have ceased to play their natural role in terms of promoting cultural and civic literacy (T. Montanari 2021). As with many other cases, in Venice and Florence the UNESCO brand has further contributed to the cities' conversion into 'museums' and increased the distortive effects that UNESCO itself has for several years been seeking to combat (D'Eramo 2014; Meskell 2018: 129).

After the pandemic

The global economic losses to the tourism industry from the pandemic amounted to 4.5 trillion US dollars in 2020 alone. The wealth produced by tourism has been practically cut in half, decreasing from 10.4 per cent of GDP (in 2019) to 5.5 per cent (in 2021). It is calculated that about 62 million jobs have been lost in the industry worldwide (−18.5 per cent; World Travel & Tourism Council 2021a: 3). According to data from the national tourist board, in 2020 the Italian cities most penalised by the pandemic were Venice (−47.3 per cent) and Florence (−45.6 per cent) (ENIT 2020: 10; Istat 2020a).

As the most up-to-date sector surveys have highlighted in 2021, the crisis caused by the pandemic has revealed the importance of a balanced economy not dependent on tourism as the main source of income. In a balanced economic system capable of withstanding unexpected market crises and contractions, tourism should account for 10 per cent of GDP at most (von Magius Møgelhøj 2021: X). The Italian situation is especially critical, because Italy now depends on tourist revenues for over 13 per cent of its GDP, the highest percentage among G20 countries, with the exception of Mexico (World Travel & Tourism Council 2021b: 7, Figure 6).[14]

However, the weakness of the economic model represented in the examples of Venice and Florence was already evident before COVID-19. Only a minimal part of the wealth produced contributed to the well-being of the community and to improving the quality of life in cities, while the pandemic further underscored the fragile nature of this economic model.

Confinement and distancing measures have further accentuated the need for public spaces to be open to everyone, especially those who live in deprived neighbourhoods with little space (Giagni 2020). Before the pandemic there had been a progressive shrinking and sanitisation of public spaces, while since, as a form of relief to food service establishments, the local authorities have granted permission to use larger public outdoor areas for free. The result is a further privatisation of community spaces and a consequent decrease in the collective enjoyment of those spaces. In addition to the collapse of the labour market, which has affected less specialised jobs, such as those connected to tourism, the pandemic has also exacerbated social inequalities (Agostini and Gisotti 2020).

Notwithstanding the problems emerging from the analyses and data, and the evidence of the unsustainability of a system founded on 'one-economy towns', political and business leaders do not seem inclined towards a change in policies and have continued to focus on making up for the losses, in terms of the number of incoming tourists and amount of revenue, as quickly as possible. During lockdown, the mayors of both Venice and Florence promised to restore balance in order to encourage the return of residents and mitigate the effects of the phenomenon of short-term rental platforms, including and above all Airbnb (Ratti 2020).[15] However, as early as summer 2021 there was a resumption of real estate investments aimed at converting buildings and properties belonging to the cultural heritage. As a result, they continue to be privatised and intended for selective access based on income. Even during the pandemic, work continued on the projects in Venice to 'rehabilitate' the islands in the lagoon and monumental buildings (Somma 2021: 143).

In March 2021, exactly one year after the first lockdown and in what was still a very serious epidemiological situation in Italy, the municipal authorities of Venice and Florence announced they had jointly produced a 'decalogue' with the aim of 'lending new appeal to Italy and its splendid cities of art as soon as it is possible to travel safely again' (Comune di Firenze, Città di Venezia 2021). The decalogue includes a wide-ranging series of measures designed to incentivise tourist activities, from food service to transport, with the addition of a few palliative measures against short-term rentals.

There are also 'rules for protecting urban decorum and safety and the development of smart control rooms for an intelligent management of cities', which echo measures designed to contain phenomena of urban decay, essentially consisting of sanitisation operations. When presenting the 'decalogue', the mayor of Venice stated, 'We cannot think that Italy will get going again without the involvement of excellences like the cities of art, which have a strong appeal as ambassadors of Italy in the world. Venice and Florence, linked together by a strong historical bond, are the symbol of the will to succeed' (Comune di Firenze, Città di Venezia 2021).

It is also worth stressing that the phenomena described above, which led to a degradation of urban and social functions, are taking place within a framework of democratic mechanisms: the local policymakers who further them enjoy the support of residents, since they are regularly elected.[16] One of the possible explanations is that the 'quick cash' economy, such as one based on short-term rentals or fast food, has replaced other sources of income in a society that is increasingly deindustrialised, but where digital or more advanced economies still struggle to establish themselves. The renting out or sale of owned residential property, given the relatively 'easy' and 'flexible' conditions offered by specialised platforms, has become a secure source of income (or at least it was so until the lockdown).

Finally, as regards the uses of cultural heritage, the pressure of real estate investors aiming to exploit residential property for tourism has increasingly impacted on the dynamics of conservation and protection. Starting from the 1990s in particular, restrictions designed to protect historical heritage have been eased in Italy, where, from the end of the 1970s, there had previously been an emphasis on strict conservation of existing buildings and protection of the architectural heritage of historic city centres, considered, since the Gubbio Charter (Guermandi and D'Angelo 2019),[17] as a single system to be preserved as a whole. This meant protecting not only the elements of greatest architectural and monumental importance, but also the urban fabric made up of lesser buildings.

As critical heritage studies has taught us, the use of cultural heritage is continually evolving and changes according to the sociopolitical context and the demands, needs and expectations of the communities it represents or is part of. Not surprisingly, the tourist exploitation of heritage largely prevalent in 'heritage towns' is in line with other natural and cultural resource commodification processes that have been ongoing for some time, in many parts of the world. Additionally, the examples discussed here have highlighted the function of cultural prestige tied to the urban environments and monumental places of the city. In this case, the urban cultural heritage becomes the stage for representations of power,[18] as it continues to exert a powerful symbolic appeal that is associated with a use that is both exclusive and excluding.

Notes

1. The research which forms the empirical basis for this chapter was conducted between December 2020 and August 2021 and the first draft of the chapter was submitted in December 2021. As such, it was written as the pandemic was still unfolding and represents an understanding of the issues as they presented themselves at that time.
2. On the depopulation of Italian historic centres, see Severini 2015.
3. At the top of the ranking are the Asian cities Hong Kong and Bangkok, and in Europe, metropolises such as London and Paris.
4. Overtourism is also one of the most debated topics in critical tourism studies; see Gibson 2021.
5. On the ineffectiveness of the policies adopted so far to combat overtourism at a European level, see Peeters et al. 2018 and A. Montanari 2020. For Venice, see Vitucci 2021, and for Florence, Semmola 2021.
6. On the specific form of gentrification due to tourism, see Cócola-Gant 2018 and Mansilla 2019.
7. As regards Italy, see Istat 2020a, b.
8. A first analysis of touristification in post-COVID times is Cañada and Murray 2021.
9. A daily update of the number of residents of the Venetian historic centre is available on the blog Venessia.com (https://www.venessia.com).
10. https://ich.unesco.org/en/RL/the-art-of-glass-beads-01591
11. On working conditions in the tourism sector in general, see Cheer 2018.
12. On cultural tourism as a form of neocolonialism, see Guermandi 2021: 115 ff.
13. Divieto di Accesso alle manifestazioni SPOrtive, or prohibition of access to sports events and urban areas, including those frequented by tourists.
14. Data for 2019.
15. In general, on the proposals to overcome the crisis caused by the pandemic and on the 'recovery vs reform' alternative, see Pasquinelli and Trunfio 2021.
16. For reasons of space, it was not possible to discuss here the movements of resistance to the mechanisms of gentrification and overtourism which also exist in Venice and Florence, as in many other European cities; see Pardo and Gómez 2019 and Gainsforth 2020.
17. The Gubbio Charter of 1960 established criteria for interventions in the historic centres of Italian cities that were based on a concept of comprehensive conservation, i.e. the need to preserve not only individual buildings of worth, but also the urban fabric or context as a whole.
18. Venice and Florence, together with other Italian heritage towns, were, not surprisingly, chosen as locations for the events of the G20 during the Italian presidency of 2021.

References

Agostini, Ilaria. 2020. Il turismo consuma l'urbanistica e il diritto alla casa. In Agostini, Fiorentino, and Vannetiello (eds), 2020: 50–53.

Agostini, Ilaria and Piero Bevilacqua (eds). 2016. *Viaggio in Italia. Le città nel trentennio neoliberista*. Roma: manifestolibri.

Agostini, Ilaria, Antonio Fiorentino and Daniele Vannetiello (eds). 2020. *Firenze Fabbrica del Turismo*. Firenze: Edizioni perUnaltracittà. Online at https://www.perunaltracitta.org/wp-content/uploads/2020/10/Firenze-fabbrica-del-turismo-Agostini-Fiorentino-Vannetiello-edizioni-perUnaltracitta-2020.pdf Accessed 27 March 2023.

Agostini, Ilaria and Maria Rita Gisotti. 2020. Politiche urbane e pratiche solidali durante la pandemia. Il panorama internazionale e un caso di studio. *Scienze del Territorio*, special issue 'Abitare il territorio al tempo del Covid': 177–185. Online at https://oajournals.fupress.net/index.php/sdt/article/view/12271/11757 Accessed 27 March 2023.

Bertasi, Gloria. 2018. L'ex fornace diventa hotel, turisti anche nelle isole. *Corriere del Veneto*, 22 June 2018.

Bianchin, Roberto. 2008. Venezia, l'ultima invasione, gli hotel si mangiano le isole. *la Repubblica*, 9 October 2008.

Bugalski, Łukasz. 2021. The Touristification of Italian Historic City Centres: The Lesson for Central Europe about the Airbnb Eruption. In *Heritage and Environment: The 5th Heritage Forum of Central Europe*. Kraków: International Cultural Centre: 281–293.

Cañada, Ernest and Murray, Ivan (eds). 2021. *#TourismPostCOVID19: Lockdown Touristification*. Barcelona: Alba Sud Editorial. Online at https://www.albasud.org/detallespublicacion.php?id=103&lan=en Accessed 26 April 2023.

Cheer, Joseph. 2018. Geographies of Marginalisation: Encountering Modern Slavery in Tourism. *Tourism Geographies* 20(4): 728–732.

Cócola-Gant, Agustin. 2018. Tourism Gentrification. In Loretta Lees and Martin Phillips (eds), *Handbook of Gentrification Studies*. Cheltenham: Edward Elgar Publishing: 281–293.

Comune di Firenze, Città di Venezia. 2021. *Città d'arte? #NONmetterledaparte: Un Decalogo di proposte per il rilancio da Firenze e Venezia*. Online at https://live.comune.venezia.it/sites/live.comune.venezia.it/files/articoli/allegati/Decalogo_Firenze_Venezia_ok.pdf Accessed 27 March 2023.

D'Eramo, Marco. 2014. Unescocide. *New Left Review* 88 (July/August): 47–53.

D'Eramo, Marco. 2017. *Il selfie del mondo. Indagine sull'età del turismo*. Milano: Feltrinelli.

ENIT. 2020. *Bollettino Ufficio Studi n. 10*. Ente Nazionale del Turismo Italiano. https://www.enit.it/storage/202206/20220627174717_bollettino-enit-n-10_fin.pdf

Fiorentino, Antonio. 2019. A chi fa gola Firenze: i nuovi padroni della città in 10 schede. *perUnaltracittà*, 17 September. Online at https://www.perunaltracitta.org/2019/09/17/a-chi-fa-gola-firenze-i-nuovi-padroni-della-citta-sintesi-finale/ Accessed 27 March 2023.

Gainsforth, Sarah. 2020. *Airbnb città merce. Storie di resistenza alla gentrificazione digitale*. Roma: DeriveApprodi.

Giagni, Tommaso. 2020. Dopo il virus, riprendiamoci le città. Anzi, cambiamole. *L'Espresso*, 5 luglio 2020.

Gibson, Chris. 2021. Critical Tourism Studies: New Directions for Volatile Times. *Tourism Geographies* 23(4): 659–677.

Guermandi, Maria Pia. 2021. *Decolonizzare il patrimonio. L'Europa, l'Italia e un passato che non passa*. Roma: Castelvecchi.

Guermandi, Maria Pia and Umberto D'Angelo (eds). 2019. *Il diritto alla città storica. Atti del Convegno - Roma*, 12 November 2018. Roma: Associazione Ranuccio Bianchi Bandinelli.

Harrison, Rodney. 2013. *Heritage: Critical Approaches*. London and New York: Routledge.

Istat. 2020a. *Movimento turistico in Italia, Gennaio-Settembre 2020*. Roma: Istat (Istituto nazionale di statistica). Online at https://www.istat.it/it/files/2020/12/REPORT_TURISMO_2020.pdf Accessed 27 March 2023.

Istat. 2020b. *Turismo d'arte in area urbana. Una proposta di indicatori*. Roma: Istat (Istituto nazionale di statistica). Online at https://www.istat.it/it/files//2021/01/Turismo-arte-area-urbana.pdf Accessed 27 March 2023.

Italia Nostra Venezia. 2021. UNESCO e Grandi Navi. Online at https://www.italianostravenezia.org/2021/07/18/comunicato-unesco-e-grandi-navi/ Accessed 27 March 2023.

LADEST dell'Università di Siena. 2018. *L'airificazione delle città. Airbnb e la produzione di ineguaglianza*. Online at https://www.myguestfriend.it/wp-content/uploads/2018/10/Airificazione-città-italiane-Univ.-Siena.pdf Accessed 27 March 2023.

Lamberti, Manuela. 2021. Il vetro artistico va in pezzi: metà delle fornaci sono chiuse. *Il Gazzettino*, 9 April. Online at https://www.ilgazzettino.it/nordest/venezia/murano_vetro_artistico_crisi_fornaci_chiuse-5886971.html Accessed 27 March 2023.

Mansilla, José. 2019. Gentrification, touristification and social class in Mediterranean cities. In Ernest Cañada (ed.), *Tourism in the Geopolitics of the Mediterranean*. Barcelona: Alba Sud Editorial: 62–65.

Meskell, Lynn. 2018. *A Future in Ruins: UNESCO, World Heritage and the Dream of Peace*. Oxford: Oxford University Press.

Mi riconosci. 2021. *Venezia e i suoi musei ostaggio del turismo* – Manifestazione 27 febbraio. Published 21 February 2021. Online at https://www.miriconosci.it/venezia-e-musei-ostaggio-del-turismo-manifestazione/ Accessed 27 March 2023.

Milano, Claudio, Joseph Cheer and Marina Novelli. 2019. Overtourism: An Evolving Phenomenon. In Claudio Milano, Joseph Cheer and Marina Novelli (eds), *Overtourism: Excesses, discontents and measures in travel and tourism*. Wallingford: CABI: 1–17.

Ministero della Cultura. 2021. *Unesco, evitata l'iscrizione di Venezia nella lista del patrimonio mondiale in pericolo*, 22nd luglio 2021.Online at https://www.beniculturali.it/comunicato/21014 Accessed 27 March 2023.

Montanari, Armando. 2020. Covid-19 as an Opportunity to Tackle the Phenomenon of Overtourism in European Historic Centres: The Case of Rome. *Il capitale culturale*, Supplementi 11: 285–305.

Montanari, Tomaso. 2020. Dolce&Gabbana prendono Firenze. E la cultura chiude. *Il Fatto Quotidiano*, 7 September.

Montanari, Tomaso. 2021. *Chiese chiuse*. Torino: Einaudi.

Moreno-Gil, Sergio and Andres Coca-Stefaniak (eds). 2020. *Overtourism and the Sharing Economy*. Special issue of *International Journal of Tourism Cities*, 6(1).

Operazione antibivacco. 2017. Operazione antibivacco. Il sindaco Nardella con gli idranti sul sagrato di Santa Croce. *La Nazione*, 31 May. Online at https://www.lanazione.it/firenze/cronaca/foto/nardella-idranti-santa-croce-1.3163368 Accessed 27 March 2023.

Pardo, Daniel and Reme Gómez. 2019. Southern Europe as an Anti-tourism Political Space. In Ernest Cañada (ed.), *Tourism in the Geopolitics of the Mediterranean*. Barcelona: Alba Sud Editorial: 86–91.

Pasquinelli, Cecilia and Mariapina Trunfio. 2021. The Missing Link between Overtourism and Post-pandemic Tourism: Framing Twitter Debate on the Italian Tourism Crisis. *Journal of Place Management and Development*. https://doi.org/10.1108/JPMD-07-2020-0073

Peeters, Paul, Stefan Gössling, Jeroen Klijs, Claudio Milano, Marina Novelli, Corné Dijkmans, Eke Eijgelaar, Stefan Hartmann, Jasper Heslinga, Rami Isaac, Ondrej Mitas, Simone Moretti, Jeroen Nawijn, Bernadett Papp and Albert Postma. 2018. *Research for TRAN Committee – Overtourism: Impact and Possible Policy Responses*. Brussels: European Union.

Poli, Simona and Massimo Vanni. 2013. Ponte Vecchio chiuso, c'è una festa privata la bellezza in affitto: così i sindaci fanno cassa. *La Repubblica*, 1 July.

Ratti, Carlo. 2020. Così un nuovo turismo salverà Venezia dalla crisi. *Corriere della Sera*, 6 August. Online at https://www.corriere.it/editoriali/20_agosto_06/cosi-nuovo-turismosalvera-venezia-crisi-d440b1bc-d817-11ea-ad6c-bda3a14094de.shtml Accessed 27 March 2023.

Segre, Andrea. 2019. Nella Venezia del 'mi sto qua'. *L'Espresso*, 24 November: 38–40.

Semmola, Edoardo. 2021. Assalto a Firenze, il fronte dei musei 'Non è stato fatto nulla per cambiare'. *Corriere Fiorentino*, 5 November.

Sequera, Jorge and Jordi Nofre. 2018. Shaken, Not Stirred: New Debates on Touristification and the Limits of Gentrification. *City* 22(5-6): 843–855.

Seraphin, Hugues, Paul Sheeran and Manuela Pilato. 2018. Over-tourism and the Fall of Venice as a Destination. *Journal of Destination Marketing & Management* 9: 374–376.

Severini, Giuseppe. 2015. Centri storici: occorre una legge speciale o politiche speciali? *Aedon* 2 (May–August). Online at http://www.aedon.mulino.it/archivio/2015/2/severini.htm Accessed 27 March 2023.

Somma, Paola. 2021. *Privati di Venezia. La città di tutti per il profitto di pochi*. Roma: Castelvecchi.

Staglianò, Riccardo. 2019. Tutta mia la città. *il Venerdì di Repubblica*, 9 August.

UNWTO. 2020. *International Tourism Highlights*. UNWTO (World Tourism Organization). Online at https://www.e-unwto.org/doi/epdf/10.18111/9789284422456 Accessed 27 March 2023.

UNWTO, CELTH and ETFI. 2018. *'Overtourism'? Understanding and Managing Urban Tourism Growth beyond Perceptions, Executive Summary*. Madrid, Spain: World Tourism Organization (UNWTO). Online at https://www.e-unwto.org/doi/epdf/10.18111/9789284420070 Accessed 27 March 2023.

Visentin, Francesco and Dario Bertocchi. 2019. Venice: An Analysis of Tourism Excesses in an Overtourism Icon. In Claudio Milano, Joseph Cheer and Marina Novelli (eds), *Overtourism: Excesses, Discontents and Measures in Travel and Tourism*. Wallingford: CABI: 18–38.

Vitucci, Alberto. 2021. Priorità, fermare l'invasione. Un piano per salvare Venezia. *La Nuova Venezia*, 2 November.

von Magius Møgelhøj, Helene. 2021. *Overtourism: The Role of Effective Destination Management*. New York: Business Expert Press.

World Travel & Tourism Council. 2021a. *Lessons Learnt during COVID-19: The Lessons Learnt So Far and How These Can Be Used to Prepare for Future Crises*. Online at https://wttc.org/Portals/0/Documents/Reports/2021/Lessons-Learnt-%20COVID-19.pdf?ver=2021-08-19-095731-037 Accessed 27 March 2023.

World Travel & Tourism Council. 2021b. *Travel & Tourism: Global Economic Impact & Trends 2021*. Online at https://wttc.org/Portals/0/Documents/Reports/2021/Global%20Economic%20Impact%20and%20Trends%202021.pdf?ver=2021-07-01-114957-177 Accessed 27 March 2023.

Yasmeen, Rabia. 2019. *Top 100 City Destinations*. London: Euromonitor International. Online at https://gate.ahram.org.eg/Media/News/2019/12/9/2019-637114875902629480-262.pdf Accessed 27 March 2023.

Zorzi, Alvise. 2019. Stefanel: all'isola della Grazia faremo qualcosa di bello e speciale. *Corriere del Veneto*, 5 May.

Part III: Digital heritages and digital futures

The future of Europe seems to be, according to the European Commission's goal for the next decade, tied to the digital. The commission's proposal, 'Path to the Digital Decade', aims to achieve 'a digital transformation of our society and economy in line with the EU's values'. Among the diverse spheres deemed to contribute to the 'prosperous digital future', digital heritage is undoubtedly one of the most crucial.

The five contributions to this section explore the challenges, constraints and advantages of digital archives and digital heritage and their role in creating and reinforcing national and/or transnational identities. By pointing out the bias underlying digital technologies, the chapters demonstrate that processes of digitisation are neither value-neutral nor producing value-neutral data. Through the process of content selection, databases, records and digital archives reflect and consolidate hierarchies of power relationships, making invisible issues of gender and ethnicity. Thus, the importance of considering digital technologies' ontological impact – how they transform the elements they aim to safeguard and how, as Geoffrey C. Bowker (2000) noted in connection to biodiversity databases, they come to shape a world in their own image – is underlined (see further discussion in Harrison et al. 2020).

As Stuart Dunn emphasises in his contribution (Chapter 10), 'digital maps are highly partial' and 'most digital mapping platforms … encode a certain perceptive bias about the world'. By examining the relationship between material objects (physical maps) and digital objects (digital maps), Dunn explores how a concern with the immaterial paves the way for connecting digital heritage with critical heritage. The demand for a critical turn in digital heritage studies echoes the call by Plets et al. (Chapter 14) for a critical digital heritage studies that 'can bring to the surface the sociopolitical agendas embedded in metadata structures that would otherwise remain invisible'.

Based on the Irish feminist commemoration on Twitter in 2016 during the centenary of the 1916 Easter Rising, Hannah K. Smyth's contribution (Chapter 11) shows how social media platforms in general, and Twitter in particular, 'act as "digital repositories" and play a 'de facto "archival role"', as the digital content they provide is openly available and continuously accumulated and transformed. Thus, digital heritage should include 'born digital' content from social media; by challenging, rather than merely reflecting, official historical narratives, social media platforms, argues Smyth, can contribute to critical heritage studies.

The present system of heritage management in Europe has its formal roots in the systematic development of national archives of archaeological and historic monuments and sites over the past 150 years. These archives were employed by national agencies as cultural heritage for administration and planning, and by many museums and research institutions. From around 1980 to the early 2000s, these heritage institutions were drivers of the digitisation of cultural heritage, as they could mobilise the necessary resources, and had the administrative need to make these archives accessible for planning in new regional and local contexts (Kristiansen 1984). This process was thus part of the integration of cultural heritage values into the wider planning systems of Europe (Plets 2016).

This is a set of issues explored in William Illsley's chapter (Chapter 12). Focused on the concept and the terminology of 'the historic environment', he explores the record-keeping process (the database) and its silences and omissions regarding minority groups. Carlotta Capurro's chapter (Chapter 13) also picks up the contemporary threads of this longer history. Her focus is Europeana, one of the key recent pieces of European digital cultural policy established by cultural heritage institutions, the European Commission and its member states. Capurro demonstrates the ways in which 'the mission of Europeana has evolved considerably: from the digital repository of European cultural heritage, it soon became a digital infrastructure in charge of supporting the digital transformation of European cultural institutions'. Furthermore, Europeana aimed to standardise technical practices, and in doing so to create 'narratives of shared European experiences' and ultimately to forge a homogeneous European heritage. Akin to World Heritage listing that enables forms of government 'at a distance' (Harrison 2016: 214), attempts by Europeana to regulate and manage digital heritage among the European member states can be seen as a particular form of European governmentality.

The final chapter by Gertjan Plets, Julianne Nyhan, Andrew Flinn, Alexandra Ortolja-Baird and Jaap Verheul (Chapter 14) articulates theoretical and critical analysis in relation with two specific case studies: the 'Enlightenment Architectures: Sir Hans Sloane's Catalogues' project and the Central Archaeological Inventory of the Flemish Government (Belgium). The chapter provides 'an overview of the ethical challenges and political agendas encoded in digital heritage projects' and aims by means of digital tools 'to recover, rather than re-encode absences'. By questioning both 'the widespread enchantment with digital heritage infrastructures in policy and academia' and 'the veneer of neutrality of digital heritage technologies', the authors plead for 'research into the ways cultural heritage is collected, ordered and governed digitally'.

In the five contributions, digital heritage is envisioned as a process that needs to be critically scrutinised rather than a mere technical operation related to preservation, management and accessibility of heritage collections. Furthermore, due to its particular position at the crossroads of the futures of Europe and of digital futures, digital heritage is, inevitably, a key arena for cultural, ethical and political tensions.

References

Bowker, Geoffrey C. (2000). Biodiversity Datadiversity. *Social Studies of Science* 30: 643–683.
European Commission (2022). Path to the Digital Decade. Online at https://ec.europa.eu/info/strategy/priorities-2019-2024/europe-fit-digital-age/europes-digital-decade-digital-targets-2030_en Accessed 3 July 2022.
Harrison, Rodney (2016). World Heritage Listing and the Globalisation of the Endangerment Sensibility. In Fernando Vidal and Nélia Dias (eds), *Endangerment, Biodiversity and Culture*. London: Routledge: 195–217.
Harrison, Rodney, Caitlin DeSilvey, Cornelius Holtorf, Sharon Macdonald, Nadia Bartolini, Esther Breithoff, Harald Fredheim, Antony Lyons, Sarah May, Jennie Morgan, and Sefryn Penrose (2020). *Heritage Futures: Comparative Approaches to Natural and Cultural Heritage Practices*. London: UCL Press.
Kristiansen, K. 1984. Denmark. In Henry Cleere (ed.), *Approaches to the Archaeological Heritage*. Cambridge: Cambridge University Press: 21–37.
Plets, G. 2016. Heritage Bureaucracies and the Modern Nation State: Towards an Ethnography of Archaeological Systems of Government. *Archaeological Dialogues* 23(2): 193–213.

10
Datafied landscapes: exploring digital maps as (critical) heritage

Stuart Dunn

Introduction

'Heritage', whether it is visible or not, pervades the physical environment. The term includes historic buildings and landscapes, our monuments and our ancient sites. It also refers to cultural objects, artefacts and artworks (a subgenre of the term often referred to as 'material culture', with the 'heritage' label remaining implicit). It includes shared stories, narratives and processes such as dance and ritual, so-called 'intangible heritage', a term formally recognised by international organisations such as the United Nations Educational, Scientific, and Cultural Organization (UNESCO).[1] The term also includes common characteristics of communities, regional and national identities, and material culture. In this wider context, what should the qualifier 'critical' in 'critical heritage' be taken to mean? In part, aligning the prefix logically with counterparts such as 'critical edition', 'critical essay' or 'critical theory', it indicates (or rather should indicate) a set of common frameworks and methodologies for understanding and interrogating all these different aspects of heritage, and more, by both professional curators and academics and the wider public. On a theoretical level, critical heritage stems from the so-called 'critical turn' in heritage studies: a perspective which imagines the past as being interpretable only in the context of the present. This 'constructivist' approach places an interpretive onus on present-day audiences to make meaning out of the material and intellectual culture of the past, rather than on curators, museum professionals, historians or other such mediators. However, for such a process of understanding to be possible, common frameworks of understanding need to exist.

The idea of 'digital heritage' adds a further layer of complexity to the question of critical approaches to heritage. 'Digital heritage' is often taken to refer to heritage collections that have been digitised, and which can be curated and augmented using methods enabled by the World Wide Web (WWW), such as crowdsourcing (e.g. Owens 2013: 121). There have been many initiatives to digitise heritage collections of various kinds, such as artistic collections, libraries and image collections, both for the purposes of preservation and for access. In the contemporary world, however, 'digital heritage' should also be taken to include 'born-digital' content which *relates* to heritage, whether tangible or intangible. This need not be limited to physical material which has been digitised (or rather the digitised products thereof), but also includes, for example, the social media activities of cultural institutions and their audiences (Coffee 2007: 377), the reception of art and culture in the digital world which can be explored with methods such as network analysis (Noble et al. 2021), as well as the use of digital analytical techniques to explore heritage which creates new content, such as annotations (Hunter and Gerber 2010: 83). Extending the idea of 'critical heritage' to cover digital cultural heritage simply requires additional shared frameworks for approaching and interrogating digital objects as well as physical ones.

This chapter looks at how the idea of the map as a particular class of object to critical heritage approaches can be applied. It will be shown that the materiality of maps and the challenges they present for digitisation, and the issues of understanding cartographic web platforms such as Google Maps and the open source OpenStreetMap as born-digital objects, show that critical heritage can form a useful bridge between the physical and digital worlds. The key thing connecting the ideas of critical heritage and digital heritage is a concern with the *immaterial*. Digitisation is a way of 'datafying' heritage, of turning it into binary information which can be processed by a machine. This in turn allows us to see critical heritage as a means of understanding processes of representation, reproduction and remediation which connect physical and digital heritage.

The datafication of heritage

The Western, Eurocentric traditions of mapping and cartography emerged from intellectual approaches to space and place dating back to at least ancient Greece (see Dunn 2019: Chapter 2). Ancient Greek philosophy drew a distinction between *chorografia*, which was the form of place which was seen, felt, traversed and interacted with at the level of the human individual; and *geografia*, which was place in the abstract: place that could be mapped, conceptualised and seen as a mathematical entity (see Dunn 2019: Chapter 2). The latter emerged from the work of Claudius Ptolemy, who tabulated the first set of coordinates, defining specific places in relation to one another. The distinction between the two types of spatial perception at once highlights the significance of subjectivity in the production of spatial data: the subjective perception is central to the chorographic idea and is specifically excluded from the geographic one.

A brief survey of the *longue durée* of heritage studies shows that the relationship between the material and the immaterial is of crucial importance; for there is an intuitive impetus to see 'heritage' as being comprised of tangible or intangible objects *inherited* from previous times (both words derive from the Latin root *inhereditare*, 'to appoint as an heir'). In contrast, however, the assumption that heritage can *only* be material underpinned much of the theory and context behind the emergence of 'scientific archaeology', based on artefact typology, in the nineteenth and first part of the twentieth centuries. The historic focus on the tangibility of heritage is, arguably, a product of post-Darwinian perspectives in this period, whereby evolutionary theory was applied to the development of artefact typologies. This perspective privileged the physical properties of objects to the exclusion of all other considerations. Augustus Lane-Fox Pitt-Rivers, the so-called founder of scientific archaeology, stated:

> The collection ... has been collected during upwards of twenty years, not for the purpose of surprising anyone ... but solely with a view to instruction. For this purpose, ordinary and typical specimens, rather than rare objects, have been selected and arranged in sequence ... The classification of natural history specimens has long been a recognised necessity in the arrangement of every museum which professes to impart useful information, but ethnological specimens have not generally been thought capable of anything more than a geographical arrangement (Pitt-Rivers 1875: 295).[2]

Ethnology based on strict principles of physical classification clearly encapsulated Enlightenment principles of progress, linearity and complexity increasing over time. In contrast, critical heritage demands that we look beyond the object, towards the social and intangible elements that it represents. This is comparable to the intellectual traditions of post-processual archaeology, with a view of the past 'which celebrates historical particularity and the individual' (Shanks 2008: 133). This critique of process (or rather the *processual* archaeology which, logically, preceded *post-processual* archaeology) rejects the centrality of *objective* fact rooted in and derived from *objects*, and sees interpretation of past events and societies as being rooted in the contemporary present.

As with processual archaeology, placing interpretation of the past in the context of the present situates critical heritage, as a container of the theoretical and the subjective as well as the objective and the tangible, as a social-cultural movement as well as an academic approach. Winter, for example, frames critical heritage as a force for social and cultural good in the world, arguing that it 'address[es] the critical issues that face the world today, the larger issues that bear upon and extend outwards from heritage' (Winter 2013: 532). Both of these perspectives start from an assumption that heritage, critically understood, exists as an integral part of contemporary society, not – say – curated collections, partitioned off and separated from the everyday world in curated environments such as museums, libraries, archives and galleries.

This perspective on heritage – one that has been highlighted and promoted by several initiatives, including the 'CHEurope' project, of which this volume is a product – is closely related to two ideas. The first of these is that heritage is transmitted through certain classes of media and/or objects, where understandings of the same object will vary from field to field. A scholar trained in the material cultural traditions of archaeology, for example, would have a different understanding of (say) an Athenian black-figure vase from the fifth century BCE than a scholar trained in visual art history. The latter might frame the object in terms of the evolution of the schools of Hellenic Classical art, of stylistic change, of technique and, as a matter of provenance, of the object's cultural and financial value (or potential value) in the commercial art markets. The former, on the other hand, would see the same vase as a product of the Athenian community, and would read its morphology, decoration, ceramic composition, physical context, findspot and chronological con-text for historical clues about the culture or cultures which produced it. Both scholars would agree, however, that the vase represents a distinct type of medium of transition with its own critical infrastructure, epis-temology and specialisms of interpretation in their respective fields. Crucially, however, they both rely for their interpretations on specialised expertise, knowledge and method. Furthermore, in the context of the critical heritage approaches as framed above, both scholars would also be likely to agree that the Athenian black-figure vase appears as a cul-tural motif in a range of day-to-day contexts, from the visual culture of the Renaissance to the artwork of Walt Disney.

As a particular *type* of heritage, Athenian black-figure vases are classifiable according to various objective criteria – of datafication. These could vary across the bespoke classification systems of individual museums dealing with the collections of classical Greece. There are also higher-level classifications designed to cross institutional boundaries, such as the CIDOC-CRM reference model, where a vase of this (conjectured) type could be assigned to the category 'E22', which is defined as 'all persistent physical objects of any size that are purposely created by human activity and have physical boundaries that separate them completely in an objective way from other objects' (CIDOC CRM 2021: 74). It is further defined in the schema as a 'subclass' of categories 'E19 Physical Object and E24 Physical Human-Made Thing'. In other words, as an object, it follows the logic and grammars of object logic.

Maps as (datafied) heritage objects

Maps and globes are a more complex form of object than this notional Athenian black-figure vase and, because of the complex relationship between the physical and the intangible which they represent, they are much harder to classify meaningfully. The field of 'carto-bibliography' presents a set of esoteric challenges for librarians precisely because maps are so much more difficult to classify, and thus to search for, than books; the field emerged through the labours of local historians and map enthusiasts (see Hyde 1972: 290). Until the last two decades of the twentieth century, when digital mapping technologies began to emerge (of which more below), maps and globes combined complex cognitive spatial information with physicality, usually paper, but also linen, plastic, metal and, in earlier periods of history, wood, stone and other such media. The term 'spatial data bearing object', although somewhat unwieldy, captures the various layers of complexity when dealing with maps and globes as classes of critical heritage.

In contrast to this, most standard definitions of the term 'map' focus only on their *informational* aspect, to the exclusion of their physicality. In the definition most widely accepted by cartographers and cartographic historians, that of Harley and Woodward, maps are defined as 'graphic representations that facilitate a spatial understanding of things, concepts, conditions, processes, or events in the human world' (quoted in Brotton 2012: 5). The definition is neutral about the medium which conveys or contains the data. The object-oriented consideration of critical heritage set out above allows us to go further: rather than expressing only a spatial understanding of the contemporary world, we can go on to classify maps (and globes) as archaeological artefacts, as works of art, as utilitarian objects and as cultural pieces. This somewhat inverts the informational definition of what a map is and introduces an additional level of complexity into the discussion, as the 'graphical representation' being 'inherited' or received is in fact an encoding of spatial characteristics of the world in both visual and physical form.

The importance of spatial information as a component of heritage, defined broadly, was recognised in the early history of mapmaking. As Abraham Ortelius noted in the introduction of the 1606 edition of his *Theatrum Orbis Terrarum*:

> Seeing that as I thinke, there is no man, gentle Reader, but knoweth what, and how great profit the knowledge of Histories doth bring to those which are serious students therein … there is almost no man be it that he have made neuver so little an entrance in to the same … for the understanding of them aright, the knowledge of Geography, which, in that respect is therefore of some – and not without just cause called **The eye of History** (Ortelius 1606: ii).

The *Theatrum* is a collection of illuminated and annotated maps covering most regions of the then-known contemporary world, but which also contained maps of the Holy Land and the Roman Empire, both, of course, important tropes for the educated elite who were Ortelius' customers. In the context of these, Ortelius' perspective is that visual, and visualised, knowledge of these regions' geography is essential for a fully rounded insight into their history. This is an important departure, with 'knowledge of Geography', as presented in the *Theatrum*, being needed alongside the *textual* testimony of history to gain such an insight.

Critical heritage therefore directs us to consider the materiality of maps, whether contemporary, historical, artistic or archaeological (or any combination of these). In some early cases, the materiality of maps emerges as a significant problem in the early days of the print revolution. This was a period, following the publication of landmark works of 'chorographical' writing such as John Leyland's *Itinerary*, compiled between 1538 and 1543, and William Camden's *Britannia* (1701), when there was much interest in printed accounts of the British landscape, which often included printed maps. However, the new industry of printing found these requirements practically and economically difficult to accommodate. Writing in 1657, the priest, antiquarian and dissident from Cromwell's purges Peter Heylyn wrote (see Dunn 2019 for further discussion):

> I did once think of beautifying the Work with as many maps as the several States and Kingdoms which are here described. But on further consideration, how much it would increase the Book both in bulk and price, and consequently of less publik use than I did intend it; I laid by those thoughts, and rested satisfied with the adding of four Maps for the four parts of the World (Heylyn 1674: i).

The publisher of the 1701 edition of Camden's *Britannia* encountered exactly the same problem:

> The last edition of our Author, Publish'd by the Ingenious Mr Gibson, met with that Acceptance in the World as might be expected. But it being a very large volume, and upon account of its Maps and other Sculptures, unavoidably high in its price, it was thought it might be of Publik Use to Publish an Abridgment of this Author, in this case without maps (Camden 1701: i).

As well as cost, the physical size of maps also presented problems for early print editions. This was part of the motivation for Abraham Otelius's *Theatrum Orbis Terrarum*, the model for the idea of the atlas. Ortelius commented in the preface to the English language 1606 edition:

> Others there are who when they have that which will buy them would very willingly lay out the money, were it not by reason of the narrownesse of the Roomes and places, broad and large Mappes cannot be so open'd or spread so that everything in them may be easily and well be seen and disceren'd (Ortelius 1606: ii).

Ortelius' concern here was that the physical space of his clients' homes was so limited that they would not be able to see all the features in their entirety. Along with the economic barriers described for their readerships by Camden and Heylyn, this shows that the idea of maps as artefacts of critical heritage cannot be detached from the history of the media in which they are conveyed; and that therefore, to the disciplinary list of characteristics of critical heritage listed above, we must also add the history of media. This will be important later when we come to consider the map in digital form.

The process of creating a map itself involves processes of datafication. Projection, the translation of spatial relations between features whose spatial relations coexist on a globe, to relations which exist on a flat plane, is just such a process, enabling the translation of information between different physical forms. Projection in itself is not a neutral process and produces perceived or perceivable biases. Take, for example, the Mercator projection, first presented by the Flemish cartographer Gerhardus Mercator in 1569, which models the Earth's features cylindrically. This has the effect of exaggerating the size of land masses as distance from the equator increases. The institutionalisation of the Mercator projection for military and commercial navigation after 1700 or so entrenched and institutionalised this perspective.

The 'eye of history' is an apt metaphor for the consideration of critical heritage seen through the lens of geographical representation. To take one example as a case study, 'The President's Globe' was commissioned in 1942 by the Office of Strategic Services (OSS, the predecessor of the CIA) for presentation to President Theodore Roosevelt; however, in the event, two globes were commissioned as Christmas gifts for Roosevelt and Prime Minister Winston Churchill (Robinson 1997). At the time, General George C. Marshall commented:

> In order that the great leaders of this crusade may better follow the road to victory, the War Department has had two 50-inch globes specially made for presentation on Christmas Day to the Prime Minister and the President of the United States. I hope that you will find a place at 10 Downing Street for this globe, so that you may accurately chart the progress of the global struggle of 1943 to free the world of terror and bondage (Robinson 1997: 143).

In the context of critical heritage, therefore, the President's Globe is a symbolic artefact, representing, in Marshall's vision of the gift, both a geographical and a metaphorical pathway to an eventual Allied victory. It can therefore be said to represent not just a geographical representation of the Earth, but a set of events, context and versions of historical significance.

Other forms of map give insight into the contemporary perceptions of landscape infrastructures as they evolve at significant points in history. For example, the *Britannia* atlas of roads by the Scottish cartographer John Ogilby (1600–1676) set out a stylised birds-eye view of 100 important turnpike routes between important conurbations, for example from York to Chester-le-Street near Durham (Ogilby 1675). These maps gave a great deal of detail about the features in the immediate vicinity of the road, while at the same time covering the entire length of the route. This 'strip map' approach mirrors Abraham Ortelius' solution to the problem posed by the physical limitations of the print medium for combining high levels of detail with large extents of coverage – the compromise that inevitably exists in any mapmaking endeavour.

Digital mapping: the latest chapter of heritage datafication?

This twin consideration of the materiality and immateriality of maps, and the epistemological tension between these, brings us to the question of maps which have no material or physical presence in the world: digital maps. Unlike the technologies of ink, vellum, paper, copper engraving and so on, the WWW requires no compromise between scale and extent. This is not to say that they do not include biases of their own: on the contrary, digital maps are highly partial. Most obviously, most digital mapping platforms use the Mercator projection system, which, as discussed above, encodes a certain perceptive bias about the world. The coverage of digital mapping tends to reflect richer parts of the world with a greater presence of internet-enabled devices (Farman 2010). In many cases, commercial platforms such as Google Maps are shaped by corporate interests with motivation to influence the behaviour of users, for example by increasing the exposure and profile of advertisers (Leszczynski 2014: 61). On some platforms which aggregate large quantities of geographic data contributed by users, there is evidence to suggest that certain features of interest to certain demographics are overrepresented at the expense of underrepresented demographics (Stephens 2013). These platforms are subjective, they are political and they thus conform to every aspect of the classification of a critical digital heritage object.

Digital mapping moves our view from a tradition of cartography whose whole history is concerned with producing spatial data bearing objects which overcome, as much as they can, the limits of materiality while all the time managing compromise between scale and detail, to a tradition in which there is no materiality at all.[3] What aspects of critical heritage, recognising that a key part of critical heritage is a shift of focus from the material to the immaterial, can we draw on to understand digital maps as heritage objects?

Most importantly, many types of contemporary digital map are not created by one cartographer, expert in the use of the technologies involved, like an Ortelius or an Ogilby. Many digital maps are created collectively by multiple users adding features cumulatively, as in the OpenStreetMap model. Alternatively, users can aggregate traces created by GPS-enabled mobile devices, thus representing not static features such as buildings, roads and forests, but the routes taken by people carrying such devices. Such aggregate maps created by either one user or multiple users can be 'transactional', meaning that they track the routes of devices as their carriers go about their daily lives, or they can be proactive, meaning that the carrier deliberately takes a certain route to create a particular pattern. 'GPS art', which uses GPS (global positioning system) technology in this way, indeed has an active community, with several prominent practitioners (e.g. Lauriault and Wood 2009).

Transactional GPS maps can reveal insights into the relationship between people and the environments they move through. Figure 10.1, for example, shows a screen capture from OpenStreetMap (OSM), the open-source, community-driven online world map that is used by many locative mobile apps, because it is free to use. One feature of OSM is the facility for users to upload GPS traces that they have created with their mobile devices and, if they wish, to share them publicly. This creates a visual profile of which routes are more popular with such users, and thus of the main directions of flow of pedestrian or vehicular traffic (although there is no immediate mechanism for distinguishing between the two types). Figure 10.1 shows the immediate environment around Regent's

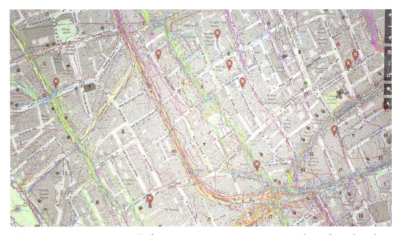

Figure 10.1 Screengrab from OpenStreetMap. Reproduced under the Open Database Licence, https://wiki.osmfoundation.org/wiki/Licence/Attribution_Guidelines

Street in Central London, and the traffic therein as depicted by GPS traces. This shows that such traffic flows predominantly north and south, between Oxford Circus and Piccadilly Circus, and west, towards Mayfair. Traffic flowing east, towards Soho, is limited by the configuration of the roads linking Regent's Street with the district. This was precisely the intent of the architect who laid out the area, John Nash (1752–1835), for reasons entirely to do with social engineering:

> [A] complete separation between the streets occupied by the Nobility and Gentry, and the narrower Streets and meaner houses occupied by mechanics and the trading part of the community … My purpose was that [Regent Street] should cross the eastern entrance to all the streets occupied by the higher classes and to leave out to the east all the bad streets (John Nash, quoted in Johnson 2006: 20).

This aggregate, transactional map therefore captures an artificial legacy of the past in the present day.

A digital map therefore represents a particular human view of the world, visualised and presented as either a static or dynamic digital object. Usually using the Mercator projection, digital maps encode much the same sorts of bias and distortion as material maps, but without the compromise between scale and detail that is inevitable in physical space. It is important to remember, however, that the WWW itself was not designed to *visualise* information, but to *connect* it in a way that makes cognitive sense to human users. As Daren Brabham has noted,

> The hypertextual nature of the web mimics the very way we think as humans … so it should come as no surprise that humans should see themselves in the medium as actors, creators, innovators, as implicated in the information flow rather than witnesses to it (Brabham 2008: 81).

Conclusion

From Ptolemy to Lane-Fox Pitt-Rivers, via Ortelius and Winston Churchill, the examples discussed above demonstrate that heritage in all its forms, like place, has always been datafied in order to be understood, transmitted and preserved. The datafied landscapes that we inhabit and navigate through our electronic devices are simply the latest iteration of this. In a hyperconnected world, human actors are implicated in the creation and cocreation of map-borne heritage, making the idea of *critical heritage* even more important.

This chapter has taken into account three factors: the presence of critical heritage as the cocreated presence of the past in the present, the presence of distinct types of medium through which culture is transferred from the past to the present, and the importance of the digital. In light of these factors, the chapter has considered objects bearing spatial data – principally maps and globes – as objects of critical heritage, as media types through which heritage is transmitted and which have been transformed by the emergence of digital environments and culture. It has argued that spatial data bearing objects such as maps have a particular place in the contemporary discourse on critical heritage, because of the unique relationship they demonstrate between complex information about the world, encoded using commonly understood grammars and abstractions, and material objects. Some examples from the early history of the print revolution show that this new form of communication presented mapmakers with challenges of both a practical and an economic nature. Overcoming these challenges involved compromise, with limits on the number of images that could be produced, and innovation in the fields of book production, layout and visual style. Heylyn, Camden, Ortelius and Ogilby all provide clear examples of this.

As noted above, 'digital heritage' in a datafied world can refer to multiple things. Much cultural content, and the meaning made by it, is stored, curated and transmitted in digital form, but an inclusive definition of heritage should also encompass born-digital material. This is a relatively unexplored aspect of critical heritage, as the majority of digital heritage discussions have focused on the digitisation of artefacts and the communication of curatorial or museum narratives on digital platforms such as social media and network analytics. While all these approaches have yielded valuable insights into how 'the digital' facilitates interaction with heritage, the question of what new forms of meaning are made by this interaction is less clear. Furthermore, the way in which any object bearing spatial information, such as a map or a globe, encodes that information is intensively subjective and partial. It aligns the presentation of the places being mapped with the purpose for which the map (or globe) was created in the first place. This does not change with maps produced immaterially in the digital realm, forming a type of digital heritage; it is simply that the partiality becomes harder to evaluate.

Notes

1. See https://ich.unesco.org
2. Quotation obtained from https://web.prm.ox.ac.uk/rpr/index.php/article-index/12-articles/427-pitt-rivers-on-collecting.html
3. It could be pointed out that the internet and the WWW are very much physical structures composed of cables, devices, transmitters, receivers and so on; but that is outside the scope of this chapter.

References

Brabham, Daren. 2008. Crowdsourcing as a Model for Problem Solving: An Introduction and Cases. *Convergence* 14(1): 75–90.

Brotton, Jerry. 2012. *A History of the World in 12 Maps*. London: Penguin.

Camden, William. 1701. *Britannia*. London: Joseph Wilde.

CIDOC CRM. 2021. Definition of the CIDOC Conceptual Reference Model, version 7.1.1, April 2021. Online at http://www.cidoc-crm.org/version/version-7.1.1 Accessed 30 March 2023.

Coffee, Kevin. 2007. Audience Research and the Museum Experience as Social Practice. *Museum Management and Curatorship* 22(4): 377–389.

Dunn, Stuart. 2019. *A History of Place in the Digital Age*. New York: Routledge.

Farman, Jason. 2010. Mapping the Digital Empire: Google Earth and the Process of Postmodern Cartography. *New Media & Society* 12(6): 869–888.

Heylyn, Peter. 1674. *Cosmography in Four Books Containing the Chorography and History of the Whole World*. London: Anne Seile & Philip Chetwind.

Hunter, Jane and Anna Gerber. 2010. Harvesting Community Annotations on 3D Models of Museum Artefacts to Enhance Knowledge, Discovery and Re-use. *Journal of Cultural Heritage* 11(1): 81–90.

Hyde, Ralph. 1972. What Future for Carto-Bibliography? *New Library World* (1972): 288–290.

Johnson, Steven. 2006. *The Ghost Map: A Street, an Epidemic and the Hidden Power of Urban Networks*. London: Penguin.

Lauriault, Tracey and Jeremy Wood. 2009. GPS Tracings – Personal Cartographies. *The Cartographic Journal* 46(4): 360–365.

Leszczynski, Agnieszka. 2014. On the Neo in Neogeography. *Annals of the Association of American Geographers* 104(1): 60–79.

Noble, Laura, Valentina Vavassori, Alan Crookham and Stuart Dunn. 2021. Networking the Archive: The Stories and Structures of Thos. Agnew's Stock Books. *ACM Journal on Computing and Cultural Heritage* 15(1): 1–14.

Ogilby, John. 1675. *Britannia, volume the first: Or, an illustration of the Kingdom of England and Dominion of Wales; by a geographical and historical description of the principal Roads thereof. Actually admeasured and delineated in a century of whole-sheet copper-sculps … By John Ogilby, Esqr; his Majesty's Cosmographer, etc.* London: John Ogilby.

Ortelius, Abraham. 1606. *Theatrum Orbis Terrarum*. Antwerp: John Norton, Printer to the King's Most Excellent Majestie in Hebrew, Greeke and Lataine.

Owens, Trevor. 2013. Digital Cultural Heritage and the Crowd. *Curator: The Museum Journal* 56(1): 121–130.

Pitt-Rivers, General Lane-Fox. 1875. Principles of Classification. *Journal of the Anthropological Institute* 4: 293–308.

Robinson, Arthur. 1997. The President's Globe. *Imago Mundi* 49(1): 143–152.

Shanks, Michael. 2008. Post-Processual Archaeology and After. In Alexander Bentley, Herbert Maschner and Christopher Chippindale (eds), *Handbook of Archaeological Theories*. London: Altamira Press: 133–144.

Stephens, Monica. 2013. Gender and the GeoWeb: Divisions in the Production of User-Generated Cartographic Information. *GeoJournal* 78(6): 981–996.

Winter, Tim. 2013. Clarifying the Critical in Critical Heritage Studies. *International Journal of Heritage Studies* 19(6): 532–545.

11
#Womenof1916 and the heritage of the Easter Rising on Twitter

Hannah K. Smyth

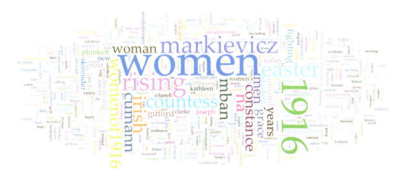

Figure 11.1 Word cloud of 'women of 1916' tweets. Generated using Voyant Tools (Sinclair and Rockwell 2016).

Introduction

This chapter focuses on the role of social media research in critical heritage studies. Empirically, it draws on research of Irish feminist commemoration on Twitter during the centenary of the 1916 Easter Rising in 2016. The chapter particularly aims to address broader questions of absence and presence and their relation to feminist methods in social media research and the future role of social media research in critical heritage studies. It draws on my doctoral thesis, which was carried out through the 'CHEurope' project (Smyth 2021). Firstly, I will introduce the research context and the 'Decade of Centenaries' within which this major commemorative moment took place and the feminist interventions it precipitated. I will then outline why I chose Twitter and the value it holds for critical heritage studies (CHS). Following on from this, I will summarise the methods used and some of the data access, ethics and privacy concerns that are paramount to any social media study, before moving on to some of the findings of my particular case study. I will conclude by returning to this reflection on the future of social media research for CHS.

The Decade of Centenaries (DoC) is a programme of national commemoration in the Republic of Ireland aiming to mark the events of 1912 to 1923 that shaped modern Ireland, in a 'tolerant, inclusive and respectful way' (Decade of Centenaries 2014). A feature of the DoC has also been the involvement of 'the public', that is to say those outside academia or professional heritage practice, in pluralising the history of the period to include diverse narratives, 'traditions', identities and new ways of exploring its heritage and legacy. The Expert Advisory Group for the centenaries programme declared that during this decade there would be an 'acknowledgement of the complexity of historical events and their legacy, of the multiple readings of history and of the multiple identities and traditions which are part of the Irish historical experience' (Expert Advisory Group on Centenary Commemorations 2020).

The hundredth anniversary of the 1916 Rising was the 'centerpiece' (Government of Ireland 2015: 6) of the DoC. Described as the 'key site of memory in twentieth century Ireland' (Daly and O'Callaghan 2014: 3), the 1916 Easter Rising was an armed rebellion against British colonial rule in Ireland. Militarily it was a failure, yet it sparked a series of events that led to the foundation of the 26-county Free State (later to become the Republic of Ireland in 1949) and the partitioning of six northern counties to become Northern Ireland, which remained in the United Kingdom. The most significant of these events were the 1918 'Sinn Féin' election that reshaped the political landscape, the War of Independence (1919–1921), the partitioning of Ireland in the Government of Ireland Act 1920, and the Anglo-Irish Treaty of 1921. Following the surrender of the 1916 insurgents, the swift trial and execution of 14 rebels at Kilmainham Gaol – including the seven signatories of the Proclamation of the Irish Republic – ensured that these men (and particularly the signatories) would become enshrined in the nationalist imagination, synonymous with the Rising and instantiating the 'ideals' of the nation. Women and their role in achieving independence – with around 300 taking part in the Easter Rising – were sidelined in Free State Ireland, and public commemoration of the Rising reflected this by focusing overwhelmingly on a small number of men, compounded by a comparative failure to capture and preserve the record of women's activism in the period.

During this commemorative decade, however, there has been a marked increase in research and publications on women and the revolution using new archival sources and particularly the digitised and freely available *Bureau of Military History (1916–1921)* (BMH)[1] and *Military Service (1916–1923) Pensions Collection* (MSPC),[2] as well as a trend towards biographies and individual stories in historical publications. A long process that began in the so-called 'revisionist' years of the 1970s and 1980s, this shift in the scholarly and public imagination is encapsulated by Crozier-De Rosa and Mackie, stating that, 'Female revolutionaries were written out of the national historical narrative in postcolonial Ireland, forming a repressed memory for almost seventy years, until feminist scholars resurrected their stories' (Crozier-De Rosa and Mackie 2018: 83).

The aforementioned BMH and MSPC collections have in no small way facilitated this acceleration of feminist research and discourse, not simply through their release to the public but through their digitisation and free availability and circulation online, including in social media spaces. Digitisation drives such as this both feed into and reflect the wider digitalising of pan-European cultural heritage (see Capurro, this volume), and are layered and value-laden acts of cultural production within and beyond commemorative agendas (Thylstrup 2018; Jensen 2021; Smyth 2022). Furthermore, the use of social media as an arena for critical debate and a spotlight on women's underrepresentation in Irish history was observed in the first half of the decade of commemorations (Casserly and O'Neill 2017: 11) and in a way that had not been possible in pre-social network anniversaries such as the 90th in 2006. The DoC was billed as a commemorative programme for 'digital natives' (Cronin 2018: 272) and social media was an active space for both 'official' and vernacular commemoration as well as for challenging authorised heritage, leaving behind a historical record of digital public engagement. Emblematic of this was the successful social media campaign in 2013, during the centenary of the 1913 Labour Lockout, to have a new tram bridge in Dublin city named after trade unionist, Irish Citizen Army activist and veteran of 1916, Rosie Hackett (The Rosie Hackett Bridge Campaign 2013).

In 2016, feminists continued to challenge exclusionary heritage and make historical women visible, evidenced by the data set collected for this study which retrieved over 45,000 tweets connected to the subject of the 'women of 1916'. If '1916' persists as the crucible of Irish national identity, social media provided a medium for engaging in a feminist critique of remembrance of the Easter Rising and of Irish history more broadly, a scholarly, public and political conversation that has not abated in the aftermath of the centenary. Commemoration, in this way, was also a reference point for critiquing the present. This study has thus traversed critical heritage, public history, digital history and digital humanities in order to illuminate how feminist discourse manifested online during the Irish commemorations. The following section will outline some of the key literature pertaining to this study and social media research in heritage more widely, setting out the value of Twitter for CHS.

Twitter for critical heritage studies

Twitter, a 'micro-blogging' social network platform, is now a commonplace tool of public communication but is also itself a source of information and a driver of debates. The extent to which Twitter has become embedded in everyday parlance in shaping other news media and public discourse demonstrates the cultural reach of the platform far beyond the boundaries of those who actually use it (Quan-Haase and McCay-Peet 2017). If it is no longer plausible to distinguish between offline and online (Richardson 2015; Miller et al. 2016: 7), this pervasiveness of social media in the contemporary world as a shaper of public discourse and as 'big data' offers clear potential for insights into the societies in which they are embedded (Cook 2012). Being 'suited for looking back in time pre- and post-critical events' (Schwartz and Ungar 2015: 90), Twitter lends itself to the study of clearly defined moments, communities, community formations or topics, a product of the codification of the hashtag and the retweet as aggregator and amplifier respectively. Reflecting this, hashtag feminism (and 'hashtag activism' more generally) 'appropriates Twitter's metadata tags for organising posts and public-by-default nature to draw visibility to a particular cause or experience' (Clark-Parsons 2019: 1–2). Unequivocally, Twitter has proved a vehicle for debate and the politics of visibility and recognition across numerous social issues in the past decade. Banet-Wiser defines the 'politics of visibility' as follows:

> The politics of visibility usually describes the process of making visible a political category (such as gender or race) that is and has been historically marginalised in the media, law, policy, and so on. This process involves what is simultaneously a category (visibility)

and a qualifier (politics) that can articulate a political identity. Representation, or visibility, takes on a political valence. Here, the goal is that the coupling of 'visibility' and 'politics' can be productive of something, such as social change, that exceeds the visibility (Banet-Wiser 2018: 22).

With this in mind, and given the affordances of the platform, it is not difficult to see how Twitter is suited to the study of critical heritage in practice, and significant commemorations in particular, with numerous examples regarding the commemoration of both recent and historical events (Paulsen 2013; Merrill 2019; Sumartojo 2020; Zamponi 2020). Clavert's work (Clavert 2018a, 2018b, 2021) on the commemoration of the First World War in France is, for example, one of the first longitudinal collections of tweet data specific to nationally and internationally significant commemorations, with several million tweets collected between 2014 and 2019 for the study of memory, historical transmission and temporalities through social networks. Interrogating transnational communication networks on the fifth anniversary of the Fukushima disaster, Rantasila et al. have been more concerned with the 'ritual discourse' of commemoration and importantly 'the potentially volatile relationship between the power of ritualising and the (counter) power of politicising the ritualised moment' that may be observed through commemoration on Twitter (Rantasila et al. 2018: 939). Such approaches have particular application for the entanglements between contemporary social tensions and heritage phenomena.

CHS is thus increasingly turning to social media spaces for insights into the ways in which societies remember, engage and challenge authorised heritage. Recent examples include Farrell-Banks' exploration of the Magna Carta – a document that holds iconic status in the British imaginary and notions of British collective memory and identity – in populist political discourse on Twitter during the anniversaries of its publication and of the Brexit referendum in June 2018, mapping this onto a typology of national identity (Farrell-Banks 2020). Bonacchi, Altaweel and Krzyzanska (2018) have applied digital humanities methods to capture and interrogate uses of the past – the 'pre-modern heritage' of Britain – to express political identities in activism around the Brexit referendum on Facebook. Bonacchi and Krzyzanska (2021) have further studied heritage-based tribalism on Twitter through the Cheddar Man DNA controversy and the deployment of ancestry and origin myths online. Both studies raise questions around 'the effects that diverse expert practices are having on the construction of specific messages, their circulation, proliferation and ultimate moulding into identities' (Bonacchi, Altaweel and Krzyzanska 2018: 172) as well as having profound implications for thinking through the shaping of 'collective memory'.

In this Irish case study, Twitter is therefore understood as a site of critical heritage and the expression of feminist identities, as well as an ephemeral record of critical engagement with the past in the present. While some have leaned on this characterisation of the internet itself as an enormous store of 'archival memory' or a digital archive, the meaning of 'archive' is loosely applied, a repository of things more than a collecting and ordering entity (de Groot 2009; Hoskins 2009; Reed 2014). In this way, social media platforms act as 'digital repositories' and play a 'de facto "archival role"', so characterised by Huvila (2015: 358), as they are incidental or semi-conscious, but also mass-accumulating as opposed to the formalised, selecting archive. Such data are, in this view, also forms of open-ended digital archives, akin to a 'living archive' (Hall 2001: 89) or a *milieu de mémoire*, in that they are continually accumulating and transforming, even as cultural institutions are capturing snapshots of the web in time for the future. As such, this research has traversed Twitter as both cultural data and cultural heritage in which the state, national cultural institutions and a historically conscious Irish public alike have a stake. Social media reflect the digitality of human interaction and 'imagined communities' (Anderson 2006) in postmodernity, bleeding into heritage politics. Tweets are thus 'ephemera of the everyday' (Samuel 2012: 27), yet they leave potent traces of experience and of a moment in time, ritual moments that are never engaged in uncritically.

Many memory institutions are now in the business of archiving social media, albeit in a highly selective way and often skewed towards official or governmental activities given the legal, ethical, preservation and access challenges that they pose as digital records. Such selectivity and reliance on more public platforms like Twitter, which cannot be taken as representative, indeed risks recreating problems of representation (Fondren and McCune 2018). Conversely, social media data sets are being independently collected for specific research and activist purposes (Catalog 2020). And despite preservation challenges, many also consider social media to be an integral aspect of their personal archives and evidence of their lives and particular perspectives on wider historical forces (Cannelli and Musso 2021; see also discussion by Elsherif 2021), as digital memorials in which 'nostalgia' and the meanings of heritage are negotiated among users of differing social and political imaginaries. Such data are thus not unproblematic artefacts of one heritage or another, a question CHS is equipped to deal with, but neither are they unencumbered by the practical and value-laden processes by which they are created, stored and later retrieved for inquiry.

Data access and ethics

Ever-changing limitations on social media research influence the kind of research that can be conducted, the kind of data we can collect and the kinds of questions we can ask. As Walker, Mercea and Bastos (2019: 1538) summarise, citing Boyd and Crawford (2012), there is a 'data access gap':

> between 'big data rich researchers', who have access to proprietary data and might be working in the interests of the company employing them, and the 'big data poor', or the broad universe of academic researchers whose findings may be of public interest but may ultimately be critical of social media platforms.

When I applied for a Twitter developer account in 2019, a requirement to utilise the premium application programming interfaces (APIs), my research intentions were deemed acceptable within the parameters set out by Twitter (Twitter Inc. 2020). Crucially, I was also later able to pay to draw down data, made possible through 'CHEurope' project funding that also supported a paid collaboration with my UCL colleague Diego Echavarría Ramírez. While I was carrying out this research, tweet data from more than seven days in the past was only available by recourse to a data purchase, and the aforementioned tendency towards topic-based Twitter research has been due in part to the restrictions on historical data collection that Twitter imposed (Boyd and Crawford 2012: 666). Twitter announced in January 2021 that free access to the full historical tweet archive would be permitted for bona fide academic researchers. This partial liberalisation of the Twitter API would, however, be short-lived; in October 2022 Twitter was acquired by the business magnate Elon Musk, a takeover which heralded numerous changes to the platform, including the ending of free API access for researchers. A new set of access tiers, announced in March 2023, means that, at the time of writing, scalable research using the API will be unaffordable for most researchers (Coalition for Independent Technology Research, 2023).[3] Developments such as this speak directly to wider concerns over a 'rapidly changing and hostile data environment' (Walker, Mercea and Bastos 2019: 1531) regarding internet research as it pertains to digital heritage. Beyond

Twitter, the 'data access gap' continues to deepen across internet cultures and social media companies,[4] with differential access between researchers (Perriam, Birkbak and Freeman 2020).

In tandem with questions of access is the 'ethics turn in social media' (Rogers 2018: 558) and the tightening of data protection regulations – safeguarding and legal privacy measures that guide how findings can be presented so as to minimise participant harm. That tweets are considered public information 'by default' when agreeing to terms of service, unless otherwise restricted through the user privacy settings, cannot be equated with unfettered mass consent (Boyd and Crawford 2012). What is legal is not always ethical and we must respect the same principles of consent, anonymity and harm avoidance as we would in any other sociological study involving human participants (Ahmed, Bath and Demartini 2017). The findings of this study have been reported in aggregation, without direct quotes, or have been significantly reworded.[5] Consent may be obtained for individual tweets, but such a mechanism should be built into the ethics committee application and into data management and research plans before undertaking data collection, as it requires thinking through the long-term implications of directly quoting an individual and their ongoing right to rescind consent.

Methods

With the caveat that 'access' remains contingent, Twitter was, at the time that this research was conducted, one of the more open social media platforms for retrieving data for heritage research (Walker, Mercea and Bastos 2019), underscoring its utility for CHS. Diego and I used Python to create a programme to retrieve data from 2016 via the Twitter Premium API and for data cleaning and processing. The keyword query that was used was created to capture, as widely as possible, tweets referring to women, 1916, and the Irish commemorations, as opposed to a much more general data set of commemorative tweets for that year. This returned around 45,000 tweets from the period August 2015 to December 2016 and around 10,000 original tweets after removing retweets.

An abundance of Twitter studies rely exclusively on big-data-driven modelling and network analysis; increasingly there are calls to balance this with more qualitative methods of analysis (Rantasila et al. 2018) and I have brought this to bear upon this data set of commemorative tweets. It became clear to me that 'meaning' could not be derived from this data set through modelling, visualisations and frequencies alone, although

MS Excel, Voyant Tools (Sinclair and Rockwell 2016) and Gephi were used to explore the data and to generate word frequencies, time-series charts and illustrative visualisations such as hashtag co-occurrences and retweet networks.

The principal approach was to code tweets into major themes emerging from the data for qualitative thematic analysis using NVivo (https://lumivero.com/products/nvivo/). Nvivo is a 'qualitative computing' software package that supports the exploration, organisation, annotation, indexing and coding of qualitative data. By iterating through keyword frequency queries in Nvivo, tweets were aggregated into 'nodes'. Coding was overall inductive, as well as adding some relevant tweets ad hoc, with labels assigned *in vivo*. Not every tweet was coded to a node; rather, this process continued until a saturation point was reached, that is to say, when no new tweets relevant to my research aims remained to be coded. These nodes were added to, revised and rearranged into larger nodes and subnodes, eventually amalgamating into five major areas of interest, with conceptual labels assigned to capture the overarching concepts of the emergent themes. These were 'Historical Information', 'Centenary Commentary', 'Absence', 'Affect' and 'Equality'. (For an extended account of the methods and programming code used to retrieve and process tweets, see Smyth and Ramírez Echavarría 2021.)

The themes of 'Historical Information' and 'Centenary Commentary' accounted for the largest portion of tweets in this data set. These were much more generalised statements and repeated similar phrasing, information and sentiments, reflecting also what Rantasila et al. describe as the 'ritual discourse' of commemoration (2018: 939). 'Centenary Commentary' also reflected an official discourse of commemoration, which by its nature focuses on the more positive sentiments of pride and honour. 'Historical Information' reflected the huge amount of scholarship, digital history projects, exhibitions, theatre productions and so on that appeared in the lead-up to or during this centenary year. A smaller theme, 'Affect', was assigned to tweets expressing affective responses, feelings of inspiration, connection and identification with the women of 1916 and their recognition in the official commemorations. 'Equality' was assigned to tweets that were most explicitly making connections between commemoration, feminism and nation and referencing present-day equality struggles like the #WakingTheFeminists and #RepealThe8th movements.[6]

Together the larger themes of 'Historical Information' and 'Centenary Commentary', though more formulaic in nature, were essential to *making visible* the women of 1916 through information diffusion and statements of recognition on Twitter, as elaborated on elsewhere (Smyth and Ramírez Echavarría 2021). I will now briefly focus on the subtheme of 'Absence', as it resonates particularly with my broader thesis, introduced above, on the digitisation of heritage archives that have been centrally implicated in a wider politics of representation in the Irish commemorations.

Absence

'Absence' resonates particularly with recent developments in the historiography of the Irish Revolution vis-à-vis the role of women, the 'democratisation' of the archives in this heightened commemorative period and the wider phenomenon of commemorating 'absent heritage' in late modernity (Harrison 2013: 169). Harrison describes the latter as 'the memorialisation of places and objects whose significance relates to their destruction or absence' that 'has developed as a significant global cultural phenomenon in which the visual and aesthetic language of heritage conservation is applied to the conservation of voids or absent spaces to maintain an "absent presence"' (Harrison 2013: 169). This 'absent heritage' can be extended to the memorialisation of subaltern/marginalised groups, for which heritage is a tool to self-define and reclaim power (Smith 2006; Cifor and Wood 2017). The approach to representation in this chapter also incorporates Bergsdóttir and Hafsteinsson's (2018) eschewing of an absence–presence binary in favour of absence as a 'relational entity' with presence regarding the marginalisation of women in heritage institutions and collections. Just as remembering is contingent on forgetting, absences, the authors contend, are integral to our understanding of what is present, or seen, in turn shaping our understandings of masculinity and femininity, and therefore having ethical implications; absence, in other words, is a political and affective matter (Bergsdóttir and Hafsteinsson 2018).

The obfuscation and 'domestication' of revolutionary nationalist women and their memory has elsewhere been shown for its role in constructing the image of the postcolonial, paternalistic Irish nation state (Crozier-De Rosa and Mackie 2018), highlighting the ways in which absence upholds patriarchal histories and shapes social roles (Smith 2008). Equally, their rediscovery demonstrates that absence is not a fixed state. Rather, absence in this way can be understood, not as a nothingness, but as having critical agency in the world (Bergsdóttir and Hafsteinsson 2018). As such, the sub-discourse of 'absence' in these commemorative tweets was tied to both restorative history-making and a feminist 'politics of visibility' in the present, with 'equality' being the 'social change' that might be produced by this practice.

The presence of absence and the tension between remembering and forgetting were recurrent in the tweets coded in this theme, with terms like 'forgotten', 'airbrushed', 'silencing', 'erasure', 'exclusion', 'hidden', 'airbrushed' and 'airbrushing' that were countered by or coexisted with words like 'herstory', 'remember' and 'recognition' (Figure 11.2). The repeated use of 'airbrushed' and 'airbrushing' demonstrates the extent to which the Elizabeth O'Farrell incident continued to be a popular leitmotif for the marginalisation of women in remembrance of the Rising. Some used variations of the term 'éirebrushed' (Ireland-brushed) to convey the particular Irishness of this silencing. These are also in reference to a theatre production of the same name that dramatised 'the untold story of the revolutionary lesbian and gay heroes of 1916 that have been airbrushed from our history until now' in May 2016, with reference to Elizabeth O'Farrell and Eva Gore-Booth as well as male rebels whose sexuality has been reappraised (The 13th International Dublin Gay Theatre Festival 2020). The centenary of the Easter Rising occurred less than a year after a historic referendum on marriage equality in the Republic, a campaign that had pushed forward the discourse on non-normative sexuality and

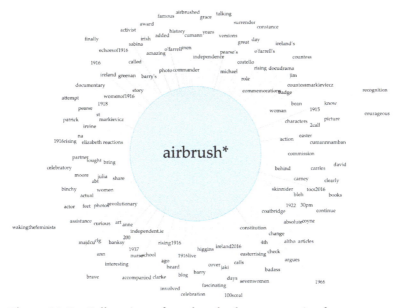

Figure 11.2 Collocations of words or hashtags stemming from 'airbrush'. Generated using Voyant Tools (Sinclair and Rockwell 2016).

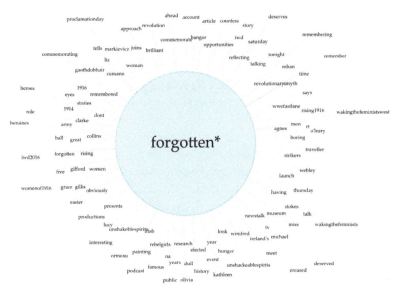

Figure 11.3 Collocations of words or hashtags stemming from 'forgotten'. Generated using Voyant Tools (Sinclair and Rockwell 2016).

in which the Irish Proclamation and its language of equality had been recalled, as so often it is in public debates on social issues in the Republic.

'Erasure' of women was further framed by some as a century of marginalisation and being actively 'written out', with many tweets commenting specifically on the relationship between Irish historiography and absence, and how women and their roles in 1916 were excluded from the historical narrative and 'communal memory'. There was repeated commentary on the 'forgotten' women, 'forgotten' stories and 'roles' of women in the Rising (Figure 11.3). The duty to remember and not to forget was communicated in many tweets, as were assertions about 'recapturing' and 'revealing' these 'untold', 'hidden' and 'unofficial' narratives or '#Herstory', reinstating women in revolutionary history. While some expressed dismay at this history of 'forgetting', statements were more often couched in active remembrance and celebration. During an official state ceremony to commemorate the women of 1916 that was held on International Women's Day, a section of a speech made by the President of Ireland at this event was quoted or referenced in several tweets:

> May I start by paying tribute to those historians who have so diligently documented the vital part that women played in the struggle for Irish freedom, thus ensuring that those who were long

described as 'the forgotten women of 1916' are not forgotten any more (Higgins 2016).

Tweets surrounding this event and #InternationalWomensDay were characterised by affective expressions of pride and honour, of feeling 'inspired' by the activism of these historical women and their official recognition. Gender equality being an implicit imperative in this international day to celebrate women, it was also explicitly connected to the acknowledgement of these women in the national heritage with references like #womenofcourage, #inclusion, #hero, #equality4all, #genderequity and #inspiringwomen. That at last the women of 1916 were 'no longer forgotten' was a phrase taken up elsewhere in media representations of their rehabilitation and ongoing critique of the integration of gender histories and feminist scholarship (Ward 2016; McAuliffe 2021).

As is evident from this vignette, 'absence' intersected with discourses of national pride and of feminism that were also manifest in the themes of 'affect' and 'equality'. The spectre of historical absence was mobilised in this space, recognising and critiquing the gendered silences of the archives, of historiography and of previous commemorations. Yet, the presencing of a once absent, feminist heritage was also framed through the ritual discourse of authorising commemoration even as it was interwoven with present-centred discourses of women's equality.

Conclusion

Twitter is a space for 'the performance of remembrance culture' (Pine 2011: 3), whether private, public, individual or collective, and for politicised engagement with heritage. Reflecting on this Irish decade of remembrance, McGarry has suggested that more than 'simply re-enacting the past, the most successful forms of commemoration allow for its energies to illuminate the possibility of alternative futures' (2016: xiv), echoing present discourses that emphasise future-making heritage imaginaries (Harrison et al. 2020). While the DoC has reaffirmed the fundamental position of the 1916 Easter Rising in the story of the nation, it has also broadened the possibilities for, indeed authorised, other historical moments, narratives or figures to act as explorations of Irishness. As this chapter has demonstrated, the heritage of 1916 was mobilised not only in the digitisation of prestige archives but also in social media discourses around the politics of gender and national identity with dialectics of absence, presence, visibility and questions of 'whose heritage?' (Hall 1999) carrying through in this space from the perspective of an engaged public.

Drawing on these experiences of empirical research utilising historical Twitter data to study Irish feminist commemoration of the centenary of the Easter Rising in 2016, this chapter has further aimed to draw attention to the significance of social media for research in heritage studies and to the ways in which social media data itself might be considered to be a form of heritage. It has also drawn attention to the ways in which the control of access to such data raises significant issues both in terms of researcher privilege and the always uncertain future of this type of critical digital heritage research. As with 'the archives', who controls but also who has access to data raises questions about the perpetuation of authorised/authorising narratives, which is as much an ethical concern as the prevention of participant harm and one that reflects on the theme of absence and the politics of representation that this case study has addressed.

Notes

1. https://www.militaryarchives.ie/collections/online-collections/bureau-of-military-history-1913-1921
2. https://www.militaryarchives.ie/en/collections/online-collections/military-service-pensions-collection-1916-1923
3. As outlined in an open letter to Twitter from a coalition of journalists, academics, researchers and community scientists in April 2023: 'The Basic tier costs $100 per month but allows researchers to collect only 10,000 tweets per month – a mere 0.3% of what could previously be collected for free in one day. The Enterprise tier, which ranges from $42,000 to $210,000 per month, is unaffordable for researchers' (Coalition for Independent Technology Research 2023).
4. For a useful overview of such restrictive actions in recent years by social media corporations and apparent moves towards a 'post-API environment', see Perriam, Birkbak and Freeman 2020.
5. Exceptions were made in this case study for publicly funded entities or verified accounts. Verified 'blue-tick' accounts are deemed to be in the public interest.
6. #WakingTheFeminists was a response to the male-dominated centenary programme announced by the National Theatre, The Abbey, in November 2015. The 'Repeal' movement sought to liberalise restrictive abortion laws in the Republic by removing the eighth amendment to the Irish Constitution (Bunreacht na h'Éireann).

References

Ahmed, Wasim, Peter Bath and Gianluca Demartini. 2017. Using Twitter as a Data Source: An Overview of Ethical, Legal and Methodological Challenges. In Kandy Woodfield (ed.), *The Ethics of Online Research*. Bingley: Emerald Publishing Limited: 79–107.

Anderson, Benedict. 2006. *Imagined Communities: Reflections on the Origin and Spread of Nationalism*. Rev. ed. London: Verso.

Banet-Weiser, Sarah. 2018. *Empowered: Popular Feminism and Popular Misogyny*. Durham, NC: Duke University Press.

Bergsdóttir, Arndis and Sigurjon Baldur Hafsteinsson. 2018. The Fleshyness of Absence: The Matter of Absence in Feminist Museology. In Wera Grahn and Ross Wilson (eds), *Gender and Heritage: Performance, Power and Place*. London and New York: Routledge: 99–112.

Bonacchi, Chiara, Mark Altaweel and Marta Krzyzanska. 2018. The Heritage of Brexit: Roles of the Past in the Construction of Political Identities Through Social Media. *Journal of Social Archaeology* 18(2): 1–19.

Bonacchi, Chiara and Marta Krzyzanska. 2021. Heritage-Based Tribalism in Big Data Ecologies: Deploying Origin Myths for Antagonistic Othering. *Big Data and Society* 8(1). https://doi.org/10.1177/20539517211003310

Boyd, Danah and Kate Crawford. 2012. Critical Questions for Big Data: Provocations for A Cultural, Technological and Scholarly Phenomenon. *Information Communication and Society* 15(5): 662–679.

Cannelli, Beatrice and Marta Musso. 2021. Social Media as Part of Personal Digital Archives: Exploring Users' Practices and Service Providers' Policies Regarding the Preservation of Digital Memories. *Archival Science* 22(2): 259–283.

Casserly, Maeva and Ciaran O'Neill. 2017. Public History, Invisibility and Women in the Republic of Ireland. *The Public Historian* 39(2): 10–30.

Catalog. 2020. *Documenting the Now*. Online at https://catalog.docnow.io/ Accessed 20 September 2020.

Cifor, Marika and Stacy Wood. 2017. Critical Feminism in the Archives. *Journal of Critical Library and Information Studies* 1(2): 1–27.

Clark-Parsons, Rosemary. 2019. "I SEE YOU, I BELIEVE YOU, I STAND WITH YOU": #MeToo and the Performance of Networked Feminist Visibility. *Feminist Media Studies* 21(3): 362–380.

Clavert, Frédéric. 2018a. Commémorations, Scandale et Circulation de l'Information: Le Centenaire de la Bataille de Verdun sur Twitter. *French Journal for Media Research. Special Issue: Le web 2.0: lieux de perception des transformations des sociétés*, 10. Online at http://french journalformediaresearch.com/lodel-1.0/main/index.php?id=1620 Accessed 6 April 2023.

Clavert, Frédéric. 2018b. Temporalités du Centenaire de la Grande Guerre sur Twitter. In Valérie Schafer (ed.), *Temps et Temporalités du Web*. Nanterre: Presses Universitaires de Paris Nanterre: 113–134.

Clavert, Frédéric. 2021. History in the Era of Massive Data. *Geschichte und Gesellschaft* 47(1): 175–194.

Coalition for Independent Technology Research. 2023. Letter: Twitter's New API Plans Will Devastate Public Interest Research. 3 April. Online at https://independenttechresearch.org/letter-twitters-new-api-plans-will-devastate-public-interest-research/ Accessed 20 April 2023.

Cook, Terry. 2012. Evidence, Memory, Identity and Community: Four Shifting Archival Paradigms. *Archival Science* 13(2–3): 95–120.

Cronin, Mike. 2018. Irish History Online and in Real Time: Century Ireland and the Decade of Centenaries. *Éire-Ireland* 52(1): 269–284.

Crozier-De Rosa, Sharon and Vera Mackie. 2018. *Remembering Women's Activism*. 1st ed. London: Routledge.

Daly, Mary and Margaret O'Callaghan. 2014. Introduction: Irish Modernity and 'the Patriot Dead' in 1966. In Mary Daly and Margaret O'Callaghan (eds), *1916 in 1966: Commemorating the Easter Rising*. Dublin: Royal Irish Academy: 1–17.

Decade of Centenaries. 2014. *Decade of Centenaries via Internet Archive*. Online at https://wayback.archive-it.org/all/20141011183618/http://www.decadeofcentenaries.com/ Accessed 7 April 2021.

Elsherif, Nermin. 2021. The City of al-Zaman al-Gamîl: (A)political Nostalgia and the Imaginaries of an Ideal Nation. *Égypte/Monde arabe* 23: 61–79. https://doi.org/10.4000/ema.14749

Expert Advisory Group on Centenary Commemorations. 2020. Initial Statement by Advisory Group on Centenary Commemorations. *Decade of Centenaries*. Online at https://www.decadeofcentenaries.com/wp-content/uploads/publications/Initial/Initial/index.html Accessed 27 August 2020.

Farrell-Banks, David. 2020. 1215 in 280 Characters: Talking About Magna Carta on Twitter. In Areti Galani, Rhiannon Mason and Gabi Arrigoni (eds), *European Heritage, Dialogue and Digital Practices*. London and New York: Routledge: 86–106.

Fondren, Elizabeth and Megan McCune. 2018. Archiving and Preserving Social Media at the Library of Congress: Institutional and Cultural Challenges to Build a Twitter Archive. *Preservation, Digital Technology and Culture* 47 (2): 33–44.

Government of Ireland. 2015. *Centenary Programme*. Dublin.

de Groot, Jerome. 2009. *Consuming History: Historians and Heritage in Contemporary Popular Culture*. London: Routledge.

Hall, Stuart. 1999. Whose Heritage? *Museums Journal* 13(49): 3–13.

Hall, Stuart. 2001. Constituting an Archive. *Third Text* 15(54): 89–92.

Harrison, Rodney. 2013. *Heritage: Critical Approaches*. London and New York: Routledge.

Harrison, Rodney, Caitlin DeSilvey, Cornelius Holtorf, Sharon Macdonald, Nadia Bartolini, Esther Breithoff, Harald Fredheim, Antony Lyons, Sarah May, Jennie Morgan and Sefryn Penrose. 2020. *Heritage Futures: Comparative Approaches to Natural and Cultural Heritage Practices*. London: UCL Press.

Higgins, Michael. 2016. Speech at an Event to Commemorate the Role of Women in the 1916 Easter Rising. *President of Ireland*. Online at https://president.ie/en/media-library/speeches/speech-by-president-michael-d.-higgins-to-commemorate-the-role-of-women-in Accessed 6 April 2023.

Hoskins, Andrew. 2009. Digital Network Memory. In Astrid Erll and Ann Rigney (eds), *Mediation, Remediation and the Dynamics of Cultural Memory*. New York: De Gruyter: 91–108.

Huvila, Isto. 2015. The Unbearable Lightness of Participating? Revisiting the Discourses of 'participation' in Archival Literature. *Journal of Documentation* 71(2): 358–386.

Jensen, Helle Strangaard. 2021. Digital Archival Literacy for (all) Historians. *Media History* 27(2): 251–265.

McAuliffe, Mary. 2021. Remembered for Being Forgotten. In Oona Frawley (ed.), *Women and the Decade of Commemorations*. Bloomington: Indiana University Press: 22–40.

McGarry, Fearghal. 2016. *The Rising in Ireland: Easter 1916*. 2nd ed. Oxford: Oxford University Press.

Merrill, Samuel. 2019. Walking Together? The Mediatised Performative Commemoration of 7/7's Tenth Anniversary. *Journalism* 20(10): 1360–1378.

Miller, Daniel, Elisabetta Costa, Nell Haynes, Tom McDonald, Razvan Nicolescu, Jolynna Sinanan, Juliano Spyer, Shriram Venkatraman and Xinyuan Wang. 2016. *How The World Changed Social Media*. London: UCL Press.

Paulsen, Martin. 2013. #Holodomor: Twitter and Public Discourse in Ukraine. In Julie Fedor, Ellen Rutten and Vera Zvereva (eds), *Memory, Conflict and New Media: Web Wars in Post-Socialist States*. New York: Routledge: 82–98.

Perriam, Jessamy, Andreas Birkbak and Andy Freeman. 2020. Digital Methods in a Post-API Environment. *International Journal of Social Research Methodology* 23(3): 277–290. https://doi.org/10.1080/13645579.2019.1682840

Pine, Emilie. 2011. *The Politics of Irish Memory: Performing Remembrance in Contemporary Irish Culture*. Basingstoke: Palgrave Macmillan.

Quan-Haase, Anabel and Lori McCay-Peet. 2017. What is Social Media and What Questions Can Social Media Research Help Us Answer? In Luke Sloan and Anabel Quan-Haase (eds), *The SAGE Handbook of Social Media Research Methods*. London: SAGE Publications: 13–26.

Rantasila, Anna, Anu Sirola, Arto Kekkonen, Katja Valaskivi and Risto Kunelius. 2018. #Fukushima Five Years On: A Multimethod Analysis of Twitter on the Anniversary of the Nuclear Disaster. *International Journal Of Communication* 12: 928–949.

Reed, Barbara. 2014. Reinventing Access. *Archives and Manuscripts* 42(2): 123–132.

Richardson, Lorna-Jane. 2015. Micro-Blogging and Online Community. *Internet Archaeology*: 39. https://doi.org/10.11141/ia.39.2

Rogers, Richard. 2018. Social Media Research After the Fake News Debacle. *Partecipazione e Conflitto* 11(2): 557–570.

Samuel, Raphael. 2012. *Theatres of Memory: Past and Present in Present Culture*. New York: Verso.

Schwartz, Andrew and Lyle Ungar. 2015. Data-Driven Content Analysis of Social Media: A Systematic Overview of Automated Methods. *Annals of the American Academy of Political and Social Science* 659(1): 78–94.

Sinclair, Stéfan and Geoffrey Rockwell. 2016. Voyant Tools. Online at https://voyant-tools.org/ Accessed for use 2020.

Smith, Laurajane. 2006. *Uses of Heritage*. London and New York: Routledge.

Smith, Laurajane. 2008. Heritage, Gender and Identity. In Brian Graham and Peter Howard (eds), *The Ashgate Research Companion to Heritage and Identity*. Abington: Routledge: 159–178.

Smyth, Hannah. 2021. *Digital Archives and the Irish Commemorative Impulse: Gender, Identity and Digital Cultural Heriatge* [Unpublished doctoral thesis]. University College London.

Smyth, Hannah K. 2022. 'Permanent Reminders': Digital Archives and the Irish Commemorative Impulse. *Éire-Ireland* 57(1–2): 166–188. https://doi.org/10.1353/eir.2022.0008

Smyth, Hannah and Diego Ramírez Echavarría. 2021. Twitter and Feminist Commemoration of the 1916 Easter Rising. *Journal of Digital History* 1(1): 142–167. https://doi.org/10.1515/jdh-2021-1006 or https://journalofdigitalhistory.org/en/article/SLCj9T3MsrEk

Sumartojo, Shanti. 2020. Tweeting from the Past: Commemorating the Anzac Centenary @ABCNews1915. *Memory Studies* 13(4): 400–415.

The 13th International Dublin Gay Theatre Festival. 2016. *International Dublin Gay Theatre Festival*. Online at http://www.gaytheatre.ie/wp-content/uploads/2016/04/Brochure_2016_Web.pdf Accessed 6 April 2023.

The Rosie Hackett Bridge Campaign – The Rediscovery of a Forgotten History by Angelina Cox, 2013. *Labour via Internet Archive*. Online at https://web.archive.org/web/20140307190506/http://www.labour.ie/blog/2013/09/03/the-rosie-hackett-bridge-campaign-the-rediscovery/ Accessed 1 April 2023.

Thylstrup, Nanna Bonde. 2018. *The Politics of Mass Digitization*. Cambridge and London: MIT Press.

Twitter Inc. 2020. Developer Agreement and Policy. *Twitter Developers*. Online at https://developer.twitter.com/en/developer-terms/agreement-and-policy Accessed 19 February 2020.

Walker, Shawn, Dan Mercea and Marco Bastos. 2019. The Disinformation Landscape and the Lockdown of Social Platforms. *Information Communication and Society* 22(11): 1531–1543.

Ward, Margaret. 2016. No Longer Forgotten: Women Activists From The Decade of Centenaries. *The Irish Times*, 1 December.

Zamponi, Lorenzo. 2020. #ioricordo, Beyond the Genoa G8: Social Practices of Memory Work and the Digital Remembrance of Contentious Pasts in Italy. In Samuel Merrill, Emily Keightley and Priska Daphi (eds), *Social Movements, Cultural Memory and Digital Media: Mobilising Mediated Remembrance*. Berlin: Springer Nature: 141–171.

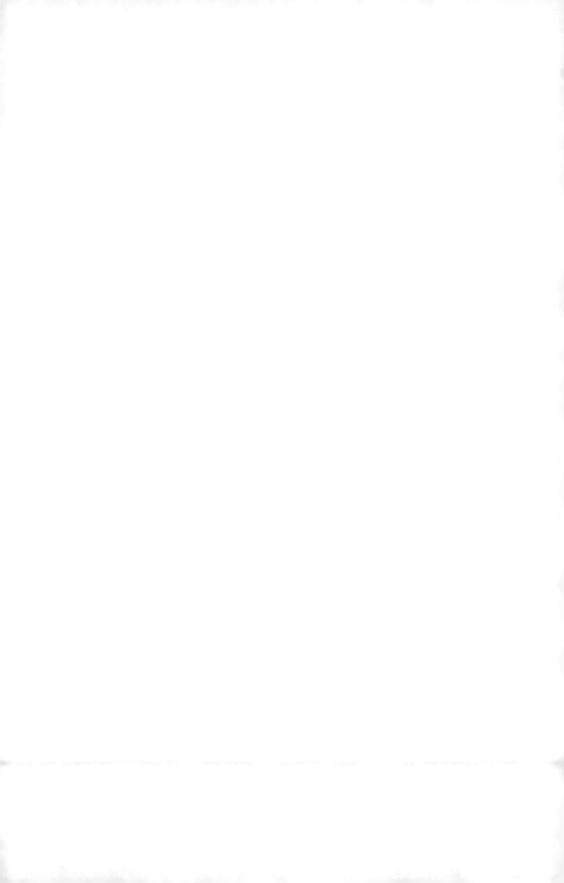

12
The material and immaterial historic environment
William Illsley

Introduction

In the social spaces of human activity, the historic environment is unavoidable, whether explicitly in the flesh and bones of heritage nomenclature, or tacitly and unacknowledged in the spaces and places through which we partake in our quotidian pursuits. Conceptually, however, the historic environment is often limited by practice and the structures and definitions applied in the processes of heritage management. While it frequently finds its way into cultural legislation (Ministry of Housing 2019; Riksdagen 2016), policy documents and practice guidelines (Baker 1977), English practice rarely achieves the broadness, community value and understanding it is assumed to have. Indeed, as Emma Waterton demonstrates, within Historic England the historic environment is not only understood to be a widely comprehended term, but also one that is inherently inclusive (Waterton 2010: 180).

For all its spatial ubiquity, the terminology and what it denotes is often poorly conceived in heritage terms. It is therefore within this context that this chapter is developed, elaborating upon the relationship between historic environment practice and heritage experience in England. Under scrutiny is the scope of the authorised and legitimised heritage praxis tied to planning and development, which alongside tourism is one of the primary drivers of the country's heritage industry. Against this background, the archaeological hegemonisation of the historic environment record in landscape terms will be explored, taking into account the manner in which current practice can be problematised through the lens of critical heritage studies. In view of this, the aim is to offer an alternative definition of the historic environment.

Further to this, there is the consideration of how this is motivated regarding digitality, both technologically and epistemologically. As a facet of heritage production, that is, 'any activity, occurring online or offline, as part of which human or non-human agents engage with the past' (Bonacchi and Krzyzanska 2019: 1237), digital heritage often bears resemblance to familiar, analogue practice in actualising the material content of the historic environment. However, in realising its full heuristic and hermeneutic potential, digitality affords the conditions for how knowledge is produced and presented (Ingvarsson 2020: 9). Remediating heritage in a digital format not only has tendencies for blurring the lines between users and creators, but also emphasises that heritage processes not only enact different realities, but also assemble different futures (Harrison 2016: 171).

Background

This chapter is coupled with my doctoral research, and the case studies therein assessing digitally accessible historic environments as a means of accessing heritage. In assessing the relationship between the historic environment and heritage, it should be clearly discerned what heritage is and what it is not. Heritage, as determined in this instance, follows Rodney Harrison's approach, defining it as a set of current attitudes and values 'formed as a result of the relationships between people and other human and non-human actors, relating to "objects, places and practices"' (Harrison 2013: 14). Heritage itself does not simply exist as a *de facto* somatic phenomenon or social behaviour' (Russell 2010: 29). Nor is it, therefore, purely tangible objects with latent value – an approach rooted firmly in the material realm. Despite this, there is a degree to which heritage is still deeply enmeshed in material culture and requires 'tangible places and objects' to 'mobilise identifications, significations and memorialisation' (Meskell 2015: 1). This requires a consistent gateway for accessibility. In this context, by abstracting historic and cultural resources within the landscape as a singular concept, the historic environment and its inventorisation through historic environment records (HERs) represents an ongoing mediation between material culture and the mobilisation of its value through the stewardship of historic environment data.

As well as considering heritage itself, the alternatives to the historic environment on an international level should be briefly discussed. As Peter Howard points out, UNESCO utilises the term 'cultural landscape', which he notes is largely accepted at international level (Howard

2009: 51). Landscapes, however, are often poorly defined and diffuse, in terms of both their physical boundaries and cultural boundedness (Denham 2017: 464), to the extent that the term 'cultural' is omitted from the European Landscape Convention. As a matter of perception, both locally and extra-locally, the landscape according to the Council of Europe has evolved 'through time as a result of being acted upon by natural forces and human beings' (Council of Europe 2021). By extension, all landscapes are to be considered 'cultural' in some way or another (Howard 2009: 51). What the convention has engendered, however, which is not truly applicable to the processes of the HER, is a shift towards the vernacular perspective and democratised participation (Howard 2009: 53). More than 20 years has passed since Stuart Hall (1999) published 'Whose Heritage? Un-settling "the Heritage", Re-imagining the Post-nation', yet analyses of heritage audiences, practices and practitioners reveals that heritage remains largely associated with ruling and middle-class white histories (Holmes-Skelton 2019: 370).

In disciplinary terms, the field of landscape archaeology is closely tied to the historic environment concept and how it is utilised. According to Tim Denham, landscape archaeology 'can be considered to be the study of artifacts, features, sites and site complexes within the broader spatial realms – both physical and meaningful – of past human experience' (Denham 2017: 465). This clearly has valid and apparent value in the heritage dynamic. However, inasmuch as there is undoubtedly an archaeological heritage in relation to the landscape – in essence the places, sites and artefacts and their vital material essence within an archaeological framework – it is not one necessarily commensurate with a wider definition of heritage as a whole (Waterton and Smith 2009: 5, 24).

Importantly, landscapes have frequently been revisited critically, particularly in the context of representativity and constructivism (Wickstead 2009). As yet, it cannot be said to be entrenched in the historic environment sector, despite frequently cross-examining the same source materials. Through the examination of the approaches of HERs in the English heritage sector, this chapter rejects the emphasis placed on fidelity to material landscapes by the planning sector via the National Planning Policy Framework (NPPF) and argues for greater recognition of the abstract and the intangible in the historic environment sector. Against the disposition that the current approach lacks an element of public discourse, the primary question is one of how digitally remediating HERs has the potential to broaden public knowledge and communicate heritage if the historic environment is determined to be a more abstract point of contact with the landscape.

Defining a historic environment

Conventionally managed by local government authorities, regional and urban level HERs are the foremost source of historic environment data in England, ahead of even Historic England's National Heritage List for England. It is through the performative process of compiling gazetteers and the association with HER data that legitimate archaeological interest in spaces with no known archaeological features is advanced. However, the record is not consistent with the historic environment itself, nor can one be comprehensive and remain outside of the historic environment. But what then constitutes the historic environment? Unlike the record, the historic environment is actualised, and has been occupied by human actors continually. One could go so far as to argue that it is a vital component of what makes space a place. But its definitions often limit themselves firmly within the realm of physical expression in the landscape. In England, the NPPF definition reigns king in terms of the utility of the term in functional practice and is the definition adopted by Historic England:

> All aspects of the environment resulting from the interaction between people and places through time, including all surviving physical remains of past human activity, whether visible, buried or submerged, and landscaped and planted or managed flora (Ministry of Housing 2019).

Timothy Darvill (2009) adds the clause 'and its associations' to the physical evidence of the past, perhaps extending the relationship to the non-physical realm but without truly offering legitimacy to the intangible elements of an environment. Problematically, Darvill also references that the explicit (UK) government usage of the term 'historic environment' is in preference to, or at least synonymous with, the term 'heritage'.

Yet the broader cultural connections to historic environments, and indeed place, are not limited to the places themselves. Representations of historic environments through music, art and literature are frequently inspired by and inspire connection to place in return, yet rarely feature in the recording process associated with HERs. Scotland takes an explicitly broader approach to defining historic environments:

> The historic environment belongs to all of us. It's part of our everyday lives. It shapes our identity. It tells us about the past, the present – and even points the way to the future.

But what is the historic environment? We see it as everything that has been created by people over time: the tangible and the intangible. It can be a place, an object, or an idea. It can be a castle, a ruined abbey, or a stone circle; a high street, a colliery or a garden; a book, an instrument – even a song or a piece of music. It's all those things that we've made, all the way up to today (Scotland's Environment 2020).

In the overall context of this PhD study, English practice is used in a comparative case study against the state-sponsored practices in Sweden. Like the Scottish one, the Swedish definition of the historic environment (*kulturmiljö*) goes beyond the material realms, specifically referencing place names (*ortnamn*) and legends/traditions (*sägner*) that are bound to places or areas (*knutna till en plats eller ett område*; Riksantikvarieämbetet 2021). While the Scottish definition has advanced beyond the definition of landscape archaeology and at least factors the present into contention, it strays uncomfortably close to a synonymous term for heritage. Nor does either the Scottish or the Swedish definition evidence any particular theoretical nuance. Thus, for my own research purposes, I have adhered to an alternative reading of the historic environment, which is as follows:

The historic environment is an assemblage defined by a common, collective and abstract space, wherein human actors interact with non-human places, objects and things – where indeed, heritage itself is negotiated. Much like the concept of heritage, the appearance of the historic environment is contingent to the means through which it is accessed, yet fulfils heterotopic criteria, in the sense that it is superficially resemblant of the spaces we recognise in the cultural landscape – viewed through a lens of subjectivity, anachronism and hybridity. There is nothing particularly historic about the historic environment. Rather than being bifurcated by material and immaterial, or tangible and intangible, or even past, present and future, it is representative of a fluid space of contemporaneousness, liable to alignment with our own moveable values and societal structures (Illsley 2022: 63).

Recording the historic environment

Arguably the primary heritage informant to the planning system, HERs fuel pre-development research and enable targeted excavation in line with national planning policy documents. Yet they are often considered as more than simply a planning tool. For illustrative purposes, Figure 12.1 plots a non-exhaustive network of the functions of a typical HER. Because of their digital gateways, HERs are considered as a universal heritage resource for specialists and non-specialists alike, a point raised by Newman (2009) in response to questions regarding the role of archaeology in critical heritage discourses. These gateways can more or less be digitally characterised by the term 'geovisualisation', which is a method incorporating layers of 'geographical, historical, archaeological, literary, philosophical, scientific, anthropological, sociological and even theological data' (Foka et al. 2021: 203) in a mapped format. In this instance, geographical information systems (GISs) draw upon HER databases to visualise a variety of heterogeneous sources – archaeological data, including records of interventions, with diverse resources such as historic buildings, historic landscape characteristics, geological data, historic mapping, as well as aerial photography, lidar data and palaeoenvironmental data.

At this point, it should be made clear that my goal in this chapter is not to delegitimise the role of archaeology in the historic environment sector. The grounding philosophy of HERs is simply to create a descriptive record to function as an empirical foundation to the planning system. Nevertheless, this does not insulate HERs from valid critique. Not only does the presentation of the HER create an 'unproblematic association between the place in the human record of the real world and place in

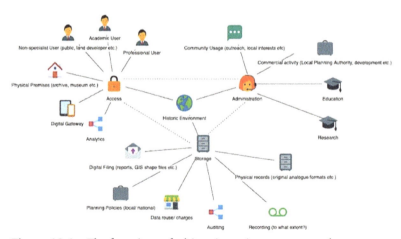

Figure 12.1 The functions of a historic environment record as a simplified network. © William Illsley.

the vectorised world of the geo-database' (Dunn 2019: 49), but also the administrative process of red-flagging potential sites of interest and value curtails the status and value judgements of a wide range of actors including architects, developers, planners and local communities. Thus, as Joel Taylor and Laura Kate Gibson highlight (2016: 417), although digitality has enabled consumption of heritage in new ways on new terms, the role of democratisation of heritage is either not yet fully understood or not yet enacted.

Contentious issues, not limited to digitality, are evident throughout the historic environment sector:

- Most of the data is archaeological or architectural in origin, sidelining intangible practices formulated by space as well as practices linked to contemporary heritage activity. While this was never the intention for the initial database, little has been done to progress towards a more culturally present system of management.
- There is rarely clear accountability as to who makes decisions and what their value is or for how long. The record-keeping process itself is a cumulative compilation by past and present archivists, with no way of determining their voices or values. There is 'an expert-defined threshold of significance' (Jeffrey et al. 2020: 886) but it is unclear what differentiation is made between fact and opinion for planning purposes (Howard 2009: 67). Anything outside of this threshold 'necessarily becomes insignificant within that conceptual framework' (Jeffrey et al. 2020: 886).
- Linked to the above, the inventories approach gained its values initially through the antiquarian gaze of the late nineteenth and early twentieth centuries. While of course archaeology has changed considerably over the past century, it is rare that individual archaeologists are accounted for in the records, nor their gender, ethnic or identity perspectives. This is a matter of practice in both instances; the inclusion of paradata within the database, alongside the prerequisite metadata, is fundamental in documenting the decision-making process. Interpretive practices take place constantly within HERs – but a level of digital intimacy, of the kind that 'affords greater exploration and reflection on the data' (Richards-Rissetto and Landau 2019: 125), is rarely fully articulated. This is a consequence of adopting a technology without considering the coinciding epistemology.
- To function as readily synthesisable resources for data reuse, a strict glossary of definitions is used for data retrieval, creating implications in terms of alterity, equity and representation. For example, in being

bound by terminology, diasporic groups are rendered invisible in the landscape, aside from at sites such as mosques or religious temples, which have attained definitions within the current scope. There is no search term for Roma or traveller sites. Thus, in the understanding of the current recording process, the implication is that marginalised or minority groups are only negotiating the historic environment via their sites of worship or are rendered invisible by the lack of appropriate metadata.

- As part of the planning system, a goal is to minimise lacunae to broaden protection, but because of the formulation of records, the goal is synthesis and aggregation through gazetteer creation, rather than heritage and place-making narratives, thus favouring the specialist community, rather than a non-specialist public. These databases are held by public bodies generally at county or urban level, but as the process of tax allocation is placed under greater scrutiny and pressure, underperforming in public-facing engagement is less and less sustainable.

Arguably, many of these difficulties can be solved, presupposing an interest in actual propositions for solutions, not least the issues of digital praxis. North of the border, while Historic Environment Scotland's Canmore database shares some of the same issues, for example the limitations of a fixed thesaurus, there is at least the possibility of public contribution and enhancement of records through a purpose-built mechanism in 'MyCanmore' (McKeague 2021). By comparison, public contributions to HERs in England are largely on an ad hoc basis, and rarely inscribed by any specific procedure.

There are already refocused efforts in England evidencing the possibility for progress. This is particularly evident through the Know Your Place structure, inaugurated in Bristol (Insole 2017) and exported to neighbouring counties, most recently to Worcester (Worcester City Historic Environment Record 2021) on the back of National Lottery Heritage funding. Here cooperation between public and institution represents, not just a form of collecting information, but a means of transmitting self-determined and culturally meaningful heritage. This in essence is Sven Lindqvist's (1978) *Gräv där du står* ('Dig where you stand') principle in action, linking the 'use of archaeology and other historical methods to understand the history of where communities stood' as well as emphasising 'the significance of history, the importance of people participating in the telling of their own histories' (Flinn and Sexton 2013: 7).

Content creation

The contents of HERs also bear scrutiny. Through their enrolment in trusted institutions, they approach immutability and are offered a level of authenticity. They are hybrid actors in their own right, mediating human responses through the performance of database searches and determining mitigating responses to development. They are both material and immaterial but removed from physical space and time. It may be scarcely recognisable, but these are digital representations of the physical entities and objects.

If we consider the network of the database as a social space and the record entries themselves as social entities, then they can be articulated through the spatial theory if we see the database not as an anthropological space but a space organised and administered by the social characteristics of certain groups and agencies – namely, archaeological exploration and its associated actants. This space is then, of course, mapped in HERs, taking on the *role* of the original place (Latour 1999: 67) but without ever actualising it.

Mapped space as a representation of human place requires construction, and is therefore often perceived as less real. Latour states, 'The more the human hand can be seen as having worked on an image, the weaker is the image's claim to offer truth' (Latour 2002: 16). The legitimacy of these truths, however, is not dependent on whether the object is material or immaterial; what is salient is how it is mediated and reflected in the production of reality (Latour 1999: 275). While one could argue that the mapped HER is semi-actualised through the gazetteer process in the routine of identifying archaeological evidence, the gazetteer process produces only the narrowest of reflections of heritage material, organised primarily by access to its non-human inhabitants. Instead, the inverse of Latour's reasoning becomes the case: the more unseen the work of the human hand, the weaker the representation's claim to truth is.

An assemblage for Europe, or beyond?

Clearly there is much to focus upon on English shores, but what of the future and a wider geographical scope? Moving beyond the emphasis on localised HER processes in planning, if we think in broader cultural terms, then there is scope for utilising these assemblages for assuaging the wider implications of social tropes and practices, such as capitalism, colonialism and European identity. If assemblage as a descriptor is understood to emphasise gathering, then this form of thinking offers a discourse on the practice of assembling in a situation where the formative elements may, or may not, cohere. In keeping with the geographic context behind the historic environment, rather than HERs coinciding with the 'archaeological record' as a given and static entity that remains to be discovered and stewarded by archaeologists (Hamilakis and Jones 2017: 82), heterogeneity and contingency can be found through assemblage thinking.

The role of digitality stewardship and the assembling of the historic environment is part of the process of revisualising the past in the present, making 'the familiar unfamiliar' (Graves-Brown 2011: 131). Now that we can connect historic environments across online and offline fields, we can bridge multiple web spaces and redefine ideas of locality and place-making (Bonacchi 2021: 1). In essence, physical proximity is no longer localised as a necessity. These vectors of digitality can be discussed in proximity to Nico Carpentier's discussion on the European assemblage. Here, the coexistence of hierarchical and non-hierarchical layers of identity at local, national and supranational levels evidences 'a sense of belonging (to a community) and sharing – of (a) similar space(s), history/ies, culture(s), religion(s), language(s) or other elements' (Carpentier 2021: 232) in relation to the entire continent.

While this concept of a European assemblage has only recently been concretely discussed by Carpentier, there are historic antecedents, particularly with regards to cultural heritage. Specifically, to some extent it mirrors the Enlightenment period concepts of European publicness. Harrison (2013: 43) and Byrne (2014: 50) draw on the idea that eighteenth-century European modernity is linked to the conceptual development of heritage through the development of the public sphere as Lefebvrian public space (Lefebvre [1974] 1991). The recording activities of seventeenth- and eighteenth-century scholars entailed transposing historic monuments 'from local forms of religious and legendary knowledge into the new knowledges of antiquarianism, archaeology, and art history … to conceive of these dispersed sites as a constellation of objects occupying a common conceptual space' (Byrne 2014: 51). This was not limited to European shores, as Byrne demonstrates via the extension of monumental recording to the Pharaonic and Islamic monuments of Egypt during Napoleon's 1789 excursion (Byrne 2014: 51).

An optimistic perspective might therefore envision HERs forming a foundational part of a Europe-wide historic environment gateway, akin to the role that Europeana fulfils in the arts sector. This is not without significant stumbling blocks, not least the dismal outlook for interoperability and collaboration in light of current sociopolitical issues such as the Brexit referendum and subsequent UK exit from the European Union. It is clear from this process that a number of premodern European heritages still permeate the thought processes of the contemporary population (Bonacchi, Altaweel and Krzyzanska 2018: 175, 187). In a similar context, Andrew Gardner (2017: 6) comments that the significance of the 'archaeological contribution to national, colonial, post-colonial and other cultural identities in modern times and across the globe' is well documented. Documentation and transmission are not necessarily the same, however, and subjects such as Brexit only serve to highlight the need for accessible and open sources of knowledge to counter misinformation and myth.

Heritage stewardship is at its most effective when informing and empowerment is the primary goal. Moving beyond the archaeological traces in the historic environment is a means for the public to make distinctions between myths, stereotypes and misinformation. The processes of mythologising and producing politically informed heritages show that the familiar is not always so benign. There remain colonial pasts and presents intertwined within the UK, as too in Europe. Objects that archaeologists separate in time are not necessarily separate in the world views of the contemporary cultures they exist in now. A case in point are the Mannlicher-Carcano and Vetterli-Vitali rifles used by the Italian armies in the 1935 invasion of Ethiopia and in the 1896 battle of Adwa that remain in use by Gumuz tribes in Ethiopia (González-Ruibal 2006: 113). This is but one example that highlights the obligation to confront 'the "open wounds" of the past in the present' (Harrison 2011: 185).

The impact of European expansion shows that two things separated by immense distance can in fact be in the very same neighbourhood, and rather than being a linear process, time can make things appear very distant from one another while they closely exist in culture (Serres and Latour 1995: 57). If the EU is to truly 'represent a way of moving forward politically that might break the cycle of nationalist and imperial projects which have dominated European history' (Gardner 2017: 19), then the interoperability of 'Linked Open Data' such as Europeana and the wealth of knowledge in historic environment contexts must be the focus of greater study. In this vein, HERs represent an operative material framework for visualising the European assemblage and its extracontinental impacts.

This requires sustainable and lasting public transmission, along with the supporting paradata and metadata used in assembling HERs. This not only adds to the public experience but also demonstrates the dynamism of the heritagisation process. The responsibility and challenge of effective stewardship is the public provision of information which engenders heuristic filtering of the plethora of information encountered daily. It is a well-informed public that is best placed to counter agendas that distort heritage for their own benefit.

Conclusion: broadening the historic environment

If the English heritage sector is to embrace a more critical discourse of heritage, then we need to understand the historic environment as both an abstract and a social space, rather than merely palimpsests of the human footprint in the cultural landscape. The current historic environment sector is largely made up of an indistinct public of historic building specialists and archaeologists, but a broader approach also requires a great range of actors to be involved in its assembling and disassembling.

In the main, the argument here is not that HERs need to be made anew, although there is certainly room to clarify the agency of those who create and maintain them. To some degree, we have to accept that if the databases are to remain fundable in the current economic and political climate, then fossilising them in the planning structure offers a degree of security. This is a strategic choice, as is the choice to limit who can contribute. The inclusion of objects of greater cultural value to contemporary communities requires a wider range of publics to upload and curate stories and material.

Folklore, landscape narratives and place names, to name but a few, all offer communities and their movements through the landscape recognition in the wider narrative of place, encouraging inclusion in the planning process. Crucially, this is a means of humanising the HER. Extrapolating data based on the Cartesian dimensions of whichever GIS software is in use may provide empirical foundation, but a more nuanced, experiential turn in practice is required.

The role of digitality should be at the heart of this. Up to now, how the hermeneutic (interpretation) and heuristic (invention) is achieved in the historic environment is largely sidelined. Technology is no longer novel enough that its performance in the historic environment should be limited to speeding up the hermeneutic process (O'Gorman 2006: 50). Holism is only possible and useful if the different parts that make up the holistic whole are properly understood (Dunn 2019: 17). That goes both for digitality as an epistemology *as well as* a technological process, and for the constitutional parts of the historic environment itself.

References

Baker, David B. 1977. Survey and the Historic Environment. In T. Rowley and M. Breakall (eds), *Planning and the Historic Environment II*. Oxford: Oxford University Department for External Studies: 1–23.

Bonacchi, Chiara. 2021. Heritage Transformations. *Big Data & Society* 8(2): 1–4. https://doi.org/10.1177/20539517211034302

Bonacchi, Chiara, Mark Altaweel and Marta Krzyzanska. 2018. The Heritage of Brexit: Roles of the Past in the Construction of Political Identities through Social Media. *Journal of Social Archaeology* 18(2):174–192. https://doi.org/10.1177/1469605318759713

Bonacchi, Chiara and Marta Krzyzanska. 2019. Digital Heritage Research Re-theorised: Ontologies and Epistemologies in a World of Big Data. *International Journal of Heritage Studies* 25(12): 1235–1247. https://doi.org/10.1080/13527258.2019.1578989

Byrne, Denis. 2014. *Counterheritage: Critical Perspectives on Heritage Conservation in Asia*. New York and London: Routledge.

Carpentier, Nico. 2021. The European Assemblage: A Discursive Material Analysis of European Identity, Europeanity and Europeanisation. *Filosofija Sociologija* 32(3): 231–239.

Council of Europe. 2021. The European Landscape Convention (Florence, 2000). Online at https://www.coe.int/en/web/landscape/the-european-landscape-convention. Accessed 14 December 2021.

Darvill, Timothy. 2009. Historic Environment. In Timothy Darvill (ed.), *The Concise Oxford Dictionary of Archaeology*. Oxford: Oxford University Press: 369.

Denham, Tim. 2017. Landscape Archaeology. In Allan S. Gilbert (ed.), *Encyclopedia of Geoarchaeology*. Dordrecht: Springer: 464–468.

Dunn, Stuart. 2019. *A History of Place in the Digital Age*. Abingdon: Routledge.

Flinn, Andrew and Anna Sexton. 2013. Research on Community Heritage: Moving from Collaborative Research to Participatory and Co-designed Research Practice. Paper presented at the Nexus, Confluence and Difference: Community Archives meets Community Informatics: Prato CIRN Conference, 28–30 October 2013, Monash Centre, Prato, Italy.

Foka, Anna, Coppélie Cocq, Phillip I. Buckland and Stefan Gelfgren. 2021. Mapping Socio-ecological Landscapes: Geovisualisation as Method. In Kristen Schuster and Stuart Dunn (eds), *Routledge International Handbook of Research Methods in Digital Humanities*. Abingdon: Routledge: 203–217.

Gardner, Andrew. 2017. Brexit, Boundaries and Imperial Identities: A Comparative View. *Journal of Social Archaeology* 17(1): 3–26. https://doi.org/10.1177/1469605316686875

González-Ruibal, Alfredo. 2006. The Past is Tomorrow: Towards an Archaeology of the Vanishing Present. *Norwegian Archaeological Review* 39(2): 110–125. https://doi.org/10.1080/00293650601030073

Graves-Brown, Paul. 2011. Touching from a Distance: Alienation, Abjection, Estrangement and Archaeology. *Norwegian Archaeological Review* 44(2): 131–144. https://doi.org/10.1080/00293652.2011.629808

Hall, Stuart. 1999. Whose Heritage? Un-settling 'the Heritage', Re-imagining the Post-nation. *Third Text* 13(49): 3–13.

Hamilakis, Yannis and Andrew M. Jones. 2017. Archaeology and Assemblage. *Cambridge Archaeological Journal* 27(1): 77–84. https://doi.org/10.1017/s0959774316000688

Harrison, Rodney. 2011. Archaeologies 'Now': Creative Interventions in the Present for the Future. *Archaeological Dialogues* 18(2): 180–196. https://doi.org/10.1017/S1380203811000250

Harrison, Rodney. 2013. *Heritage: Critical Approaches*. London and New York: Routledge.

Harrison, Rodney. 2016. Archaeologies of Emergent Presents and Futures. *Historical Archaeology* 50(3): 165–80.

Holmes-Skelton, Georgina. 2019. For Everyone?: Finding a Clearer Role for Heritage in Public Policy-making. *The Historic Environment: Policy & Practice* 10 (3–4): 363–379. https://doi.org/10.1080/17567505.2019.1645801

Howard, Peter. 2009. Historic Landscapes and the Recent Past: Whose History? In John Pendlebury, Lisanne Gibson and Professor Brian Graham (eds), *Valuing Historic Environments*. Oxford: Routledge: 51–66.

Illsley, William R. 2022. Assembling the Historic Environment: Heritage in the Digital Making. Doctoral dissertation, University of Gothenburg.

Ingvarsson, Jonas. 2020. *Towards a Digital Epistemology: Aesthetics and Modes of Thought in Early Modernity and the Present Age*. Cham: Palgrave Macmillan.

Insole, Peter. 2017. Crowdsourcing the Story of Bristol. In Sherene Baugher, Douglas R. Appler and William Moss (eds), *Urban Archaeology, Municipal Government and Local Planning*. Cham: Springer: 53–68.

Jeffrey, Stuart, Siân Jones, Mhairi Maxwell, Alex Hale and Cara Jones. 2020. 3D Visualisation, Communities and the Production of Significance. *International Journal of Heritage Studies* 26(9): 885–900. https://doi.org/10.1080/13527258.2020.1731703

Latour, Bruno. 1999. *Pandora's Hope: Essays on the Reality of Science Studies*. Cambridge, MA, and London: Harvard University Press.

Latour, Bruno. 2002. What Is Iconoclash? Or Is There A World Beyond The Image Wars? In Peter Weibel and Bruno Latour (eds), *Iconoclash: Beyond the Image-Wars in Science, Religion and Art*. Cambridge, MA: MIT Press: 16–38.

Lefebvre, Henri. [1974] 1991. *The Production of Space*. Translated by Donald Nicholson-Smith. Oxford: Blackwell Publishing.

Lindqvist, Sven. 1978. *Gräv där du står: Hur man utforskar ett jobb*. Stockholm: Bonnier.

McKeague, Peter. 2021. More Than Monuments. *GEO: connexion* 20(3): 45–47.

Meskell, Lynn. 2015. Introduction: Globalising Heritage. In Lynn Meskell (ed.), *Global Heritage: A Reader*. Chichester: Wiley Blackwell: 1–21.

Ministry of Housing, Communities and Local Government. 2019. *National Planning Policy Framework*. London: HMSO.

Newman, Martin. 2009. Devil's Advocate or Alternate Reality? Keeping Archaeology in Heritage. In Emma Waterton and Laurajane Smith (eds), *Taking Archaeology Out of Heritage*. Newcastle upon Tyne: Cambridge Scholars Publishing: 170–191.

O'Gorman, Marcel. 2006. *E-Crit: Digital Media, Critical Theory and the Humanities*. Toronto: University of Toronto Press.

Richards-Rissetto, Heather and Kristin Landau. 2019. Digitally-Mediated Practices of Geospatial Archaeological Data: Transformation, Integration and Interpretation. *Journal of Computer Applications in Archaeology* 2(1): 120–135. https://doi.org/10.5334/jcaa.30

Riksantikvarieämbetet. 2021. Definition av kulturarv och kulturmiljö. Online at https://www.raa.se/kulturarv/definition-av-kulturarv-och-kulturmiljo/ Accessed 14 December 2021.

Riksdagen. 2016. Kulturmiljölag. *1988: 950*. Stockholm: Sveriges Riksdag.

Russell, Ian. 2010. Heritage, Identities and Roots: A Critique of Arborescent Models of Heritage and Identity. In George S. Smith, Phyllis Mauch Messenger and Hilary A. Soderland (eds), *Heritage Values in Contemporary Society*. Walnut Creek: Left Coast Press: 29–41.

Scotland's Environment. 2020. Historic Environment. Scottish Environment Protection Agency. Online at https://www.environment.gov.scot/our-environment/people-and-the-environment/historic-environment/ Accessed 20 August 2020.

Serres, Michel and Bruno Latour. 1995. *Conversations on Science, Culture and Time*. Translated by Roxanne Lapidus. Ann Arbor: University of Michigan Press.

Taylor, Joel and Laura Kate Gibson. 2016. Digitisation, Digital Interaction and Social Media: Embedded Barriers to Democratic Heritage. *International Journal of Heritage Studies* 23(5): 408–420. https://doi.org/10.1080/13527258.2016.1171245

Waterton, Emma. 2010. *Politics, Policy and the Discourses of Heritage in Britain*. Basingstoke: Palgrave Macmillan.

Waterton, Emma and Laurajane Smith. 2009. *Taking Archaeology Out of Heritage*. Newcastle upon Tyne: Cambridge Scholars Publishing.

Wickstead, Helen. 2009. The Uber Archaeologist. *Journal of Social Archaeology* 9(2): 249–271. https://doi.org/10.1177/1469605309104138

Worcester City Historic Environment Record. 2021. Explore Worcester: Share Your Stories. Know Your Place Worcester. Online at https://kypworcester.org.uk/contact/. Accessed 6 May 2021.

13
Digitality as a cultural policy instrument: Europeana and the Europeanisation of digital heritage

Carlotta Capurro

Introduction

Europeana, the online platform aggregating digital heritage data produced by cultural institutions in the member states, is one of the most prominent digital cultural projects promoted by the European Commission (EC). The platform, inaugurated in 2008, resulted from a robust political will voiced by six heads of state in a letter addressed to the president of the EC in 2005 (Chirac et al. 2005). Today, *europeana.eu* is the largest public aggregator of cultural heritage data in Europe, with over 60 million digital objects provided by over 4,000 cultural heritage institutions, including libraries, archives, museums and audiovisual collections. It has become the most extensive and most significant digital cultural project and driver of heritage digitisation in Europe.

The creation of Europeana can be framed as part of a global phenomenon that has profoundly transformed the heritage field since the advent of digital technologies. New digital innovations have led to a revolution in the way heritage objects have been curated, documented, studied, shared and – in consequence – defined and valued in the public sphere. This ongoing process has been labelled the *digital turn* and has revolutionised every discipline interested in studying or curating the past (Nicholson 2013). Cultural heritage institutions have produced digital resources for various purposes (Bury 2019), which, due to the creation and widespread use of interactive online heritage platforms like Europeana, are increasingly contributing to identitarian discourses alongside the more traditional forms of heritage.

Due to the versatility of digital support, digital cultural heritage has largely been perceived as a neutral working tool (Cameron and Kenderdine 2007). Despite some early conceptual debates in archaeology and archival studies that questioned the advantages and modes of sociality produced by digital technology, the broader field of heritage study has underestimated the sociopolitical aspects of the digitisation of the heritage sector (Walch 1994; Wheatley and Gillings 2002). The technical aspects of digital heritage have been widely debated, while less attention has been paid to the politics and the cultural implications, that is, how people are impacted by digital engagement with cultural heritage or by the process whereby objects are selected to be digitised (Cameron 2007).

Throughout this chapter, digital heritage is conceived as the *entanglement* of physical objects, their digital remediation and the set of information created to describe them – the metadata (Capurro 2021). Like traditional forms of heritage, digital heritage is *socially assembled*, representing a non-objective construction of the past (Geismar 2013). As such, the use of digital heritage has cultural, ethical and sociopolitical implications. Furthermore, digital heritage gives access to *information* related to heritage. The digital artefact is immersed in a network of connections with people, cultural meanings and technical qualities, revealing what values are embedded in its status as a heritage object (Forte 2003). From a critical perspective, digital heritage reflects the cultural environment in which it is created while defining its sociopolitical context, becoming an agent in creating future scenarios. Ultimately, the selective understandings of the past and the cultural assumptions encoded into digital heritage contribute to creating people's historical framework, which informs their practice and actions.

Digital collections are also autonomous cultural artefacts. Many studies have investigated how brick-and-mortar museums have developed their policies of collecting, ordering and presenting material (Bennett et al. 2017), while these processes have not received the same critical attention within the digital context. Cultural institutions can be compared with what Latour (1988) calls *centres of calculation*, where materials with different provenance are brought together and ordered according to specific criteria. These criteria are critical for selecting the objects to be collected, as they determine what is worth including in the collection. At the same time, both the actions of collecting and ordering inform the praxis of governance of the institution and are, in turn, shaped by governmental logic. In terms of Foucault's concept of governmentality, this governmental logic consists of a combination of discourses, practices and technologies used by cultural institutions to control peoples' behaviours and understanding (Foucault et al. 1991). Within the digital sphere, cultural institutions exercise the same prerogatives when digitising, documenting and sharing their collections online (Cameron 2007). Therefore, it is crucial to investigate the infrapolitics embedded in digital collections in order to assess how digital cultural heritage is used today to build narratives around identities and the past, and the role of digital infrastructures in this process.

This chapter analyses how digital heritage has become instrumental to the identity politics promoted by the European Union (EU). Although the digitisation of the cultural sector is a global phenomenon, the European case represents an indicative entry point to analyse its broader cultural implications, due to the massive political support it has received. Over the past two decades, the EC has actively invested in digitising the cultural sector and promoting the online accessibility of cultural heritage. To this end, consistent funds were allocated to projects designed to foster cooperation between member states and to support them in digitising their cultural resources and sharing them on the web or through new technological infrastructures.

Europeana and the EU policy framework

This contribution focuses on the historical development of Europeana, exploring the political will that led to the creation of the digital repository and how it is functional in promoting the core principles of EU policy. Following its historical development allows analysis of Europeana in its double role as a product of European cultural policies and a key actor in the digitisation of the cultural sector. This work shows how Europeana has used its infrastructure to *conduct* the digitisation of the cultural sector. Thanks to a comprehensive approach that considers the different aspects of the Europeana initiative, this work brings light to the cultural implications of its digital infrastructure and its political role as the two inseparable dimensions in which Europeana operates. Such an approach reveals the relationship between the actions of *representation*, *regulation*, *identity* and *meaning production* through which Europeana works (Hall 1997).

Europeana has been the topic of many publications describing the technical features of its service, while its societal or institutional role has received only marginal consideration (Petras and Stiller 2017).

The few notable exceptions that have dealt critically with Europeana have limited their analysis to a single element, such as the user interface or the digital collection (Valtysson 2012; Almási 2014; Valtysson 2020; Stainforth 2016; Thylstrup 2018). Therefore, they have failed to approach Europeana as a whole, underestimating the cultural and social implications of all its components.

Aiming to offer a holistic understanding of Europeana, this chapter firstly analyses how it has been conceived as a political and cultural product through the joint action of cultural heritage institutions, the EC and the member states. Then, by analysing the development of the Europeana initiative, the chapter discusses how it has shaped digital cultural heritage policy in Europe, on the one hand as an advocate for cultural institutions in the EC policy debate, and on the other as the provider of a European standardised infrastructure for dealing with digital heritage online.

The methodology employed to study Europeana and its impact combines two techniques. The first is the critical analysis of the documentary sources released by both the European institutions and Europeana. These documents were retrieved through archival research on the online archives of the EU and Europeana. Second, the documentary resources are complemented by information collected during interviews conducted with several employees of the Europeana Foundation during an ethnography of the institution that I carried out at its headquarters in The Hague in the Netherlands.[1] The words of Europeana employees produce a clear image of how Europeana perceives its role and identity within the European cultural heritage panorama.

The European policy framework

The introduction of culture as an instrument to reinforce a European sentiment of collective belonging represented a turning point in the political agenda of the EC (Shore 2000). In the 1970s, it became clear that the economic and legislative union was not enough to create a union of the heterogeneous European people (Haas 2004). To make the project relevant for each citizen, the European institutions adopted a strategy of *imagining communities* similar to how nation-states in the nineteenth century tried to encode the nation in their inhabitants' hearts and minds (Anderson 1983; Hobsbawm and Ranger 2010). Therefore, bringing to light the common traits defining *European culture*, in which all citizens of the member states could recognise themselves, became instrumental to the survival of the European project, and cultural projects were introduced among the commission's primary objectives.

Milestones in this process were the promulgation of the Solemn Declaration on European Union in 1983 and the Maastricht Treaty in 1992. The EU Solemn Declaration explicitly addressed Europe's history and culture to improve citizens' recognition of Europe, inviting each member state to 'promote a European awareness' and undertake joint action in cultural areas (European Council 1983). A step further was Article 128 of the Maastricht Treaty, which offered a legal framework for EU actions, adding culture to the list of areas under European competence.[2] In this way, the treaty initiated the creation of structured funding schemes to finance cultural initiatives. These documents made the construction of collective European identity and memory an integral part of the cultural agenda of the commission (De Witte 1987; Shore 2000; Sassatelli 2006; Calligaro 2013).

The EC used its budget to finance various cultural projects promoting the core principles of its cultural policy. Since 2000, the commission has financed four main actions explicitly dedicated to culture, investing €2,851 million, according to data from the commission's Community Research and Development Information Service (CORDIS, https://cordis.europa.eu/en; Figure 13.1).[3] Furthermore, several initiatives have been promoted to foster European awareness through concrete cultural heritage actions, such as the annual nomination of the 'European Cities of Culture' (Patel 2014), the assignation of the 'European Heritage Label' (Lähdesmäki 2014; Lähdesmäki et al. 2020), the Museum of European Culture (Cadot 2010) and the House of European History (Kaiser 2017;

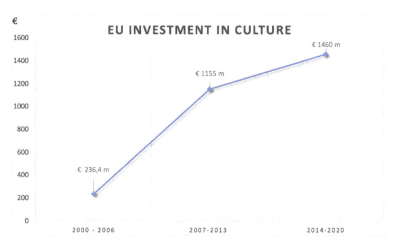

Figure 13.1 The European Commission's investments in culture between 2000 and 2020. Data aggregated from the documentation available on CORDIS.

Jaeger 2020). All these initiatives had the scope to bring Europe closer to its citizens while normalising a narrative of *Europeanness* encompassing local and national identitarian discourses (Shore 2000).

Introducing digitality to the EU cultural policy

In this cultural policy framework, the EC envisioned a central role of technologies in facilitating the diffusion of a common *European identity*. During the 1990s, the commission initiated the construction of a European *information society*, aware of digital data's growing economic, political and cultural roles. In this context, new technologies were crucial for creating and distributing information. The commission promoted a common regulatory framework, instrumental for enabling a high level of internal interoperability among the member states and capable of influencing the global market (EU Publications Office 1995: 17). According to the EC, 'the information society provides the opportunity to facilitate the dissemination of European cultural values and the valorisation of a common heritage' (European Commission 1994b: 14).

In 2000, the EC launched the eEurope Action Plan, promoting the creation of an 'information society for all' by boosting the development and use of the internet and internet-related technologies and services (Liikanen 2001). The plan actively encouraged the digitisation of cultural heritage, asking member states to promote it and support cultural institutions (Thylstrup 2018). To this end, the EC financed several projects dedicated to achieving interoperability between digital practices in each member state and across cultural domains. The following part of this chapter describes the projects funded by the EC to realise its digital cultural policy and how the creation of the European Digital Library – eventually renamed Europeana – was vital in harmonising the digital practices of European cultural institutions.

The digitisation of European cultural heritage: libraries take the lead

During the 1990s, libraries started exploring the potential of digital technologies to share information about their collections on the internet. With the support of the EC, national libraries throughout Europe took on a leading role in the digital shift of the cultural sector (Jefcoate 2006). Between 2001 and 2009, The European Library (TEL) project

Table 13.1 Projects for the creation of The European Library (TEL). Data aggregated from the documentation available on CORDIS.

Project title	Duration	EU budget
TEL	February 2001 – January 2004	€1,977,527
TEL-ME-MOR	February 2005 – January 2007	€1,399,919
TELplus	October 2007 – December 2009	€3,250,000
Total		*€6,627,446*

received about €6.6 million for creating a set of agreed digitisation policies and technical standards (Table 13.1). Under the coordination of the Conference of European National Librarians (CENL), TEL worked to create unified access to the digital catalogues of all its members. It was the first project addressing the issue of uniformising the multiple information structures used by the national libraries (Woldering 2004). The project resulted in the launch of the *TheEuropeanLibrary.org* portal in 2005.

TEL represented a successful collaborative effort: institutions with different cultural backgrounds and missions, at diverse stages of their digital transformation and with varied budgets, developed a joint strategic plan for their development (Collier 2005). The creation of a pan-European service led to harmonising several aspects of the internal workflows, the general objectives and the business plans of the institutions involved. It was a first step towards standardising content and procedures, opening the way for establishing European digital development in the cultural sector. Therefore, it was unsurprising that the commission used the experience of TEL as a starting point for the creation of Europeana, the digital repository for all the cultural heritage data of the member states.

The EU versus Google: towards the creation of Europeana

The European plans for digitising cultural heritage institutions experienced a sudden jolt when, in 2004, Google announced its Google Books project. Several European countries were concerned about the appropriation of shared cultural heritage by a private (American) actor, the issue of respect for copyright and the dominance of English language cultural resources on the internet (European Commission 2005a). Therefore, on 28 April 2005, the heads of six European member states signed a joint letter calling for the creation of a *bibliothèque numérique européenne*, an online library of all European bibliographic collections. The letter described European cultural heritage as a treasure of diversity and a testimony to the universality of the continent in relation with the rest of the world (Chirac et al. 2005). To preserve the cultural position of Europe in the future 'geographies of knowledge', they called for joint action in the digitisation and publication of this material online.

The EC swiftly responded to this call. In a letter of 7 July, President Barroso (2005) endorsed the requests, recognising that the digitisation and online availability of cultural heritage were crucial for creating a European knowledge-based economy and society. Barroso assigned the preparation of an official communication about the opportunities and challenges of creating such a European digital library to Viviane Reding, the then Information Society and Media Commissioner, and Ján Figel', the Commissioner for Education, Training, Culture and Youth (European Commission 2005c). The EC accepted a leading role in the digital shift of European cultural heritage institutions, as both a coordinator and a financial sponsor of the project.

On 29 September 2005, in front of the CENL assembly, Reding outlined her view of a European digital library, proposing the creation of a network of online collections connecting all European heritage institutions (Reding 2005). In the commission's view, the European digital library had a more ambitious scope than the Google Books project, providing access to all digital heritage resources. While each member state would have the responsibility to implement and facilitate the digitisation process of its cultural institutions, an organisation coordinated by the commission would work towards the implementation of standardised practices, reducing legislative obstacles and ensuring adequate financial support for the action.

Next, Reding (2005) explained that the commission would facilitate the creation of the European digital library, acting on two levels: first, politically, by providing assurance of the European authorities' constant political support for the action; and second, strategically, by advocating the advice of experts from the cultural sector. The commission made over €90 million available under various funding schemes to support the plan. In this way, the creation of the European digital library became the most extensively funded cultural action in Europe. The substantial amount of money allocated is proof of the strong political will that supported the technical developments required to create a unified digital library of European cultural heritage.

CENL prepared a proposal to create a cross-domain portal. The European Digital Library (EDL) project was initiated in November 2006, focused on constructing a digital library for showcasing digital heritage from all cultural domains. The project grouped together representatives from the heritage, knowledge and IT sectors and addressed the issue of the interoperability of the diverse content held by European heritage institutions. The project's main result was a functioning prototype of the portal for digital cultural heritage from European institutions named *Europeana* – meaning 'European things' – to immediately describe the platform's purpose and content.

The portal went live in November 2008, offering about two million digital heritage objects (European Commission 2008). During the inauguration of the service, Barroso (2008) presented Europeana as a 'shop window' and a 'digital doorway' to European culture 'in all its glorious diversity'. Aware of the portal's role in constructing a European identity, he stressed that 'Europeana has the potential to change the way people see European culture. It will make it easier for our citizens to appreciate their own past, [and] become more aware of their common European identity.'

Europeana as an instrument of digital governmentality

Over time, the mission of Europeana has evolved considerably: from the digital repository of European cultural heritage, it soon became a digital infrastructure in charge of supporting the digital transformation of European cultural institutions. The initiative's progress did not depend only on political support from the EC and the member states. Europeana needed to mobilise as many cultural institutions as possible while expanding its digital collection. To make this possible, between 2008 and 2010, the commission financed a series of projects to transform the Europeana prototype into a functioning and stable service (Purday 2009). In this phase, strategic decisions on the Europeana infrastructure were taken, and much attention was devoted to extending the digital collection and the network of content providers. Then, between 2011 and 2014, Europeana became an operational service consolidating its infrastructure and services. Lastly, between 2015 and 2019, Europeana focused on outreach and creating a significant impact on society. The following part of the chapter shows how Europeana, conceived as a digital resources aggregator, has also become a central actor in designing and enforcing European digital cultural policy by shaping its operational infrastructure.

Europeana's content

The main operative obstacle to creating a European heritage platform was harmonising all digital heritage objects. Libraries, archives, museums and audiovisual collections have very different standards for producing and documenting their collections, which are often incompatible. These differences are determined by the heterogeneous nature of the heritage, the vocabularies of the various authorities documenting the resources, which are discipline- or domain-dependent, and the reference models for the metadata sets in use. To accommodate such a multitude of descriptions within the same digital collection, Europeana had to design an architecture capable of bringing this variety of data together.

The first fundamental decision with a significant impact on the Europeana service's architecture regarded the nature of the collected objects. In line with Reding's view of the European digital library as a network, Europeana was not designed as a repository of digital heritage but as an aggregator of *surrogates* of the digital resources (Purday 2009). Surrogates are composed of three main elements: (1) a set of metadata describing the object, (2) a thumbnail for its preview on Europeana and (3) a URL linking the surrogate to the full-resolution digital object preserved on the server of the owner institution (Gradmann, Dekkers and Meghini 2009). This choice allowed Europeana to overcome the issues posed by the diversity of digital resource file formats, leaving the owner institutions responsible for digital conservation and accessibility. On the other hand, partner institutions kept control over their digital collections. Thanks to the surrogate model, Europeana could achieve a leading role in the governance of cultural heritage information on the web with minimal investment in the management of digital resources.

The second constitutional decision shaping Europeana's contents structure involved establishing an optimal way to describe the resources, accommodating the 'information perspectives' of the different cultural domains within the same digital library (Aloia et al. 2011). Introduced in 2010, the Europeana Data Model (EDM) was then conceived as a standard for interoperability, allowing each data provider to use its preferred metadata standard and vocabulary of reference (Isaac and Clayphan 2013). In designing the EDM, representatives of all cultural domains worked together to identify its requirements, resulting in a metadata model where every domain could reuse each other's data (Charles and Olensky 2014). Thanks to its open model, the EDM could accommodate the variety of cultural heritage documentation in an unambiguous model, symbolising the European motto 'Unity in Diversity' with its semantic structure (Capurro and Plets 2020).

To facilitate browsing the resources and highlight their *European value*, Europeana started to curate the digital collection. By creating curated collections, Europeana (2015) aimed to 'build and sustain an active online community of interest for the wider cultural heritage sector in Europe'. A team of curators worked to bring the best stories and quality content into the spotlight. By selecting topics and stories that reveal the commonalities between the member states, curators bring to light the European value of the resources (field notes, May 2019). In this way, heritage is used to create linkages among different realities and promote a feeling of unity and shared *European identity* (Capurro 2021). Since 2014, curated collections have acquired a prominent place on Europeana, thanks to the launch of the *Europeana Collections* interface, and have gained a central place in the new *Europeana Experience* interface.

The digital service

Critical to Europeana's success was the definition of its operative infrastructure. This consisted of a framework for facilitating content providers' sharing of their collections on the portal. To this end, Europeana devised a supply chain working at the national, domain or thematic levels, based on a network of data aggregators. They are institutions acting as intermediaries, supporting data providers in mapping their resources according to the EDM, gathering the metadata and verifying its quality before uploading to Europeana. When working at the national level, these institutions were identified by governments as national aggregators. In contrast, those working at the thematic or domain level resulted from specific projects funded by the EC (Purday 2009). Content aggregators are grouped in the Europeana Aggregators' Forum, where they share experiences and best practice (Europeana 2021).

In 2018, Europeana flattened the structure of the aggregation model by transferring to aggregators the role of expertise hubs (Europeana Foundation 2016). Aggregators were entrusted to facilitate the digital transformation of heritage institutions, supporting them in adhering to Europeana's standardised practices. In this way, Europeana was positioned at the centre of a Europe-wide network of cultural institutions, united by shared digital procedures. This infrastructure simplifies Europeana's work by reducing the number of organisations uploading content to the database. It also facilitates the penetration of Europeana's standards into cultural heritage institutions, which are closely supported in their digitisation processes. Therefore, Europeana imposes its technical and operative requirements on institutional procedures by constructing its operative infrastructure, creating a network of *European cultural institutions* adopting common standards and digital working procedures (Capurro and Plets 2020).

Europeana's governance

Lastly, it was crucial to define Europeana's governance. In 2007 the EDL Foundation, later renamed the Europeana Foundation, was established to run the service. It was the legal entity owning and taking responsibility for the progress of the digital library, applying for funding and employing dedicated personnel. Two collegial bodies managed the foundation: the Board of Participants and the Executive Committee. The former, which included representatives of Europeana's partners and content providers, elected the Executive Committee and supervised its activities. The latter oversaw the foundation's day-to-day management, making decisions on budget and development strategies. Therefore, the governance of the foundation was devised as a distributed model that enhanced the representation of Europeana's partners (Europeana Foundation 2010).

The Council of Content Providers and Aggregators (CCPA) was created as a collegial advisory body grouping together the cultural institutions partnering with Europeana. The CCPA elected representatives to sit on the foundation's board: in this way, cultural institutions could express their views on Europeana's future. In 2011, the CCPA was renamed the Europeana Network Association, including all the practitioners interested in cooperating with Europeana. Members shared expertise in an international and cross-domain environment, contributing to the creation of Europeana's best practices. Therefore, the Network represents a *community of practice* operating around the digital heritage (Lave and Wenger 1991). It is a resource of know-how for the smaller institutions with few internal resources, and a driver of the standardisation of the cultural heritage sector. The website Europeana Professional was created to facilitate knowledge exchange, collecting the documentation of all technologies and services developed by Europeana. It occupies a central role in disseminating the digital practices promoted by Europeana.

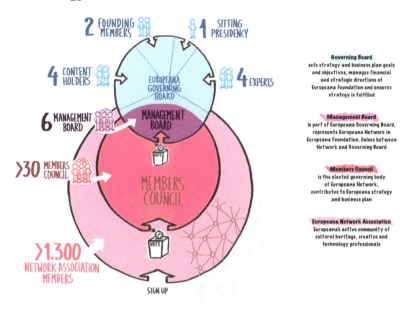

Figure 13.2 Governance of the Europeana Foundation, as presented in the 2017 Business Plan. © Europeana. Reproduced under the Creative Commons licence CC BY-SA.

In 2015, Europeana's governance became more inclusive (Figure 13.2). Firstly, the Europeana Network was registered as an independent association, adopting a representative structure. Members elected the Member Council, which elected the association's Management Board. Composed of six representatives, the board also had the task of representing the association to the Europeana Foundation Governing Board. Within this renewed structure, the Network Association gained a predominant role in the functioning of Europeana.

Secondly, a political representative of the country holding the EU presidency was included on the Europeana Foundation's Governing Board. In 2017, the number of national representatives sitting on the board increased to three, including the predecessor and the successor of the country holding the presidency (field notes, June 2019). While Europeana has always had to account for its results to the commission, this transformation embedded political control into the initiative's governing structure. Through its representatives, the commission gained an active role in steering the direction of Europeana's development from the inside; working with the representatives of the cultural sector sitting on the board, they devised a digital strategy abiding by the EU cultural policy guidelines.

With the democratisation of its governance, Europeana became an effective instrument for enacting EU digital cultural policy specifically addressed to (national) heritage institutions. Through their open participation in the work and decision-making organs of Europeana, cultural institutions became actors in designing a digital practice in line with the EC policy guidelines. Once promoted by Europeana, these standard procedures gradually entered the workflow of Europeana's content providers. Therefore, by democratising the foundation's governance, Europeana gained a central position in designing and implementing the harmonisation of the digital practice of cultural institutions.

Europeana's infrapolitics

Since its inauguration, Europeana has outgrown the aims of a digital archive of European heritage. In an analysis of the technical, cultural and political choices behind the construction of its infrastructure, Europeana can be conceptualised as an instrument of European *governmentality*, acting upon multiple levels of the construction of *Europeanness*.

Firstly, it facilitates the collaboration of international partners within the framework of EU-financed projects. By promoting a common modus operandi through the definition of standardised best practices, Europeana has constructed a network of *European institutions*. Secondly, it discursively produces *European heritage* by curating a transnational collection of digital resources. By accommodating opposite and potentially conflicting perspectives on selected topics within the same collection, Europeana constructs narratives of shared European experiences. Lastly, it brings together a community of practitioners, creatives and end users around its collection, creating a *European (cultural) audience*. All these aspects are made possible by Europeana's governance and infrastructure.

As a policy actor, Europeana promotes its technical standards to the cultural sector. Although not an official body of the EU, Europeana has been given the power to address the digital development of the cultural sector. Thanks to its infrastructure, Europeana implements European top-down policies, incorporating them into the bottom-up attempts generated within its community, adopting and normalising the EU rhetorical discourse on European heritage. Europeana successfully implements the EU's digital cultural policy through the Network Association and the Aggregators' Forum.

Conclusion

This chapter has analysed how the EC has conceived and implemented cultural policy and digital policy and how they were mutually influenced in the digital cultural sector, leading to the creation of Europeana, a political and cultural product. The EC has used culture to promote citizens' European identity and a sense of belonging to a joint European culture. Due to the encompassing nature of digitality, the policy designed to lead Europe's digital transformation soon included the cultural sphere. The official EU documents narrate the digital transformation as a medium to democratise access to culture, sharing cultural content with citizens using innovative channels. Conceived as the most ambitious European cultural project ever, with the aim of aggregating digital resources from all the member states, Europeana has become a central actor in designing and enforcing a European digital cultural heritage policy.

The creation of Europeana exemplifies how the EC designed and financed digital cultural actions oriented towards reaching interoperability between the digital practices in different member states and across cultural domains. By promoting the cooperation of cultural heritage actors within Europe-wide networks through their participation in Europeana, the commission created a digital cultural policy that shaped the digital identity of cultural institutions. Thanks to the enthusiastic support of the members of the Europeana Network Association from the bottom, and the recommendations of Ministries of Culture from the top, heritage institutions have had to adapt their data to the new standards when sharing their collections on Europeana. In this way, the Europeana infrastructure subtly produces the Europeanisation of national cultural heritage institutions through the introduction of standardised technical practices.

It is possible to conclude that Europeana has played a crucial role in the governance of the cultural sector. Thanks to the creation of democratically approved digital procedures and in line with the main EC guidelines, Europeana has become an intermediary organisation leading the digital transformation of European cultural institutions. Digitisation has not only transformed their practices and methodologies but has also forced them to adhere to common standards and procedures. By promoting international cooperation and financing projects that align with the required parameters, through Europeana the EU has implemented a digital cultural policy that has successfully shaped the identity of European cultural institutions.

Acknowledgements

The Ethical Committee of Utrecht University has approved this work. I would like to thank those interviewed at Europeana for the information provided. A special thank you to the reviewers and the editors for their valuable feedback and support.

Notes

1. This information relies on field notes taken between 2017 and 2020, as a result of meetings with the staff of the Europeana Foundation, participation in events promoted by Europeana, and a research residency at the Europeana Foundation between May and July 2019. During this residency, 11 employees of the Europeana Foundation agreed to be formally interviewed. Their identities and positions remain confidential.
2. Article 128 of the Maastricht Treaty was firstly amended in Article 151 of the Treaty of Amsterdam (1997), then in Article 167 of the Treaty on the Functioning of the European Union (2009).
3. Two previous actions, Raphael (1997–1999) and Ariane (1997–1998), financed projects dedicated respectively to the restoration and preservation of cultural heritage and of books and reading. Raphael had a budget of 30 million ECU (European Currency Unit), while Ariane had 7 million ECU.

References

Almási, Zsolt. 2014. Europeana: The European Identity Transfigured for and through the Digital. In Zsolt Almási and Mike Pincombe (eds), *Transfiguration of the European Identity*. Newcastle upon Tyne: Cambridge Scholars Publishing: 61–84.

Aloia, Nicola, Cesare Concordia and Carlo Meghini. 2011. Europeana v1.0. In Maristella Agosti, Floriana Esposito, Carlo Meghini and Nicola Orio (eds), *Digital Libraries and Archives.* Communications in Computer and Information Science. Berlin: Springer: 127–129.

Anderson, Benedict. 1983. *Imagined Communities: Reflections on the Origin and Spread of Nationalism*. London: Verso.

Assmann, Aleida. 2007. Europe: A Community of Memory? *Bulletin of the German Historical Institute Washington, DC*, No. 40: 11–26.

Barroso, José Manuel. 2005. *Barroso Letter on the European Digital Library*, 7 July 2005. European Commission. Online at https://web.archive.org/web/20210729073146/https://digital-strategy.ec.europa.eu/en/library/timeline-digitisation-and-online-accessibility-cultural-heritage (website accessed through the WayBack Machine) Accessed 26 April 2023.

Barroso, José Manuel. 2008. Europeana: *A Shop Window on Europe's Cultural Heritage*. SPEECH/08/632. European Commission - PRESS RELEASES. Online at https://europa.eu/rapid/press-release_SPEECH-08-632_en.htm Accessed 26 April 2023.

Bee, Cristiano. 2008. The 'Institutionally Constructed' European Identity: Citizenship and Public Sphere Narrated by the Commission. *Perspectives on European Politics and Society* 9(4): 431–450.

Bennett, Tony, Fiona Cameron, Nélia Dias, Ben Dibley, Rodney Harrison, Ira Jacknis and Conal McCarthy. 2017. *Collecting, Ordering, Governing: Anthropology, Museums, and Liberal Government*. Durham: Duke University Press.

Borgman, Christine. 2015. *Big Data, Little Data, No Data: Scholarship in the Networked World*. Cambridge, MA: MIT Press.

Bradford, Anu. 2020. *The Brussels Effect: How the European Union Rules the World*. Oxford: Oxford University Press.

Bury, Stephen. 2019. Museum Libraries and Archives in the Digital 21st Century. In Tula Giannini and Jonathan Bowen (eds), *Museums and Digital Culture: New Perspectives and Research*. Springer Series on Cultural Computing. Berlin: Springer International Publishing: 483–490.

Cadot, Christine. 2010. Can Museums Help Build a European Memory? The Example of the Musée de l'Europe in Brussels in the Light of 'New World' Museums' Experience. *International Journal of Politics, Culture and Society* 23(2–3): 127–136.

Calligaro, Oriane. 2013. *Negotiating Europe: EU Promotion of Europeanness since the 1950s*. Europe in Transition: The NYU European Studies Series. New York: Palgrave Macmillan US.

Cameron, Fiona. 2007. Beyond the Cult of the Replicant: Museums and Historical Digital Objects – Traditional Concerns, New Discourses. In Fiona Cameron and Sarah Kenderdine (eds), *Theorizing Digital Cultural Heritage: A Critical Discourse*. Cambridge, MA: MIT Press: 49–76.

Cameron, Fiona and Sarah Kenderdine (eds). 2007. *Theorizing Digital Cultural Heritage: A Critical Discourse*. Media in Transition. Cambridge, MA: MIT Press.

Capurro, Carlotta. 2021. *Digitising European Culture: Europeana and the Government of Digital Cultural Heritage*. Utrecht: Utrecht University.

Capurro, Carlotta and Gertjan Plets. 2020. Europeana, EDM and the Europeanisation of Cultural Heritage Institutions. *Digital Culture and Society* 6(2): 163–189.

Charles, Valentine and Marlies Olensky. 2014. *EDM Mapping Refinement Extension Report*. pro. europeana.

Chirac, Jacques, Schroeder, Berlusconi, Zapatero, Kwasniewski and Gyurcsány. 2005. *The letter to Barroso*, 28 April 2005. European Commission. Online at https://web.archive.org/web/20210729073146/https://digital-strategy.ec.europa.eu/en/library/timeline-digitisation-and-online-accessibility-cultural-heritage (website accessed through the WayBack Machine) Accessed 26 April 2023.

Collier, Mel. 2005. The Business Aims of Eight National Libraries in Digital Library Co-operation: A Study Carried out for the Business Plan of The European Library (TEL) Project. *Journal of Documentation* 61(5): 602–622.

Delanty, Gerard. 1995. *Inventing Europe: Idea, Identity, Reality*. Basingstoke: Macmillan.

De Witte, Bruno. 1987. Building Europe's Image and Identity. In Albert Rijksbaron and Max Weisglas (eds), *Europe from a Cultural Perspective: Historiography and Perceptions*. The Hague: Nijgh and Van Ditmar Universitair: 132–139.

EU Publications Office. 1995. *Europe and the Global Information Society: Recommendations to the European Council: Conference G7 – Raport BANGEMANN*. Brussels: EU Publications Office.

European Commission (ed.). 1994a. *Growth, Competitiveness, Employment: The Challenges and Ways Forward into the 21st Century. White Paper (Parts A + B)*. Luxembourg: Office for Official Publ. of the EC.

European Commission. 1994b. *Europe's Way to the Information Society: An Action Plan*. COM(94) 347 final. EU publications.

European Commission. 2005a. *Annex to the Communication from the Commission 'i2010: Digital Libraries'*. COM(2005) 465 final. EUR-Lex.

European Commission. 2005b. *i2010: Digital Libraries*. COM(2005) 465. EUR-Lex.

European Commission. 2005c. *New Strategy on European Digital Libraries Unveiled*. News. CORDIS.

European Commission. 2008. EUROPEANA – *Europe's Digital Library: Frequently Asked Questions*. MEMO/08/724. European Commission – PRESS RELEASES.

European Council. 1983. *Solemn Declaration on the European Union*. Bull. EC 6-1983.

European Council. 2000. *Presidency Conclusions on the Lisbon European Council*. European Council.

Europeana. 2015. *Transforming the World with Culture: Next Steps on Increasing the Use of Digital Cultural Heritage in Research, Education, Tourism and the Creative Industries*. The Hague: Europeana Foundation.

Europeana. 2021. 'EAF – Europeana Aggregators Forum'. Online at https://pro.europeana.eu/page/aggregators. Accessed April 2021.

Europeana Foundation. 2010. *2010 Annual Report and Accounts*. Den Haag: Europeana Foundation.

Europeana Foundation. 2011. *2011 Annual Report and Accounts*. Den Haag: Europeana Foundation.

Europeana Foundation. 2015. *2015 Business Plan*. Den Haag: Europeana Foundation.

Europeana Foundation. 2016. *2016 Business Plan*. Den Haag: Europeana Foundation.

Europeana Foundation. 2020. *About Us – Europeana*. Online at https://www.europeana.eu/en/about-us Accessed November 2020.

Europeana Network Association. 2018. Europeana Network Association Statutes. Online at https://pro.europeana.eu/files/Europeana_Professional/Europeana_Network/Association_Updates/Governance_documents/europeana-network-association-bylaws.pdf Accessed 29 April 2023.

Forte, Maurizio. 2003. Mindscape: Ecological Thinking, Cyber-Anthropology and Virtual Archaeological Landscapes. *BAR International Series*, No. 1151: 95–108.

Foucault, Michel, Graham Burchell, Colin Gordon and Peter Miller (eds). 1991. *The Foucault Effect: Studies in Governmentality: With Two Lectures by and an Interview with Michel Foucault*. Chicago: University of Chicago Press.

Geismar, Haidy. 2013. Defining the Digital. *Museum Anthropology Review* 7(1–2 Spring–Fall): 254–263.

Geismar, Haidy. 2018. *Museum Object Lessons for the Digital Age*. London: UCL Press.

Gradmann, Stefan, Makx Dekkers and Carlo Meghini. 2009. *Europeana Outline Functional Specification for Development of an Operational European Digital Library*. EDLnet Project.

Haas, Ernst. 2004. *The Uniting of Europe: Political, Social and Economic Forces, 1950–1957*. 3rd ed. Contemporary European Politics and Society. Notre Dame, IN: University of Notre Dame Press.

Hall, Stuart. 1997. The Work of Representation. In Stuart Hall, Jessica Evans and Sean Nixon (eds), *Representation: Cultural Representations and Signifying Practices*. Thousand Oaks: SAGE Publications: 13–74.

Hassan, Robert. 2020. Digitality, Virtual Reality and The 'Empathy Machine'. *Digital Journalism* 8(2): 195–212.

Hassan, Robert and Thomas Sutherland. 2017. *Philosophy of Media: A Short History of Ideas and Innovations from Socrates to Social Media*. London and New York: Routledge.

Hobsbawm, Eric and Terence Ranger (eds), 2010. *The Invention of Tradition*. Cambridge: Cambridge University Press.

Isaac, Antoine and Robina Clayphan. 2013. *Europeana Data Model Primer*. Online at https://pro.europeana.eu/files/Europeana_Professional/Share_your_data/Technical_requirements/EDM_Documentation/EDM_Primer_130714.pdf Accessed 29 April 2023.

Jaeger, Stephan. 2020. *The Second World War in the Twenty-First Century Museum: From Narrative, Memory and Experience to Experientiality*. Berlin and Boston: De Gruyter.

Jefcoate, Graham. 2006. Gabriel: Gateway to Europe's National Libraries. *Program: Electronic Library and Information Systems* 30(3): 229–238.

Kaiser, Wolfram. 2017. Limits of Cultural Engineering: Actors and Narratives in the European Parliament's House of European History Project. *JCMS: Journal of Common Market Studies* 55(3): 518–534.

Kaiser, Wolfram, Stefan Krankenhagen and Kerstin Poehls. 2014. *Exhibiting Europe in Museums: Transnational Networks, Collections, Narratives and Representations*. New York and Oxford: Berghahn Books.

Lähdesmäki, Tuuli. 2014. Transnational Heritage in the Making: Strategies for Narrating Cultural Heritage as European in the Intergovernmental Initiative of the European Heritage Label. *Journal of European Ethnology* 44: 75–83.

Lähdesmäki, Tuuli, Viktorija Čeginskas, Sigrid Kaasik-Krogerus, Katja Mäkinen and Johanna Turunen. 2020. *Creating and Governing Cultural Heritage in the European Union: The European Heritage Label*. London: Routledge.

Latour, Bruno. 1988. *Science in Action: How to Follow Scientists and Engineers through Society*. Cambridge, MA: Harvard University Press.

Lave, Jean and Etienne Wenger. 1991. *Situated Learning: Legitimate Peripheral Participation*. Cambridge: Cambridge University Press.

Liikanen, Erkki. 2001. *eEurope – An Information Society for All*. SPEECH/01/180. European Commission – PRESS RELEASES.

Littoz-Monnet, Annabelle. 2012. Agenda-Setting Dynamics at the EU Level: The Case of the EU Cultural Policy. *Journal of European Integration* 34(5): 505–522.

Nicholson, Bob. 2013. The Digital Turn: Exploring the Methodological Possibilities of Digital Newspaper Archives. *Media History* 19(1): 59–73.

Patel, Kiran Klaus (ed). 2014. *The Cultural Politics of Europe: European Capitals of Culture and European Union since 1980s*. Routledge/UACES Contemporary European Studies 24. London: Routledge.

Petras, Vivien and Juliane Stiller. 2017. A Decade of Evaluating Europeana: Constructs, Contexts, Methods and Criteria. In Jaap Kamps, Giannis Tsakonas, Yannis Manolopoulos, Lazaros Iliadis and Ioannis Karydis (eds), *Research and Advanced Technology for Digital Libraries*. New York: Springer International: 233–245.

Purday, Jon. 2009. Think Culture: Europeana.eu from Concept to Construction. *The Electronic Library*, November.

Reding, Viviane. 2005. *The Role of Libraries in the Information Society*. CENL Conference, Luxembourg, 29 September 2005. SPEECH/05/566. European Commission Press Release.

Sassatelli, Monica. 2006. The Logic of Europeanizing Cultural Policy. In Ulrike Hanna Meinhof and Anna Triandafyllidou (eds), *Transcultural Europe: Cultural Policy in a Changing Europe*. London: Palgrave Macmillan: 24–42.

Sassatelli, Monica. 2009. *Becoming Europeans: Cultural Identity and Cultural Policies*. London: Palgrave Macmillan.

Schlesinger, Philip. 2017. The Creative Economy: Invention of a Global Orthodoxy. *Innovation: The European Journal of Social Science Research* 30(1): 73–90.

Shore, Cris. 2000. *Building Europe: The Cultural Politics of European Integration*. London and New York: Routledge.

Stainforth, Elizabeth. 2016. From Museum to Memory Institution: The Politics of European Culture Online. *Museum and Society* 14(2): 323–337.

Thylstrup, Nanna Bonde. 2018. *The Politics of Mass Digitization*. Cambridge, MA: MIT Press.

Tsilas, Nicos. 2011. Open Innovation and Interoperability. In Laura DeNardis (ed.), *Opening Standards: The Global Politics of Interoperability*. The Information Society Series. Cambridge, MA: MIT Press: 97–118.

Valtysson, Bjarki. 2012. Europeana: The Digital Construction of Europe's Collective Memory. *Information, Communication & Society* 15(2): 151–170.

Valtysson, Bjarki. 2020. *Digital Cultural Politics: From Policy to Practice*. New Directions in Cultural Policy Research. Cham, Switzerland: Palgrave Macmillan.

Walch, Victoria Irons. 1994. *Standards for Archival Description: A Handbook*. Chicago: Society of American Archivists.

Wheatley, David and Mark Gillings. 2002. *Spatial Technology and Archaeology: The Archaeological Applications of GIS*. London: Taylor & Francis.

Woldering, Britta. 2004. The European Library: Integrated Access to the National Libraries of Europe. *Ariadne*, No. 38. Online at http://www.ariadne.ac.uk/issue/38/woldering/ Accessed 14 April 2023.

14

De-neutralising digital heritage infrastructures? Critical considerations on digital engagements with the past in the context of Europe

Gertjan Plets, Julianne Nyhan, Andrew Flinn,
Alexandra Ortolja-Baird and Jaap Verheul

Enchantment with digital heritage and 'overtrust' in technology

Over the past two decades, digital media and platforms in heritage institutions in Europe[1] have been framed within celebratory discourses of accessibility, transparency and efficiency (Cameron and Kenderdine 2010; Musiani and Schafer 2017). In a suite of policy documents across Europe, ranging from funding tenders within, for example, the Horizon 2020 framework of the European Union (EU) to the programmes of national heritage agencies, digital technologies and platforms have been embraced as the solution to challenges of preservation, conservation and accessibility. During the COVID-19 pandemic, during which brick-and-mortar heritage spaces were closed, digital heritage was further embraced, not only as a temporary emergency solution, but as offering foundational perspectives on the future. Successful digital exhibitions, augmented reality (AR) apps, recommender systems, guided virtual tours and 3-D immersive websites showcased the capacity of digital heritage to expand audiences, to render both objects and intangible heritage visible and to inculcate new forms of engagement and sociality (Samaroudi, Rodriguez Echavarria and Perry 2020; European Heritage Days 2020).

An expectant attitude towards the digitalisation of heritage collections is strongly encouraged by the EU, which has adopted digital cultural heritage as a policy instrument to foster European cultural identity (Thylstrup 2019: 57–77). Through funded institutions such as Europeana, the EU has stimulated the digitisation of many aspects of the cultural sector in the member states – although the material cultural heritage held in Europe is far from fully digitised (see Nauta, van den Heuvel and Teunisse 2017). Recently the president of the European Commission even heralded the arrival of the 'Digital Decade' and how Europe will take an active role in achieving 'the digital transformation of our society and economy by 2030' (Leyen 2021). Interestingly, in these policy projections digital heritage is deployed to deliver this comprehensive digital transformation of European society (Capurro 2021).

Yet the emergent body of critical work on digital heritage (e.g. Cameron and Kenderdine 2010; Musiani and Schafer 2017) is still rarely incorporated in contemporary digital heritage projects, especially outside academia. Many stakeholders continue to perceive digital systems as neutral tools enabling the objective preservation and presentation of the past. However, any digital application is a social construct, defined by a set of complex and highly culturally specific internal workings and standardisations (e.g. Hauswedell et al. 2020). Furthermore, technical experts, despite their important role in digital heritage projects, are often not recognised as key players and practitioners encoding highly specific understandings of the past in the digital form (e.g. Griffin and Hayler 2018).

The veneer of neutrality of digital heritage technologies is both understandable and problematic. First, 'technology overtrust' (Hardé 2016; Ullrich, Butz and Diefenbach 2021) is an outcome of the highly complex nature of the digital. Digital technologies require expert knowledge to understand their inner workings and the – often cultural, racialised and hegemonic – choices encoded in them. In a sense they have become 'black boxed' (Latour 1999): due to their complex design and often smooth working, we are unaware of the inner functions, human labour and decision-making structures defining a digital platform. Many tools and platforms have become input–outcome systems, but what happens behind the scenes remains invisible and the impact on the final product unknown.

Second, we tend to be uncritical of these inner workings because of our historically located optimism vis-à-vis technology and infrastructure as vehicles of modernity (Edwards 2003). Because technological innovations have so drastically benefited our livelihoods since the Industrial Revolution, 'modern' society has become *enchanted* by technological infrastructure (Harvey and Knox 2012). As a result, these successes from the past can be projected onto new technologies, producing 'excessive optimism' (Clark, Robert and Hampton 2015).

Although this overtrust in digital heritage is understandable, it is also at odds with the critical turn in heritage studies. Over the past decades, the power structures and discourses enacted by cultural heritage institutions have been discussed at length (Smith 2006; Bennett 1995). Beyond academia, more and more practitioners engage with these critical ideas and strive for a more inclusive curation of the past. At the same time, also within sociology (e.g. Marres 2017), media studies (Manovich 2001) and anthropology (Pink et al. 2016; Geismar 2018), there is increased attention to the power structures that technology (re)produces. In digital humanities and archival studies, the inherent biases in data selection, digitisation priorities, metadata structures and workflows have been critically evaluated (Thylstrup 2019; Kim 2018; Dobson 2019). Recently, research on the assumptions, stereotypes and biases of race, ethnocentrism and gender encoded in algorithms have received similar attention (Noble 2019; Mandell 2019; Risam and Josephs 2021; McPherson 2012).

Despite a 'critical turn' in our engagement with (in)tangible heritage and discussions in media studies on the biases in digital infrastructure, the 'digital turn' in the heritage sector has not received similar scrutiny. Digital heritage is an expansive field where there is plenty of room to critically explore different technology-driven engagements with the past, ranging from AR applications (Stichelbaut, Plets and Reeves 2021) to virtual museums (Perry et al. 2017). In this chapter, we will interrogate the sociocultural affordances of so-called 'digital heritage infrastructures', large digital platforms where digital data and heritage objects are stored and made available (often online) for both expert and non-specialist audiences. Generally speaking, they comprise both digital archives open to the public and research infrastructure that scholars mine almost on a daily basis for their research. As governments have very high expectations of digital infrastructures, a steep increase in funding has produced a proliferation of digital archives and heritage platforms (Benardou et al. 2019).

Towards digital infrastructure literacy: platforms and the government of people

Infrastructure has become a cornerstone of our 'modern' condition, regulating our daily actions and political subjectivities. At the same time, because of the prevalence of infrastructures today, they escape the untrained eye. Over two decades ago, Bowker (1994) showed how mundane information technologies and infrastructures strongly influence how scientists collect, order and interpret their data. He strongly called for an *infrastructural inversion* (Bowker 1994) and to 'struggle against the tendency of infrastructure to disappear' (Bowker and Leigh Star 1999: 34) and spotlight how databases impact researchers and scholars.

Recently, anthropology has adopted this quest to make the sociopolitical impact of infrastructures on ordinary people visible (Larkin 2013). By zooming in on the effects of physical infrastructure such as radio transmitters (Larkin 2008), pipelines (Plets 2020) and roads (Harvey and Knox 2012) on people's actions and subjectivities, anthropology has triggered a broader interest in the humanities and social sciences on the social effects of infrastructure beyond the walls of the laboratory and technology park.

Although tangible infrastructures have received considerable attention, also over the past year the affordances of digital infrastructures in (re)producing or challenging power structures have been exposed (Bergère 2019; Uimonen 2019). Especially, e-government portals (Leenes 2005) and social networks (Miller 2011) have been identified as the new pipes, grids and road systems of our social arena. These studies have theorised that the standards and protocols that define these often well-intentioned and highly necessary applications or platforms indirectly – albeit strongly – nudge social action in specific directions.

The widespread nature and strong implications of contemporary digital infrastructures have perhaps been best described by van Dijck, Poell and de Waal (2018) as a reality of the 'platform society' we are all a part of. Today, major advances in computing power have ensured that our fields of practice have become infiltrated by platforms through which both new enterprises and legacy institutions operate. Platforms are digital architectures that are carefully 'designed to organise interactions between users – not just end users but also corporate entities and public bodies' (2018: 4). Through their design, they not only replicate certain social structures, but also create new ones.

Despite their structuring of our sociopolitical ecosystem, digital platforms have – just like tangible infrastructures – remained largely invisible to both users and scholars. Fast-paced infrastructures such as social media or digital information platforms are considered as mundane basic services, rather than as the intricate and carefully designed technologies that they are. As noted by Star (1999: 382), the 'invisible quality of working infrastructure becomes visible when it breaks: the server is down, the bridge washes out, there is a power blackout'. It was only in

2016 that the considerable cultural impact of basic digital infrastructure came to light, when Facebook got caught up in the Cambridge Analytica scandal during the 2016 US presidential campaign (Confessore 2018; Cadwalladr and Graham-Harrison 2018). Suddenly the black box was opened, and people became aware of the algorithms and protocols structuring our digital arena.

This emerging interest in the hidden power of digital infrastructures and platforms has direct relevance for heritage scholars and practitioners. Within the field there is consensus that the politics of collecting, ordering, describing and curating objects in traditional GLAM institutions (galleries, libraries, archives and museums) are imbued with processes of governing and disciplining subjects (Bennett 1995). Recent work has even more strongly tied the politics of 'collecting, ordering and governing' information at these institutions with the nation-building and colonial projects of the nineteenth and twentieth centuries (Bennett et al. 2017). In short, invisible selection criteria, taxonomies and protocols in the curation of heritage objects intrinsically structure the narratives and heritage objects made available to the public.

While similar cultural forces are at work in digital heritage infrastructures, the digitality adds additional challenges of technology and governmentality (see Capurro and Plets 2021; Thylstrup 2019). Complex software architectures and specialist programming languages make it incredibly difficult to reveal and understand invisible biases and choices. Therefore, research into how cultural heritage is collected, ordered and governed digitally is essential to develop a critical tool kit for understanding digital infrastructures. Ultimately, such a reflective lens would enable practitioners and academics to see digital technologies not just as useful tools, but also as powerful conceptual schemes that impact how we organise and represent the past. However, if we want to fully understand the politics, inner workings and impact of digital infrastructures, we need to examine these mechanisms on the micro-level of specific collections.

This chapter will therefore present two very different digital heritage platforms that both contribute to a finer-grained understanding of the sociality of digital infrastructures. First, the 'Enlightenment Architectures: Sir Hans Sloane's Catalogues' project will be discussed. This case enables us to explore the issue of absence of marginalised and minority voices in digital collections, and strategies for overcoming this. Subsequently, a case study on the Central Archaeological Inventory of the Flemish Government (Belgium) addresses the impact of digital heritage portals on their users, and how digital infrastructures can encourage their users to reproduce banal nationalist framings of the past.

'Enlightenment Architectures': Sir Hans Sloane's catalogues

Sir Hans Sloane (1660–1753) was a physician, naturalist and secretary, and later president of the Royal Society as well as of the Royal College of Physicians in the UK. During his lifetime, Sloane assembled a collection of some 70,000 objects from all over the world. By the time of his death, his collection comprised over 50,000 books and manuscripts, thousands of natural history objects, ethnographic materials, antiquities, hundreds of prints, drawings and more. Sloane financed some of his collection with the gains he made from his entanglements in the transatlantic slave trade: he owned shares in slave-trading companies and married into a plantation-owning family (Delbourgo 2017). Upon his death, he bequeathed his collection to the British nation, an action that became a catalyst for the British Museum Act 1753. Following the creation of the Natural History Museum and the British Library out of the British Museum, Sloane's objects formed the foundational collections of three key national cultural heritage institutions in the UK.

During his lifetime, Sloane and his amanuenses labelled and described the objects aggregated by his collecting practices in some 54 manuscript catalogues, of which about 40 are extant. These catalogues list what was once in Sloane's collection, along with additional information that can include, inter alia, notes on objects' provenance, date of acquisition and catalogue numbers. Not only that, they also impart, through the information they do and do not record, what Sloane and his contemporaries did and did not value; thus they postulate a complex set of interrelationships between, on the one hand, objects and the worlds and humans whence they were extracted, and on the other hand, the worlds and humans with whom those objects would be formally collocated in manuscript catalogues and, over the longer term, in the context of the museum and museum technologies.

As 'core documents of museum structure and meaning' (Ortolja-Baird et al. 2019), the eighteenth-century catalogues compiled by Sloane and his amanuenses have remained in continuous use by curators of the aforementioned national institutions. Although the link between the present-day collections and the historical catalogues is currently broken, as this case study will explore, Sloane's catalogues raise fundamental questions about the limits of current digital infrastructures for heritage remediation, representation and navigation, including their propensity to reanimate and perpetuate problematic social, cultural and racial scripts in ostensibly techno-utopian digital environments.

The case study that follows has emerged from the 'Enlightenment Architectures' project (2016–2021), which sought to make the information-bearing aspects of Sloane's catalogues machine readable, as a precursor to the computationally assisted analysis of his foundational collection and its documentation.[2] Thus, to identify and interrogate the highly complex information architecture of Sloane's catalogues, the project sought to encode a subset of five of these catalogues in line with the Guidelines of the Text Encoding Initiative (TEI; https://tei-c.org/guidelines/), an internationally recognised standard for the representation of texts in digital form. This process forced questions that were unexpected at the outset of the project about the issue of absence and bias in early modern archival documents and the potential for the perpetuation of such absences that digital humanities approaches may give rise to, albeit unintentionally. The case study that follows summarises the key outcomes of the 'Enlightenment Architectures' project in this regard.[3]

Many of the objects in Sloane's catalogues are recorded in detail. For some objects, however, little is given about their provenance, as there is only sporadic documentation of the routes by which objects made their way into his collection, through whose hands they passed, their exact origins and how they were acquired. It has been argued that Sloane acted as a centre-point around which his collection was built and organised by a network of lesser-known and now largely forgotten individuals (Delbourgo 2017). The agency of these individuals in the decision-making around collection and ordering practices accordingly matters. Yet, while much scholarship has focused on recovering the vast network of individuals who built, organised and documented Sloane's collection, we still have only a rough picture of these individuals, especially the non-hegemonic ones. This issue is important as many individuals were part of Sloane's network due to the growth of global trade and imperial expansion, and the forms of colonialism of which Sloane was a part. While Sloane collaborated with a wide network of individuals, many of those from beyond Europe who –willingly or unwillingly – 'contributed' to the collection were either enslaved, coerced or unremunerated for their efforts, and their identities are irretrievable as Sloane remained silent about how he acquired objects from colonial contexts.

Personal names are a feature of Sloane's texts that we sought to encode in order to understand more about those individuals and their interrelationships mentioned in the catalogues as having contributed to Sloane's collection in some way. As we used automated named-entity recognition and manual annotation to identify and encode the names of mentioned individuals (Humbel et al. 2021), we increasingly wondered about those individuals who are *not* named in the catalogues. Those individuals' names may be absent but an echo of their agency, and a trace of their presence, is, in some nebulous way, enfolded in the catalogues. After all, the existence of an object in Sloane's collection indicates that it was made, worked, sold and transported by human beings (in examples of artificial, not natural items). As we worked, we began to conceptualise these nameless individuals as presences who 'haunt' the catalogues, in the sense that they participate in a dialectic of trace and absence that is detectable only from certain viewpoints and is rarely anchorable to a specific location in the catalogue. But how can one encode the ghosts and the 'haunting' of an early modern archival document? Encoders can usually tag an individual only if they are actually 'there' in some concrete or anchorable way in a text, for example, if they are textually embodied in a person, name or metaphor. Although in some cases it might be possible to view an object name or category of knowledge as a proxy for their presence, this would require further fundamental long-term research and would not result in clear-cut identifications in all instances.

It was in the process of thinking through how absence, and absent individuals and groups, could be modelled and encoded in the catalogues that we were alerted to how positivist, and hence limiting, encoding schemes like the TEI, which hold a place of pre-eminence in the digital humanities, can be (Figure 14.1). If a feature of a text is present, and recognised as such by the encoder, then they can tag it (directly or with stand-off mark-up) and proceed to study that textual feature in other ways. But what can be done when an anchor point cannot be found, when an absence is textually unmoored? And what can be done when we suspect that a milestone in a catalogue should be associated with individuals whose identities are unknown and probably unknowable?

These questions may initially seem abstruse, but there is much at stake in them. The individuals who contributed objects and knowledge to Sloane's collection were part of his network due to the growth of global trade and imperial expansion, and the forms of colonialism and the transatlantic slave trade of which Sloane was a part, having married into a plantation-owning family. That these individuals were omitted from Sloane's catalogues is crucial to understanding the sociocultural and economic contexts of his collecting, the hierarchies of esteem and knowledge that his collecting practice emanated from and the ideologies of race that overarched his documentation and practices of attribution. The absences in Sloane's catalogues are caused by personal and societal ideological biases of data selection, and further informed by imperatives for that data to conform to taxonomies of collection.

```
<div3>
  <ea:catnum>-1386.</ea:catnum>
  <p>An Indian grater the bone of a fish w <hi rend="sup">t</hi>. which they grated<lb/>
sev<hi rend="sup">ll</hi>. of their med&apos;cinall roots. From
<persName>M <hi rend="sup">r</hi>.
    Winthorp.</persName> Sturgeon?</p>
  <p><add rend="pencil">221. w</add></p>
</div3>
```

Figure 14.1   Excerpt from Sir Hans Sloane's Catalogue of Fossils including Fishes, Birds, Eggs, Quadrupeds (Volume V). While 'Mr Winthorp', thought to be Mr John Winthrop (1714–1779), 'mathematician, physicist and astronomer and acting president of Harvard University in 1769 and 1773' (http://viaf.org/viaf/ 11132722), is recorded as having given Sloane this object, it is attributed and marked up in line with the Text Encoding Initiative. Those individuals from whom this object was sourced, extracted or otherwise acquired and the source of the contextual information about the use of the object remain unspecified in the eighteenth-century catalogue and likewise in the twenty-first-century remediation of it.

Research and interpretation which do not recognise and account for these biases and absences simply reinforce and reinscribe these fundamental prejudices and preferences. The absences in Sloane's catalogues thus speak to the inherent subjectivities of data collection and documentation, be it analogue or digital, recalling how 'the concept of *data* as a given has to be rethought through a humanistic lens and characterised as *capta*, taken and constructed' (Drucker 2011: 1). The absences also raise crucial questions about the extent to which such subjectivities continue to shape current data-driven approaches to the analysis of digitised documents. However unintentionally (see also McPherson 2012), the positivist orientation of the TEI (and perhaps future initiatives) to modelling Sloane's catalogues risks the further perpetuation of historical absences and, indeed, their activation and amplification in new ways as historical data sets are made machine readable and are combined and recombined in new systems and applications.

Two questions thus follow: regarding the particular context of Sloane, how might we use digital tools to recover, rather than re-encode, absences in and from his catalogues? From a broader perspective, what steps might be taken to gaining deeper understandings of how data-driven approaches to cultural heritage historical documents might not perpetuate the silence of individuals who have already been marginalised in the historical record? These are the urgent critical questions to which we will be attending in the next iteration of this project, called 'The Sloane Lab: Looking back to build future shared collections', following the award of a multi-million-pound grant from the Towards a National Collection programme led by the Arts and Humanities Research Council.[4]

Digital archaeological inventories and the production of national frameworks

Over the past half-century, the cultural heritage field in Belgium has drastically evolved. Over the course of the twentieth century, Flemish nationalist movements, in concert with Walloon regionalism, challenged the unitarian Belgian nation-state. From the 1970s–1980s onwards, Belgium evolved towards a federal state, culminating in 1993 in the formal establishment of Flemish, Walloon and Brussels governments and parliaments. Although many competences remained on the Belgian level (e.g. military and foreign affairs), cultural policy was transferred to the regions. Nationalist and regionalist movements wanting to expand cultural sovereignty were keen to mobilise culture as part of their nation-building portfolio.

In this struggle, heritage played a role. Whereas the Middle Ages (Flemish cities and art) became part of the political portfolio of the Flemish nation builders, archaeological heritage received very little political attention. This contrasted sharply with the politicisation of archaeology in Wallonia to craft a strong regional metanarrative (Van Looveren 2014: 456–457). While there was an absence of such a politicised discourse about archaeology in Flemish public opinion, the way archaeologists used the concept of 'Flanders' in their analyses started to shift.

A close reading of a selection of archaeological texts revealed that contemporary territorialisations were projected onto archaeological periods, even when these present-day administrative boundaries had no relevance. For example, earlier texts would mention the 'Belgian' Bronze Age. More recent works would explore 'Flanders' in the Roman period. To study these shifts in territorialisation in archaeological knowledge practices, all archaeological literature (in Dutch) produced by Belgian archaeologists since 1945 was subjected to data-driven digital analysis (mainly text mining; see Plets, Huijnen and van Oeveren 2021). Word frequency analysis was used to map these changed spatialisations of the past. By looking at which geographical signifiers with identitarian values (e.g. Belgium, Europe and Flanders) were used in descriptions and interpretations of the past, evolutions in everyday banal nationalist discourses were traced (Billig 1995). The outcomes of this study showed that 'Belgium' was the main geographic framework used until the mid-1970s (Figure 14.2). Flemish framings of archaeology, however, started in 1975 and became dominant in the mid-1990s, while Belgian signifiers have decreased significantly.

Discussions within the social sciences remind us of the widespread nature and strong impact of so-called methodological nationalism. Methodological nationalism can be best described as the 'assumption that the nation/state/society is the natural social and political form of the modern world' (Wimmer and Glick Schiller 2002: 301), meaning that the nation-state is too often used as the dominant frame of analysis in describing and analysing heritage in past and present. Building on Billig (1995), Wimmer and Glick Schiller argue that this is not without repercussions, since by routinely using the nation-state in an almost 'banal' way in scholarly discourse, present-day national imaginations become naturalised.

The above-mentioned quantitative research clearly suggests that archaeologists use shifting banal nationalist frameworks in their engagement with the past. This methodological nationalism is not limited to specialist reports and texts but can also be found in communication with the public about archaeological artefacts found in the territory of

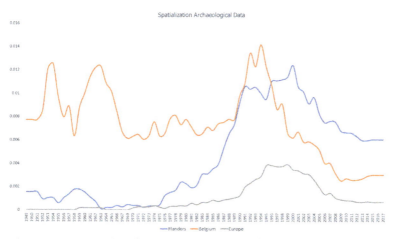

Figure 14.2 Results of text mining analysis of territorial signifiers used in archaeological texts in conjunction with descriptions of archaeological phenomena (for full methodology, see Plets, Huijnen and van Oeveren, 2021).

Flanders (see Plets 2016). Interviews with key archaeologists in 2019 indicated that most of these professionals were unaware of the national framework that they reproduce – inconspicuousness is an intrinsic characteristic of banal nationalism (Billig 1995). Furthermore, most interviewees did not identify with the Flemish nationalist movement and were sceptical of many of the initiatives of the Nieuw-Vlaamse Alliantie (New Flemish Alliance) – a secessionist party striving for the full independence of Flanders. Recent polling suggests that inhabitants of Flanders do not univocally support these policies and are not against re-federalising some areas of government.[5]

Clearly, this banal nationalist framework is neither the product of flag-waving nationalisation of archaeology by the state, nor a deliberate political infiltration of archaeology with national ideas by archaeologists. Rather, field conditions beyond archaeology shape the spatialisation of archaeological data. First, Flanders has become a key point of reference in the media, popular culture and education. This has helped in naturalising the geographical signifier 'Flanders' as a container for analysis. Second, praxeological perspectives teach us to also foreground everyday practices, rather than only discourses circulating in a thought collective, in exploring how knowledge is produced (Mol 2003).

We contend that digital governmentality plays a crucial role in this process of heritage spatialisation. First-hand experience with archaeological research, participatory observation of archaeological knowledge practices and interviews all indicate a very strong dependence on, or even overtrust in, the digital libraries and GIS-based information platforms that are managed by the Flemish agency for immovable (i.e. archaeological and architectural) heritage. Flemish governmental portals position digital archaeological reports and data as the only gateways to the archaeological heritage of Flanders. This overabundance of digital data is recurrently used in archaeological practice.

The study of recent excavation reports, MA and PhD dissertations, and interviews with archaeologists teach us that everyday archaeological work is strongly dependent on the information infrastructure managed by the Flemish government. A central digital database is *Centrale Archeologische Inventaris* (CAI; Central Archaeological Inventory), an online GIS-based database of all sites and significant archaeological finds that is designed, curated and continuously updated by the Flemish agency. It was mainly promoted at the turn of the millennium as a spatial planning tool (Meylemans 2004) for sites and monument records. As detailed by its designers (Van Daele, Meylemans and De Meyer 2004), the database is also purposely designed as a research instrument that should occupy a central role in the archaeological process. Furthermore, the 2013 archaeological legislation detailing the standards for archaeological field reporting even requires consultation and careful interpretation of the CAI as part of publication practices.[6] Clearly more than a spatial planning tool, the database constitutes a carefully designed node in – legally curtailed – archaeological practice.

The design of the CAI shows it was intended as a research infrastructure since the database goes beyond the mere localisation of sites or listing of bibliographical references. In its multi-layered design, there is significant attention to scholarly interpretations of sites and finds: standardised interpretations that are distilled from both old and recent reports by database managers. Because of its detail and the relative ease of searching for sites that it enables, it has also become a workhorse for most archaeologists. Almost any archaeologist looking for comparable sites uses this database and the interpretations listed. In addition to the CAI, the Flemish heritage agency also hosts a digital library (https://oar.onroerenderfgoed.be/) where most recent archaeological reports and articles are freely accessible.

In his seminal *Archive Fever* (1996), Derrida explores the nature and politics of archives in the modern world. He argues that archives, whether in digital or brick-and-mortar form, are political institutions influencing people's actions. Accordingly, archives are as much about the future as they are about the past, since '(t)he archivisation produces as much as it records the event' (Derrida 1996: 17).

One of the key selections that archives make is what is included and what is not. This will structure what users will use and what in the long term will be found significant. In the case of the CAI, one of the fundamental choices was the exclusion of archaeological data from Wallonia, which is understandable because it falls outside the responsibility of the Flemish heritage agency. However, because of the ease of using a digital portal, the difficulty of looking beyond the boundaries and the legal position of the inventory in archaeological legislation, Flanders has become a methodological artefact and container within which comparison and analysis happen. The power of the platform and abundance of data have created a frame of reference within which heritage valuation takes place. Clearly, government-funded and -controlled digital heritage portals not only provide information, but also direct its users to heritage phenomena pertaining to their territory and sovereignty.

Conclusion: developing critical digital heritage studies

In our age of digital abundance, cultural heritage, too, is collected, pre-served and made available in digitised form. This offers huge benefits for users, heritage institutions and governments alike. Digitised sources become readily accessible, not only for researchers, museum curators, civil servants and many other professionals, but also for increasingly wider audiences of amateur scientists and interested citizens. New search and analytical tools allow them to discover unexpected treasures or hard-to-find nuggets of information. Even more promising and poten-tially transformative in unexpected ways is the ability to interconnect data collections in linked-data structures within wider digital ecosys-tems, such as Europeana. No wonder that the EU and national and local governments invest large budgets in digitising their heritage collections.

It is no surprise that the digital transformation of our society has permeated our cultural heritage collections. However, the digital turn also raises a number of fundamental questions about the way the data are coded, structured and embedded in larger infrastructures. The emergent field of critical heritage studies can and should be applied to understand the consequences for the heritage field. Critical *digital* herit-age studies can ask crucial questions about how we can foster complex and ethical uses and reuses of digital heritage collections and how digital technology can make visible, obviate and not re-amplify the dynamics of bias, absence, exploitation and power asymmetry that are inherent in European cultural heritage collections.

Our case studies demonstrate that critical assessment of the emerg-ing cultural heritage infrastructures can reveal social power structures, silences, and geopolitical and identitarian assumptions embedded in data structures. Critical digital heritage studies can bring to the surface the sociopolitical agendas embedded in metadata structures that would otherwise remain invisible yet have wide-ranging consequences for the interpretation of heritage collections. The 'Enlightenment Architectures' project exposed the consequences of digitising early eighteenth-century catalogues that replicated colonial power structures and the intricate social hierarchies within Sloane's extensive workforce of often anony-mous employees. The process of digitisation raises questions about orthography and disambiguation of named entities, most particularly of the many people and places that mirrored the ambiguous web of discov-ery, conquest and appropriation underlying Sloane's collection itself. But the process of coding within the unrelentingly positivist regime of the TEI also brought to light the many absences, silences and hidden figures that threatened to disappear in an irreversible blackout in the digitised representation of the catalogues. The critical approach to digital heritage studies not only helps us to prevent the silencing of marginalised individuals in the historical record collections, but urges us to decolonise the digital cultural archive.

The case study of the central digital repository designed by the government of Flanders to record all sites and significant archaeological finds likewise shows that data and metadata structures are not neutral. The collection that is designed, curated and continuously updated by the Flemish agency reflects the changing spatialisation of local archaeology, as the geographical attribute 'Flemish' became attached to the metadata, replacing 'Belgian', and finds from Wallonia disappeared from purview. This methodological nationalism reflected the changing boundaries of political and linguistic identities within Belgian society from the 1970s onwards. As this central archaeological portal serves a wide range of official, academic and amateur users, this shift in data structure, in turn, has both obvious and more subtle consequences for the construction of collective heritage. The reterritorialisation of culture can result in budget reallocation, changing archaeological practices and a politicised sense of place.

In all these cases, digitalisation of cultural heritage does not so much cause but rather reveal or even emphasise the sociopolitical structures that undergird heritagisation, often in invisible ways that seem neutral or objective. This confirms that digital infrastructures can create new realities. In other words, to paraphrase Oscar Wilde, life tends to imitate digital heritage, far more than digital heritage imitates life. And this anti-mimetic consequence of the digital turn requires thorough academic reflection on the enchantment with – if not overtrust in – digital heritage infrastructures. This creates an urgent need for interdisciplinary critical digital heritage studies that interrogate how digital archives and digital cultural heritage impact those who engage with them, particularly in terms of their emotional response and the expression of individual and collective identities.

Notes

1. Although the infrastructures used to deliver and access digitised material are global ones (Thylstrup 2019: 57), the digitisation of primary and secondary sources and material culture across the globe has shaped, and been shaped by, a broad range of local and situated contexts and agenda (e.g. Crymble 2021: 50; Hauswedell et al. 2020). Thus, the predominately European picture presented in this chapter should not be interpreted as a normative or global one (see Risam 2018: 5–6). Rather, the questions and perspectives pursued here can usefully

be brought into conversation with other (inter)national and situated contexts so as to build a more comprehensive dialectology of digitisation and its social, cultural, institutional and conceptual entanglements across the globe.

2. This project, entitled 'Enlightenment Architectures: Sir Hans Sloane's catalogues of his collections' (2016–2019), was funded by a Leverhulme Trust Research Project Grant and led by Kim Sloan (British Museum) and Julianne Nyhan. The project was a collaboration between the British Museum and UCL, with further expertise contributed by the British Library and the Natural History Museum. For a wider overview of the project and the wider project team, see https://reconstructingsloane.org/enlightenmentarchitectures/

3. The following case study is based on the following open-access publications, which allow it to be reshared with attribution: Ortolja-Baird et al. (2019); Ortolja-Baird and Nyhan (2022).

4. See: https://gtr.ukri.org/projects?ref=AH%2FW003457%2F1

5. Over the past years, polls have been held in the Flemish media about the degree of support for the Belgian state and for Flemish nationalism and independence. Multiple studies show that a majority of people support the Belgian state and are not in favour of a Flemish nation-state. A majority seem to find Belgium and Belgian identity still highly relevant. See results of 2021 poll online at https://www.vrt.be/vrtnws/nl/2021/05/21/is-de-vlaming-een-flamingant-of-toch-liever-meer-belgie/, accessed 17 April 2023.

6. Ministerieel besluit tot bepaling van de minimumnormen voor de registratie en documentatie bij archeologisch onderzoek met ingreep in de bodem en de wijze van rapportering https://codex.vlaanderen.be/PrintDocument.ashx?id=1020865&datum=2013-01-01& geannoteerd=false&print=false, Article 76.

References

Benardou, Agiatis, Erik Champion, Costis Dallas and Lorna Hughes. 2019. *Cultural Heritage Infrastructures in Digital Humanities*. London: Taylor & Francis.

Bennett, Tony. 1995. *The Birth of the Museum: History, Theory, Politics*. London: Routledge.

Bennett, Tony, Fiona Cameron, Nélia Dias, Ben Dibley, Rodney Harrison, Ira Jacknis and Conal McCarthy. 2017. *Collecting, Ordering, Governing: Anthropology, Museums, and Liberal Government*. Durham, NC, and London: Duke University Press.

Bergère, Clovis. 2019. 'Don't Tax My Megabytes': Digital Infrastructure and the Regulation of Citizenship in Africa. *International Journal of Communication* 13: 4309–4326. https://ijoc.org/index.php/ijoc/article/view/11493/3187

Billig, Michael. 1995. *Banal Nationalism*. London: Sage.

Bowker, Geoffrey. 1994. *Science on the Run: Information Management and Industrial Geophysics at Schlumberger, 1920–1940*. Cambridge, MA: MIT Press.

Bowker, Geoffrey and Susan Leigh Star. 1999. *Sorting Things Out: Classification and Its Consequences*. Cambridge, MA: MIT Press.

Cadwalladr, Carole and Emma Graham-Harrison. 2018. Revealed: 50 Million Facebook Profiles Harvested for Cambridge Analytica in Major Data Breach. *The Guardian*, 17 March 2018. https://www.theguardian.com/news/2018/mar/17/cambridge-analytica-facebook-influence-us-election

Cameron, Fiona and Sarah Kenderdine (eds). 2010. *Theorizing Digital Cultural Heritage: A Critical Discourse*. Cambridge, MA: MIT Press.

Capurro, Carlotta. 2021. *Digitising European Culture: Europeana and the Government of Digital Cultural Heritage*. PhD dissertation, Utrecht University.

Capurro, Carlotta and Gertjan Plets. 2021. Europeana, EDAM and the Europeanisation of Cultural Heritage Institutions. *Digital Culture & Society* 6(2): 63–189.

Clark, Brent, Robert, Christopher and Stephen Hampton. 2015. The Technology Effect: How Perceptions of Technology Drive Excessive Optimism. *Journal of Business Psychology* 31(1): 87–102.

Confessore, Nicholas. 2018. Cambridge Analytica and Facebook: The Scandal and the Fallout So Far. *The New York Times*, 4 April 2018. https://www.nytimes.com/2018/04/04/us/politics/cambridge-analytica-scandal-fallout.html

Crymble, Adam. 2021. *Technology and the Historian: Transformations in the Digital Age*. Urbana: University of Illinois Press.

Delbourgo, James. 2017. *Collecting the World: The Life and Curiosity of Hans Sloane*. London: Allen Lane.

Derrida, Jacques. 1996. *Archive Fever: A Freudian Impression*. Translated by Eric Prenowitz. Chicago and London: University of Chicago Press.

Dobson, James E. 2019. *Critical Digital Humanities: The Search for a Methodology*. Urbana: University of Illinois Press.

Drucker, Johanna. 2011. Humanities Approaches to Graphical Display. *Digital Humanities Quarterly* 5(1). http://www.digitalhumanities.org/dhq/vol/5/1/000091/000091.html

Edwards, Paul. 2003. Infrastructure and Modernity: Force, Time and Social Organisation in the History of Sociotechnical Systems. In Thomas Misa, Philip Brey and Andrew Feenberg (eds), *Modernity and Technology*. Cambridge, MA: MIT Press: 285–325.

European Heritage Days. 2020. How Digital Technologies Enhance the Cultural Heritage Experience during COVID-19 Pandemic. 4 June 2020. Online at https://www.european heritagedays.com/EHD-Programme/Press-Corner/News/How-digital-technologies-enhance-the-cultural-heritage-experience-during-COVID19-pandemic Accessed 17 April 2023.

Geismar, Haidy. 2018. *Museum Object Lessons for the Digital Age*. London: UCL Press.

Griffin, Gabriele, and Matt Steven Hayler. 2018. Collaboration in Digital Humanities Research – Persisting Silences. *Digital Humanities Quarterly* 12(1). http://digitalhumanities.org/dhq/vol/12/1/000351/000351.html

Hardé, Patricia. 2016. When, How and Why Do We Trust Technology Too Much? In Sharon Tettegah and Dorothy Espelage (eds), *Emotions, Technology and Behaviors*. Cambridge: Academic Press: 85–106.

Harvey, Penny and Hannah Knox. 2012. The Enchantments of Infrastructure. *Mobilities* 7(4): 521–536.

Hauswedell, Tessa, Julianne Nyhan, M. H. Beals, Melissa Terras and Emily Bell. 2020. Of Global Reach yet of Situated Contexts: An Examination of the Implicit and Explicit Selection Criteria that Shape Digital Archives of Historical Newspapers. *Archival Science* 20: 139–165. https://doi.org/10.1007/s10502-020-09332-1

Humbel, Marco, Julianne Nyhan, Andreas Vlachidis, Kim Sloan and Alexandra Ortolja-Baird. 2021. Named-Entity Recognition for Early Modern Textual Documents: A Review of Capabilities and Challenges with Strategies for the Future. *Journal of Documentation* 77(6), 1223–1247. https://doi.org/10.1108/JD-02-2021-0032

Kim, Dorothy. 2018. Building Pleasure and the Digital Archive. In Elizabeth Losh and Jacqueline Wernimont (eds), *Bodies of Information: Intersectional Feminism and the Digital Humanities*. Minneapolis: University of Minnesota Press: 230–260.

Larkin, Brian. 2008. *Signal and Noise: Media, Infrastructure and Urban Culture in Nigeria*. Durham, NC: Duke University Press.

Larkin, Brian. 2013. The Politics and Poetics of Infrastructure. *Annual Review of Anthropology* 42: 327–343.

Latour, Bruno. 1999. *Pandora's Hope: Essays on the Reality of Science Studies*. Cambridge, MA: Harvard University Press.

Leenes, Ronald. 2005. Local e-Government in the Netherlands: From Ambitious Policy Goals to Harsh Reality. Institute of Technology-Assessment working papers, Vienna, Austrian Academy of Sciences. Online at http://epub.oeaw.ac.at/?arp=0x0010b26f Accessed 2 March 2022.

Leyen, Ursula von der. 2021. State of the Union: Path to the Digital Decade. Text, European Commission, 15 September 2021. Online at https://ec.europa.eu/commission/presscorner/detail/en/ip_21_4630 Accessed 17 April 2023.

Looveren, Jonas Van. 2014. *IJdele Hoop? Een Politiek-Institutionele Geschiedenis van Archaeologische Monumentenzorg in België (1830-1991/3)*. Antwerpen: Universiteit Antwerpen.

Mandell, Laura. 2019. Gender and Cultural Analytics: Finding or Making Stereotypes? In Matthew K. Gold and Lauren F. Klein (eds), *Debates in the Digital Humanities 2019*. Minneapolis: University of Minnesota Press. https://dhdebates.gc.cuny.edu/read/untitled-f2acf72c-a469-49d8-be35-67f9ac1e3a60/section/5d9c1b63-7b60-42dd-8cda-bde837f638f4#ch01

Manovich, Lev. 2001. *The Language of New Media*. Cambridge, MA: MIT Press.

Marres, Noortje. 2017. *Digital Sociology: The Reinvention of Social Research*. Malden, MA: Polity.

McPherson, Tara. 2012. Why Are the Digital Humanities So White? Or Thinking the Histories of Race and Computation. In Matthew K. Gold (ed.), *Debates in the Digital Humanities*. Minneapolis: University of Minnesota Press. https://dhdebates.gc.cuny.edu/read/untitled-88c11800-9446-469b-a3be-3fdb36bfbd1e/section/20df8acd-9ab9-4f35-8a5d-e91aa5f4a0ea#ch09

Meylemans, Erwin. 2004. Drie jaar Centrale Archeologische inventaris: een overzicht en stand van zaken. In *CAI-I De opbouw van een archeologisch beleidsinstrument*, IAP-Rapporten 14, Instituut voor het Archeologisch Patrimonium, Brussel: 9–28.

Miller, Daniel. 2011. *Tales from Facebook*. Cambridge: Polity.

Mol, Annemarie. 2003. *The Body Multiple Ontology in Medical Practice*. Durham, NC: Duke University Press.

Musiani, Francesca and Valérie Schafer. 2017. Digital Heritage and Heritagization. *RESET*, no. 6 (November). https://doi.org/10.4000/reset.806

Nauta, Gerhard Jan, Wietske van den Heuvel and Stephanie Teunisse. 2017. *D4.4 Report on ENUMERATE Core Survey 4. Europeana DSI 2 – Access to Digital Resources of European Heritage, Europeana*. Online at https://pro.europeana.eu/files/Europeana_Professional/Projects/Project_list/ENUMERATE/deliverables/DSI-2_Deliverable%20D4.4_Europeana_Report%20on%20ENUMERATE%20Core%20Survey%204.pdf Accessed 27 April 2023.

Noble, Safiya Umoja. 2019. Toward a Critical Black Digital Humanities. In Matthew K. Gold and Lauren F. Klein (eds), *Debates in the Digital Humanities 2019*. Minneapolis: University of Minnesota Press. https://dhdebates.gc.cuny.edu/read/untitled-f2acf72c-a469-49d8-be35-67f9ac1e3a60/section/5aafe7fe-db7e-4ec1-935f-09d8028a2687#ch02

Ortolja-Baird, Alexandra and Julianne Nyhan 2022. Encoding the Haunting of an Object Catalogue: On the Potential of Digital Technologies to Perpetuate or Subvert the Silence and Bias of the Early-Modern Archive. *Digital Scholarship in the Humanities* 37(3): 844–867. https://doi.org/10.1093/llc/fqab065

Ortolja-Baird, Alexandra, Victoria Pickering, Julianne Nyhan, Kim Sloan and Martha Fleming. 2019. Digital Humanities in the Memory Institution: The Challenges of Encoding Sir Hans Sloane's Early Modern Catalogues of His Collections. *Open Library of Humanities* 5(1): 44. https://doi.org/10.16995/olh.409

Perry, Sara, Maria Roussou, Maria Economou, Hilary Young and Laia Pujol. 2017. Moving Beyond the Virtual Museum: Engaging Visitors Emotionally. *2017 23rd International Conference on Virtual System and Multimedia (VSMM)*, Dublin, Ireland, 31 Oct.–4 Nov. 2017: 1–8. Online at https://ieeexplore.ieee.org/document/8346276 Accessed 27 April 2023.

Pink, Sarah, Heather Horst, John Postill, Larissa Hjorth, Tania Lewis and Jo Tacchi. 2016. *Digital Ethnography: Principles and Practice*. London: Sage.

Plets, Gertjan. 2016. Heritage Bureaucracies and the Modern Nation. Towards an Ethnography of Archaeological Systems of Government. *Archaeological Dialogues* 23(2): 193–213.

Plets, Gertjan. 2020. Promising Pipelines and Hydrocarbon Nationalism: The Sociality of Unbuilt Infrastructure in Indigenous Siberia. *Social Anthropology* 28(4): 843–861.

Plets, Gertjan, Pim Huijnen and David van Oeveren. 2021. Excavating Archaeological Texts: Applying Digital Humanities to the Study of Archaeological Thought and Banal Nationalism. *Journal of Field Archaeology* 46(5): 289–302. https://doi.org/10.1080/00934690.2021.1899889

Risam, Roopika. 2018. *New Digital Worlds: Postcolonial Digital Humanities in Theory, Praxis and Pedagogy*. Illustrated edition. Evanston, IL: Northwestern University Press.

Risam, Roopika and Josephs, Kelly Baker (eds). 2021. *The Digital Black Atlantic*. Minneapolis: University of Minnesota Press. https://doi.org/10.5749/9781452965321

Samaroudi, Myrsini, Karina Rodriguez Echavarria and Lara Perry. 2020. Heritage in Lockdown: Digital Provision of Memory Institutions in the UK and US of America during the COVID-19 Pandemic. *Museum Management and Curatorship* 35(4): 337–361. https://doi.org/10.1080/09647775.2020.1810483

Smith, Laurajane. 2006. *Uses of Heritage*. London: Routledge.

Star, Susan Leigh. 1999. The Ethnography of Infrastructure. *American Behavioural Scientist* 43(3): 377–391.

Stichelbaut, Birger, Gertjan Plets and Keir Reeves. 2021. Towards an Inclusive Curation of WWI Heritage: Integrating Historical Aerial Photographs, Digital Museum Applications and Landscape Markers in 'Flanders Fields' (Belgium). *Journal of Cultural Heritage Management and Sustainable Development* 11(4): 344–360. https://doi.org/10.1108/JCHMSD-04-2020-0056

Thylstrup, Nanna Bonde. 2019. *The Politics of Mass Digitization*. Boston, MA: MIT Press.

Uimonen, Paula, 2019. Muse and Power: African Women Writers and Digital Infrastructure in World Literature. *Anthropology and Humanism* 44(1): 20–37.

Ullrich, Daniel, Andreas Butz and Sarah Diefenbach. 2021. The Development of Overtrust: An Empirical Simulation and Psychological Analysis in the Context of Human–Robot Interaction. *Frontiers in Robotics and AI* 8. https://doi.org/10.3389/frobt.2021.554578

Van Daele, Koen, Erwin Meylemans and Mathieu De Meyer. 2004. De Centrale Archeologische Inventaris: een databank van archeologische vindplaatsen. In: *CAI-I, De opbouw van een archeolo- gisch beleidsinstrument*. IAP-Rapporten 14, Instituut voor het Archeologisch Patrimonium, Brussels: 29–48.

van Dijck, José, Thomas Poell and Martijn de Waal. 2018. *The Platform Society: Public Values in a Connective World*. Oxford: Oxford University Press.

Wimmer, Andreas and Nina Glick Schiller. 2002. Methodological Nationalism and Beyond: Nation-State Building, Migration and the Social Sciences. *Global Networks* 2(4): 301–332.

Part IV: Postcolonial legacies: 'European' heritages beyond Europe

Each of the chapters in this part of the book engages with what might be understood to be broadly 'European' forms of heritage or heritage practices outside Europe, or the impacts of non-European heritages on the idea of what constitutes European heritage itself. They provide an important and expanded framework through which to consider the impacts and colonial legacies of Europe and its approaches to 'past presencing' (Macdonald 2013) and imperial nostalgia or 'postcolonial melancholia' (Gilroy 2004) in a global context.

Both the chapter by Beverley Butler and Fatima Al-Nammari (Chapter 15) and that by Vittoria Caradonna (Chapter 18) focus on the ways in which heritage interventions – in the former case, an exhibition in London, and in the latter, an alternative boat cruise in Amsterdam – can contest stereotypes of refugees and other displaced peoples and produce new, more sympathetic understandings of their experience. Framed within the context of the Council of Europe and United Nations focus on the need to develop a global European conscience, Butler and Al-Nammari explore the potential for an expanded notion of European heritage which is sympathetic and open to refugees and asylum seekers. Similarly, Caradonna argues that in the absence of an engagement with the contemporary political situations and colonial histories of the places from which refugees have been forced to flee, such initiatives will only ever serve to emphasise rather than reduce the inequalities and prejudices that underpin such negative stereotyping.

The other two chapters in this section consider contested statues, plaques and memorials in the USA and Brazil respectively. Márcia Lika Hattori's chapter (Chapter 17) focuses on plaques and memorials related to state violence in the city of São Paulo, Brazil. She argues for an expanded concept of negative heritage which deals not only with recent conflicts, but also with longer colonial histories of dominance, repression and exploitation. Further, she questions the efficacy of plaques and monuments as memorial or pedagogical devices in Brazil, arguing that they employ a 'logics of remembrance' based on a standard approach to memorialising repression that has been developed in other parts of the world. Randall McGuire's contribution (Chapter 16) explores the phenomenon of contested statues in the southwestern USA, where the counter-heritages of First Nation and Hispanic/Latino communities come into conflict with one another and are each co-opted and utilised to advance Anglo-American interests, complicating conventional understandings of authorised heritage discourses in European colonial settler societies.

The chapters in this part of the book each in their own way argue for an expanded notion of European heritage which can account for the impact of European expansionism on the wider world, and the ways in which global colonial histories continue to inform postcolonial presents. Such an expanded notion of heritage would necessarily resist nationalistic narratives of history, emphasising diversity of cultural expressions and forms. A reconfigured notion of what constitutes European heritage will be vital in realising a more inclusive and less politically, economically and socially fragmented European future.

References

Gilroy, Paul. 2004. *Postcolonial Melancholia*. New York: Columbia University Press.
Macdonald, Sharon. 2013. *Memorylands: Heritage and Identity in Europe Today*. London: Routledge.

15
Heritage pharmacology and 'moving heritage': making refugees, asylum seekers and Palestine part of the European conscience

Beverley Butler and Fatima Al-Nammari

Discover the stories of people, animals and objects in exile, as told by refugees and researchers in London and the Middle East. Today, around 68.5 million refugees, asylum seekers and internally displaced people are trapped in a state of temporary permanence across the world. This free exhibition draws together poems, photographs and archival materials selected by people with experience of being displaced from their homes. Working closely with UCL researchers, people in London, Lebanon and Jordan chose objects that challenge public perceptions of what it means to be a refugee ('Moving Objects: Stories of Displacement' exhibition).[1]

Both the Council of Europe and the United Nations embodied these aims and hopes. At its origin the Council was about much more than human rights, though this was one, perhaps the most significant, manifestation of the conscience that had grown out of the twentieth century's two terrible wars … It is not a conscience that any one part of the horrors of the war can claim exclusively … That conscience which cannot be exclusive must be universally set against all violence and oppression wherever it manifests itself (Coleman 1999: 13).

The Palestinian diaspora should reach out to 'people of conscience' at all levels in EU capitals and in the US to call for international action, she [Ashrawi] noted. 'We have reached a turning point in which Palestinians everywhere are rising up together and saying "Enough is enough, we can't be ignored any more"', she said. 'Palestinians in Jordan, in Lebanon, in Europe and in the US are rising up to say: "Palestinian people need to have their rights"', she said (comments of Hanan Ashrawi, reported in Rettman 2021).

Introduction: moving heritage

In this chapter, we argue the urgent need for critical heritage studies, heritage institutions and heritage work of all kinds to take on the moral/ethical imperative of making refugees, asylum seekers and particularly Palestine part of the European conscience. We explore the salience this has for 'heritage wellbeing' and 'heritage health' by situating these dynamics within Butler's conceptualisation of 'heritage pharmacology' (Butler, Forthcoming) while simultaneously grounding our chapter in a case-study context of the exhibition 'Moving Objects: Stories of Displacement' held from March to October 2019 in the Octagon Gallery, UCL.

The exhibition's guiding motif – moving objects – was conceived in order to reflect upon the 'migration of persons, animals[2] and objects across time and space', as led by 'stories of displacement', and as told by those with lived experience of such tropes. By drawing on empirical fieldwork and creative collaborations undertaken by UCL researchers with refugees and asylum seekers,[3] the exhibition thus addressed the ways in which heritage 'moves us and moves with us in complex, intimate ways' (exhibition text panel). The exhibition and accompanying workshops explored the extent to which diverse objects and intangible heritage forms and forces can 'move us', in terms of 'inviting, demanding, requiring different forms of emotional and political engagement with questions of displacement'. Writ larger still, the exhibition sought to 'challenge public perceptions of what it means to be a refugee' (exhibition text panel).

Taking forward the comments of Coleman and of Ashrawi,[4] cited above, we are concerned more particularly with the imperative of Europeans, and more specifically still heritage practitioners, as 'people of conscience' to recognise their responsibilities and obligations to respond to calls for solidarity from those *in extremis*. This is especially important given the significant commitments by the Council of Europe (COE) and the United Nations (UN) to manifesting 'European conscience' and 'world conscience' respectively, and more particularly within heritage policy and programming.[5] Indeed, in the context of Brexit Britain and the wider European resurgence of right-wing nationalisms that are in turn inextricably bound up in so-called 'culture wars', there is an urgent need for such interventionism. The ongoing waves of refugee crises demand new impetus in terms of the need for the academy, cultural institutions, activists and others to counter negative media stereotypes and engage in quests to create new heritage solidarities in both the present moment and as centred within future directionalities. These are tropes that the global COVID-19 pandemic, ongoing and recent conflict in Palestine/Israel and contemporary events in Ukraine have brought into sharp relief.

Exhibition as journey and quest

The 'Moving Objects' exhibition was structured to mimic journeys and experiences of displacement and thus there was no prescribed linear pathway or set order, but rather visitors were given a sense of the different contexts of enforced movement and containment synonymous with refugee and asylum-seeker experiences. The human experience of the loss of home was placed within wider tropes of endangerment affecting other animals, habitats and environments. In discussion with co-curators, it was thus decided to divide the exhibition into four subthemes chosen and displayed in four distinct cases/sections:

- Being in Place
- Out of Place
- Talking Objects
- Challenging Views

Each of these subthemes and the related cases explored different aspects of human mobility, immobility, displacement, memory and heritage, by bringing together material such as objects, poems, visual pieces and archival materials selected, cocreated and analysed through co-curation workshops and research projects based at UCL. Many of these materials emerged through object handling, craft, writing, film and photography workshops in cities and camps, including Beirut and the Baddawi camp (Lebanon), UCL and the Helen Bamber Foundation (London, UK), and the Jerash, Talbieh and Zarqaa camps (Jordan).

In the majority of the text that follows, we focus on the 'Talking Objects' case as the specific section that we co-curated with Palestinians living in selected refugee camps in Jordan, based on long-term research (Butler and Al-Nammari 2016, 2018). First, however, we give a brief overview of the other three cases to provide overall context.

'Being in Place'

The case 'Being in Place' opened up global perspectives on climate change and endangerment and explored how 'habitat destruction, climate change and altering land use affect humans, other animals and things'. In terms of 'moving objects', an emphasis was placed on how the objects selected in this case 'represent ongoing global pressures which can impact human and animal rights, values, conflict, trade and what is lost or gained from losing a sense of place'. As an intentionally sparse case, items in this section included a taxidermy pangolin from the UCL collections[6] and accompanying reflections on animal endangerment. A trap was also chosen, to reflect on 'Indigenous hunting vs industrial farming' and on 'how the challenges faced in terms of climate change and endangerment might force us to reconsider Indigenous notions of being in place'.

'Out of Place'

The case 'Out of Place' addressed the motif of moving objects in terms of 'overlapping/multiple experiences of displacement and dispossession' with a focus on the Middle East and more specifically Palestinian refugees living in camps in Lebanon and Jordan. This case raised questions about and problematised descriptors of 'refugee', 'local', 'stranger' and 'hospitality', and thus of 'who [is] assumed to have [the] right and ability to welcome and host the other'. Images and the creative works of co-curators gave insights into contemporary life in refugee camps. Examples of such drawings, photographs, poetry and prose from writing workshops were suspended from the ceiling of the case while the 'ground of Palestine' was symbolically and literally present in archaeological form.

A poem entitled 'The Wall',[7] written to reflect on a piece of original wall in a refugee home in the Baddawi camp, Lebanon, built in the mid-1950s, explored, in poetic form, this object's 'moving', multi-layered agency. This wall was not only explored as a 'barrier between neighbours and us', but also as a 'moving object capable of redefining itself by itself' as new layers of plastering see 'the wall' 'multiply' 'over time'. Beneath the poem was a brick from 'Ancient Jericho', labelled 'Joshua's wall', selected from the UCL Institute of Archaeology (IoA) collections.[8] Such juxtapositioning brought contemporary strata of the refugee camp into relationships with deep-time excavations of Palestine and with colonial archaeologies that were returned to in the

'Talking Objects' case. The overtones of 'The Wall' also prompt reflections on the 'Separation Wall'[9] that marks the landscape of Palestine/Israel and that, again, re-emerge in the 'Talking Objects' case.

'Challenging Views'

The section 'Challenging Views' reiterated the overall goal of the exhibition as quest – that of challenging media and government negative stereotypes of refugees and asylum seekers – and sought to create new solidarities. A subversive example here saw asylum seekers from the Helen Bamber Foundation select Francis Galton's finger-printing machine from the UCL collections for display. The item is inextricably bound up in the 'negative heritage' of eugenics[10] and, more specifically, the use of fingerprints as synonymous with the identification of criminals, and also with the genre of identity cards, passports and papers, the possession of which may guarantee free movement, the absence of which may lead to further displacements and/or encampments. Members of the Helen Bamber photography club responded to this item by creating a backdrop of purposely blurred fingerprints, thus thwarting the possibility of identification and so resisting and acting back on such objects and on the powers that authorised them historically and in the present day.

The exhibition was also made available online through a 'virtual tour' and digital archive, so that it could be accessed by those unable to see it in London. This was particularly important given the co-curation of the exhibition with communities in the Middle East, whose ability to access 'heritage' in UK museums is limited by the legacies of colonialism. Virtual workshops and object-handling sessions were also held for co-curators to reflect upon 'how collections can be formed and "reformed" in relation to conflict and displacement' and 'how displaced people themselves relate to and reinterpret artefacts "housed" and "labelled" by UCL museums' (including collections specifically relating to Palestine held at UCL's IoA).

Ultimately, these workshops provided a space for people with lived experience of being displaced from their homes to imaginatively explore their own heritage, and to place alongside the above-mentioned collections objects, images and narratives that participants identify as 'empowering' in contexts of displacement. This process also enabled an examination of the benefits of critical approaches to heritage, and thus of 'challenging who the archive is for, what it is and who can interpret it' (exhibition text panel).

Heritage pharmacology: critical framework

The question of the *pharmakon* first arose in contemporary philosophy with Jacques Derrida's commentary on the *Phaedrus* in 'Plato's Pharmacy'. ... The *pharmakon* is at once what *enables* care to be taken and that *of which* care must be taken ... a pharmacology – that is, ... a discourse on the *pharmakon* understood *in the same gesture* in its curative and toxic dimensions (Stiegler 2013: 2–4; emphases in original).

Empowered by efficacious forces objects have the capacity to move us and move with us in complex, intimate ways. They 'speak' to and of experiences of displacement, marginalisation and conflict. In this context just as persons preserve, protect and care for empowered objects they reciprocate by acting as significant loci for repair, revitalisation and recovery of persons and 'lost' worlds.

In this case we juxta-pose contemporary, ancient and fabulous and futuristic objects, images and words. These are potent and powerful entities that both speak of and transcend diverse temporalities, territories and traditions. They creatively weave together the 'real' in complex acts in which the repossession of wholeness is grasped at in poetry, art, craft, magical thinking, wish-fulfilment, histories, memories and story-telling that in turn communicate oft-hidden truths while creating new facts on the ground (introductory panel, 'Talking Objects').

To move our journey forward to the 'Talking Objects' case, as a specific outcome of co-curation with Palestinians living in selected refugee camps in Jordan, we take Butler's (Forthcoming) concept of 'heritage pharmacology' as our encompassing critical framework to radically recast heritage in terms of its interactions and efficacies (Butler 2016) as a particularly potent pharmacology of care. We place core concepts and practices of heritage and Stiegler's above-cited philosophic reflections 'on pharmacology' (2013) in critical dialogue, with the aim of gaining mutual insights into 'care' as that which links together the two domains of heritage and health, as otherwise distinct discourses, concepts, technics and practices. Stiegler's own pursuit of 'pharmacological questions' builds on Derrida's work and recasts 'pharmacology' – a term usually reserved for that branch of the biomedical sciences dealing with drugs and their interactions and efficacies – for the deconstructionist lexicon. Here the alternatively and/or simultaneously 'curative and toxic dimensions' of the pharmakon/pharmacology take in wider philosophical-political and cultural-psychological dynamics vis-à-vis health and care. Pharmacology in this sense is concerned with responding to experiences and feelings of loss by establishing mutually constituted modes of care and protection. These manifest as diverse expressions of spirit, creative lifeworlds, modalities of resilience and 'object-work'. Ultimately, Stiegler reiterates, pharmacology is led by the quest/ion of 'What makes life worth living?' (Stiegler 2013: 4).

Our own concern with heritage, health and wellbeing pursues these same interests. In the 'Talking Objects' case, we addressed heritage as a quest for such efficacies. Thus, while 'heritage pharmacology' invests us in the quest/ion of pharmacology as ultimately a concern with 'What makes life worth living?' (Stiegler 2013) within both the poetics and realpolitik of Palestine, this quest/ion is paralleled by the inclusion by co-curators of the Palestinian poet Mahmoud Darwish's poem 'On this Earth'[11] in the 'Talking Objects' case. Darwish, dubbed Palestinian 'poet laureate', famously uses this poem to position the land of Palestine as an efficacious cosmology of the centre and, in so doing, as the epitome of all 'that which makes life worth living'.

Heritage work and/as object-relations

With reference to the efficacies of Stiegler's own thesis (2013), we also pursue the quest/ion of how 'heritage pharmacology' can best be grasped as a highly potent psychodynamic field of 'object-relations'. Recast further as a field of potential 'moving objects', one would wish that 'we' 'all' could have at our disposal the combined efficacies of the imaginative-practical 'object-work' outlined by Stiegler, as acts of attachment, detachment and praxis – and as operative within our heritage care repertoires and as a means to bring 'healthy' change and transformation to our diverse worldings. Object-work in this sense has the capacity to expand the efficacies of communion to alternative constellations and cosmologies, notably including spiritual, esoteric/countercultural object-relations. As such, these are 'moving object-relations' that resist being pressed into the exclusive service of power – including that of the COE and UN/UNESCO – as authorised heritage discourse, including new top-down 'heritage wellbeing' tropes.

However, experiences of enforced displacement and encampment obstruct, block and traumatically break with the efficacies of such object-work. Here then emerges the need to acknowledge more fully the pharmakonic ambivalences of heritage. In 'Plato's Pharmacy', Derrida does this by critically recuperating the ancient Greek etymology of *pharma-kon* as that which is alternatively and/or simultaneously 'poison-cure' (Derrida 2004). What particularly interests us in Stiegler's subsequent recasting of 'pharmacology' as an alternative model of dynamic psycho-cultural-political interactions and efficacies is the foundational and formative role it has in terms of instituting care, thus he identifies the 'pharmakon' precisely as 'at once what *enables* care to be taken and that *of which* care must be taken' (Stiegler 2013: 4; emphases in original).

Drawing on Winnicott's work, Stiegler argues that encounters with the 'pharmakon' and 'pharmakonic object(s)' are the lynchpin of object-relations and of transitional, psychic developmental pathways. Crucially, the pharmakon introduces 'us/the psyche/mental life' to social worlds and invests us in them. In the wider sense, it inculcates in us the phar-makonic efficacies of 'cultural things' and creative acts synonymous with heritage and/as 'memory-work'. Care is thus the bulwark around which memory-work, psychic-bodily health, identity, relationships, creativity and spirit are simultaneously forged and embedded within a dynamic 'pharmakonic milieu' and in tropes of care that manifest as particularly potent strains of 'arche-pharmacologies' (Stiegler 2018; see also Butler, Forthcoming).

In the 'Moving Objects' exhibition, accompanying workshops and in particular the 'Talking Objects' case, co-curators were committed to exploring these double-edged efficacies of heritage as that which has the agency to displace and dispossess, yet, alternatively and/or simultane-ously, to provide 'significant loci for repair, revitalisation and recovery of persons and "lost" worlds'. Pursuing the latter, in the 'Talking Objects' case we focused on how heritage is capable of ' "speaking" to and of expe-riences of displacement, marginalisation and conflict'. With a specific interest in heritage work as part of place-making in Palestinian refugee camps, we reiterate the sentiments expressed in our exhibition text that centres upon the relationalities and reciprocities vis-à-vis 'heritage well-being' and 'heritage care' in such contexts thus: 'Just as persons preserve, protect and care for empowered objects, they reciprocate.' Not only was heritage explored as a potential locus for gaining a sense of wholeness and healing, but also in terms of its efficacies in mapping across and col-lapsing virtual, spiritual and 'real' worlds of operational action.

Within our overarching 'heritage pharmacology', and writ larger still within the 'Talking Objects' case, co-curators sought to articulate a move-ment that was capable of 'speaking to and of' the spirit of *sumud*, an effica-cious force that is synonymous with Palestinian heritages of steadfastness, resistance and wellbeing. *Sumud* thus positions wellbeing, health and care as vitalities that yet again cross over spiritual registers and, crucially, also become materialised as part of the realpolitik, as 'facts on the ground' and as action. In creating the 'Talking Objects' case, co-curators were thus able to grasp and commune with the efficacies of 'Palestine' and 'home/homeland' as a potent 'arche-pharmacology of care' by means of imaginatively grounded object-relations and/as 'heritage-work'.

'Talking Objects': Palestinian heritage quests

> Workshop participants opened their discussions of 'heritage' ('turath' in Arabic) by focusing upon Palestinian embroidery. The cross-stitch dress, or 'thobe', was particularly valued as multi-layered 'heritage object', with motifs, designs and patterns that relate to specific Palestinian cities, locales and villages. Collectively they embody a unifying Palestinian identity. Embroidery speaks powerfully of women as creators, custodians and transmitters of heritage. 'The thobe is the unique fingerprint of Palestinian heritage and identity' (panel, 'Talking Objects').

The specific 'Heritage Workshops' held with Palestinians living in Jordanian refugee camps that guided our quest provided the specific narrative movement and structure of the 'Talking Objects' case (Figure 15.1). The viewer was thus taken on a journey of displacement that replicated the perspectives of Palestinian refugees as co-curators. It moved through further subthemes and experiences that can be usefully recast as a dynamic 'pharmakonic milieu' operating within heritage and visions of Palestine as an encompassing 'arche-pharmacology of care' (Stiegler 2018):

- Talking Turath/Heritage
- Exile/Nafy – Displacement and Repossession
- Home/Watan – Wholeness and Fragments of Place
- Promise/Wa'ad – Visions of Fulfilment

'Talking Turath/Heritage'

Forward movement was initiated as co-curators pursued the theme of 'Talking Turath' (Figure 15.2). It was here that the traditional Palestinian *thobe* (cross-stitch embroidery dress) was positioned as the epitome of

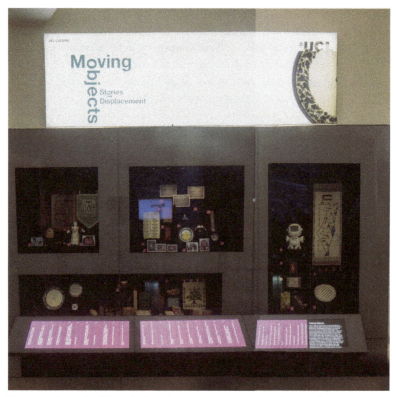

Figure 15.1 'Talking Objects' case, 2019. © Beverley Butler.

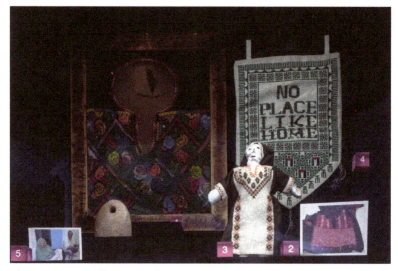

Figure 15.2 'Talking Turath/Heritage' theme, 2019. © Beverley Butler.

Palestinian heritage, and powerfully described by one refugee camp co-curator as 'the unique fingerprint of Palestinian heritage and identity'. The multi-layered efficacies of the *thobe* were explored in terms of the complex use of embroidery motifs that 'speak of and to' diverse Palestinian locales while giving them a unity and by celebrating the role, creativities and efficacies of women who are thus positioned at the centre of heritage transmission. Items displayed included an embroidered front panel (*qabbah*) that was invested with particular transformational powers. An accompanying text read:

> It [the *qabbah*] can be recycled, reused and transported when cut from an old dress and placed on a new one. The panels continue to be used by younger women to learn embroidery skills and thereby engage in rituals of cultural transmission. The thobe as 'mobile' heritage and as 'fused' or 'bridging' object thus connects refugees in Jordanian camps with their Palestinian origins.

While the selection started with contemporary items of significance made and/or owned by refugee co-curators, these were juxtaposed with items chosen from UCL collections (notably the aforementioned IoA collections relating to Palestine). Collectively, these items and the exhibition text reflected upon contemporary and deep time:

> Ancient arts of weaving [that] resonate across time from the material traces of ancient Gaza and Jericho to the makers and wearers of Palestinian textiles today. Cloth long vanished in the humid ground is tangible in the robe of a man incised on a scarab charm, in the dress pin that fastened a garment in a city near Gaza 36 centuries ago. Spindle and loom weight still echo the chatter of the weaving-hall (exhibition text panel).

An excerpt from Palestinian literature selected by co-curators drew these elements and efficacies together:

> I want to sew the times together. I want to attach one time to another, to attach childhood to age, to attach the present to the absent and all the presences to all the absences, to attach exiles to homeland and to attach what I imagined to what I see now (Barghouti 2005, *I saw Ramallah*).

'Exile/Nafy – Displacement and Repossession'

The second movement addressed the loss of home/homeland while also featuring the subsequent repossession of heritage (Figure 15.3). Poetry and other art forms selected from refugee camps sought to articulate the violence of the 1948 Nakba ('catastrophe'), the 1967 Naksa ('setback'/ 'relapse') and the ongoing profound ruptures synonymous with enforced movement, displacement and/or detainment. Thus, the pharmakonic underside of heritage as synonymous with painful experiences of harm, violence, dispossession and encampment was explored, while simultaneously and/or subsequently heritage was turned around to provide a locus of repossession. Such experiences and struggles are captured in an extract from the Palestinian intellectual Edward Said's (2012) *Reflections on Exile* that co-curators used to frame this section:

> Exile is strangely compelling to think about but terrible to experience. It is the unhealable rift forced between a human being and a native place, between the self and its true home: its essential sadness can never be surmounted. And while it is true that literature and history contain heroic, romantic, glorious, even triumphant episodes in an exile's life, these are no more than efforts meant to

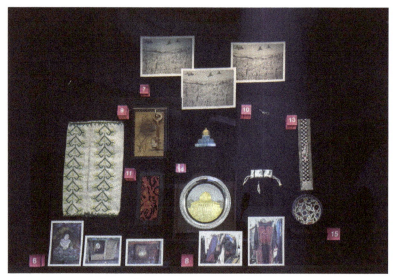

Figure 15.3 'Exile/Nafy – Displacement and Repossession' theme, 2019. © Beverley Butler.

overcome the crippling sorrow of estrangement (Said 2012, quoted on exhibition text panel).

The artwork of Khalil Ghaith, an artist who lives and works in Baqa camp, gave expression to the trauma of loss and more specifically the 'yearning for home'. One of his paintings featured an excerpt from another poem by the Palestinian poet Mahmoud Darwish that reads, 'I yearn for my mother's bread, and my mother's coffee, and my mother's touch'. The focus then turned to explore how:

> 'Palestine' is brought to the refugee camps in various ways. As 'heirlooms' (*mirath*)/'kept objects'/'inheritance'(*irth*) – jewellery, crafts, photographs, title-deed documents – and as items that feature recurrent symbols and motifs (exhibition text panel).

Often dubbed 'Little Palestines', the camps are home to such items, some original, some 'remade'. Examples of such heritage were brought to workshops held in the camps; some were photographed and some were loaned for the exhibition.

It was here, too, that co-curators explored the efficacies of 'Heritage as Sumud', thus making a direct link between heritage and (or as) health, and simultaneously highlighting the accompanying object-work. The text read:

> Palestinian heritage is associated with the Arabic term 'sumud': steadfastness, perseverance, resilience, solidarity and wellbeing. An example is the now iconic map and key well known to Palestine refugees. Many refugees still have the original keys to their homes in Palestine, it is an important symbol of attachment and national pride. Keys are often displayed to express the desire to return home and as a sign that the homeland is not forgotten.

The following text, written by a co-curator living in a camp, accompanied a particular key displayed in the exhibition:

> We have to resist the injustice that happened … we have been wronged, we have to carry symbols of our lands. Even though we have never visited Palestine we have to remember her and our rights. It is a sign of belonging, of not letting go, of persisting, even though we are third generation, the map [also] teaches my children [about the homeland] just like it taught me.

Such items were used to further explore how 'dreams' of repossessing Palestine as a 'lost object' are grasped and materialised in diverse ways. Here, the practice of traditional *dabka* dancing was highlighted by many co-curators, as was the preparation of traditional Palestinian food that creates 'sensoria' within the camps; writ larger, too, examples and images of vibrant street art were used in the case that similarly featured recurring symbols that define what might be called a Palestinian heritage canon. In these ways, the exhibition reiterated how 'camps act as alternative, dispersed archives, museums and as commemorative, memorial networks dedicated to repossessing – collecting, curating, representing – Palestine as "lost object" and "living culture"'.

'Home/Watan – Wholeness and Fragments of Place'

The topic of 'Home/Watan' was then explored in more depth and placed within the 'dream' of fragments of place being transformed into wholeness (Figure 15.4). This part of the 'Talking Objects' case was visually rich, displaying a wealth of objects old and new, and was led by a core question that binds Palestinian heritage up in much controversy:

> How should we best 'speak' about the land of Palestine? An object possessed by sacred narratives? The Promised Land of Milk and Honey? As lost homeland? As witness to many possessional acts: of pilgrims, crusaders and ancient to modern colonising projects? And/or as a place that folklore populates with supernatural forces of ghouls and jinn that 'speak' of alternative wisdoms, cures and curses? A land that possesses us and acts back? (exhibition text panel)

Here too co-curators drew on items from the IoA's collections, notably from what has been referred to as the 'Petrie Palestinian collection' – Sir Flinders Petrie being an early archaeological pioneer who has been afforded many accolades, including that of 'Father of Archaeology' and, more specifically, 'Father of Palestinian Archaeology'. As stated in the text panel quoted below, and as critically explored by Butler (2022), Petrie and 'his' Palestinian collection were *the* crucial element in the founding of the IoA. Co-curators also again drew on items excavated by Kathleen Kenyon (who has been called the 'Mistress of Stratigraphy') relating to 'ancient Jericho'. The accompanying text read:

> 'Palestine' emerges as an object of the Biblical archaeological imagination before becoming increasingly subject to scientific enquiry.

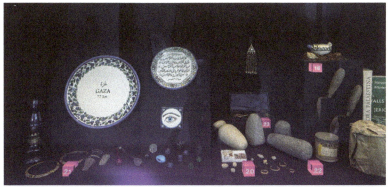
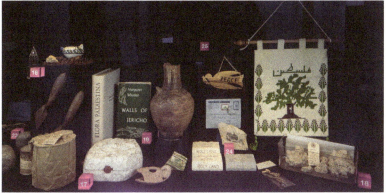

Figure 15.4 'Home/Watan – Wholeness and Fragments of Place' theme, 2019. © Beverley Butler.

Items displayed here from the Flinders Petrie Tell-el-Ajjul,[12] where a town flourished in the second millennium BC just south of modern Gaza city, and Kathleen Kenyon's excavations at the iconic site of Jericho 'speak' of this transformation. Such objects narrate the origins of ancient civilizations, the origins of archaeology and the origins of UCL Institute of Archaeology (IoA). Creating a home for what was dubbed Petrie's 'Homeless Palestinian collection' initiates academic archaeological study.

The colonial patriarchs and matriarchs, however, were themselves strategically displaced in order to bring marginalised constituencies into view. The text reads:

> Here we de-centre and recast our archaeologists as bearing witness to experiences of movement and stories of displacement. Excavating in the 1930s, Petrie was present at a period of increasing

tensions. He commented on the struggle of the Bedouin. In 1952–1958, Kenyon led excavations at Jericho, on the West Bank of the Jordan. The finds from the town site narrate the origins of civilizations, as the excavators from abroad commented on the arrival of Palestinian refugees as the latest stratum in the life of the place. The objects from these excavations too resist incorporation into the archaeological story alone, resonating with a sense of places and persons too powerful to reduce to one narrative. The distributed finds from such excavations followed the paths of later Palestinian exile to America, Europe and Australia.

The exhibition thus iterated the therapeutic, healing value of 'moving objects' that resist being pressed into the service of exclusivist possession by top-down oriental-colonialist narratives authorised by power. Thus, as migrant, exiled and moving objects, the distributed Palestinian collections (plural) were opened to the vision of new possibilities of 'rehoming' and to greater efficacies of circulation. Co-curators also took their cue to open up the efficacies of Palestine to acknowledge the wider, popular, folkloric heritages that effectively exposed the limitations of scientism. Alternative efficacies were drawn out vis-à-vis how objects are communed with to provide protection, amuletic and/or medicinal, and to explore the healing powers of such diverse material. One example here under the heading of 'anointing, adorning – pharmakonic materials' explores the efficacies of 'poison-cure' that operate across human, animal, spiritual, natural and supernatural worlds. The text reads:

> Depending on the dose, the medicinal plant may be cure or poison, the two meanings in the Greek term pharmakon, entangling use in practice with the seemingly exact history of weighing. Beyond the museum labels 'packet of seeds', 'cosmetic vessel', 'weight', the objects open themselves to the overlapping spheres of bodily adornment, pharmacist prescription, ritual anointing and sustenance in contemporary Palestine.

Here seeds and pestles from Jericho and a calcite vessel and rock crystal lozenge weight from 'Ancient Gaza' (Tell el-Ajjul) were juxtaposed next to diverse items that are turned to as deep-time and contemporary loci for care and wellbeing practices. These included beads, amulets to protect from the evil eye and protective koranic scripts. The same section also contained the Mahmoud Darwish poem that contains the refrain: 'We have on this land that which makes life worth living' – efficacious words that echo Stiegler's (2013) claim that the question of pharmacology is ultimately bound up in the quest for 'what makes life worth living'. This was positioned between a souvenir, a contemporary ceramic lamp emblazoned with 'From the Land of Milk and Honey', from the Old City of Jerusalem, and some soil from Palestine. The soil highlights, from the Palestinian perspective, that the ongoing quest for wholeness of place and the search for the 'good life' are deeply compromised and obstructed by ongoing violent displacements and the land grabs that bring back into view 'The Wall'. The panel here reads:

> This soil displayed here is from the Cremisan Valley located on the seam line between the West Bank and Jerusalem. The valley is one of the last remaining green areas of greater Bethlehem. It is a site associated with a long heritage of wine making. The area is however at risk as the construction of the Wall threatens to annex it from the nearby village of Beit Jala.[13]

'Promise/Wa'ad – Visions of Fulfilment'

The concluding part of the 'Talking Objects' case addressed 'Promise/ Wa'ad' and, as such, spoke of 'visions of fulfilment' (Figure 15.5). Given that the Palestinian struggle is ongoing, co-curators drew on the imaginative efficacies of heritage and how these relate to the realpolitik, thus emphasising that:

> The task of articulating future promise – like that of Scheherazade in *A Thousand and One Nights* weaving her intricate tapestry of storytelling – illustrates how acts of creativity bind the mundane to the magical in articulations of desire, wish-fulfilment and dream-work. It 'speaks' to and of imperatives to communicate oft-hidden truths and wisdoms while in turn creating the possibilities of generating new realities on the ground.

Here objects included fantastic, creative interventions that use 'desire, wish-fulfilment and dream-work', and often humour and satire, to rework heritage pharmacologies of care as loci of hope and of action. This strategy saw the creation of 'counterfactual' objects too, in the

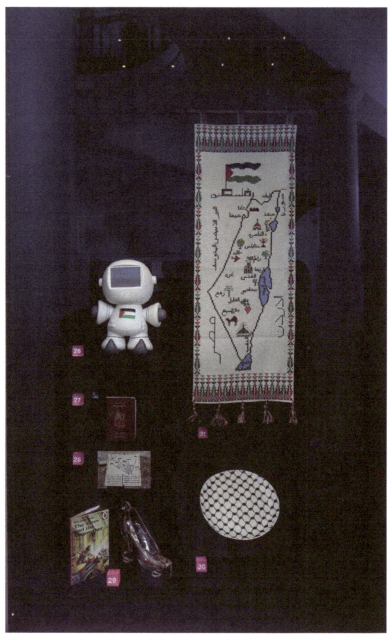

Figure 15.5 'Promise/Wa'ad – Visions of Fulfilment' theme, 2019. © Beverley Butler.

sense that Palestine was recast and projected onto iconic events, narratives and objects. An example is the 'Bethlehem passport' created by the Open Bethlehem campaign.[14] As an exercise in wish-fulfilment, pastiche and *sumud*, this object subverted the notion of papers and documentation based on exclusionary demands of national sovereignty that limit freedom and travel to others as non-citizens. This passport as a 'moving object', however, represents a significant statement made at a time when the city of Bethlehem itself continues to be increasingly closed off and Bethlehemites encamped and besieged. As the exhibition text continues:

> The quotation inside this passport reads: 'In that the bearer of this passport is a citizen of Bethlehem, that they recognise this ancient city provides a light to the world, and to all people who uphold the values of a just and open society'. The Bethlehem passport was launched in 2005 as part of a protest campaign against the Wall and to keep Bethlehem 'open'. It has been granted to more than 3,000 supporters worldwide.

Another object displayed here, a 'Palestinaut', saw Palestine imaginatively and subversively inserted within an iconic event. This artwork was one of 500 similar sculptures that are usually displayed in a group as part of an installation, and relates to the Palestinian artist Larissa Sansour's film *A Space Exodus*.[15] As stated in the accompanying text panel:

> The film re-imagines one of America's finest moments of space exploration as a Palestinian triumph. It posits the idea of a first Palestinian into space and referencing Armstrong's moon landing, it interprets this theoretical gesture as 'a small step for a Palestinian, a giant leap for mankind'.

A second item, a ceramic plate also created by Sansour, held particular efficacy in that it distilled, if not stripped bare, the underpinning logic/premise/efficacies of archaeology – notably, those put in place by Flinders Petrie, whose monikers also included that of 'Father of Pots' (see Butler 2022). The plate – presented as an archaeological find and decorated with a design that echoes the keffiyeh (an iconic symbol of Palestine) – highlighted the archaeological preoccupation with pots/ceramics as the archaeological litmus test or basis for recognising the existence of ancient civilisations, while simultaneously providing a locus of reimagining. Locating this artwork at the 'cross-section between science-fiction, archaeology and global politics', Sansour has argued that when the 'real' becomes 'surreal', alternative worlds of critique need to be created. Indeed, the artwork in all its pseudo-authenticity is articulated as an act of 'narrative terrorism' and thus as a strategy to move beyond the impasse synonymous with the 'archaeology wars' and the over-politicised instrumentalisation and weaponisation of archaeology, particularly in the Israeli/Palestinian context. In response, Sansour projects her narrative into a fictional future in which the 'replicant plate' is one of thousands manufactured by a 'rebel leader' who deposits archaeological ceramics back in time for archaeologists to find, thus 'setting up an elaborate operation in order for the future generations of Palestinians to obtain the basic privileges that history has so far denied', and thus 'de facto creating a nation' through 'actions' that act as alternative 'historical interventions'.[16]

A further item made by co-curators transformed a transparent mould of a high-heeled shoe, turning it into an alternative fairy-tale 'glass slipper' that was inspired by the following quote from Palestinian lawyer-intellectual Raja Shehadeh:

> Such is the despair of Palestinian refugees and deportees about ever setting foot on the soil of their country that in Hebron, whose people are famous for their entrepreneurial spirit, a shoemaker has produced a shoe that contains a small amount of Palestinian soil in the sole (Shehadeh 2015, quoted on exhibition text panel).

The themes and efficacies of home and homeland were further iterated within diverse story-telling genres:

> From Ma'ruf the Shoemaker in *A Thousand and One Nights*, the Brothers Grimm's story of the elves giving a poor shoemaker a helping hand, to the glass and ruby slippers worn by Cinderella and Dorothy; footwear in fantasy and fairy tale evokes transformational potencies. Popular wisdom and wish-fulfilment illuminate new pathways and possibilities, led by moral-ethical acts of gifting, and by the fulfilment of promise that begins and ends at home.

The 'Talking Objects' case ended where it began, with Palestinian embroidery – this time in the form of a map bought from Ramallah, a familiar and recurring 'moving object'. The accompanying panel read:

> Most Palestine refugees' homes – and those of diaspora Palestinians – have some version of this map in them and still use the names of

towns, cities and villages embroidered on it to reference their place of origin. They refer to these as home.

A more general reflection was made in these terms:

> How do 'we' and 'others' carry a vision of home/homeland with us? How might such visions transform into new futures of promise? From ancient to modern times map-making acts as a powerful tool of possession, dispossession and repossession. Maps depicting what Edward Said referred to as a 'tiny sliver of land in the Eastern Mediterranean' are often deeply contentious. Here a map embroidered by a refugee is rooted in a pre-1948 rural vision of Palestine transmitted across the generations.

A final postscript returned to refugee voices and visions of home and featured a popular heritage ritual engaged in by refugees in Jordan, in which people travel from their camp to visit viewing sites, such as Mount Nebo and Umm Qais, where Palestine can be seen – a ritual offering some comfort and consolation in the vision of close proximity to their ancestors/homeland and to the enduring promise of fulfilment. This final element was accompanied by a quotation from one such alternative pilgrim, who reflects, 'Knowing that when it is sunrise here [in Jordan] it is sunrise in Palestine, brings bitter-sweet feelings of happiness and of longing.'

Conclusions: Palestine in the European conscience

> Blake also realised the central significance of Imagination (he always used a capital I). For him it was not just an aesthetic or aesthetic extra, but the working of the Spirit that gives meaning to the political … One of the prerequisites of a 'celestial Europe' [is] … [t]o paraphrase the words of William Blake, 'We cannot rest until we have created many Jerusalems in Europe's green and pleasant lands' (Coleman 1999: 14, 33).

> We have on this land that which makes life worth living (Darwish).[17]

Our shared journey through the 'Moving Objects' exhibition and 'Talking Objects' case as a critical movement led by the voices of refugees and asylum seekers has sought to articulate diverse insights and the complexities that such experiences of displacement expose. In our conclusions, we re-engage with the urgent quest/ion of placing such actors, and the wider stories of displacement, within the 'European conscience'. Our critical recasting of the exhibition within conceptualisations of 'heritage pharmacology' – as 'moving' efficacious fields of object-work and object-relations that resist exclusivity as they collapse across imaginative, political and cultural worldings – ultimately pursues calls for justice that intensify the need to make the case for an ethics of moral thought rooted in 'heritage care' as that which takes in such facts on the ground.

In particular, our chapter demonstrates how and why contemporary Palestinians look to 'Palestine' as a vibrant 'arche-pharmacology of care', and yet in the European conscience, they still exist in a state of exception. This is not to say that Palestine does not exist in a European discourse of its relations to the Middle East and/or within Europe itself; only that, in the absence of rights (in terms of a nation-state, citizenship and so on), there is neither a presumed ethics of justice nor an ethics of care that might be assumed to flow from within that discourse. Indeed, in an increasingly exclusivist Brexit Britain and right-wing nationalist Europe, Coleman's (1999) iterations and Blakean paraphrasing of creating 'many Jerusalems in Europe's green and pleasant lands' as manifestations of conscience[18] are confronted by the imperative of reconnecting with such tropes within Palestinian heritage quests and/as 'pharmacologies of care'. The cruel irony of excluding those for whom the ground of Jerusalem itself is looked to as an efficacious 'arche-pharmacology' and as a 'manifestation of conscience' from this exclusivist European vision of 'just' futures exacerbates the situation by reiterating old and creating new politics of possession that must be opened up.

As demonstrated, within the 'world as exhibition', imagination is employed to adopt a unique position within articulations of 'conscience' that are capable of crystallising attempts to possess the efficacies of things. Notably, these creative-imaginative efficacies emerge to define themselves as part of expressions of *sumud* synonymous with both everyday acts of life-making and the quest/ion of what makes life worth living. Thus, what we care about and who we care for are fundamental questions in any 'ethics of care'. In recognition of such socially and culturally embedded object worlds of 'heritage pharmacology', we, and our co-curators, call on 'people of conscience' to pursue this imperative in the hope of inspiring attitudes and actions that move 'us all' towards a future European conscience that we feel is sadly lacking at present.

Acknowledgements

We wish to thank Prof. Helen Chatterjee, Prof. Elena Fiddian-Qasmiyeh and Prof. Stephen Quirke at UCL for their collegiality. We acknowledge the co-curators who made this exhibition possible and extend to them our sincere thanks and ongoing gratitude. Their lived experience of displacement, of refugee camps and/or of seeking asylum underpins the critical movement of the exhibition as manifestations of conscience that require response and responsibility vis-à-vis a new heritage pharmacology/'ethics of care'.

Notes

1. https://www.ucl.ac.uk/culture/whats-on/moving-objects-exhibition
2. We use animals here to mean non-human animals.
3. See https://refugeehosts.org/, https://www.geog.ucl.ac.uk/research/research-centres/migration-research-unit, https://culturehealthresearch.wordpress.com/forced-displacement-and-cultural-interventions/, and https://www.culturehealthandwellbeing.org.uk/ in partnership with https://www.helenbamber.org/ and Chatterjee et al. (2020).
4. Hanan Ashrawi is a Palestinian politician, legislator, activist and scholar.
5. Council of Europe: see https://www.coe.int/en/web/culture-and-heritage/cultural-heritage; United Nations (UNESCO): see https://whc.unesco.org/en/
6. For information on these collections, see https://www.ucl.ac.uk/culture/
7. https://refugeehosts.org/2018/05/22/the-wall/
8. For information on these collections, see https://www.ucl.ac.uk/culture/institute-archaeology
9. See https://www.un.org/unispal/document/auto-insert-207980/
10. See https://www.ucl.ac.uk/culture/projects/bricks-mortals
11. See https://asitoughttobe.wordpress.com/2010/08/24/on-this-earth-what-makes-life-worth-living-3/ Note that this poem is sometimes translated as 'On this Land'.
12. It is crucial to point out that the Palestinian collection relates to pre-1948 Palestine and that two sites, Tell Gemmeh and Tell el Fara, are now within contemporary Israel. See https://www.ucl.ac.uk/archaeology/research/directory/petrie-palestinian-project. 'Moving Objects' thus focused on Tell el Ajjul.
13. See https://www.europarl.europa.eu/doceo/document/E-7-2013-004944_EN.html?redirect
14. https://www.openbethlehem.org/become-a-bethlehem-citizen.html
15. https://larissasansour.com/A-Space-Exodus-2009
16. https://www.lawrieshabibi.com/exhibitions/45/; https://www.lawrieshabibi.com/video/8-larissa-sansour-interview-with-blue-coat-liverpool/ 2017.
17. https://asitoughttobe.wordpress.com/2010/08/24/on-this-earth-what-makes-life-worth-living-3/
18. In the UK, this vision led to operational care in the form of the founding of the National Health Service being manifest as a 'New Jerusalem'.

References

Barghouti, Mourid. 2005. *I saw Ramallah*. London: Bloomsbury.

Butler, Beverley. 2016. The Efficacies of Heritage: Syndromes, Magics and Possessional Acts. *Journal of Public Archaeology* 15 (2–3): 113–135.

Butler, Beverley. Forthcoming. On Heritage Pharmacology: Rethinking 'Heritage Pathologies' as Tropes of Care. *Journal of History of Human Sciences*.

Butler, Beverley. 2022. Rehoming Flinders Petrie's 'Homeless Palestinian Collection'. *Jerusalem Quarterly* 90: 37–57.

Butler, Beverley and Fatima Al-Nammari. 2016. 'We Palestinian Refugees': Heritage Rites and/as the Clothing of Bare Life: Reconfiguring Paradox, Obligation and Imperative in Palestinian Refugee Camps in Jordan. *Journal of Contemporary Archaeology* 3(2): 147–159.

Butler, Beverley and Fatima Al-Nammari. 2018. 'We Palestinian Refugees': Heritage Rites and/as the Clothing of Bare Life: Reconfiguring Paradox, Obligation, and Imperative in Palestinian Refugee Camps in Jordan. In Yannis Hamilakis (ed.), *The New Nomadic Age: Archaeologies of Forced and Undocumented Migration*. Bristol, CT: Equinox: 29–41.

Chatterjee, Helen, Clelia Clini, Beverley Butler, Fatima Al-Nammar, Rula Al-Asir and Cornelius Katona. 2020. Exploring the Psychosocial Impact of Cultural Interventions with Displaced People. In Elena Fiddian-Qasmiyeh (ed.), *Refuge in a Moving World: Tracing Refugee and Migrant Journeys Across Disciplines*. London: UCL Press: 323–347.

Coleman, John (ed.). 1999. *The Conscience of Europe*. Strasbourg, France: Council of Europe.

Derrida, Jacques. 2004. *Dissemination*. London: Continuum.

Rettman, Andrew. 2021. EU Impunity for Israel Creating 'Horror' in Gaza. *EUobserver*, 17 May 2021. Online at https://euobserver.com/world/151851 Accessed 19 April 2023.

Said, Edward. 2012. *Reflections on Exile: And Other Literary and Cultural Essays*. London: Granta Books.

Shehadeh, Raja. 2015. *Language of War, Language of Peace: Palestine, Israel and the Search for Justice*. London: Profile Books.

Stiegler, Bernard. 2013. *What Makes Life Worth Living: On Pharmacology*. Translated by Daniel Ross. Cambridge, UK, and Malden, MA: Polity Press.

Stiegler, Bernard. 2018. *The Neganthropocene*. Edited and translated by Daniel Ross. London: Open Humanities Press.

16
How to tell the good guys from the bad guys … or not

Randall H. McGuire

Introduction

On 15 June 2020, a crowd of Indigenous people and their primarily Anglo-American allies assembled at the municipal museum in Albuquerque, New Mexico (Romero 2020). They gathered there to protest a sculpture called *La Jornada*, meaning 'the journey'. *La Jornada* illustrates, in bronze, the conquistador Juan de Oñate leading a column of settlers to found the Spanish colony of New Mexico. Everyone in New Mexico agrees that Oñate was a brutal conqueror and Indian people still hate him after four centuries. The crowd chanted, splashed red paint on Oñate and put a chain around his neck to topple the effigy. Hispanic counter-protesters attempted to stop the desecration, and a right-wing militia group joined them. Gunshots were heard and an Anglo-American ally fell wounded as people screamed and fled. The police arrested the shooter. At first glance, it seems clear who the 'good guys' and the 'bad guys' are at the Albuquerque Museum. But the history and contemporary social context of these monuments and the groups they represent complicate how we tell the good guys from the bad guys … or not.

Authorised heritage discourses and settler states

Imperialistic expansion spread European colonial heritages beyond Europe. This was especially the case where European conquerors and colonists established settler states by seizing territory and replacing or displacing Indigenous populations through genocide, assimilation and/or more subtle means (Wolfe 2006; Veracini 2010). Subjugating Indigenous peoples required colonisers to seize control of the narrative, to conquer history itself. They established social structures, ideologies and institutions to impose authorised heritage discourses (AHDs; Smith 2006) that demean or co-opt Indigenous peoples and legitimate the settler state.

The formation of a settler state was not an event, but rather an unending process of struggle (Kauanui 2016). This struggle exposes 'difficult heritage' (Macdonald 2016; Miller and Schmahmann 2017). Indigenous peoples resist their domination and the AHD that shapes and legitimates that oppression. They engage in a critical heritage praxis to further their liberation and emancipation (see Querin 2020 for an example in Brazil). They formulate counter-heritages to motivate their own people and to recruit disaffected members of the European descendent majority. This praxis materialises in street demonstrations, vandalisation of buildings and the defacing and destruction of statues.

The inherent struggle of heritage in settler states creates difference and a dynamic AHD laden in contradiction. The AHD is not fixed but rather depends on the nature of difference in the settler state and historical context. Non-Indigenous and Indigenous groups will read the same monument in completely different ways. The AHD appropriation of Indigenous heritage romanticises the native. It leads disaffected members of the dominant European descendent community to support Indigenous heritage (Deloria 1998). Indigenous peoples struggle to recruit and control the disaffected but often these descendants of the conquerors create new appropriations. The AHD changes and morphs through time in a dialectic with Indigenous counter-heritage. The AHD eventually must change its appropriations of Indigenous heritage to accommodate those counter-heritages as mainstream 'heritage' or give up power and control of the historical narrative (Harrison 2013).

The AHD of every settler state must resolve two inherent contradictions: (1) that Europeans established the state on lands clearly taken from Indigenous people and (2) that Indigenous people survive as minorities within the state (McGuire 2008: 77–79). Some settler state AHDs deny the humanity of the Indigenous population, demonising them to justify their physical and/or cultural destruction. Other AHDs co-opt or appropriate Indigenous counter-heritages by appropriating Indigenous history and culture in a transient and/or marginal way that benefits the European descendants. We see such appropriation in many, many cases, including México (McGuire 2008: 157–163), Brazil (Querin 2020), Australia (Byrne 1996) and New Zealand (Brown 2013).

We see these contradictions and appropriations in the AHD of the USA (McGuire 1992). In the nineteenth century, the AHD attributed archaeological sites in the USA to a lost race of 'Mound Builders' who were annihilated by red savages who invaded the continent a few hundred years before the European conquest. At the turn of the twentieth century, the AHD declared Native Americans to be the 'First Americans' (that is, the first immigrants to the nation). Calling Indians the 'First Americans' gives Indian people a transient role in the US national heritage and appropriates Indian heritage for the settler state. In the southwestern USA, a legacy of dual colonialism complicates this solution and manifests itself in recent demonstrations and attacks on statues celebrating Hispanic/Latino heroes.

Traditionally in the western USA, we distinguish three major ethnic/racial groups. Native American or Indian nations originally inhabited the region. They speak a variety of Indigenous languages and identify with their specific nations. Spain (and later México) conquered New Mexico and California, and the conquerors' descendants speak Spanish. Most of these descendants are mestizos of mixed Indian and Spanish ancestry. The term 'Hispanic' emphasises Spain, and the term 'Latino' emphasises Latin America. More specific identities (Hispanos, the first Spanish inhabitants of New Mexico; Californios, the first Spanish inhabitants of California; and Chicanos, Mexican-American people who migrated from México) exist within these broad categories. English-speaking Euro-Americans are referred to as 'Anglos'.

Spain established the first settler state in the region during the seventeenth and eighteenth centuries. In the mid-nineteenth century, the USA conquered Mexican New Mexico and California and marginalised the Indigenous and Spanish-speaking populations of the region. The mestizo Spanish speakers did not fit into the AHD of the USA because they were both Indigenous and European. As Rubén Mendoza (2015) points out, 'Hispanic contributions have long been deemed secondary to an authentic American history.' In this context of shifting AHD and competing counter-heritages, it can be difficult to tell who are the good guys and who are the bad.

Critical heritage praxis in the streets

Following the 25 May 2020 murder of George Floyd in Minneapolis, Minnesota, cities in the USA erupted with demonstrations against anti-Black racism. Black Lives Matter protesters, African-Americans and their allies filled the streets with marches to protest the police murder of another Black man and to disrupt the country's racist structures. These demonstrations spread globally, with hundreds of protests, including ones in virtually every European country. The history of structural racism in the USA becomes material in statues that glorify slave holders and Confederate heroes. Protesters tore down, defaced and painted over numerous Confederate statues and many municipalities removed statues to protect them from vandalism. In numerous cities, right-wing militias and the Ku Klux Klan confronted the protesters to defend the statues. Here a left-wing critical politics confronts Black racism, and it seems very clear who are the bad guys and the good, both in bronze and on the streets.

Very quickly the protests expanded to confront oppression and racism against Native Americans. Indigenous peoples and their allies assailed statues that materialised their oppression. Across the country, activists tore down, defaced and painted over statues of Christopher Columbus. In New Mexico, they reviled bronze images of Juan de Oñate and in California, they abused statues of Junípero Serra. In New Mexico and California, these protests confronted and undermined Hispanic people's counter-heritage. In many ways, they reinforced the Anglo-driven AHD of Latino people and obscured the oppression by Anglo-Americans of both Indigenous peoples and Latino peoples.

Juan de Oñate, the last conquistador

In 1542, Charles I of Spain issued the New Laws of the Indies for the Good Treatment and Preservation of the Indians. These laws forbade the *Conquista*, a practice that originated in the Spanish reconquest of the Iberian Peninsula. A Spanish nobleman would finance a *Conquista* and in return the Crown would grant him rights of *encomienda*. These rights allowed the conquistador to demand tribute and forced labour from the people of the conquered region. In return, the Crown expected the conquistador to convert the subjugated population to Catholicism and to defend them against heathens. Conquest and the *encomienda* led to many grave abuses of Indigenous peoples, and leaders in the Catholic Church (most notably Bartolomé de Las Casas) argued for its abolition. The king agreed and the New Laws placed control of Indigenous populations with the church.

In 1595, the Crown gave Juan de Oñate permission to raise money for a *Conquista* in Nueva México (Simmons 1993). To enlist Spanish settlers and soldiers, Oñate offered recruits rights of *encomienda* even though the

New Laws had abolished these rights. Oñate executed a brutal conquest of Nueva México, attacking and reducing the Indigenous Pueblo Indian towns. He also did not tolerate dissent from his settlers, executing individuals who opposed him. The Spanish settlement survived by demanding tribute in corn, cloth and women from the Indigenous Pueblos.

In 1599, warriors at the Pueblo of Acoma killed a dozen Spanish soldiers sent to collect tribute. Oñate ordered an attack on the Pueblo, and his soldiers slaughtered hundreds of Acoma people. The Spanish enslaved many of the children and cut the right foot from 24 surviving warriors. Even for his time, Oñate's brutality was extreme. The viceroy summoned him to Mexico City, where a tribunal convicted him of crimes against Indigenous people and Spanish settlers.

For the Indigenous people of New Mexico, especially the Pueblo Nations, Juan de Oñate brought Spanish tyranny (Burnett 2020; Pérez and Ortega 2020). The processes of colonisation, attacks on their religion and their oppression begin with Oñate. The modern Pueblo of Acoma have always opposed any memorialisation or glorification of the conquistador. Numerous Native Americans argue that they, the original inhabitants, deserve the dominant voice in a counter-heritage.

Many Hispanos take a very different view of Oñate and his role in history (Burnett 2020). They have been discriminated against since the USA subjugated New Mexico in 1848 and they embraced Oñate as a symbol of their resistance to that discrimination and marginalisation (Romero 2020). For them, Oñate founded Hispano culture in New Mexico. He brought Catholicism, the Spanish language and livestock. They recognise his brutality but see his accomplishments as surpassing his crimes (Pérez and Ortega 2020: 2; Burnett 2020).

Statues to the last conquistador began to appear around the turn of the twenty-first century, spurred on by the 400th anniversary of the Spanish conquest. They reflect a movement by Hispano people to formulate their own counter-heritage in order to resist discrimination and to establish themselves as victors in New Mexican history. In 1997, the Hispano community of Alcalde, New Mexico, established an Oñate Monument Centre with an equestrian statue of the conquistador (Figure 16.1). Albuquerque is the largest city in New Mexico, with a slight majority Hispano/Mexican-American population. On its 400th anniversary, in 2004, the city erected *La Jornada*. Two years later, the Latino-majority city of El Paso, Texas, erected an equestrian statue to the conquistador at the city airport.

These bronze Oñates promptly attracted protests that continue today. In one of the most evocative acts of dissent, an Acoma man

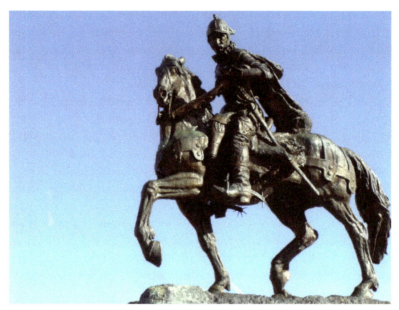

Figure 16.1 Equestrian statue of Juan de Oñate, Alcalde, New Mexico, 2006. © Advanced Source Productions. Available at https://commons.wikimedia.org/wiki/File:Equestrian_statue_of_Juan_de_O%C3%B1ate.jpg, and reproduced under the Creative Commons licence CC BY 2.0.

amputated the right foot from the newly erected Alcalde bronze (Romero 2017). Protesters gathered to oppose the El Paso statue before its dedication. In 2017, someone painted the reconstructed right foot of the Alcalde Oñate red and sprayed graffiti on the monument.

Protests intensified as demonstrations against anti-Black racism surged in the summer of 2020. Native Americans and (primarily) Anglo allies attacked Oñate. In El Paso, unknown persons daubed the bronze statue with graffiti and red paint. In Albuquerque, the protest at *La Jornada* turned violent. Because of this incident, the city of Albuquerque removed the Oñate statue on the same day that county authorities removed the Alcalde equestrian sculpture.

Junípero Serra: missionary saint

Spain's 1542 New Laws gave control of Indigenous peoples to the Catholic mendicant orders (Dominicans, Franciscans, Augustinians and Jesuits).

The laws defined a process of *reducción* (reduction) to pacify and convert Indigenous peoples. The missionaries used a combination of guile, force and enticement to reduce scattered Indigenous communities into missions. The military would establish presidios (military bases) to protect the missionaries, to control Indians in the missions, to catch Indians escaping the missions and to bring Indians into the missions. *Reducción* opened land for Spanish settlement. The friars would remain in control of Indian people until they had fully converted them and made them loyal subjects of the Spanish Crown. At this point, the mission would become a parish church. For almost 300 years, the Spanish used this mission–presidio system in North and South America.

In 1769, the Franciscan friar Junípero Serra began the Spanish missionisation of Alta California (the US state of California). Missionisation would continue for 54 years, with the establishment of four presidios and 21 missions. Father Serra personally established nine missions. He died in 1784. Alta California became part of an independent México in 1821, and in 1833, the Mexican government secularised all missions. Serra and his fellow missionaries sought to open the gates of heaven to the Indigenous people. To help native peoples thrive economically, the padres introduced livestock, new crops and new crafts. They created each mission as a self-sustaining enterprise, and they worked communally with the *neophytes* (Indians on the mission). Soldiers and settlers often sought to abuse and enslave Indian people. Father Serra and other padres opposed these efforts. He also wrote a 33-point bill of rights for Indigenous people living in missions and delivered it to the viceroy of New Spain, in México City (CNA Staff 2020). Many Native Americans entered the missions to seek protection from abuse and enslavement (Hackel 2013).

Modern critics of Serra dismiss the benefits of the missions for native peoples and instead view them as concentration camps. Although the laws of New Spain required that the *reducción* be done voluntarily, soldiers had to force Indians into the missions. The padres did not allow the *neophytes* to leave the missions and they sent soldiers to capture and return any Indians who stole away. Conversion to Catholicism necessitated that the *neophytes* first discard their Indigenous religious beliefs and norms. In front of each church stood a whipping post. Friars flogged *neophytes* who maintained Indigenous religious practices, who failed to practise or resisted Catholic ritual or who violated Spanish norms (especially sexual norms). Few if any of the missions could maintain a resident population (Beebe and Senkewicz 2015). Due to disease, physical abuse and low levels of fertility, populations consistently declined, and the missionaries sent soldiers out to capture more Indians. On numerous occasions, Indians rose in revolt against the missions. As Native American professor of literature Deborah A. Miranda said in an interview for *The Atlantic* (Green 2015: 47), 'Serra did not just bring us Christianity. He imposed it. He did incalculable damage to a whole culture.'

In the 1940s, the Catholic Church initiated the long process of canonising Serra. In 1985, the pope declared Serra to be 'Venerable'. At this point, Native American activists amplified their critique of Serra, demanding that the church deny him sainthood (Lind 2015; Green 2015). In 2015, Pope Frances canonised Saint Serra after calling him 'one of the founders of the United States' (Pineda 2018: 286). Activists and demonstrators filled the streets, and statues of the new saint became targets for their wrath. That fury seemed unabated when, five years later, the killing of George Floyd sparked massive demonstrations in the streets and renewed attacks on statues.

There are many more statues of Saint Serra than of Juan de Oñate, and they have a longer and more complex history. In 1891, Jane Elizabeth Lathrop Stanford, wife of Leland Stanford (both non-Catholics), erected a granite statue to Father Serra in Monterey, California. The statue in Golden Gate Park, San Francisco, was built in 1907 (Figure 16.2). In 1922, the Catholic Church erected a wooden statue of Father Serra at his grave, in the Carmel mission. Since then, other statues of the friar have appeared in the community of Carmel-by-the-Sea. In the 1930s, many other communities and the Catholic Church erected statues of him. The 1931 inclusion of Friar Serra as one of two statues representing the state of California in the United States Capitol may have inspired this wave of bronze Serras. That year, the state legislature erected a copy of the US Capitol statue in Sacramento, the state capital of California. People continued to put up sculptures of Serra throughout the 1970s, including a cartoonish 8-metre-tall concrete Serra that points across Interstate Highway 280 (the Junípero Serra Freeway). No complete list of Father Serra statues exists for California, but dozens stand. In addition, there are statues of Father Serra in Las Palmas, Mallorca, where he was born, and in Querétaro, México, where he worked before going to California.

Just as no complete list exists of Serra statues, no precise list exists for statues vandalised or removed. Following Serra's canonisation, demonstrators attacked and vandalised at least five statues. In Monterey, someone decapitated the saint with a sledgehammer (Figure 16.3; Herrera 2017). At other sites, demonstrators splashed red paint, sprayed graffiti and attached ropes or chains to pull the statues down. In 2020,

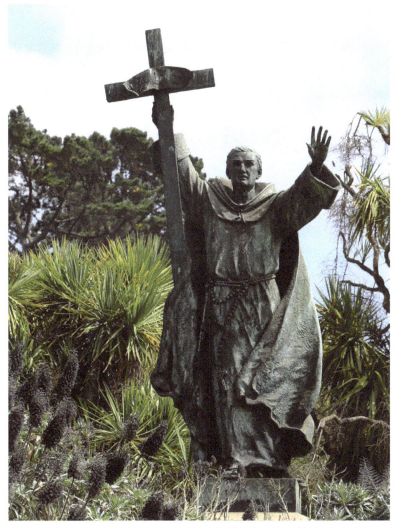

Figure 16.2 Statue of Junípero Serra in Golden Gate Park, San Francisco, 2015. © Burkhard Mücke. Available at https://commons.wikimedia.org/wiki/File:Jun%C3%ADpero_Serra_%28Statue%29.JPG and reproduced under the Creative Commons licence CC BY-SA 4.0.

activists once again struck down Serra statues, attacking at least six images of the saint. Out on Interstate 280, during the night, Anglo allies sprayed red paint on the 8-metre-tall concrete Serra (Bay Area Anarchists 2021). In at least five other cases, the owners of the statues removed them before demonstrators could damage them.

Just as in New Mexico with the Oñate statues, supporters of the memorials flocked to defend the bronze Serras. Groups of Catholics, primarily Latinos, gathered around statues to protect Serra with their bodies. Although heated verbal exchanges occurred in several places, I have found no accounts of violence. The vandalism deeply distressed many Catholics, and in several cases, supporters made the vacant statue pedestals into small altars, burning candles and leaving flowers. In reaction to the damaged Serras, the Spanish Embassy to the United States stated that 'defending the Spanish legacy in the US is a priority' and called for 'the memory of our rich shared history [to] be protected' (Liu 2020). Despite the official Spanish position, activists in Mallorca spray-painted the word *racista* ('racist') on the bronze Serra there.

The good guys and the bad guys

My discussions to this point have largely followed the popular narrative of a critical heritage praxis that confronts the racism against and oppression of Indigenous people in New Mexico and California. This praxis pits Native American activists and their allies against Latino peoples (Green 2015). The popular narrative hardens the categorical boundaries that separate Anglos, Latinos and Native Americans (Pineda 2018: 289). This narrative, however, largely ignores the role of the AHD created by Anglo-Americans at the end of the nineteenth century and used by them to appropriate Latino and Indigenous heritages in order to marginalise Latino and Indigenous peoples (Beebe and Senkewicz 2015).

La Leyenda Negra ('the black legend')

We might think of *la Leyenda Negra* as the first AHD applied to Hispanic peoples in the Americas. Spreading from the Netherlands to England, for centuries it shaped the image of Hispanic peoples in the Anglophone world, including the USA.

Adversaries of Spain took what began as an internal debate that led to some of the first humanitarian laws in global history and transformed it into anti-Spanish propaganda. In the early sixteenth century, the Dominican friar Bartolomé de Las Casas became an advocate for the Indians. He defended their humanity, questioned their slaughter by the conquistadors and opposed their exploitation in the *encomiendas*. In his

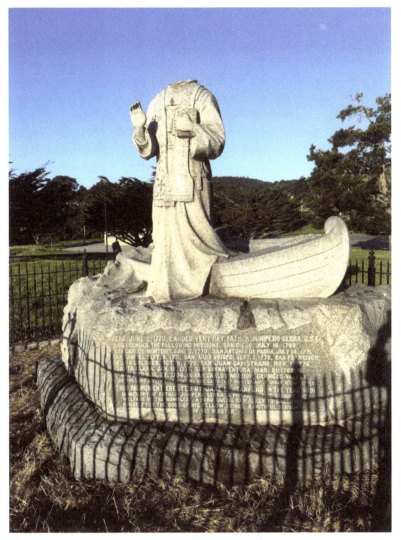

Figure 16.3 Decapitated statue of Father Junípero Serra, Monterey, California, 2015. © Tzerrer. Available at https://commons.wikimedia.org/wiki/File:Father_Junipero_Serra_late.jpg and reproduced under the Creative Commons licence CC BY-SA 4.0.

Short Account of the Destruction of the Indies, he recounted the atrocities that Indian peoples had suffered. He appealed to the Spanish king to change policies and to protect the Indians. His advocacy led to the New Laws of 1542. In 1566, the Netherlands rose in revolt against Spanish rule, and the Dutch published an edition of the book with lurid graphics.

An illustrated English edition soon followed, and the legend became a mainstay of English anti-Spanish propaganda.

La Leyenda Negra demonised the Spanish. It held that they were inhumanly cruel, intolerant, tyrannical, indolent and bloodthirsty. Advocates of the legend argued that Spain's Moorish past had racially tainted the nation's moral character, making Spaniards different from the pure Europeans to the north (Mignolo 2007). *La Leyenda Negra* crossed the Atlantic with English settlers. The demonisation of the Spanish grew into the demonisation of all Hispanics in the Americas (de Ortego y Gasca 2020). The first Anglo accounts of California identified the missions as slave plantations filled with death (Rawls 1992). Josiah Gregg (1844: 119) summarised the history of Santa Fe, New Mexico, as tainted by a 'sordid lust for gold and power, which so disgraced all the Spanish conquests in America; and that religious fanaticism – that crusading spirit, which martyrised so many thousands of the aborigines of the New World under Spanish authority'. Many scholars have argued that the legend still slanders Latinos today (de Ortego y Gasca 2020) and affects discussions of important political issues, including immigration, civil rights and the pulling down of statues (Pineda 2018: 298–300).

Treaty of Guadalupe Hidalgo

The USA defeated México in a war that lasted from 1846 to 1848. In the Treaty of Guadalupe Hidalgo, México ceded an area about the size of western Europe. The cession represented about half of the territory that México claimed as a nation, and it increased the size of the USA by more than a third. The lands that México ceded, however, contained few Mexicans. They were inhabited by Indigenous peoples who recognised the claims of neither nation. The US Congress had debated taking more or all of México. Opponents to this plan argued that adding so many Mexicans to the USA would undermine democratic institutions and foster cultural and racial decay. They believed that Mexicans were cruel, lazy, intolerant and racially tainted (*la Leyenda Negra*). The Mexican cession included significant Mexican populations only in Texas, New Mexico and California.

The treaty contained protections for the citizens of México who remained in the ceded region. It made these Mexicans citizens of the USA, and the USA agreed to respect their civil and property rights. In New Mexico, Mexican citizens included Spanish-speaking Hispanos and Pueblo Indians who lived in permanent villages, engaged in agriculture and practised Catholicism. In California, Spanish speakers identified as Californios. In both communities, wealthy families claimed pure Spanish ancestry but, in both cases, most Spanish-speaking people were mestizos with mixed Indigenous and Spanish ancestry. México had secularised the California missions just 15 years before and although this act also made the 'mission's' Indians citizens of México, most of these people lived in servitude to the Californios who had taken up mission lands (Hughes 1975).

Hispanos, Mexican-Americans and Latinos

The inclusion of tens of thousands of Californios and Hispanos into the USA troubled Anglo-Americans. Many wanted to profit from one of the largest land grabs in world history, but the treaty protected Mexican civil and property rights. Anglo-Americans ignored and/or manipulated the treaty to take control of the politics and economies of California and New Mexico. Also, the new citizens did not fit into existing racial categories and oppositions. *La Leyenda Negra* labelled these people as immoral, culturally inferior and indolent. It insinuated that they were racially tainted, no matter how pure their Spanish blood.

The California gold rush (1848–1855) flooded California with Anglo-Americans who seized political and economic control of the territory. The Indigenous peoples suffered with the Anglo takeover (Madley 2016). During the 78 years of the Spanish/Mexican period (1770–1848), disease, disruption of traditional life, violence and enslavement had reduced the Indigenous population by about a third. During the gold rush and after, disease and disruption of native life continued to kill many people, but the Anglos also launched a systematic campaign of genocide (Madley 2016). In more than 370 massacres, Anglos slaughtered Native Americans, killing between 9,500 and 16,000 people. In 30 years, Anglos reduced the Indigenous population of California by 90 per cent.

New Mexico did not experience a massive influx of Anglos, and Hispanos comprised the majority of the population into the early twentieth century. Upon taking power, the USA moved to pacify the region. In 1863–1864, Kit Carson led US troops in a bloody, scorched-earth campaign against the Navajo Indians. In the late 1860s, a group of Anglo businessmen, attorneys and land speculators formed the Santa Fe ring, which controlled New Mexico's politics and economy into the early twentieth century (Caffey 2014). The ring disenfranchised Hispano voters and swindled them out of their Spanish land grants.

The largest influx of Latino peoples into California and New Mexico came during and following the Mexican Revolution (1910–1920). It has been estimated that a million and a half Mexicans entered the USA at this time (de Ortego y Gasca 2020). Their descendants outnumber the Hispanos and Californios in modern New Mexico and California. Today, California has a population of over 39 million people and New Mexico around 2 million people. In California and New Mexico, there is no majority ethnic/racial group, but in both states the Latino population equates to about 40 per cent of inhabitants.

Baron L. Pineda (2018) discusses the ambiguity of Latino racial identity in terms of the Father Serra controversy in California. In general, Anglos categorise Latinos as non-White. The racial system of the USA has traditionally been built around a Black/White axis and/or a Native/White axis. In these oppositions, the Latino category becomes an intermediate category – that is, 'Brown' people between Whites and Blacks, and 'Mestizos' in between Whites and Indians. Pineda argues (2018: 291) 'that the American racial system effectively prevents Latinos from identifying as Native American (and vice versa) to the detriment of both Latinos and American Indians'. He notes that the secularisation of Serra as a founder of California performs ideological work to 'Americanise' California, the Catholic Church and the California missions.

Cultural appropriation as authorised heritage discourse

At the end of the nineteenth century, Anglo intellectuals rejected an AHD based in *la Leyenda Negra*. They sought to Americanise California and New Mexico with romantic cultural appropriations from both Indigenous and Latino peoples (Rawls 1992; Wilson 1997). Their work and advocacy resulted in a Mission Myth and a Myth of Santa Fe, both of which continue today.

James Rawls (1992) traces the origin of the Mission Myth to the novel *Ramona*, written by Helen Hunt Jackson, published in 1884 and still in print. This romantic story contrasted the rapacious greed of Anglo-Americans with the holiness and kind-heartedness of the old mission padres. The padres watched over happy and childlike Indians. The book became immensely popular as a largely Anglo audience embraced a vision of the good old Spanish Days. The railroad had opened California to tourists, and they wanted to see the missions mentioned in the novel. This sparked a movement to restore and reconstruct the missions, many of which lay in ruins at the time. An Anglo scholar, Charles F. Lummis, led these efforts and William Randolph Hearst raised money to fund them. By the 1890s, the Anglo elite of California had accepted the Mission Myth and were actively building an AHD around it. In 1891, the Stanfords put up the granite Serra in Monterey.

Early in the twentieth century, the Mission Myth became part of the California elementary school curriculum. Up until the first decade of the twenty-first century, California textbooks repeated the myth (Imbler 2019). Generations of fourth-grade students did the 'Mission Project', where they built a model of a mission. The state curriculum required the Mission Project until 2017, and some teachers still have their students make model missions (Imbler 2019).

Critique of the Mission Myth began in the first half of the twentieth century (Rawls 1992). The first reference to missions as concentration camps occurred in the 1940s. By the second half of the twentieth century, scholars had rejected the romanticism of the myth, and recognised that the missions were abusive of Indigenous people. Some challenged the myth with versions of *la Leyenda Negra* (Castillo 2015). Fuelled in part by the disputes over Father Serra's sainthood, Indigenous critics elaborated a popular critique (Imbler 2019). As Jonathan Cordero, a Ramaytush Ohlone-Chumash activist and sociology professor, said in a newspaper interview, 'persistent use of talking points reinforces the romantic myth of the missions that has and continues to inhibit justice for California's Native peoples' (Escobar 2020).

The Myth of Santa Fe exists to attract tourists and to create a distinct civic identity. Anglo-American newcomers quite consciously created the city's alluring image by commodifying Native American and Hispano cultures. In 1912, the Anglo-dominated city government decided to remake the city in a distinctive tri-cultural (Indian, Hispano and Anglo) style (Wilson 1997). The myth presented the city to visitors as a harmonious tri-cultural community. Advocates of the myth used rhetoric and a uniform architecture to obscure ongoing class/ethnic frictions. The myth did/does not include the Chicanos who made/make up the majority of the Latinos and the greater part of the working class. Over time, the state government embraced the Myth of Santa Fe and extended it to all of New Mexico.

Edgar Lee Hewett, director of the Museum of New Mexico, and his staff appropriated select aspects of Pueblo and Hispano culture to create a unique Santa Fe (Wilson 1997). Despite the tri-cultural claim of the myth, these efforts excluded aspects of Anglo culture. The myth is most evident in architecture. Here the museum staff wrote building codes for new construction and the city launched an aggressive campaign to refurbish existing edifices in this style. In 1919, the museum staff established a Santa Fe fiesta to celebrate the history of the tri-cultural city. The museum encouraged a revival of Indian and Hispano art and laid the foundation for the modern markets for these arts.

Critiques of the Myth of Santa Fe focus on its invention and the frictions that it hides. Cynics refer to the city as the 'Adobe Disneyland'. Chris Wilson (1997) details the process of this invention. The frictions often reveal themselves in struggles over heritage and identity. Frank G. Pérez and Carlos F. Ortega (2020: 1) recognise the Myth of Santa Fe as a hegemonic ADH: 'New Mexico's tourism economy relies on and heavily emphasizes the state's ties to Indian cultures, colonial Spain, and Anglo settlers, while it simultaneously downplays the state's Mexican/ American peoples.' Native Americans sawing off Oñate's foot and pulling down his statues challenges the harmony of the myth.

Why these myths? The simplest answer is for profit (Rawls 1992; Wilson 1997). In both cases, the myths spawned tourism that today forms a major part of the economy. The pull of the exotic that lured tourists also brought more Anglos to settle and buy real estate. In each case, we can also drop the word 'myth' and replace it with the word 'style'. Mission Style and Santa Fe Style define architectural and interior designs that became popular throughout most of the western USA. Rawls (1992) notes how advertisers link their products to the myth and use of mission images to sell their products. Santa Fe hosts a thriving market in Indian art and a smaller market in Hispano art. Indian and Hispano artists benefit from these markets but primarily Anglos control the business. Beyond profit, however, Anglos sought to Americanise exotic places.

In most of the USA, Anglo (White) settlers displaced and dominated Indigenous peoples, killing them, removing them, marginalising them and replacing them with many, many more Anglos. This near-total replacement and overwhelming Anglo numerical dominance did not happen in California and New Mexico. In both contemporary states, Latino and Anglo population numbers remain about equal (around 40 per cent). So, if not by replacement, how could California and New Mexico be Americanised? Anglo elites appropriated the culture and history of the Indigenous and Latino people to make an AHD that they controlled and profited from. They adopted Indigenous and Latino styles and artefacts as decorations that legitimated their presence in somebody else's land. Although they Americanised the heritage of the regions, they did not Americanise the people. They did not make Indians and Latinos fully empowered citizens with the same rights as Anglos.

Latino peoples manipulated the AHD to advance their own interests. Latinos in California exploited the Mission Myth to make their contributions to US history primary and not secondary (Pineda 2018). They used the Serra debate to claim a victor's role in California's history by identifying Serra not just as the founder of the mission system but also as the founder of modern California. Hispanos in New Mexico both deployed and challenged the Myth of Santa Fe. Within a generation, the Hispano community took control of the Santa Fe fiesta and transformed it to extol Catholic piety and celebrate their ethnic purity as Spaniards (Wilson 1997: 4). Their memorialisation of Oñate played into the myth's celebration of the colonial Spanish, but the conflicts this memorialisation engendered with Native Americans contested the harmony of the myth.

The myths, however, also work against Latino counter-heritage. The advocates for Oñate and Serra (popular, scholarly and religious) all know and admit that the myths paint a false picture of harmony. In both cases, they recognise that the Spaniards abused Indigenous people. But they argue that Oñate's accomplishments surpassed his crimes and that Serra protected Indian people from even greater abuse outside the missions. Their critics, however, attack the myths rather than the real history, easily demonstrate that abuses occurred and clandestinely invoke *la Leyenda Negra*.

The myths obscure the violence and the abuse of Indigenous people at the hands of the Anglo-American conquerors. Oñate's destruction of Acoma was terrible, but was it worse than Kit Carson's war on the Navajo? Carson's army killed hundreds of people, destroyed crops and homes, mutilated and tortured, and removed the Navajo to a reservation far from their homeland. Thousands of Indians died in California missions from disease, disruption of their lives and abuse, but there is no evidence that the padres wished to exterminate the Indigenous people. This cannot be said for the Anglos who in the middle of the nineteenth century attacked villages and slaughtered Indian people with the express goal of exterminating Indigenous peoples from California.

Conclusion

In the southwestern USA, Indian and Hispanic/Latino counter-heritages clash. Indigenous protesters and their allies attack, deface and destroy monuments to Hispanic/Latino individuals demonised by their heritage. They see the origins of their oppression in these individuals, and they assault Spanish statues to liberate Indigenous lives in the present. But the demons of the Indigenous counter-heritage also have a heritage of oppression. Anglos defeated the Mexican settler state and seized control of the narrative to construct an AHD to shape and legitimate the inclusion of the southwest into the US settler state. In its most modern form, this AHD appropriates Indian and Hispanic/Latino counter-heritages to advance Anglo interests. In its original form, it demonised Indigenous peoples as savages and embraced *la Leyenda Negra*.

Anglos found the concepts of the savage and *la Leyenda Negra* in European colonial heritages. As with all other European-derived settler states, the AHD of the USA had to resolve two inherent contradictions: (1) that the European state exists on stolen lands and (2) that the Indigenous victims of this theft still live as minorities within the state. To resolve these contradictions, the AHD must conquer history itself. Such conquests, however, are always incomplete, complex and filled with unanticipated contradictions because they are opposed. Oppressed peoples engage in a critical heritage praxis that advances counter-heritages to undermine the AHD that forms and legitimates their oppression. But as we see in the southwestern USA, these complex struggles may pit colonised groups against each other and the AHD. Such struggles may leave us wondering who are the 'good guys' and who are the 'bad guys'.

Acknowledgements

I would like to thank the volume editors for inviting me to join this project and for their detailed and useful comments on my chapter. Cinthia Campos read and commented on an early draft and Rubén Mendoza provided me with citations and comments.

References

Bay Area Anarchists. 2021. Junipero Serra Statue Vandalized in San Mateo County. Online at https://www.indybay.org/newsitems/2021/02/07/18839832.php Accessed 20 April 2023.

Beebe, Rose Marie and Robert Senkewicz. 2015. *Junípero Serra: California Indians and the Transformation of a Missionary*. Norman: University of Oklahoma Press.

Brown, Deidre. 2013. Traditional Identity: The Commodification of New Zealand Maori Imagery. Paper presented at the IPinCH Cultural Commodification, Indigenous Peoples and Self-Determination Public Symposium, University of British Columbia. Online at https://www.youtube.com/watch?v=HYa2kxL9EFY Accessed 20 April 2023.

Burnett, John. 2020. Who Was Juan de Oñate? A Look at the Conquistador's Violent Legacy in New Mexico. *National Public Radio, Weekend Edition Saturday*, 11 July 2020. Online at https://www.npr.org/2020/07/11/890000884/who-was-juan-de-o-ate-a-look-at-the-conquistadors-violent-legacy-in-new-mexico Accessed 20 April 2023.

Byrne, Denis. 1996. Deep Nation: Australia's Acquisition of an Indigenous Past. *Aboriginal History* 20: 82–107.

Caffey, David. 2014. *Chasing the Santa Fe Ring: Power and Privilege in Territorial New Mexico*. Albuquerque: University of New Mexico Press.

Castillo, Elias. 2015. *A Cross of Thorns: The Enslavement of California's Indians by the Spanish Missions*. Fresno, CA: Craven Street Books.

CNA Staff. 2020. Archbishop Cordileone Applauds Prosecution of St Junipero Serra Statue Vandalism. *Catholic News Agency*. 13 November 2020. Online at https://www.catholicnews agency.com/news/46592/archbishop-cordileone-applauds-prosecution-of-st-junipero-serra-statue-vandalism Accessed 7 May 2023.

Deloria, Phillip. 1998. *Playing Indian*. Hartford, CT: Yale University Press.

de Ortego y Gasca, Felipe. 2020. La Leyenda Negra/The Black Legend: Historical Distortion, Defamation, Slander, Libel and Stereotyping of Hispanics. *Latino Stories*. Online at https://latinostories.com/the-black-legend-stereotyping-of-hispanics/ Accessed 20 April 2023.

Escobar, Allyson. 2020. Controversial Junípero Serra Supported by Some Indigenous Catholics, California Mission Workers. *National Catholic Reporter.* 11 August 2020. Online at https://www.ncronline.org/news/justice/controversial-jun-pero-serra-supported-some-indigenous-catholics-california-mission Accessed 20 April 2023.

Green, Emma. 2015. Is the Pope Trying to Redeem Colonialism? *The Atlantic*, 23 September 2015. Online at https://www.theatlantic.com/politics/archive/2015/09/junipero-serra-pope-francis-colonialism/406306/ Accessed 20 April 2023.

Gregg, Josiah. 1844. *Commerce of the Prairies*, Vol. 1. New York: Henry G Langley.

Hackel, Steven. 2013. *Junípero Serra: California's Founding Father*. New York: Hill and Wang.

Harrison, Rodney. 2013. *Heritage: Critical Approaches*. London: Routledge.

Herrera, James. 2017. Head Reattached to St. Junipero Serra Statue in Monterey. *Mercury News*, 28 February 2017. Online at www.mercurynews.com/2017/02/28/head-reattached-to-st-junipero-serra-statue-in-monterey/ Accessed 20 April 2023.

Hughes, Charles. 1975. The Decline of the Californios. *The San Diego Journal of History* 21(3): 1–31.

Imbler, Sabrina. 2019. Is the End Coming for a Problematic California Grade School Tradition? *Atlas Obscura*. Online at https://www.atlasobscura.com/articles/california-mission-models Accessed 20 April 2023.

Kauanui, Kēhaulani. 2016. A Structure, Not an Event: Settler Colonialism and Enduring Indigeneity. *Lateral* 5(1): 23–31.

Lind, Dara. 2015. Junipero Serra Was a Brutal Colonialist. So Why Did Pope Francis Just Make Him a Saint? *Vox*, 24 September 2015. Online at https://www.vox.com/2015/9/24/9391995/junipero-serra-saint-pope-francis Accessed 20 April 2023.

Liu, Natalie. 2020. Spanish Icons Take Hit in US War on Statues. *Voice of America*, 26 June 2020. Online at https://www.voanews.com/usa/race-america/spanish-icons-take-hit-us-war-statues Accessed 20 April 2023.

Macdonald, Sharon. 2016. Is 'Difficult Heritage' Still 'Difficult'? *Museum International* 67: 6–22.

Madley, Benjamin. 2016. *An American Genocide: The United States and the California Indian Catastrophe, 1846–1873*. New Haven, CT: Yale University Press.

McGuire, Randall. 1992. Archaeology and the First Americans. *American Anthropologist* 94(4): 816–836.

McGuire, Randall. 2008. *Archaeology as Political Action.* Berkeley: University of California Press.

Mendoza, Rubén. 2015. Review of: *A Cross of Thorns: The Enslavement of California's Indians by the Spanish Missions*, by Elias Castillo. *Choice Reviews*, 53(1): 45.

Mignolo, Walter. 2007. What does the Black Legend Have to do with Race? In Margret Greer, Walter Mignolo and Maureen Quilligan (eds), *Rereading the Black Legend: The Discourses of Religious and Racial Difference in the Renaissance Empires.* Chicago: University of Chicago Press: 312–324.

Miller, Kim and Brenda Schmahmann (eds). 2017. *Public Art in South Africa: Bronze Warriors and Plastic Presidents*. Indianapolis: Indiana University Press.

Pérez, Frank G. and Carlos F. Ortega. 2020. *Deconstructing Eurocentric Tourism and Heritage Narratives in Mexican American Communities: Juan de Oñate as a West Texas Icon*. London and New York: Routledge.

Pineda, Baron L. 2018. 'First Hispanic Pope, First Hispanic Saint': Whiteness, Founding Fathers and the Canonisation of Friar Junípero Serra. *Latino Studies* 16: 286–309.

Querin, Camilla. 2020. Heritage Sites: How Afro-Brazilian and Indigenous Communities Leverage Archaeology and Architecture to Protect Their Histories and Challenge the Hegemonic Heritage Discourse. *Latin American and Latinx Visual Culture* 2(1): 82–91.

Rawls, James. 1992. The California Mission as Symbol and Myth. *California History* 71(3): 342–361.

Romero, Simon. 2017. Statue's Stolen Foot Reflects Divisions Over Symbols of Conquest. *New York Times*, 30 September 2017.

Romero, Simon. 2020. Man Is Shot at Protest Over Statue of New Mexico's Conquistador. *New York Times*, 15 June 2020.

Simmons, Marc. 1993. *The Last Conquistador: Juan de Oñate and the Settling of the Far West.* Norman: University of Oklahoma Press.

Smith, Laurajane. 2006. *Uses of Heritage.* London: Routledge.

Veracini, Lorenzo. 2010. *Settler Colonialism: A Theoretical Overview.* London: Palgrave Macmillan.

Wilson, Chris. 1997. *The Myth of Santa Fe: Creating a Modern Regional Tradition.* Albuquerque: University of New Mexico Press.

Wolfe, Patrick. 2006. Settler Colonialism and the Elimination of the Native. *Journal of Genocide Research* 8(4): 387–409.

17
Traumatic heritage: politics of visibility and the standardisation of plaques and memorials in the city of São Paulo, Brazil

Márcia Lika Hattori

Introduction

This text explores public policies and the standardisation of plaques and memorials, part of the contested landscapes related to state violence (Ayán-Vila 2008; Barreiro and Fábrega-Álvarez 2019; van der Laarse 2013: 72) in the city of São Paulo, Brazil. These plaques have been claimed by social movements to visualise subjects, collectives, places and events. Drawing on critical heritage studies (González-Ruibal and Hall 2015; Harrison 2013; Rico 2008; Smith 2006), I question the creation of plaques and monuments as reparation and pedagogical action and attempt to understand how this obeys certain rationalities, intentionalities and logics of remembrance based on a standardised way of approaching repressive periods developed in different parts of the world (David 2017). In this volume on critical heritage studies and the 'futures of Europe', I nuance aspects related to the Western European heritage practice and thought applied in the Global South, specifically in the Brazilian context.

In 2017, a plaque in memory of victims of the dictatorship was unveiled at the Volkswagen factory in the metropolitan region of São Paulo. According to newspapers at the time, it was a form of reparation and support for human rights and carried out at the factory's initiative. The unveiling of the plaque took place together with the delivery of a report commissioned by the Volkswagen company to investigate human rights violations it had committed during the military dictatorship.

The report states that 'Volkswagen was unreservedly loyal to the military government and shared its economic and domestic policy objectives' (Kopper 2017: 130). The automotive corporation regularly informed the regime about the trade union activities of its workers. There was a 'blacklist of politically undesirable workers'. As a result, six workers were arrested and one tortured at the factory. It should also be stated that the report mentioned no evidence of institutionalised collaboration between the company and the repressive state. In fact, Lúcio Bellentani, who was tortured by political police agents in one of the factory's rooms, told the *Deutsche Welle* news agency of his dissatisfaction with the report, indicating that the company wanted to control the narrative of its past and was not being honest when it came to taking specific action: 'The report is weak, it doesn't have a lot of documentation. I don't think the company has opened all its files to the historian'[1] (Struck 2017: 1).

The initial proposal from a group of employees aimed to create a memorial site to the workers' struggle, a proposal vehemently rejected by the company (Vannuchi 2020). The inauguration of the plaque was the response. Questioned about why the plaque does not name the persecuted workers, the factory president said it was a plaque in line with the company's values, claiming, 'What happened here happened in all companies. It was a systematic process of the military regime' (Struck 2017: 1). The text of the plaque translates into English as follows:[2]

> In memory of all the victims
> of the military dictatorship in Brazil.
> For Human Rights, Democracy
> Tolerance and Humanity.
> Volkswagen

This history of sanitising and simplifying the memory of violence and human rights violations committed there, via the unveiling of a plaque to 'repair' and affirm the company's commitment and 'values' in relation to this issue, led me to reflect on the processes that these kinds of initiatives involve: their material making, types of materials, messages and more specifically, the visibility of these plaques, whether public or private. Plaques and monuments regarding resistance to the last dictatorship in Brazil have been created since the 1990s and have the objective of permanence, visibility and attracting people's attention to the 'hidden' history of the place where the plaque or monument is located. The raw materials used for many of these monuments are usually concrete or a type of stone, materials that evoke permanence, durability and rigidity, something seen in many examples in South America such as *El Ojo que Llora* in Peru (Moraña 2012), the memorial of *Patio 29* in Chile (Aguilera 2013) and *Parque de la Memoria* in Argentina (Battiti 2018), to name a few. Commonly, these memorials carry the inscribed names of victims and details about what happened at a particular place.

This style of plaque is most commonly used in public policies related to memories of silenced resistance and in the context of policies of reparation. In this sense, I agree with Carol Kidron (2020), who calls for a self-reflexive critique on memorialisation as a new form of humanitarian governance. Commonly, human rights defenders operate under an unquestioned assumption: that proper memorialisation of a traumatic past is essential for both democracy and human rights. From this derives an economy related to a certain morality of remembrance that evokes a list of actions – ways of 'being' that should be followed to combat and counter traumatic pasts (David 2017).

Contextualising Brazilian military dictatorship (1964–1985)

The 1964 *coup d'état* in Brazil began the 'regime of the generals', with the dismissal of the democratically elected president João Goulart. Brazilian historiography holds that the coup, and the subsequent dictatorship, should not be considered exclusively military, but rather civil-military, since it was supported by important segments of society, namely the large rural landowners, the São Paulo industrial bourgeoisie, a large part of the urban middle classes and the conservative and anti-communist sector of the Catholic Church.

Under the dictatorship, the authoritarian government's ideal model for a Brazilian citizen's body, attitudes and behaviours was supported by a Christian ideology of family and morality (Quinalha 2017: 318). All those categorised outside this ideal were classified as internal enemies (Padrós 2012) and considered subversive, dangerous or deviant. The idea of 'dangerous' groups included (at different times and different levels of repression) members of the LGBTQI+ community and those classified as communists or even artists. There were many other 'undesirable' groups also associated with ideas of subversion and/or social disorder.

The military regime constituted an extensive legislation of exception and a broad administrative-institutional structure. This legislation gave legal meaning to a sphere of action that was itself extra-legal, characteristic of the state of exception (Agamben 2005; J. Teles 2020). Indeed, the dictatorship was able to move with skill in the blurred area between the legal and de facto situation. The new laws were materialised in a network of military, political and intelligence agencies, some institutional, others clandestine (Soares 2016). Based on the idea that the internal enemy could be any person or group, the principle of the rule of law was inverted, and everyone became a suspect until proven the contrary (J. Teles 2015).

The repression against opponents of the regime was coordinated by the hierarchy of the armed forces. Their teams worked daily with an intensive zeal on imprisonment, torture, death and disappearances (Godoy 2015: 45; Joffily 2008: 304). During the 21 years of military dictatorship, this 'legal' and 'clandestine' apparatus perpetrated a vast number of human rights violations. In addition to the clandestine detention centres created for this purpose, the forensic institutes (IML), funeral services, public cemeteries and the Military Justice were all involved in operations carried out to cover up the assassination and disappearance of politically persecuted people (Hattori 2021).

Despite significant historiographical focus during the last decades on members of different guerrilla groups who fought against the dictatorship, I highlight here other groups who were persecuted in a context of generalised repression. I cite cases to emphasise how race, class and gender were all used by the authoritarian state to justify their actions. This is particularly relevant in the persecution of Indigenous groups, peasants, LGBTQI+ groups and women, many of whom were perceived as undesirable or dangerous.

An analysis based on feminist theories and contemporary archaeology demonstrates how, in a female prison in Rio Grande do Sul state, the incarceration landscape was used by the repressive state to maintain the dehumanising conditions to which female political prisoners were subjected, including isolation and solitary confinement, and the implications thereof. If male and female prisoners entered the detention centre both considered as enemies and subversives, the way in which space was used in the treatment of these groups showed deliberate gender bias. These procedures were guided by a misogynistic logic which authorised the persecution of people through different stages of humiliation and punishment, a dehumanisation based on gender. For example, female political prisoners were often housed in a section of the prison formerly used as a dog kennel (Baretta 2020: 87).

In parallel, the feminist resistance movement began at the apogee of the dictatorship. Between 1970 and 1978, the number of females registering as trade union members grew by 176 per cent. This was the birth of 'women's work' within the trade unions and, not without resistance, they soon formed into groups, collectives focused on the rights of women and their demands. During this period, the feminist press also became more prevalent, publishing important alternative newspapers (M. Teles 2018) and unifying their actions while strengthening the organisation and the success of the movement – in 1978, the Movement for Amnesty was initiated by women; in 1979 came the Movement for the Struggle for Day Care Centres in Housing, and, in 1979, 1980 and 1981, the Congresses of the Women of São Paulo, whose decisions supported the Constituent Assembly process (Instituto Vladimir Herzog 2020).

Municipal and state governments carried out a concerted hunt for the LGBTQI+ population in Brazil. The process of 'cleansing' and 'sanitising' was mainly carried out through *rondões* (roundups), police patrols and censorship actions. However, human rights violations by the police did not cease with the transition to democracy. In 1987, during the peak of the AIDS epidemic, the mayor of São Paulo, Jânio Quadros, with the support of the Civil and Military Police, initiated Operation Tarantula. The goal was to attack the LGBTQI+ population under the pretext of fighting AIDS, leading to numerous arrests and murders (Ocanha 2018: 89). Despite living with the fear generated by repression and 'compulsory heterosexuality', the 1970s represented a time of greater freedom for the LGBTQI+ movement, something witnessed with the publication of the alternative newspaper *Lampião da Esquina* and the rise of the first organised groups to fight back against the regime, the Brazilian Homosexual Movement (MHB) and SOMOS, both inaugurated in 1978. Even if having a homo-affective relationship was not considered a crime by the Penal Code, the legal instrument used to persecute this movement was vagrancy, which gave police the power to decide who could be arrested (Vieira and Fraccaroli 2018).

Hundreds of peasants and Indigenous people were killed or disappeared in the midst of disputes over land ownership in the country. It is estimated that at least 1,196 peasants and 8,350 Indigenous people (originating from ten different native groups) died as victims of the direct or indirect action of the Brazilian State during this period (CNV 2014: 205).

The transition to democracy was an extremely controlled process, carried out from above, controlled by the elites. Two main legacies can be discerned: the deepening of social inequality promoted by the dictatorship's economic model, and the institutionalisation and sophistication of the use of torture and state violence. The nationalisation of the military police from 1969, under the command of the army, gave rise to a policy of policing with military weapons. This scenario shaped the political transition, and during the democratic period certain continuities of practices like violence, control, and also negligence and omission are a state policy in relation to certain populations.

Plaques, monuments and visibility

The object analysis here focuses on plaques and monuments erected over the last several decades which make reference to the last military dictatorship in Brazil (Fabri 2013). They are places of inscription, a territorial marking, and represent a legacy linked to the power of perpetuation (Le Goff 1978), a dispositive (Foucault 1992) that shapes the collective imagination (Nora 1997).

Because of the difficulties involved in more extensive mapping, I have omitted certain components from analysis: grassroots memorials, graffiti and interventions such as posters erected during the 2018 elections (Brito 2017; Margry and Sánchez-Carretero 2011). Despite their ephemeral nature, these artefacts represent social action in public spaces. In São Paulo there are many such objects and places: graffiti (Figure 17.1), artistic interventions, ecumenical masses organised by relatives, social movements, silent marches and other activities. The use of photographs of the disappeared, usually on posters, during demonstrations also evokes existence, a strong transnational visual and emotional aesthetic that personifies and individualises each disappeared person.

When the names of these victims are read out at demonstrations, they are followed by the crowd shouting 'Presente, hoje e sempre' ('Present, today and always'), a powerful ritual in which place and photograph (object) become a political instrument reflecting the social struggle that mothers, wives, daughters and granddaughters endure when taking images of the lost and persecuted to galleries or emblazoning them on clothing, posters and flags in various public spaces.

My work analyses 'conditions of visibility', as proposed by the archaeologist Felipe Criado-Boado (1995), to describe the efforts of different groups, supported by the use of plaques and monuments (Table 17.1), to draw attention to this memory of resistance and public policies related to reparation. I argue that this type of analysis can be a

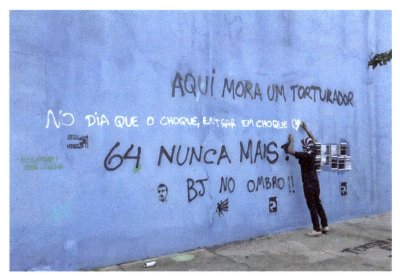

Figure 17.1 Graffiti on the front wall of a known collaborator's house. Organised by the social movement Levante Popular da Juventude as part of the *'escrachos populares'*. © Douglas Mansur.

Table 17.1 Plaques and monuments related to memories of repression and resistance in the city of São Paulo.

Plaque or monument	Address	Year
Arco do Presídio Tiradentes	Avenida Tiradentes esquina com a Praça Coronel Fernando Prestes	1985
Monumento de Perus	R. Ernesto Diogo de Faria, 860 - Perus, São Paulo - SP, 05215-000, Brazil	1993
Carlos Marighella	Alameda Casa Branca, Jardins. São Paulo	1999
Isis Dias de Oliveira	Praça Isis Dias de Oliveira, São Paulo - SP	1999
Memorial imprescindíveis - Placa Faculdade de Medicina da USP	Av. Dr. Arnaldo, 455 - Cerqueira César, Pacaembu - SP, 01246-903, Brazil	2006
Memorial imprescindíveis - Placa PUC - SP	R. Monte Alegre, 984 - Perdizes, São Paulo, 05014-901, Brazil	2006

(*continued*)

Table 17.1   (Cont.)

Plaque or monument	Address	Year
Memorial da Resistência	Largo General Osório, 66 - Santa Ifigênia, São Paulo - SP, 01213-010, Brasil	2009
Ana Rosa Kucinski	Av. Prof. Lineu Prestes, 748 - Butantã, São Paulo, 05508-900, Brazil	2014
Memorial aos Membros da Comunidade USP Vítimas do Regime da Ditadura Militar	Rua do Anfiteatro, Cidade Universitária, São Paulo	2017
Alexandre Vannuchi Leme	R. do Lago, 562 - Butantã, São Paulo - SP, 05508-080, Brazil	2013
Monumento em Homenagem aos Mortos e Desaparecidos Políticos	Parque Ibirapuera - Vila Mariana, Brazil	2014
Memorial da Luta Pela Justiça	Avenida Brigadeiro Luís Antonio, 1249.	2014
Memorial dos Crimes de Maio e das Vítimas de Genocídio	Centro de Culturas Negras. R. Arsênio Tavolieri, 45 - Jabaquara, São Paulo - SP, 04321-030, Brazil	2016
Jardim Para não dizer que não falei de flores	Av. Flor de Vila Formosa, s/n - Vila Formosa, São Paulo, 03366-010, Brazil	2016
Placa Cemitério Perus	R. Ernesto Diogo de Faria, 860 - Perus, São Paulo - SP, 05215-000, Brazil	2017
Placa Cemitério Vila Formosa	Av. Flor de Vila Formosa, s/n - Vila Formosa, São Paulo, 03366-010, Brazil	2017
Placa Cemitério Campo Grande	Av. Nossa Sra. de Sabará, 1371 - Campo Grande, São Paulo - SP, 04685-003, Brazil	2017
Placa Maria Antonia	R. Maria Antônia, 258/294 - Vila Buarque, São Paulo - SP, 01222-010, Brazil	no information
Jardim Cálice	R. Ernesto Diogo de Faria, 860 - Perus, São Paulo - SP, 05215-000, Brazil	2016

fundamental way of accessing knowledge that is not accessible through words and narratives, that is, of confronting what cannot be verbalised, thereby allowing hidden realities of the past and present to be uncovered (Buchli and Lucas 2001). Here, I place emphasis on my own past experiences (Ingold 2002; Lee and Ingold 2006; Tilley 2016) of participation, unveiling plaques and attending demonstrations and commemorations.

In this cartography (via the contested meanings of different places in the public space), there is a fundamental aspect that could be termed a 'will to visibility' (Criado-Boado 1995). Is there a will to visibility in the case of these plaques and monuments? Depending on the place and the conditions of visibility, with whom are these plaques attempting to engage? Do they only evoke a policy of reparation grounded in Brazil's response to the condemnation of the Inter-American Court of Human Rights and the fulfilment of certain actions? And/or, in fact, have they given new meaning to those places and made visible those subjects whose repression sought to erase their existence?

I emphasise that in the Global North, many terms have been proposed for this kind of heritage – that which is negative (Meskell 2002), uncomfortable (Morgan 1993), difficult (Logan and Reeves 2008) or dissonant (Tunbridge and Ashworth 1996), or which hurts (Uzzell and Ballantyne 1998). However, in (ex)colonial contexts, the idea of traumatic heritage is not only related to conflict, war or dictatorship, but can also be extended to a much broader temporal memory 'that hurts'. In the Brazilian case, most of this traumatic heritage is related to colonial baroque architecture (Chuva 2017) and to the coloniser's memorials, statues that represent a terrible period for Indigenous groups which often entailed attempts at genocide (Marins 2008) and violence against Africans forcibly displaced.

Public policies and the creation of plaques and monuments

The plaques and monuments created over the last 35 years, since the end of the dictatorship in the city of São Paulo, are analysed here across the period 1985 to 2021 in terms of their visibility in public space. An analysis of where plaques have been erected in São Paulo over time provides important information for understanding the constitution of this counter-hegemonic memory in the landscape and the efforts undertaken to make the memory of resistance visible (Figure 17.2).

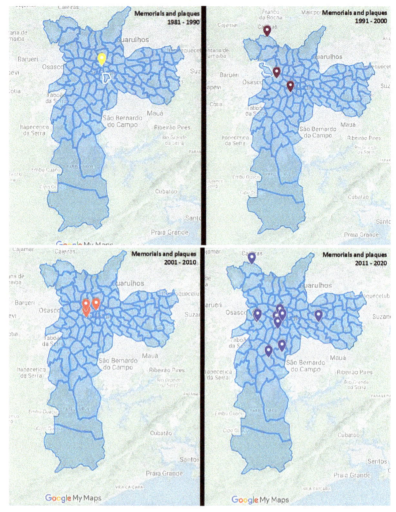

Figure 17.2 Memorials and plaques in the city of São Paulo, 1985 to 2020. © Márcia Lika Hattori.

Heritage policies had already recognised several sites as symbols of resistance against the regime even before the dictatorship ended (Neves 2014). Heritage policies are implemented in very different ways. From one perspective, these represented the first state actions related to the memory of dictatorship. From another, truth commissions and investigations usually only take place after the dictatorship has fallen, although there are exceptions, as in Argentina. In Brazil, examples of that include the case of a clandestine detention centre (DOPS), Tiradentes prison gate and the building of the Faculty of Philosophy for the University of São Paulo, on the site where the Battle of Maria Antonia[3] took place.

The 1990s heralded the discovery of the Perus mass grave, and the construction of a monument on the site (designed by the architect Ruy Ohtake). It was one of the initiatives promoted by the former mayor Luiza Erundina, but there were many others, such as the creation of a parliamentary commission of inquiry, which relatives of disappeared people recognise as the first truth commission in Brazil. At the request of relatives involved with the association known as 'Comissão de Familiares de Mortos e Desaparecidos Políticos', the commission conducted archival research and was the driving factor in bringing to light the dictatorship's crimes and erecting the monument.

Two other initiatives were undertaken at the end of the decade, paying tribute to two National Liberation Alliance (ALN) militants. These were in different central neighbourhoods, as can be seen in Figure 17.2. The two plaques were created after pressure from family members and former guerrillas who were part of this resistance group.

From 2001 to 2010, the number of plaques was reduced and public policies from both the municipalities and federal government were centralised in colleges, specifically at the Pontifícia Universidade Católica and the School of Medicine of the Universidade de São Paulo. Here plaques have a more individualised nature, referring to former students and employees who were persecuted and murdered by the dictatorship.

A decentralisation of these inscriptions was not seen until the 2010s, when there was a profusion of actions related to the implementation of numerous truth commissions and greater public debate, along with new policies and a focus on municipal public cemeteries where the victims of repression are buried. Monuments, plaques and gardens were built as part of the 'politics of memory' and even street names were changed. The memorial gardens that combined tree planting, plaques and stone paths were seen in the same light as new cemetery projects being proposed by the municipal administration. The cemeteries were public spaces and often popular places to visit, usually the only green areas in the neighbourhood and full of stories of the people of São Paulo.

Between 2013 and 2017, with the work of various truth commissions now in motion (set up in collaboration with the National Truth Commission), there was a change in São Paulo's policies on memory and truth. During the administration of Mayor Fernando Haddad (2013–2017), the Secretariat for Human Rights and Citizenship was created with a specific brief for historical memory. Among public policies such as the creation of forensic teams, a municipal truth commission and artistic projects related to the topic, there were three equally important projects. The first was called 'Ruas da Memória' ('Streets of Memory') and aimed to change street names that paid homage to torturers or people who were part of the system of repression. The second was related to the creation of memorials and plaques, and the third was a project mapping sites of resistance and repression, which was carried out in collaboration with the group responsible for managing the Memorial da Resistência. This resulted in the publication of *Memórias Resistentes, Memórias Residentes* ('Resistant Memories, Resident Memories'; SMDHC 2016). Researchers and activists affiliated with the memorial mapped more than 37 sites that constituted this terrorscape (van der Laarse 2013: 72), all of them part of the machinery of repression, from buildings to clandestine burial sites and detention and torture centres. In total, more than 80 memorial sites represent expressions of resistance, ranging from theatres to religious institutions, research centres and factories.

Despite decentralisation, six plaques and monuments (35 per cent) are located on university campuses. Five are at the University of São Paulo (USP), a public space, albeit with restricted access for those not associated with the university. The other is at the Pontifical Catholic University of São Paulo, a private university usually only frequented by students, employees and teachers. These are tributes related to victims who had links to these universities, as either students or employees.

The plaques' central location implies they are sited in areas with high people movement, especially pedestrian movement. However, if we observe each plaque and monument from the perspective of how it is experienced, using the criteria of location, pedestrian movement, fencing, signage, height of buildings, access and visualisation, 65 per cent are in low-visibility areas, 11 per cent in medium-visibility areas and 23 per cent in areas classified as high-visibility. The dimensions of the monument also have an influence on this analysis, although this is not a crucial factor. In other words, although there seems to be a policy of making memory of resistance visible, most of it is not seen by the city's inhabitants.

Visible plaques and monuments

Carlos Marighella was a politician and founder of one of the revolutionary groups that fought against the dictatorship. He was murdered in 1969 in São Paulo. The monument erected in his honour on the street where the police killed him is classified as high-visibility. This is a result of an accumulation of factors in which dimensions are of lesser importance (it is on the pavement of a street) than pedestrian movement, the busy street and its location in the city. Despite its small size, the monument has suffered numerous acts of vandalism. It has been removed (J. Teles 2015) and graffitied repeatedly with references to extreme right-wing groups such as the Comando de Caça aos Comunistas, a representation of lingering transgenerational tensions and an example of an active site of power where political memory is presented and reproduced.

Inaugurated in 2014, another highly visible monument is the Monument in Tribute to the Dead and Disappeared (Figure 17.3). Raised in a dominant public place, it stands facing the largest park in the city on one of its busiest avenues. It is a place where three large monumental, sculptural and architectural landmarks are found. This monument, created by the Secretariat of Human Rights and Citizenship, disputes other São Paulo identities and stories. Nearby is the former DOI-CODI[4] clandestine detention centre, the stage for one of the largest marches for memory, truth and justice in 2019 and again in more recent times for protest against the authoritarian Bolsonaro government.

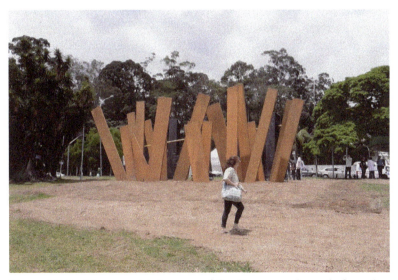

Figure 17.3 Monument in honour of the disappeared people from the dictatorship of 1964–1985 at the Ibirapuera Park. © Douglas Mansur.

Non-visible plaques and monuments

The Dom Bosco cemetery plaque was installed in 2017 at the conclusion of the Municipal Truth Commission's work. The installation involved the participation of politicians, social movements and family members of the disappeared, some of whom had also served on the truth commissions. Like other plaques, this one contains the names in alphabetical order of the 32 people buried there along with others either in the mass grave or still missing. This model of naming and, therefore, recognising disappearance and human rights violations makes those absent visible again. Despite its content, the memorial, made of cement and metal, is located at the end of the cemetery's administrative building, in a car park where hardly anyone passes by. It exists, but is not visible. On one occasion when I was at the cemetery, it was busy and there was a funeral taking place, but even so, nobody passed by the plaque.

In Figure 17.4, the red lines indicate routes taken by people during the week, as recorded during ethnographic observation. On the right is the burial courts entrance; usually people enter the cemetery through the main gate and head straight to there. Alternatively, they pass through the administration building where the funeral rooms are located and then follow a path to the burial area. Due to its dimensions and the fact that the text can be seen from a distance, the monument built in the 1990s on the location where the mass grave was found is quite visible. In fact, on numerous occasions when I was at the monument, people visiting the cemetery had left flowers or lit candles for their loved ones, leaving them near the monument. Remnants of candle wax

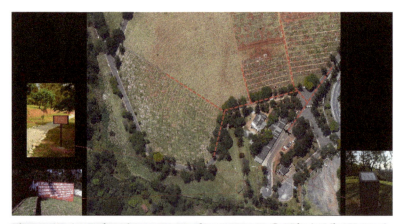

Figure 17.4   Pedestrian routes at the cemetery. © Márcia Lika Hattori.

and plastic flowers can commonly be seen around the monument. On one occasion, I approached a person placing candles there and she told me that although she had no family connection to the monument, the story seemed very impactful to her.

The same does not occur in the area where the plaque is located, at the end of the administrative building. At ground level, it has little dialogue with the monument and is even less visible to those who pass through the administration and funeral rooms.

Exploring plaques, pedagogy and elections

Did the resignification or contextualisation provided by the plaques enable other readings or pedagogies at the places where they were installed? When comparing the sites of plaques and monuments with the presidential election results of 2018 that elected the far-right candidate Jair Bolsonaro (whose statements have often been openly pro-dictatorship), it is clear that the neighbourhoods where Bolsonaro won in São Paulo are those where the most monuments and plaques are found (Figure 17.5). This observation is not intended to diminish the importance of these plaques and memorials but to question their use as a pedagogical tool.

More ethnographic and sociological data are needed to extend this exploratory analysis so as to understand the relationship between the rise of the extreme right in these traditionally conservative neighbourhoods and the plaques and memorials. Did the movement which increased in popularity during the 2010s generate a far-right reaction against these policies or not? This is a subject for future research.

Some reflections: a perspective on the never-again pedagogy from the visibility of plaques and monuments

This chapter aims to contribute to discussions about the concept of negative heritage based on critical studies of heritage and to scrutinise its use in the context of the Global South, more specifically in a country that endured more than 300 years of colonisation. Accordingly, when we refer to negative heritage, it is not only that related to war, dictatorship or conflict, but rather encompasses a broader perspective and a much longer history. Similarly, from a public policy perspective, I demonstrate how histories of resistance to the dictatorship are inscribed in the city of São Paulo and how, based on the concept of traumatic heritage, different social movements and

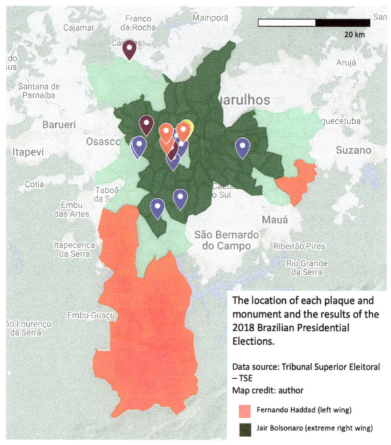

Figure 17.5 The location of each plaque and monument and the results of the 2018 Brazilian presidential elections (electoral data from Tribunal Superior Eleitoral). © Márcia Lika Hattori.

relatives' associations have seen it as one of the material ways to make visible the existence and struggle of those murdered by repression.

Throughout the democratic period, actions have been taken due to pressure from these groups, and public policies have developed, especially in the 1990s and in 2010, associated with greater public debate on the subject, for example through the discovery of mass graves and the resulting investigations, and the many truth commissions operating in the country since 2010. The materiality that constitutes the landscapes of repression and resistance presented here is often barely visible and is, for the most part, sited in places with a very low circulation of people, such as university campuses.

As demonstrated, a considerable number of plaques and monuments are located at two universities. With restricted access, these sites reinforce the representation of the victim as a middle-class university student, a very restricted perspective that has already been questioned by social movements and research related to the topic. In other words, despite public policies and efforts by civil society and family groups to create plaques and monuments, the places where they are installed and the visibility they have in the city reinforce the view of a dictatorship that affected a specific group and not society as a whole.

The issue of the visibility of these plaques, as addressed here in the case of the Volkswagen factory and through further detailed spatial analysis, raises the question of whether this is the most effective way to expose society's conflicts based on a transnational or cosmopolitan model (Bull and Hansen 2016; David 2017).

Nevertheless, monuments and plaques, when located in highly visible places, as in the case of the Carlos Marighella Monument, create a tension that ultimately combats the disappearance of the political memory of the dictatorship in the public sphere. The many objections against the installation of the monument, the efforts of Marighella's comrades and family to preserve it there, and the numerous graffiti, many with references to the dictatorship, such as the 'Comando de Caça aos Comunistas' (CCC) – all of these things may not be pedagogical but they expose a more complex side of the process of democratic transition and the need to discontinue the legacies of the dictatorship.

Notes

1. Author's translation.
2. Author's translation.
3. The battle was between students from two neighbouring universities in the centre of São Paulo. It left one dead and many injured.
4. In Portuguese: Departamento de Operações de Informações – Centro de Operações de Defesa Interna.

References

Agamben, Giorgio. 2005. *State of Exception*. Translated by Kevin Atteil. Chicago: University of Chicago Press.

Aguilera, Carolina. 2013. Londres 38 y Patio 29: Vacíos Llenos de Recuerdos: La Configuración de Espacios de Memoria a 40 Años Del Golpe Militar En Chile. *Revista de Geografía Espacios* 3(8): 98–116.

Ayán-Vila, Xurxo. 2008. El Paisaje Ausente: Por Una Arqueología de La Guerrilla Antifranquista En Galicia. *Complutum* 19(2): 213–237.

Baretta, Jocyane Ricelly. 2020. *Uma Arqueologia Do Inferno: Misoginia e Feminização Através Do Aparato Material Da Ditadura Em Porto Alegre/RS (1964/1985)*. PhD thesis, Universidade Federal de Pelotas – UFPel, Pelotas, Brazil.

Barreiro, David and Pastor Fábrega-Álvarez. 2019. La Commune n'est pas Morte. *Vestígios-Revista Latino-Americana de Arqueologia Histórica* 2(13): 141–164.

Battiti, Florencia. 2018. Itinerarios de Un Proyecto Curatorial: Parque de La Memoria-Monumento a Las Víctimas Del Terrorismo de Estado. Sala PAyS y El Centro de Documentación y Archivo Digital. *Ciudad de Buenos Aires, Argentina. Aletheia* 9(17).

Brito, Ana Paula. 2017. *Escrachos Aos Torturadores Da Ditadura: Ressignificando Os Usos Da Memória*. São Paulo, Brazil: Expressão Popular.

Buchli, Victor and Gavin Lucas. 2001. *Archaeologies of the Contemporary Past*. London: Routledge.

Bull, Anna Cento and Hans Lauge Hansen. 2016. On Agonistic Memory. *Memory Studies* 9(4): 390–404.

Chuva, Márcia. 2017. *Os Arquitetos Da Memória: Sociogênese Das Práticas de Preservação Do Patrimônio Cultural No Brasil (Anos 1930–1940)*. Rio de Janeiro: Editora UFRJ.

CNV. 2014. Comissão Nacional da Verdade. Relatório Final. Vol. 2, T. 5. Imprensa Oficial. Brasil: 1-1996.

Criado-Boado, Felipe. 1995. The Visibility of the Archaeological Record and the Interpretation of Social Reality. In Alexandra Alexandri, Victor Buchli, John Carman, Ian Hodder, Jonathan Last, Gavin Lucas and Michael Shanks (eds), *Interpreting Archaeology: Finding Meaning in the Past*. New York: Psychology Press: 194–204.

David, Lea. 2017. Against Standardisation of Memory. *Human Rights Quarterly* 39(2): 296–318.

David, Lea. 2020. *The Past Can't Heal Us: The Dangers of Mandating Memory in the Name of Human Rights*. Cambridge: Cambridge University Press. https://doi.org/10.1017/9781108861311

Fabri, Silvina M. 2013. Lugares de Memória e Marcação Territorial: Sobre a Recuperação Dos Centros Clandestinos de Detenção Na Argentina e Os Lugares de Memória Na Espanha. *Cuadernos de Geografía: Revista Colombiana de Geografía* 22(1): 93–108.

Foucault, Michel. 1992. *Vigilar y Castigar: Nacimiento de La Prisión. Criminología y Derecho*. 20th ed. Madrid: Siglo XXI.

Godoy, M. 2015. *A Casa Da Vovó: Uma Biografia Do DOI-Codi (1969–1991), o Centro de Sequestro, Tortura e Morte Da Ditadura Militar: Histórias, Documentos e Depoimentos Inéditos Dos Agentes Do Regime*. São Paulo, Brazil: Alameda.

Goff, Jacques Le. 1978. Documento/Monumento. In Ruggiero Romano (ed.), *Enciclopedia Einaudi*. Torino, Italy: G. Einaudi: vol. V, 38–47, 38.

González-Ruibal, Alfredo and Martin Hall. 2015. Heritage and Violence. In Lynn Meskell (ed.), *Global Heritage: A Reader*. Oxford: John Wiley & Sons: 150–170.

Harrison, Rodney. 2013. *Heritage: Critical Approaches*. Abingdon and New York: Routledge.

Hattori, Márcia Lika. 2021. Undressing Corpses: An Archaeological Perspective on State Violence. *Journal of Contemporary Archaeology* 7(2): 151–168. https://doi.org/10.1558/jca.41494

Ingold, Tim. 2002. *The Perception of the Environment: Essays on Livelihood, Dwelling and Skill*. London: Routledge.

Instituto Vladimir Herzog. 2020. *Memórias Da Ditadura*. Online at https://memoriasdaditadura.org.br Accessed 9 May 2023.

Joffily, Mariana Rangel. 2008. *No Centro Da Engrenagem: Os Interrogatórios Na Operação Bandeirante e No DOI de São Paulo (1969–1975)*. PhD thesis, Universidade de São Paulo – USP, São Paulo, Brazil.

Kidron, Carol A. 2020. The 'Perfect Failure' of Communal Genocide Commemoration in Cambodia: Productive Friction or 'Bone Business'? *Current Anthropology* 61(3), 304–334. https://doi.org/10.1086/708843

Kopper, Christopher. 2017. A VW do Brasil durante a Ditadura Militar brasileira 1964–1985 Uma abordagem histórica. Report. 1–138. Online at https://www.volkswagenag.com/en/group/history.html

Lee, Joe and Tim Ingold. 2006. Fieldwork on Foot: Perceiving, Routing, Socialising. Locating the Field: Space, Place and Context. *Anthropology* 42: 67–86.

Logan, William and Keir Reeves. 2008. *Places of Pain and Shame: Dealing with 'Difficult Heritage'*. New York: Routledge.

Margry, Peter Jan and Cristina Sánchez-Carretero. 2011. *Grassroots Memorials: The Politics of Memorializing Traumatic Death*. New York: Berghahn Books.

Marins, Paulo César Garcez. 1999. O Parque Do Ibirapuera e a Construção Da Identidade Paulista. *Anais Do Museu Paulista: História e Cultura Material* 6(1): 9–36.

Marins, Paulo César Garcez. 2008. Trajetórias de Preservação Do Patrimônio Cultural Paulista. *Terra Paulista: Trajetórias Contemporâneas*. São Paulo, Brazil: Cenpec/Imesp.

Meskell, Lynn. 2002. Negative Heritage and Past Mastering in Archaeology. *Anthropological Quarterly* 75(3): 557–574.

Moraña, Mabel. 2012. El Ojo Que Llora: Biopolítica, Nudos de La Memoria y Arte Público En El Perú de Hoy. *Latinoamérica: Revista de Estudios Latinoamericanos* 54: 183–216.

Morgan, Hiram. 1993. Empire-Building: An Uncomfortable Irish Heritage. *The Linen Hall Review* 10(2): 8–11.

Neves, Deborah Regina Leal. 2014. *A Persistência Do Passado: Patrimônio e Memoriais Da Ditadura Em São Paulo e Buenos Aires. 2014*. PhD thesis, Universidade de São Paulo, São Paulo, Brazil.

Nora, Pierre. 1997. *Les Lieux de Mémoire*. Vol. 3. Paris: Gallimard.

Ocanha, Rafael Freitas. 2018. Repressão Policial Aos LGBTs Em São Paulo Na Ditadura Civil-Militar e a Resistência Dos Movimentos Articulados. In James Green, Marcio Caetano, Marisa Fernandes and Renan Honório Quinalha (eds), *História Do Movimento LGBT No Brasil*. São Paulo, Brazil: Alameda Casa Editorial: 79–90.

Padrós, Enrique Serra. 2012. Ditadura Brasileira: Verdade, Memória ... e Justiça? *Revista Historiae, Rio Grande* 3(3): 65–84.

Quinalha, Renan Honorio. 2017. *Contra a Moral e Os Bons Costumes: A Política Sexual Da Ditadura Brasileira (1964–1988)*. PhD thesis, Universidade de São Paulo, São Paulo, Brazil. https://www.teses.usp.br/teses/disponiveis/101/101131/tde-20062017-182552/pt-br.php

Rico, Trinidad. 2008. Negative Heritage: The Place of Conflict in World Heritage. *Conservation and Management of Archaeological Sites* 10(4): 344–352.

SMDHC. 2016. *Memórias Resistentes, Memórias Residentes: Lugares de Memória da Ditadura Civil-Militar no Município de São Paulo*. São Paulo, Brazil: Prefeitura Municipal de São Paulo.

Smith, Laurajane. 2006. *Uses of Heritage*. London and New York: Routledge.

Soares, Inês Virgínia Prado. 2016. Nuevas Perspectivas Para La Arqueología de La Represión y La Resistencia En El Brasil Después de La Comisión Nacional de Verdad. *Arqueología* 22(2): 379–397.

Struck, Jean-Philip. 2017. Informe de Volkswagen No Satisface a Víctimas En Brasil. *Deutsche Welle*, 15 December 2017. Online at https://p.dw.com/p/2pSdP Accessed 21 April 2023.

Teles, Janaína de Almeida. 2015. Ditadura e Repressão: Locais de Recordação e Memória Social Na Cidade de São Paulo. *Lua Nova* 96 (Sep-Dec). https://doi.org/10.1590/0102-6445191-220/96

Teles, Janaína de Almeida. 2020. Eliminar 'Sem Deixar Vestígios': A Distensão Política e o Desaparecimento Forçado No Brasil. *Revista M. Estudos Sobre a Morte, Os Mortos e o Morrer* 5(10): Dossiê n. 10: Dispositivos Estatais e Construção Social de Mortos. https://doi.org/10.9789/2525-3050.2021.v5i10.265-297

Teles, Maria Amélia de Almeida. 2018. *Breve História Do Feminismo No Brasil e Outros Ensaios*. São Paulo, Brazil: Alameda Casa Editorial.

Tilley, Christopher. 2016. Phenomenological Approaches to Landscape Archaeology. In Bruno David and Julian Thomas (eds), *Handbook of Landscape Archaeology*. London and New York: Routledge: 271–276.

Tunbridge, John and Gregory Ashworth. 1996. *Dissonant Heritage: The Management of the Past as a Resource in Conflict*. London: John Wiley & Sons.

Uzzell, David and Roy Ballantyne. 1998. Heritage That Hurts: Interpretation in a Postmodern World. In Rob Ballantyne and David Uzzell (eds), *Contemporary Issues in Heritage and Environmental Interpretation: Problems and Prospects*. London: The Stationery Office: 152–171.

van der Laarse, Robert. 2013. Beyond Auschwitz? Europe's Terrorscapes in the Age of Postmemory. In Marc Silberman and Florence Vatan (eds), *Memory and Postwar Memorials*. New York: Palgrave Macmillan: 71–92.

Vannuchi, Camilo. 2020. Acordo Com a Volks Precisa Avançar Na Reparação Histórica. UOL, Notícias, 25 September 2020. Online at https://noticias.uol.com.br/colunas/camilo-vannuchi/2020/09/25/acordo-com-a-volks-precisa-avancar-na-reparacao-historica.htm Accessed 21 April 2023.

Vieira, Helena and Yuri Fraccaroli. 2018. Violência e Dissidências: Um Breve Olhar Para as Experiências de Repressão e Resistência Das Travestis Durante a Ditadura Militar e Os Primeiros Anos Da Democracia. In James Green, Marcio Caetano, Marisa Fernandes and Renan Honório Quinalha (eds), *História Do Movimento LGBT No Brasil*. São Paulo, Brazil: Alameda Casa Editorial: 357–377.

18
Lampedusa here and there: activating memories of migration in Amsterdam's historic centre – a resource for whom?

Vittoria Caradonna

Throughout the second decade of the 2000s, the name Lampedusa has become synonymous with Europe's migration crises and with catastrophe: a tiny island occupying an area of approximately twenty square kilometres periodically submerged by a human tide of people looking to escape wars and poverty, desertification and disaster. Or alternatively, a human tide made of possible terrorists and sneaky economic migrants coming to threaten Europe's way of life. Whichever narrative we decide to subscribe to, the images are there: boats and dinghies filled to the brim, the harbour or the detention centre crammed with people. Lampedusa is here and there: its name is not only an ominous symbol for people planning to cross the Mediterranean, but has also been turned into something akin to a banner and a brand, under which different groups attempt to push forward and give substance to a variety of claims.[1]

In this chapter I argue that the ongoing 'European migrant crisis' produces a particular use of memory, which attributes to present-day refugees and asylum seekers a role analogous to that of witness. This category is central to the post-Holocaust 'global memory imperative' (Levy and Sznaider 2006; Alexander 2002) and to the human rights paradigm that was born out of this constellation of memory, identity and politics that is central to the maintenance of the European project while also influencing access to membership of the European Union (EU). The duty to protect those fleeing wars, religious persecution and natural disasters is one of the main tenets of this template: but are all refugees and asylum seekers framed as equally deserving of hospitable reception? What are the limits of Europe's welcome?

For my research I employ a critical heritage studies perspective to examine how the heritagisation of contemporary migration functions as a resource, and as a contested space, to negotiate and re-evaluate past, present and future timelines of belonging in 'postcolonial' societies. Here, by combining insights from memory studies, migration and citizenship studies, critical race studies and decolonial thought, I will focus on a relatively small project, called Rederij Lampedusa or Lampedusa Cruises (RL henceforth), which, since 2015, has offered 'alternative cruises' over Amsterdam's canals and the River Ij. The tour guides are a crew of refugees and asylum seekers from different countries who tell stories about the city's past and present as a migratory hub and about their own journey towards Europe. My analysis is based on direct observation of different types of tours over the course of two years (2017–2019), structured interviews with the project's coordinators and tour guides, and the analysis of a range of documents and media: from newspaper articles about the project to YouTube videos featuring the crew, its social media channels and RL's annual reports.

Cultural participation through projects on the heritage of migration ticks most boxes: it attends to the self-image of openness and tolerance of the city in this case, and Europe in broader terms, while consolidating the script of a society open to diversity and it fulfils the criteria of social responsibility of partners while positioning the people running these projects as 'helpers' or 'allies'. But the insistence on sourcing stories from real-life refugees and the use of names such as Lampedusa reveal something more, and this chapter seeks to explore the following questions: what does it mean to materialise imagery connected to the island in the middle of Amsterdam's historic city centre? What does connecting past and present memories of migration achieve during the tours? Who benefits from the experience of being in the presence of 'real refugees' and 'real boats'?

'Most people think I came by boat because I'm a refugee, but I came by aeroplane'

Rederij Lampedusa was initiated by the artist Teun Castelein in 2015 with the support of the municipality of Amsterdam and several Dutch funding bodies such as the Amsterdamse Fond voor de Kunst, the Mondrian Fund and Stichting DOEN. During the spring and summer months, RL offers canal tours for 35 euros per person (previously donation-based) and, for 350 euros, private tours in the form of shuttle services to the De Parade theatre festival or tailored educational school trips (Rederij Lampedusa 2020). Twice a month there is an event called 'Friday Afternoon with *Mr Friday*' (*Mr Friday* being a boat name), which is free of charge and offers a varying cultural programme addressing the theme of migration from different sides, in partnership with organisations like the photography museum FOAM or the storytelling group Mezrab.

Because of their legal position, crew members who have refugee or asylum seeker status cannot receive a regular salary and, instead, they are given compensation through a state-run volunteering scheme called *vrijwilligersvergoeding* ('volunteer allowance') that cannot exceed five euros per hour or 170 euros per month. The other people collaborating with RL are employed as freelancers. The core team is composed of Castelein; Felice Plijte, who oversees all organisational matters; and Dafne Gotink, who is responsible for producing the texts. In addition, RL has also established partnerships with several organisations such as the ZEP theatre group, the Mediamatic art centre, the Volkshotel, which offers guests the chance to sail with RL, and Booking.com, which assists with marketing and ICT solutions as part of their social responsibility programme (Rederij Lampedusa 2020). The operations of RL are managed through the Stichting Gelukszoekers ('Fortune-Seekers' Foundation'). The term *gelukszoekers* is used disparagingly by the Dutch right to indicate that migrants leave their country to find their 'fortune' in the West. The foundation therefore aimed at reappropriating this word and launched with a campaign advocating for the idea that '[t]o us, everyone is welcome. Whether you're on the run from war or simply looking for a better life. The world is ours and everyone is in pursuit of happiness' (Stichting Gelukszoekers n.d.).

The original idea behind RL was to find ways to counteract how the media portrayed the 'refugee crisis' and how, in turn, the public perceived 'newcomers': 'I think that the traumatic imagery that has been used by the media … in the long term it's not helping the case,' says Castelein in my interview with him (Castelein 2018). Images of 'mass immigration' scare people in the Netherlands and Europe, he continues, convincing them that the only solution is to close borders. With RL, instead 'we focus on individuals and we do it in our poster campaigns, in our movies or if there is the media or the BBC coming' (Castelein 2018). When I ask him what motivated him to undertake such a project, he jokingly replies that maybe he is becoming 'just like my father … because my father is a social worker so maybe is in our DNA that if you see the potential of working in a collective, that if you help each other people do grow … you stimulate each other and it's wonderful' (Castelein 2018). It took two years of negotiation with the Italian authorities but finally, in 2015, he was granted permission to transport two boats to Amsterdam: the bigger one, originating from Libya, was named *Alhadj Djuma* or *Mr Friday*, while the smaller one, from Tunisia, was called *Hedir*. Later, in 2018, a third boat, named *Gamela* and heralding from Egypt, was added to the fleet.[2]

The first time I joined a canal tour was in September 2017 at the beginning of my research project and not long after having moved to Amsterdam. I arrived a few minutes late and found that the rest of the visitors had already arrived: it was a small group composed mostly of older people who appeared to be Dutch, along with a mother and daughter visiting from the United States and another person who asked permission to audio-record our guide, Tommy Hatim Sherif (after the tour I learned that this person was another researcher from the University of Amsterdam). The ship's captain, Yusuf Adam Suali, started the engine and, upon leaving the dock, Sherif asked if we could guess how many people it carried during the crossing of the Mediterranean. The answer was 76, in striking contrast with the regulations of the Dutch navy which state that such a small vessel can only contain a maximum of 14 people. Upon learning this, the small audience let out an audible gasp.

The tour paints contemporary Amsterdam as a welcoming melting pot, a unique city embracing over 180 nationalities in its population. As we pass historical sights, Sherif uses the landmarks visible from the boat to anchor his stories about the city, which flourished thanks to the contribution of famous emigres but also thanks to assets accumulated by slave traders and plantation owners. He then starts recalling his journey to Amsterdam: Sherif was a writer and activist in Cairo and worked at a TV station in the city when in 2012 he started helping refugees arriving from Syria. He recounts that when a friend questioned him about helping people that (he thought) would end up stealing their houses and jobs, Sherif answered 'today I'm helping them, maybe tomorrow I'll be a refugee' (Sherif 2017). His prediction came true when, following al-Sisi's coup in 2013, he had to live in hiding and then flee Egypt and claim asylum in the Netherlands: 'most people think I came by boat because I'm a refugee, but I came by aeroplane' (Sherif 2017). His style of storytelling is dynamic and captivating, the jokes land at the right time and the more sobering parts are told in a very accessible manner. The audience and I feel engrossed by his story which, at times, is in stark contrast to the beauty and calm of an end-of-summer afternoon cruise on the Amsterdam canals.

After leaving the bustle of the canals, Captain Yusuf Suali begins to tell us how he reached the Netherlands from Somalia. But he is interrupted by the police approaching on a boat and ordering Suali to follow them to a designated spot where they can conduct their inspection. The reason why we are being halted is not immediately clear: while Sherif explains the nature of our activities onshore, the mostly Dutch audience still in the boat is inclined to protest. Luckily, with a phone call to Teun Castelein, the situation is quickly resolved. As we return safely to the docks, everybody comments on the bitter irony of learning that we were stopped for being 'too many' on a boat that at one point had to hold 76 people.

Since then, every time I have joined a tour it has been very different from the previous one: the rhythm and atmosphere of the tours depended largely on how the tour guide approached the storytelling. During the 'Friday Afternoon' events, presentation would be more or less structured, the communal moments with food and music more or less efficacious. I noticed a common occurrence when guests were invited to ask guides questions: the less knowledgeable a member of the audience appeared to be about the 'migration crisis', the more personal the queries would get.

Memory as resource

The multi-layered relationship between trauma, memory and witnessing shapes contemporary narratives that engender the figure of 'the refugee' as a powerful political and moral symbol: as witnesses and survivors of violence, refugees are objects of humanitarian piety, who are asked to tell their stories to provide testimony of the horrors they endured and of the resilience and courage they displayed during the journey to safety. In this framing, Europe becomes a metaphor for safety and hope, and yet, at the same time, the figure of the 'illegal migrant', bargaining their laissez-passer into EU borders through fake testimonies, is mobilised to justify stricter migration policies and increasing securitisation (on the moralising usage of this distinction, see, for example, Hage 2016; Kallius, Monterescu and Rajaram 2016; and Holmes and Castañeda 2016). But as noted by Gurminder K. Bhambra, among others, it is the distinction between citizen and migrant/refugee that needs to be questioned since it originated at a time when many European states were empires and this legal formulation was 'established not simply in terms of issues of *mobility*, but rather the colour of those who moved' (emphasis in the original; Bhambra 2017: 401).

In the narrative of Europe as 'a monocultural/ethnic/racial/lingual nation', refugees are placed outside of European history. Public discourse skirts around the fact that migrants – almost invariably lumped together instead of identified as Afghans, Somalis, Sudanese or Syrians – come from countries that 'were colonised by European nations or have been subjected to European imperial powers' and that now are still the object of 'international negotiations on global trade and development' in the theatre of conflicts and peace negotiations in which the formerly European colonisers play leading roles (Gutiérrez Rodríguez 2018: 18). Current migration regimes are still based on racial grammars that frame *strangers* to the city/nation/Europe 'to be governed through restrictions, management devices and administrative categories such as "refugee", "asylum seeker" or a variety of migrant statuses' (Gutiérrez Rodríguez 2018: 24).

The *borderisation* of Europe (Cuttitta 2014) and the exacerbation of policies regarding both entry and integration are explained as humanitarian endeavours: such measures are presented as necessary to prevent 'illegal migration' through trafficking (see Pallister-Wilkins 2015). But at the same time, they are there to protect citizens from *too many* arrivals by vetting who is allowed to enter and who is allowed to stay through a variety of devices: from the creation of Frontex, the European Border and Coast Guard Agency in charge of EU border management, to repatriation and even pushback-at-sea operations becoming more and more customary, to the establishment of 'reception centres' in which to hold asylum seekers and refugees for a varying amount of time while they wait for their cases to be 'processed', to increasingly more stringent civic integration exams (see De Leeuw and van Wichelen 2014 on the evolution of naturalisation requisites in the Netherlands). Without this complex infrastructure, European societies are painted as being under the constant threat of terrorism, petty criminals arriving en masse and the dangers of *letting in* people whose culture is perceived as being *too* different for successful integration.

The preliminary stage for accessing refugee status (or subsidiary forms of protection) is based upon a specific type of witnessing, one that relies on establishing the exact amount of trauma an asylum seeker has experienced and the degree of truthfulness of the story they are telling. Didier Fassin and Richard Rechtman point out that the '[r]ecognition of trauma, and hence the differentiation between victims' hinges on whether politicians, aid workers and immigration officers can 'identify with the victims, in counterpoint to the distance engendered by the otherness of the victims ... The assessment of trauma is then also 'an assessment of "good" and "bad" victims, or at least a ranking of legitimacy among victims' (Fassin and Rechtman 2009: 282). Personal memories of violence therefore effectively constitute the possibility of obtaining a ticket to safety,[3] but after the first, prolonged hurdle of obtaining a residence permit, these memories continue to be a resource for turning the abstract figure of the refugee into a subject that is worthy of cultural if not political recognition – and *us* into an empathetic public. This is not only attempted by large and small organisations campaigning for improved recognition of refugees and asylum seekers. Memory is also a resource for a wider governmental project in which the public commemoration of deadly incidents caused by the border regime coexists with the humanitarian efforts of the former colonial metropole/EU: each shipwreck, each disaster is met with a presentist urge to memorialise.

Such responses vary in scale and intent: from a cross made with material from sunken boats exhibited at the British Museum in London to spontaneous memorials. Recently, a relic from the 2015 shipwreck that caused the deaths of more than 800 people has been turned into a piece of art called *Barca Nostra* ('Our Ship') and exhibited at the 58th Biennale di Venezia as a 'monument to contemporary migration, engaging real and symbolic borders and the (im)possibility of freedom of movement, of information and people' while highlighting 'our mutual responsibility representing the collective policies and politics that create such wrecks' (La Biennale di Venezia 2019).

In 2019, on the sixth anniversary of a 2013 shipwreck that killed over 360 people off the coast of Lampedusa, the EU-funded project 'Snapshots from the Borders' launched a petition to make 3 October the 'European Day of Memory and Welcoming' through a series of events held in 28 European capitals, including Amsterdam, where RL participated with its tours in the day-long event (*Snapshots from the Borders* n.d.). I argue that by transferring admissions of responsibility to the domain of memory and cultural expressions (museum exhibitions, films and plays, workshops and conferences), actual political responsibility is dispersed and rendered fuzzy while the policies that underpin the spectacle of the border remain unchanged or become even stricter (on the concept of *border spectacle*, see De Genova 2013). As the official commemoration of disasters gains traction as a tool for self-reflexivity and an expression of regret, the intimacies between migration policies and a selective and top-down heritagisation of the 'crisis' are pushed out of view. So too is the fact that the 'refugee crisis' resurfaces within a specific conjuncture of racism in Europe in which 'colonial legacies of the construction of the racialised Other are reactivated and wrapped in a racist vocabulary, drawing on a racist imaginary combined with new forms of governing ... through migration control' (Gutiérrez Rodríguez 2018: 17–18).

A multidirectional project?

It is difficult to pinpoint the position of RL among the entanglements between institutional, top-down approaches to memorialisation and grassroots initiatives that aim to counteract predominant narratives about migration. When asked about the concept behind the project, Castelein first calls it drolly 'a very aggressive hobby' (Castelein 2018). On a more serious note, he adds that he believes that through the team's 'playful but also sometimes questionable approach', RL manages to reach out to people newly arrived in Amsterdam to learn together 'how they can find their way to contribute to our society' (Castelein 2018). Gotink (2018) recalls that, in the beginning, several people found the idea of using boats from Lampedusa quite offensive: she does not specify who they were, but an article titled 'Lampedusa Boutique Activism', which was published in 2016 in a magazine for Italian speakers living in the Netherlands, focused on 'the ethical implication of using aesthetic representations of the plight of asylum seekers to make a consumer product' (Sfregola and Polo 2016). Gotink argues, however, that RL's provocative spirit is needed:

> Because it makes visible a lot of things that people don't normally want to see or want to be confronted with. As soon as you bring it out in the open, people are like 'you can't do it, it's stigmatising', but the whole concept is about destigmatising if you ask me. Because it's pretty joyful: they tell a story and talk about themselves ... they want to be something else than 'refugees' (Gotink 2018).

The RL narrative follows two main threads: the comparison between migrants of today and those of the past, both arrived in the Netherlands escaping something, both capable of contributing to Dutch society; and the authenticity of their stories through sensorial and emotional registers, engendered through storytelling based on their personal memories and through the tangible reminder of Mediterranean crossings provided by the boats. Karina Horsti conceives their function as a 'mobile memory site' providing 'an authentic experience – not by preserving the boat as it was during the crossing, but by renovating it for use' (Horsti 2019: 60). She argues that, as 'material remnant of the border spectacle in the Mediterranean', boats could potentially contribute 'to make bordering visible to the citizens of a country implicated in the creation of the European border' (Horsti 2019: 61). This dialogue between past histories and current memories appears to follow the model of what Michael Rothberg calls the multidirectionality of memory. The scholar coined this concept to account for how the capacity to remember historical tragedies does not operate as 'struggle over scarce resources': instead memory is always 'subject to ongoing negotiation, cross-referencing and borrowing' (Rothberg 2009: 3); according to Rothberg, collective memories of different violent histories 'emerge in dialogue with each other' (Rothberg 2019: 20) and thus can become a resource to activate against nationalism and populism since they have the potential to create 'new forms of solidarity and new visions of justice' (Rothberg 2009: 5).

In the case of RL, the guides, by telling their personal stories of migration, insert themselves in this 'multidirectional network', and, as Horsti notes, this along with the analogous struggles of immigrants of the past could potentially produce solidarity in the public, who, upon hearing their stories and sensing the physical presence of the boat, would perhaps stop conceiving contemporary migration as 'sudden crisis' and instead look at it as 'a continuum of mobilities that have shaped societies for centuries' (Horsti 2019: 62). But it is another point raised by the author that I find significant: according to Horsti, in fact, '[t]he presumed suffering of those who crossed the border or died at the border becomes part of the object's imagined biography. The "authenticity" of the object then increases the value of the "new" artefact or event' (Horsti 2019: 4) – in this case, the tours.

Whereas for the people working behind the scenes of RL, it is important not to spectacularise the arrival stories, crew member Sami Tsegaye feels that, at times, tour participants 'like to ask about what they don't understand and sometimes they ask too much, questions that are too personal' (Tsegaye 2018). Reflecting on his experience in the asylum system, he shares the conviction that for those joining the tours it is fundamentally impossible to comprehend or even 'imagine life as a refugee' (Tsegaye 2018). Gotink is mindful that during tours, 'sometimes it's also about putting "the refugee" on a pedestal … like "oh you're the refugee, please talk to us!"' (Gotink 2018). She recalls the feeling of 'looking for difference' at the time when she first started to put together the RL tours and was looking for guides with a connection to the topic of migration: 'Who's an immigrant? Whose parents are immigrants? What's interesting to say about migration?' she would ask herself while assembling the team of storytellers (Gotink 2018).

In the beginning, actors with a migration background gave the tours, while later RL established a collaboration with the ZEP theatre group to develop a script and train asylum seekers so they could tell their own stories. Throughout this process, she was acutely aware that she was no longer 'seeing people as Amsterdammers' and that even the famous emigres featured on the tours are ultimately boxed in the category of 'immigrant': 'you are stigmatising them again to destigmatise it [migration]', she points out; 'it's like you are going into the ditch to come out of it, to do something good' (Gotink 2018).

This complexity, while it does not negate the similarities with a multidirectional model, certainly reveals its 'flaws' or, rather, the points of rupture between what the project seeks to achieve – to provide an avenue for being seen as 'something else than "refugees"' (Gotink 2018) – and the narrative it perhaps inadvertently pushes forward. RL also intends to enable refugees 'to find their way to contribute to our society' (Castelein 2018), or at least to give them a sense of purpose while they are stuck in legal limbo or until they are authorised to work. Thus, the self-presentation of the crew members revolves around their agency: through their stories, the public can learn about how they extricated themselves from difficult situations, how they faced multiple challenges after their arrival and how they persevered to make this new, strange society into a home for themselves. For instance, Tommy Hatim Sherif recognises that his work with RL has given him a sense of purpose and opened a lot of doors for him through media attention, which in turn led to work opportunities in theatres and storytelling events. He simultaneously says that storytelling 'is like therapy' because 'every time I tell my story I see more details', but also that these are 'hard memories, so sometimes it's just a bit heavy … but I have to accept it because this is my work and I love my work' (Sherif 2019).

Due to a structural lack of subsidy in the cultural sector, in order to access funding, projects need to be structured around topics of proved societal relevance – such as the *migrant crisis* – and around participatory goals, which must include as much diversity as possible. And although in RL's case storytelling is the result of a collaborative effort, the overvaluation of agency in refugee 'success stories' works in line with implicit goals of cultural policy at both local and EU level: participation and outreach programmes become the stage on which to show successful examples of integration – mutually culturally enriching, a victory over many struggles. With this observation, I do not mean to single out RL as an example of bad practice or as a project born out of disingenuous intentions. Rather, I would like to underline how any cultural or heritage projects that wish to engage with people who occupy a vulnerable position cannot do without the financial or infrastructural support of a system that rewrites agency as a mixture of grit and flexibility – as a completely depoliticised personal asset, which is needed to succeed in carving a place for oneself in society.

In a later work, Rothberg (2019) uses the terms 'differentiated solidarity' or 'long-distance solidarity' for the ways in which subjects who are implicated in structures of domination and oppression can take responsibility for dismantling them. But this move cannot happen within the confines of an event, or in this case a boat tour, that in the attempt at sensitising its public ends up replicating a narrative that presents Amsterdam – a stand-in for Europe – as a safe haven and refugees as a kind of 'citizens-in-waiting', whose humanity will eventually be recognised and deemed worthy of the affordances of safety and belonging promised by 'full' citizenship.[4] After succeeding in surviving the journey, the extended stay in an asylum seekers' centre, the interruption of their family and professional lives, the instability and lack of prospects, now as 'newcomers' they only need to persist and offer up a performance of availability and flexibility to whoever asks for it – to the border patrol agent, the immigration officer, the police, but also to the eyes of concerned citizens and whoever wants to know *more*. Each tour is different from the other, guides may go 'off-script' and conversations could go deeper so a narrative of progress, despite adversities, is not transmitted without discrepancies or moments of pause. But by attempting to redraw the figure of the refugee into that of newcomer – not much different from the many expats living in Amsterdam – RL ends up obscuring the inner workings of a system that is steeped in racial thinking and that determines the price of inclusion through a careful distribution of state protections and state violence.

'Please the guest'

Castelein is aware of the one-sidedness behind that the fact that 'personal stories get more interest' and therefore he would like the tours to be more standardised to avoid the crew members having to rehash painful memories. Speaking of them doing the storytelling, he realises they might 'have the feeling that they have to please the guests':

> I don't want to tell their misery all the time, then it's a sell-out of their drama and that's definitely not what I want. Mo [crew

member Mohammad Al Masri], for example, wanted to do a full re-enactment of his journey. I asked him why he wanted to do it and if it was because he sensed that people wanted that ... and he said yes.

... [c]uriosity is something human and we focus on migration ... that's our topic. So, I understand why people expect to know from newcomers the story of their journey. It's a communicational challenge to turn it the other way: 'we're just another shipping company that focuses on Amsterdam but we have a crew of newcomers' (Castelein 2018).

Each time I returned to the tour, I noticed the audible gasp the audience lets out once they learn how many people these boats originally carried. Gotink underlines that as soon as the public hears the story of how many people originally travelled on that same vessel across the Mediterranean, 'the experience of being on the boat changes and the story becomes very real all of a sudden' (Gotink 2018). She believes that it is important to always give the exact number 'because it's so easy to forget', but also wonders whether sometimes the reaction from the public could boil down to wanting 'to be seen as a good person, you want to perform your own humanity' (Gotink 2018).

Recalling my experience onboard, I share with her my response to the storytelling: 'you're in public, so you have to have a reaction. I also probably did something like that during my first cruise – maybe I gasped, maybe later on I laughed at something else' (fieldnotes 2018). And each time I returned, I took on the role of researcher – notepad in hand, trying to capture with my pen what was happening around me and observing the audience's reactions. The audience varied in composition: sometimes I could spot other academics, while at other times there were families, or people visiting Amsterdam, and one time there was a small group of young people who had been volunteering at Moria – the Reception and Identification Centre on the Greek island of Lesvos known for its terrible living conditions. Around me I could see focused expressions and friendly faces, but also sceptical looks or hands raised to ask what was going to be an invasive question. Shock or frustration or a feeling of powerlessness would meet the parts of the story involving traumatic memories. But there were also moments of levity thanks to the guides, and moments of sharing food and listening to music.

The point, however, is not to determine whether such reactions are authentic or not. Broadly they do seem to follow a specific pattern across storytelling: 'human' curiosity always follows the initial surprise, and the replies to questions posed by the audience elicit more surprise. Curiosity and surprise, whose outward expressions might be exaggerated by being in public, need to be analysed not just as individual reactions but as affordances of the specific audiences, who board the boats in the very centre of Amsterdam. This location, not just geographical but also epistemological, allows for particular ways of knowing and not knowing. It gives people permission for wanting to know more, to access an intimate, bone-deep understanding not of the phenomenon of migration, or the history of Amsterdam as a city of arrival, but of how it feels to leave a home behind and to seek safety elsewhere. Ida Danewid calls this disconnect the 'drowned memory space' that divorces the migrant *crisis* from 'Europe's long history of empire and racial violence' (Danewid 2017: 1679).

My direct observation of the interactions between the public, including myself, and the crew members on board the RL boats has led me to conclude that what needs to be closely examined, in this and other similar projects, is not the performance through which 'refugees' negotiate their presence in the country, but *our* performance as in the efforts made to produce and propagate the idea that there is such a thing as 'bad' integration (restrictive, punishing, assimilationist) and good integration (joyful, culturally enriching and sensitive) and that regretfully both are necessary. Or rather a necessary evil, since the price to pay for failing to integrate correctly – deportation, detention, death – always lingers.[5]

Conclusion

RL and other projects featuring the voices of 'real refugees', regardless of their artistic, social or economic value, gain legitimacy by tackling issues like migration and border crossings that are both topical and dramatic. But RL ends up renouncing any real possibility to 'act upon the present' (De Cesari 2012) by delimiting its role to pragmatism: the idea of mixing bits and pieces of Amsterdam's old and new heritage of migration to change the narrative surrounding 'newcomers' ends up reinforcing the image of Europe as a safe haven and land 'where there is a future' (Castelein 2018). Castelein and his collaborators put real care into their work and into their efforts to establish collaboration with their migrant crew on equal footings. But in the attempt to portray them at once as 'something more than refugees' and new Amsterdammers deserving of a chance just like everybody else, the project ends up reinforcing a strange disconnect: they are like us but not quite like us.

What I seek to highlight throughout this chapter is that projects such as this one, although eminently cultural and without political ambition, are still presented as the Trojan horse through which progress will be ushered into society. And yet, as long as the memory space that connects colonial and imperial afterlives to contemporary migration remains 'drowned', these projects will remain the back door through which to reinforce the global performance of knowing certain things and of not knowing others – of wilfully choosing to believe that 'they are here' because we/Europe let them in.

Here I aim to identify some of the threads that connect the complex usages of personal memories of migration to a wider European (and EU) notion of conditional hospitality that hinges on unidirectional demands for authenticity and openness. Critical heritage studies is moving towards studying how heritage is produced and preserved with a particular idea of the future in mind and taking as a starting point the key issues of our time (Harrison et al. 2020). Reflecting on the 'present moment', the late Lauren Berlant wrote that it 'increasingly imposes itself on consciousness as a moment in extended crisis, with one happening piling on another' (Berlant 2011: 5). A decade after the publication of Berlant's seminal book *Cruel Optimism* (2011), 'crisis ordinariness' is still intensifying and intruding on our notion of futurity. And after several years of a global pandemic, her reasoning about precariousness and cruelly optimistic attachments to fantasies of the 'good life' resonate more than ever.

As promises of security – material and emotional – crumble around us, and yet we keep clutching at them, what does the future look like? And which Europe-to-come can be imagined? Heritage projects that question the processes of 'storying' the present (Hall 2005 need to pull apart the notion of hope for a better tomorrow and expose the exclusionary politics that feed on it. Journeys towards Europe, across the Mediterranean and/or from locations where 'imperial debris' (Stoler 2008) pollutes the lives of people cannot be heritagised without first a journey into Europe, into its skin folds: looking from up close at what we are expected to forget.

Acknowledgements

The Ethics Committee of the University of Amsterdam has reviewed and accepted this research project.

Notes

1. Only in very few cases has the name been reappropriated, one example being the groups called 'Lampedusa in Hamburg' and 'Lampedusa in Berlin', through which self-organised former 'Lampedusans' have campaigned for access to basic rights and services in Germany. This example shares a lineage with the often-overlooked protest practices happening on the island itself. These subversive acts have taken different forms over the years, from arson to symbolic occupations of public soil to lip sewing, but are 'easily contained and neutralised on Lampedusa', where any insurgent push is obstructed from view by the pervasive spectacle of 'bare life' through which the island is rendered 'the ideal stage to naturalise the distinction between the taken-for-granted, politically qualified life of the citizen and the debased and desperate existence of the migrant' (Dines, Montagna and Ruggiero 2015: 437).
2. Castelein's first visit to Lampedusa dates to 2012 and his submission to the Identifying Europe edition of the Twente Biennale of Contemporary Art. It consisted of a tongue-in-cheek video in which he played the part of an entrepreneur looking to sell the 'yachts' from one of the island's landfills which became known as 'boat cemeteries' (Twente Biennale 2013). As observed by his colleague Dafne Gotink, today Castelein is reluctant to speak about this first contact with Lampedusa because he no longer stands behind the video and its content (Gotink 2018). But what stayed with him after the experience was the desire to make something with the boats he saw abandoned on the island.
3. An interesting read that explains the point of view of public officers working for the Dutch Immigration and Naturalization Service (IND), the Central Agency for the Reception of Asylum Seekers (COA) and the Repatriation and Departure Service (DT&V) is a 2015 joint publication titled *One in a Million: Eleven Stories about the People behind the Asylum Application*, which collected the personal testimonies of officers from all three organisations detailing the challenges they encounter on the job. Several of these vignettes focus on the difficulty of ascertaining whether migrants' stories are true and whether their improbability is due to memory loss because of trauma (IND, COA and DT&V 2015).
4. In *Provincializing Europe: Postcolonial Thought and Historical Difference* (2009), Dipesh Chakrabarty elaborates the idea of the 'waiting room' to describe how the idea of Europe as the original site of modernity has been used both to justify the denial of 'self-government' to colonised countries 'not yet' ready for independence, and later in the so-called 'Third World' to specify the period of time that is needed before transitioning to 'capitalist modernity' (Chakrabarty 2009). I borrow the concept of the wait to describe the conditionality underscoring the position of 'newcomers' and the fragmented temporality characterising not only their lives while they wait for their status to be recognised, or for naturalisation, but the lives of their children and children's children who must contend with the label 'of migration background' and its ramifications.
5. Critical race and migration scholars have drawn attention to the various 'projects of illegalisation' that sustain contemporary state power. These not only target migrants through the constant threat of deportation, but also target different categories of minoritised citizens exposed to 'disavowal, disenfranchisement and effective de-naturalisation or de-nationalisation' (De Genova and Roy 2020: 352).

References

Alexander, Jeffrey. 2002. On the Social Construction of Moral Universals: The Holocaust from War Crime to Trauma Drama. *European Journal of Social Theory* 5(1): 5–85.

Berlant, Lauren. 2011. *Cruel Optimism*. Durham, NC: Duke University Press.

Bhambra, Gurminder K. 2017. The Current Crisis of Europe: Refugees, Colonialism and the Limits of Cosmopolitanism. *European Law Journal* 23(5): 395–405.

Castelein, Teun. 2018. Personal interview with Vittoria Caradonna.

Chakrabarty, Dipesh. 2009. *Provincializing Europe: Postcolonial Thought and Historical Difference*. Princeton, NJ: Princeton University Press.

Cuttitta, Paolo. 2014. 'Borderising' the Island Setting and Narratives of the Lampedusa Border Play. *ACME: An International Journal for Critical Geographies* 13(2): 196–219.

Danewid, Ida. 2017. White Innocence in the Black Mediterranean: Hospitality and the Erasure of History. *Third World Quarterly* 38(7): 1674–1689.

De Cesari, Chiara. 2012. The Paradoxes of Colonial Reparation: Foreclosing Memory and the 2008 Italy–Libya Friendship Treaty. *Memory Studies* 5(3): 316–326. https://doi.org/10.1177/1750698012443888

De Genova, Nicholas. 2013. Spectacles of Migrant 'Illegality': The Scene of Exclusion, the Obscene of Inclusion. *Ethnic and Racial Studies* 36(7): 1180–1198.

De Genova, Nicholas and Ananya Roy. 2020. Practices of Illegalisation. *Antipode* 52(2): 352–364.

De Leeuw, Marc, and Sonja van Wichelen. 2014. Institutionalizing the Muslim Other: Naar Nederland and the Violence of Culturalism. In Philomena Essed and Isabel Hoving (eds), *Dutch Racism*. Leiden, the Netherlands: Brill: 337–354.

Dines, Nick, Nicola Montagna and Vincenzo Ruggiero. 2015. Thinking Lampedusa: Border Construction, the Spectacle of Bare Life and the Productivity of Migrants. *Ethnic and Racial Studies* 38(3): 430–445.

Fassin, Didier and Richard Rechtman. 2009. *The Empire of Trauma: An Inquiry into the Condition of Victimhood*. Princeton, NJ: Princeton University Press.

Gotink, Dafne. 2018. Personal interview with Vittoria Caradonna.

Gutiérrez Rodríguez, Encarnación. 2018. The Coloniality of Migration and the 'Refugee Crisis': On the Asylum-Migration Nexus, the Transatlantic White European Settler Colonialism-Migration and Racial Capitalism. *Refuge: Canada's Journal on Refugees, 34*(1): 16–28. https://doi.org/10.7202/1050851ar

Hage, Ghassan. 2016. État de Siège: A Dying Domesticating Colonialism? *American Ethnologist* 43(1): 38–49. https://doi.org/10.1111/amet.12261

Hall, Stuart. 2005. Whose Heritage? Un-Settling 'the Heritage', Re-Imagining the Post-Nation. In Jo Littler and Roshi Naidoo (eds), *The Politics of Heritage: The Legacies of 'Race'*. London and New York: Routledge: 37–47.

Harrison, Rodney, Caitlin DeSilvey, Cornelius Holtorf, Sharon Macdonald, Nadia Bartolini, Esther Breithoff, Harald Fredheim, Antony Lyons, Sarah May and Jennie Morgan. 2020. *Heritage Futures: Comparative Approaches to Natural and Cultural Heritage Practices*. London: UCL Press.

Holmes, Seth and Heide Castañeda. 2016. Representing the 'European Refugee Crisis' in Germany and beyond: Deservingness and Difference, Life and Death. *American Ethnologist* 43(1): 12–24. https://doi.org/10.1111/amet.12259

Horsti, Karina. 2019. Curating Objects from the European Border Zone: The Lampedusa Refugee Boat. In Karina Horsti (ed.), *The Politics of Public Memories of Forced Migration and Bordering in Europe*. Palgrave: Macmillan: 53–70.

IND, COA and DT&V. 2015. One in a Million: Eleven Stories about the People behind the Asylum Application. Immigratie-en Naturalisatiedienst (IND; Immigration and Naturalization Service), Centraal Orgaan opvang asielzoekers (COA; Central Agency for the Reception of Asylum Seekers) and Dienst Terugkeer en Vertrek (DT&V; Repatriation and Departure Service), September 2015. Online at https://www.dienstterugkeerenvertrek.nl/documenten/brochures/2016/11/01/one-in-a-million Accessed 2 May 2023.

Kallius, Annastiina, Daniel Monterescu and Prem Kumar Rajaram. 2016. Immobilizing Mobility: Border Ethnography, Illiberal Democracy and the Politics of the 'Refugee Crisis' in Hungary. *American Ethnologist* 43(1): 25–37. https://doi.org/10.1111/amet.12260

La Biennale di Venezia. 2019. Biennale Arte 2019 | Christoph Büchel. La Biennale di Venezia. 13 May 2019. Online at https://www.labiennale.org/en/art/2019/partecipants/christoph-b%C3%BCchel Accessed 10 April 2023.

Levy, Daniel and Natan Sznaider. 2006. *The Holocaust and Memory in the Global Age*. Translated by Assenka Oksiloff. Philadelphia, PA: Temple University Press.

Pallister-Wilkins, Polly. 2015. The Humanitarian Politics of European Border Policing: Frontex and Border Police in Evros. *International Political Sociology* 9(1): 53–69. https://doi.org/10.1111/ips.12076

Rederij Lampedusa. 2020. Hand-out 2020. Online at https://www.dropbox.com/s/pwlnmwrw zvyr4cv/Hand-Out-2020.pdf?dl=0 Accessed 23 April 2023.

Rothberg, Michael. 2009. *Multidirectional Memory: Remembering the Holocaust in the Age of Decolonisation*. Redwood City, CA: Stanford University Press.

Rothberg, Michael. 2019. *The Implicated Subject: Beyond Victims and Perpetrators*. Redwood City, CA: Stanford University Press.

Sfregola, Massimiliano and Francesca Polo. 2016. Lampedusa Boutique Activism. *+31mag*, 28 August 2016. Online at https://www.31mag.nl/en/lampedusa-boutique-activism-2/ Accessed 24 April 2023.

Sherif, Tommy Hatim. 2017. Personal interview with Vittoria Caradonna.

Sherif, Tommy Hatim. 2019. Personal interview with Vittoria Caradonna.

Snapshots from the Borders – Small Towns Facing the Global Challenges of Agenda 2030. n.d. Online at http://www.snapshotsfromtheborders.eu/ Accessed 30 June 2020.

Stichting Gelukszoekers. n.d. About Us. Online at https://ikbeneengelukszoeker.nl/about-us/ Accessed 23 April 2023.

Stoler, Ann Laura. 2008. Imperial Debris: Reflections on Ruins and Ruination. *Cultural Anthropology* 23(2): 191–219. https://doi.org/10.1111/j.1548-1360.2008.00007.x

Tsegaye, Sami. 2018. Personal interview with Vittoria Caradonna.

Twente Biennale. 2013. *VPRO De Avonden - Teun Castelein - Barca Da Lampedusa*. Online at https://www.youtube.com/watch?v=EG8q4rrmi_I Accessed 24 April 2023.

Afterword

Barbara Kirshenblatt-Gimblett

Heritage studies has entered a new chapter, marked by the word 'critical', and this volume advances that project in bold new directions. 'Critical' heritage parallels developments in the museum field more generally, with the shift from the 'new museology', which ushered in museum critique more than five years ago, to the 'critical museum', which puts those critiques into practice. This shift prompted the International Council of Museums to write a new definition of 'museum' to better reflect a more activist mission for museums.

A similar shift is signalled by the term 'critical heritage'. During a period of major changes in the world order, indeed in the planetary order, heritage and museums are caught in the crosshairs of our state of emergency: the pandemic, climate crisis, right-wing nationalism and autocracy, erosion of democratic values and norms, violation of human rights, war and genocide, and nuclear threat. While heritage is commonly understood as a legacy from the past, heritage management is about the present and future not only of heritage assets, but also of those who are responsible for them.

The present is the context for interpreting the past, and the public has an important collaborative role to play. Taking a cue from processual archaeology, critical heritage is not only about the 'assets', whether tangible or intangible, but also about how we, not only the specialists but also the public, think about them and how we live with the built and natural heritage that surrounds us, whether buildings that are endangered by climate change, while they also contribute to it, or our disappearing landscapes. In a word, that which we designate heritage is part and parcel of our lived reality. To recognise the integral place of heritage in contemporary society is to practise critical heritage.

As this volume demonstrates, however noble the intentions and proclamations, definitions of heritage and interventions on its behalf are highly political, whether the context is colonial or postcolonial, communist or post-communist, liberal democracy or illiberal democracy, at the centre or on the periphery, serving the majority or the minority, the rooted or the uprooted, the territorial or diasporic, during war or peace, or from the bottom up or top down. Heritage critique, a subject taken up throughout this volume, is a necessary first step in the project of critical heritage, understood as a set of practices that grow out of critique and that subject themselves to critique. The goal is not just to do heritage better, but to do so critically.

Envisioning

This volume has the great virtue of bringing together a wide range of theoretical perspectives and documentation of projects that put critical heritage principles into practice. A key theme in this volume is participatory design. Design is understood here as a methodology, a process of discovery, a way to imagine solutions collaboratively. Central to imagining is envisioning in the broad sense of the term: ways of seeing, representing and making visible. Worth noting is a subtle shift in vocabulary from noun to verb – from map to mapping, image to imaging, imagination to imagining. While visualising information is not new – the pioneering work of Edward R. Tufte comes to mind – new tools and new applications are being brought to bear in the critical heritage field.[1] They are also related to the project of forensic architecture pioneered by Eyal Weizman.[2] What these approaches have in common is their performative efficacy, their power to do what they are about. In other words, imaging not only 'shows' or 'represents', but also 'does'. By bringing about something new that moves people to act, imaging becomes an agent in critical engagements with heritage.

Maps are both heritage in their own right and tools in critical heritage practice. As discussed in this volume, they are instruments of 'cartographic reasoning', whether flat, spherical, topographical as in scale models, or digital. Note the distinction in Greek philosophy between *chorographia*, an embodied spatial practice, and *geografia*, a descriptive spatial practice. The former refers to experiencing space haptically as one moves through it, and the latter to 'earth describing', as in drawings. As this volume demonstrates, mapping not only describes, but also brings into being. Imaging mediates landscapes and brings geo-aesthetics into critical heritage debates. How we see shapes what we see and, in turn, what we envision and do going forward.

As Eyal Weizman has declared, 'Mapping is power'.[3] That power is exponentially increased by a wide variety of new technologies. A signal contribution of this volume is its exploration of geovisualisation, the imaging of everything on and below the Earth's surface, both natural and cultural, including historical, literary, philosophical and even theological data, as Anna Foka and others have argued. This broad understanding of geovisualisation returns 'geography' to its early modern status as an omnibus discipline that encompasses the natural and social sciences – geography as the study of all that is on, below and above the earth's surface. Assisted by aerial photography, light detection and ranging technology (lidar), ground-penetrating radar and 3-D rendering technologies, geovisualisers can not only see more and see differently, but also make temporal inferences from spatial array and expose processes and impacts.

Several participatory design projects discussed in this volume leverage the power of geovisualisation to engage communities in thinking critically and creatively about reconciling heritage and environmental priorities and demonstrate how the remapping of memorial landscapes can bring forward otherwise non-commemorated sites of past violence. A particularly powerful example that might be added to those discussed in this volume is The Legacy Museum: From Enslavement to Mass Incarceration, which opened in Montgomery, Alabama, in 2018, as a complement to the National Memorial for Peace and Justice, otherwise known as the National Lynching Memorial. Together, they offer local communities tangible ways to memorialise racial injustice in the past and today. Taking inspiration from the Memorial to the Murdered Jews of Europe in Berlin, the Lynching Memorial reverses the iconic stelae in Berlin. Rather than rising from the ground like grave markers, they hang ominously from the ceiling, each of the 805 rusting steel beams bearing the name of the town and names of those who were lynched there. Outside, lying on the lawn, are the same beams, waiting for someone to claim the one from their town and bring it home. Inside the museum are jars of earth collected from lynching sites. The museum and memorial are in opposition to the many museums, historical sites and monuments dedicated to the role of the Confederacy, the 11 southern states that fought to defend the institution of slavery during the American Civil War. They lost that war and are now also losing monuments to their Confederate heroes as protesters demand their removal, a topic taken up in this volume.

In landscapes 'pregnant with the past', violence is hidden in plain view – whether lynching, manhunts, deportations, or death marches. Critical heritage projects marking sites of violence inscribe that history onto the landscape, making the map and the territory coterminous, whether in the form of a memorial 'ribbon' embedded on pavements to mark the borders of the Warsaw ghetto or of the 'stumbling stones' (Stolpersteine) marking the houses where Jews deported to their death once lived. The former literally draws a line on the ground; the latter pinpoints sites. Each in its own way combines the principles of *chorographia*, an embodied spatial practice, and *geografia*, a descriptive spatial practice. Both disrupt the quotidian by laminating reminders of past violence on the spaces in which we live today.

Chorographia, moving through space, is equally consequential and theoretically interesting, as Lucius Burckhardt's concept of strollology and walking as an art practice attest. Several artists come to mind: Richard Long's *A Line Made by Walking* and Janet Cardiff's exquisite soundwalks, to mention but two.[4] I have long believed that walking is as much a defining feature of the exhibition and heritage experience as seeing. These artists bring forward the haptic sense, the orientation of the body in and through space, as it relates to the visual and other senses.

Involuntary movement and displacement are considered in this volume within an expanded notion of European heritage that includes refugees and asylum seekers and mobility itself as a site of critical heritage. Syrian refugees in Portugal who were 'guests' receiving food become 'hosts' who share their culinary heritage with others. Asylum seekers become tour guides to their migrant experiences, an ambivalent role, in the case of Amsterdam. The ultimate question for 'heritage pharmacology' as envisioned in this volume is 'What makes life worth living?', especially in the face of the devastating loss and displacement experienced by refugees, migrants and asylum seekers living today in various parts of Europe. At the heart of heritage pharmacology is the commitment to make these newcomers an integral part of European consciousness and conscience, a topic explored specifically in relation to Palestinians. Heritage pharmacology is premised on the etymology of 'curate', from the Latin *curare*, 'to take care of'. Caring, both 'taking care' and 'taking care of', are fundamental to critical heritage. In 2018, doctors began prescribing visits to the Montreal Museum of Fine Arts as therapy, and other museums have followed suit, most recently in Belgium.

The digital turn

The digital turn in the heritage field is described in this volume as the 'datafication of heritage', whereby new objects are created from the binary information that digitisation produces. Those new digital objects include digital maps and mapping applications, virtual reality versions of heritage sites, databases of heritage objects and much else. While digitisation might appear neutral as a machine technology, it is anything but, as a critical heritage approach makes clear. As several essays in this volume demonstrate, metadata structures, invisible to the user, often replicate unexamined assumptions and biases, especially in historical collections and those formed in colonial contexts. Those assumptions are consequential for the interpretation of those collections. A first step is to make those metadata structures visible. The next step is to intervene.

This issue did not begin with digitisation; even the physical arrangement of books on library shelves is shaped by such unexamined assumptions.[5] Nor are digital projects that are designed to integrate diverse collections and make them widely available neutral, as the chapter on Europeana shows. This project does not simply standardise the management of information and technological infrastructure. By bringing the digitised heritage of Europe into a single 'space', Europeana also aims to create a shared sense of what it means to be European, consistent with the insight that archives, like heritage itself, are not only about caring for the past, but also produce something new for the future. Critical heritage practices can make these processes transparent.

Several chapters in this volume distinguish digital remediations of tangible and intangible heritage from objects that are born digital, with no prior existence in the material world, but that are powerful agents in that world, blurring the line between online and offline. These self-archiving phenomena – Twitter, Facebook, Instagram, TikTok, Mastodon, WeChat, Telegram – open up spaces for grassroots activism that bring visibility and voice to excluded groups and challenge authorised commemorations and the heritage they enshrine. A vivid case in point is the use of media in shining a light on the role of women in Irish history, relating that heritage in a critical way to contemporary issues and creating a historical record in the process. Social media as it emerges from the Irish case study, in contrast with Europeana, is more of an uncurated and open-ended repository in the making, a 'living archive', in the words of Stuart Hall, than a project to collect, curate and order what already exists. As the Irish case reveals, this repository in the making is not only commemorative, but also evidence of the present being experienced as already historical. Documents of the present are created in real time. Social media posts are at once ephemeral in a spontaneous interactive flow and an enduring digital archive. They have become platforms for emerging forms of critical heritage that are at once born-digital and simultaneously digital archives created in real time in the service of 'future-making heritage imaginaries', as Rodney Harrison and colleagues have discussed elsewhere (Harrison et al. 2020).

Absence/erasure

The Irish case leverages the intangible and ephemeral to make the absent present, include the excluded and make visible the invisible – not through monuments as such, but through live performance, whether marches, vigils and commemorations, or by mobilising memory and discourse through social media. Such efforts might lead to the creation of monuments and museums that materialise the rallied heritage and lend it an enduring place in the memorial landscape. They can also do their memorial work in the opposite way, by conserving the void created by destruction or erasure, what Rodney Harrison refers to as 'absent spaces' and 'absent presence',[6] a reminder of what was once there and the circumstances of its disappearance. This is neither 'forgetting' nor 'defuturing', but rather absence as the form that remembering takes.

I am reminded of Oskar Hansen's unrealised anti-monument for Auschwitz-Birkenau, developed with his team in Warsaw. 'The Road' consisted of a long, black asphalt path, a kilometre in length and 80 metres wide, running diagonally across the camp, petrifying whatever lay beneath it, the diagonal one arm of an erasing X. Everything man-made on either side of the road, the barracks, crematoria and barbed wire, would be left to the ravages of time, to entropy, which would set the biological clock in motion as flora and fauna slowly returned. Consistent with Hansen's concept of 'open work', this memorial offered visitors a blank slate for their individual reflections and personal gestures – the leaving of stones by Jewish visitors and votive candles by Catholic visitors, as well as flowers, messages and photographs. 'The Road' won the competition organised by the International Auschwitz Committee in 1957 – Henry Moore headed the jury – but was rejected by the former prisoners and was also opposed by some members of the jury. Today, every effort is being made to preserve the site, from the barracks and crematoria to the massive piles of shoes confiscated from those who were murdered there – a daunting and costly undertaking. 'The Road' is critical heritage *avant la lettre* – a refusal of the monumental, of official narratives, authorised heritage discourse and preservation protocols, while creating an opening for reflection and personal gestures. In writing about this monument, which was conceived during Poland's communist period, Marta Maliszewska describes critical narration in Nietzschean terms as 'putting history on trial', with the verdict always guilty, and draws on Walter Benjamin's proposal to 'brush history against the grain'.[7]

Generations and structures of feeling

Reflecting on the role of willed forgetting in 'defuturing' and on willed remembering in the Irish case, I am reminded of Karl Mannheim's classic 1928 essay, 'The Problem of Generations' (Mannheim [1928] 1952). As he writes, 'Individuals who belong to the same generation, who share the same year of birth, are endowed, to that extent, with a common location in the historical dimension of the social process' (p. 290). To highlight the significance of generations, he asks the reader to imagine what our social life would be like 'if one generation lived on forever and none followed to replace it' (p. 294). The importance of new generations, in his view, is what he calls 'fresh contact', coming 'into contact anew with the accumulated heritage' (p. 293). This brings with it 'some loss of accumulated cultural possessions' (p. 294), but also 'it facilitates re-evaluation of our inventory and teaches us both to forget that which is no longer useful and to covet that which has yet to be won' (p. 294). Forgetting, as frequently noted in the present volume, is as important as remembering. What would it be like if we were cursed with remembering everything or with forgetting everything and starting from scratch?

The acceleration of change is a key factor in the formation of generations, in contrast with the *longue durée* of the early modern period, when 'the tempo of change is so gradual that new generations evolve away from their predecessors without any visible break' (Mannheim [1928] 1952: 302). In contrast, a quickened tempo of social and cultural change will produce generational awareness, whereas if the pace is too fast, age groups will be too close to each other to form a distinct generation with its own awareness. Some have suggested that 'cohort' would be more precise than 'generation' as a way of referring to people of similar age who have experienced a particular historical event or period. This volume is replete with examples of critical heritage practices arising from the fresh contacts of new generations and their historical formation and consciousness.

Raymond Williams (1977) adds to Mannheim's notion of generations an affective dimension and relates generation to historical location. He distinguishes between feeling ('meanings and values as they are actively lived and felt') and ideology ('formally held and systematic beliefs'), noting that they are of course interrelated in practice:

> Methodologically, then, a 'structure of feeling' is a cultural hypothesis, actually derived from attempts to understand such elements [affective elements of consciousness and relationships] and their connection in a generation or period, and needing always to be returned, interactively, to such evidence (Williams 1977: 132–133).

Critical heritage as theory and practice must account for 'affective elements of consciousness', understood as changing structures of feeling and their historical location. What Mannheim calls 'fresh contacts', Williams refers to as 'new formations of thought', but feeling, rather than thought, is central to his thinking, as he wants to capture something that may be felt before it can be thought. Mannheim and Williams are particularly relevant to the Irish case in this volume, its attention to 'restorative history-making' and a feminist 'politics of visibility', a generational development with its own structure of feeling.

Time

Among the most interesting contributions of this volume are reflections on time, understood as critical engagement with a past that is more open than the future. Inspired by the work of Jan Assmann, several chapters argue that it is the past that keeps on changing, while the future is increasingly determined by the past. In one chapter, water, specifically water in Mexico City, becomes a metaphor for thinking about time – geological, social, cultural, political – as fluctuations in a malleable past that change our expectations of what is to come. In another chapter, 'defuturing' as a critical heritage practice is about curating the past in relation to the present by deciding what to 'defuture' through a participatory process of contestation and negotiation. Among the most dramatic examples are the monument wars, which expose the uses and abuses of a past in multiple presents – the present of the monument's creation, which might be distant from the event commemorated, and the present moment, which might be distant from the time when the monument was created. The Civil War monuments in the USA are a case in point, as noted above.

Dangers of success

I turn now to classic examples of built heritage, the crises they are facing and what a critical heritage approach might offer. Among the most vulnerable heritage sites are those that are victims of their own success. Venice and Florence, as discussed in this volume, have been completely transformed by their success as tourist destinations. Fewer and fewer local inhabitants remain as what were once their homes become short-term rentals for tourists. Hollowed out, the community infrastructure has been replaced by a tourism infrastructure. Public assets have been privatised and no longer serve what remains of the local community. Tourism, which was to boost the local economy and the economic viability of heritage sites, is now the enemy, as heritage assets are sanitised and commoditised. The pandemic has not only exacerbated the problem but also revealed the weaknesses of this economic model and the limits of 'destination management' to address the crisis. It is not enough to delocalise and divert tourist flows, ban cruise ships from the Venice lagoon or pursue a degrowth policy. The authors propose bringing together the 'orthodox' top-down approach to managing heritage and a 'heterodox' bottom-up approach. The transformation of these cities is so profound that even if the built heritage is protected, the intangible heritage of the vibrant local communities who once lived there is not.

*

Critical Heritage Studies and the Futures of Europe offers an exceptional range of theoretical approaches and case studies that advances the project of critical heritage in theory and practice. Arising from a fruitful international collaboration, this book considers Europe not only in its own right but also in relation to other places and to global issues. In the process, the contributors expand the very notion of Europe and how it is constituted through diverse heritage practices. At the very heart of this volume is the participation of local communities in envisioning what the future of their past might be.

Notes

1. Tufte, Edward. 2001. *The Visual Display of Quantitative Information* (second edition). Cheshire, CT: Graphics Press. Tufte's other books can be found at https://www.edwardtufte.com/tufte/books_vdqi Accessed 25 April 2023.
2. Forensic Architecture: https://forensic-architecture.org/ Accessed 25 April 2023.

3. Weizman, Eyal. 2022. *Forensic Architecture: Mapping Is Power* (interview). Louisiana Channel. Louisiana Museum of Modern Art, Humlebæk, Denmark. Online at https://channel.louisiana. dk/video/forensic-architecture-mapping-is-power Accessed 25 April 2023.
4. Dapena-Tretter, Antonian and Richard Long. 2014. Passage as Line: Measuring Toward the Horizon. *Iowa Journal of Cultural Studies* 15(1): 103–116; Cardiff, Janet and George Bures Miller. *Walks*. Online at https://cardiffmiller.com/walks/ Accessed 25 April 2023.
5. The 145-year-old Dewey Decimal System has been accused of racism and sexism: 'For example, Black history is not part of American history; "women's work" is a separate category from jobs; non-Christian religious holidays are situated with mythology and religion and LGBTQ+ works were once shelved under "perversion" or "neurological disorders" before landing in the "sexual orientation" category.' Joseph, Christina. 2021. Move Over, Melvil! Momentum Grows to Eliminate Bias and Racism in the 145-year-old Dewey Decimal System. *School Library Journal*, 18 August 2021. Online at https://www.slj.com/story/move-over-melvil-momentum-grows-to-eliminate-bias-and-racism-in-the-145-year-old-dewey-decimal-system Accessed 25 April 2023.
6. Harrison, Rodney. 2013. *Heritage: Critical Approaches*. Abingdon and New York: Routledge.
7. Maliszewska, Marta. 2017. The Road Monument by Oskar Hansen — Critical Narration and Commemoration Discourse. *The Polish Journal of Aesthetics* 47(4): 129–142. On the concept of anti-monument and counter-monument, see Young, James. 1992. The Counter-Monument: Memory against Itself in Germany Today. *Critical Inquiry*, 18(2): 267–296.

References

Harrison, Rodney, Caitlin DeSilvey, Cornelius Holtorf, Sharon Macdonald, Nadia Bartolini, Esther Breithoff, Harald Fredheim, Antony Lyons, Sarah May, Jennie Morgan and Sefryn Penrose. 2020. *Heritage Futures: Comparative Approaches to Natural and Cultural Heritage Practices*. London: UCL Press.

Mannheim, Karl. [1928] 1952. The Problem of Generations. In Paul Kecskemeti (ed.), *Essays on the Sociology of Knowledge*: Collected Works, Volume 5. New York: Routledge: 276–322.

Williams, Raymond. 1977. *Structures of Feeling, Marxism and Literature*. Oxford, UK: Oxford University Press.

Index

absence and absent heritage, 200–3, 249, 250–2, 354
Action for Climate Empowerment (ACE), 27
adaptation (climate change), 26, 34, 35, 46
agency, 111–12
aggregators, data, 233–4
Ahmed, Sara, 114
Airbnb, 144, 151–2, 153, 167
Alhalabi, Lara, 60–1
Amsterdam, Lampedusa Cruises (RL) project, 330–3, 336–42
'Anglos' and Anglo-Americans, 289, 291, 298, 301–5, 306
Anthropocene, 92, 94, 95–7, 98–9, 103
anthropology, 246
Appadurai, Arjun, 3
archaeology, 179–80, 211, 216
    Central Archaeological Inventory of the Flemish Government (Belgium), 252–5, 257
    Palestinian, 278–80, 283–4
    records, 214–15, 217, 218, 219
archives
    meaning of, 196
    nature and politics of, 255
Ashrawi, Hanan, 265–6
Ashworth, Gregory, 145–6, 149
assemblages, 213, 217–20
assimilation and integration, refugees, 52, 53, 54, 56, 58–62
Assmann, Aleida, 110
asylum seekers and refugees
    Lampedusa Cruises (RL) project, 330–3, 336–42
    memory as resource, 333–6
    See also food practices, Syrian refugees in Lisbon; Palestinian asylum seekers and refugees, heritage pharmacology and 'moving heritage'
Auschwitz-Birkenau monument (The Road), 354–5
authorised heritage discourse (AHD), 3, 34, 127, 306
    cultural appropriation, 302–5
    La Leyenda Negra, 298
    and settler states, 289–91

balanced economy, importance of, 166, 167
Banet-Weiser, Sarah, 194–5
Baraasyrianfood initiative, 61

Barca Nostra, 335
Barghouti, Mourid, 275
Barroso, José Manuel, 230, 231
Bartolomei, Luca Di, 58
'Being in Place' ('Moving Objects' exhibition), 268
Belgium, Central Archaeological Inventory of the Flemish Government, 252–5, 257
Bellentani, Lúcio, 310
Berardi, Franco, 8
Bergsdóttir, Arndis, 200
Berlant, Lauren, 342
'Bethlehem passport', 283
Bhambra, Gurminder K., 333
Bildwissenschaft ('science' of the image), 91, 93–4, 95, 101
Black Lives Matter protests, 6, 291–2
Blake, William, 285
Bolsonaro, Jair, 323, 324
Bonacchi, Chiara, 195–6
borderisation of Europe, 334
born-digital, 188, 353–4
Bosch, Johan Van Den, 133–5
Boyd, Danah, 197
Brabham, Daren, 187
Brazil. *See* plaques and memorials in São Paulo, Brazil
Britannia (Camden), 183
Britannia (Ogilby), 184–5
buildings
    conservation of, 45–6
    embodied carbon in, 40–5
    energy efficiency and usage, 37–40, 41–3, 44
Byrne, Denis, 218

California, 291, 295, 296, 300–1, 302–3, 304–5
Cambridge Analytica scandal, 247
Camden, William, 183
campaign groups, museum injustices, 16
cancer patients. *See* objects and wellbeing (cancer patients)
Canmore database (Historic Environment Scotland), 216
Caracciolo, Lucio, 52
Cárcamo de Dolores, 117, 118
Carpentier, Nico, 218
Carson, Kit, 301, 305
'carto-bibliography', 181

Castelein, Teun, 330, 331–2, 336, 339–40, 341, 343
catastrophes, 97, 98
Central Archaeological Inventory of the Flemish Government (Belgium), 252–5, 257
Chakrabarty, Dipesh, 343
'Challenging Views' ('Moving Objects' exhibition), 269
'CHEurope: Critical Heritage Studies and the Futures of Europe' project, 6–8, 10
chorographia, 350, 352
cities. *See* geo-aesthetic research, megacity landscapes; overtourism and COVID-19 pandemic; (over)touristification of European historic cities; participatory design (PD) and historical landscapes; water and urban heritage
'city grabbing', 165
climate change
    'Moving Objects' exhibition, 268
    See also museums, rethinking for climate emergency
climate change mitigation discourse, heritage as agent in, 33
    authorised climate discourse, 34–5
    conclusion and discussion, 45–7
    embodied carbon in historic buildings, 40–5
    energy efficiency, 37–40
    historic environment sector to be part of solution, 36–7
    risk, threats and adaptation, 35–6
Coleman, John, 265, 285, 286
colonial museums, 3
Colson, Katrien, 136–7
Comarca Minera Geopark, 101, 103
commemorations, use of Twitter, 195
commodification of cultural heritage, 164, 166, 168–9
Confederate statues, 292
conflict in participatory design (PD), 139–40
conquistadors, 292–4, 298–300
conservation
    of historic buildings, 45–6
    of nature, 101
    and overtourism, 168
    paradigm, 145–6
contested monuments in United States (US), 289, 291–2
    Juan de Oñate, 293–4
    Junípero Serra, 296–8, 299
COP26 (26th Conference of the Parties to the UNFCCC), 16, 19, 31
    Reimagining Museums for Climate Action (RMCA) exhibition at, 23–5
Cordero, Fernando, 96–7
Council of Content Providers and Aggregators (CCPA), 234
COVID-19 pandemic
    and digital heritage, 243
    and tourism, 143–4, 150, 151
    See also overtourism and COVID-19 pandemic
Crawford, Kate, 197
'crisis ordinariness', 342
critical digital heritage studies, developing, 256–7

critical heritage
    meaning of, 177, 349–50
    perspectives on, 180
Critical Heritage Studies and the Futures of Europe project, 6–8, 10
'critical museum', 349
Crozier-De Rosa, Sharon, 193
cruise ships, 160–1
Crutzen, Paul, 95
cultural and religious identity. *See* food practices, Syrian refugees in Lisbon
cultural appropriation, 302–5
cultural heritage
    centrality to Europe, 1
    commodification of, 164, 166, 168–9
    digital, and European Union (EU), 243–4
    restitution of, 6
    See also digital (heritage) platforms; Europeana and Europeanisation of digital heritage
'cultural landscape', 210–11
cultural policy. *See* Europeana and Europeanisation of digital heritage
curated digital collections, 233

Darvill, Timothy, 212
Darwish, Mahmoud, 271, 277, 281, 285
'DASPO urbano', 165
'data access gap', 197–8
data aggregators, 233–4
datafication of heritage, 178–81
    digital mapping, 185–7
    maps, 181–5
Decade of Centenaries (DoC), 192–3
defuturing, 128, 355, 356
'degrowth concept', 153
Denham, Tim, 211
Derrida, Jacques, 255, 270, 271–2
design, participatory, 350, 351
    See also participatory design (PD) and historical landscapes
destination management, 158
De Urbanisten, 116
Dewey Decimal System, 358
digital collections, 224–5, 233
digital governmentality, 231–2, 236, 247, 254
digital heritage
    developing critical digital heritage studies, 256–7
    'enchantment' with, and 'overtrust' in technology, 243–5
    infrastructures, 245–7
    meaning of, 178, 224
    See also Europeana and Europeanisation of digital heritage; historic environment; maps and digital heritage
digital (heritage) platforms, 246–7
    Central Archaeological Inventory of the Flemish Government (Belgium), 252–5, 257
    'Enlightenment Architectures' project, 248–52, 256–7
'digital turn', 223, 245, 352–4
Dijck, José van, 246
Dirkx, Luc, 136
Dom Bosco cemetery, 322–3

Duffy, Aidan, 42–3
Dundee Museum of Transport, 21

Easter Rising. *See* Twitter, Easter Rising
feminist commemoration research
Ecologising Museums, 17
economy, importance of balanced, 166, 167
eEurope Action Plan, 228
Elephant in the Room, 21
embodied carbon in historic buildings, 40–5
embroidery, Palestinian, 273–5, 284–5
encomienda, 292–3
energy concept of cities, 96–7
energy efficiency and usage, buildings, 37–40,
41–3, 44
'Enlightenment Architectures' project,
248–52, 256–7
environmental mastery, 71
'envisioning', 350–2
erosion, 92, 96–9, 101
Escobar, Arturo, 126
ethics, and social media, 198
ethnology, 179
Europe
centrality of cultural and natural
heritage to, 1
and migrants, 333–6, 342
nationalism, and critical heritage
studies, 2–6
Europeana and Europeanisation of digital
heritage, 223–5, 353
conclusion, 237–8
content of Europeana, 232–3
creation of Europeana, and Google
Books, 229–31
digital governmentality, 231–2, 236
digital service, 233–4
EU/European policy framework, 225–8
governance, 234–6
infrapolitics, 236–7
introducing digitality, 228
libraries, 228–9
Europeana Data Model (EDM), 232–3
Europeana Foundation, 234, 235
Europeana Network Association, 234, 235
European assemblage, 217–20
European Commission (EC). *See* Europeana
and Europeanisation of digital heritage
'European conscience', 266–7, 286
'European culture', 226–7
European Digital Library (EDL), 230–1
European historic cities. *See* (over)
touristification of European historic
cities
European Library, The (TEL), 228–9
'European migrant crisis', 63, 329–30,
331, 335–6
Syrian refugees in Portugal, 52, 59, 62
European Union (EU)
and digital cultural heritage, 243–4
migration policy, 334–5
See also Europeana and Europeanisation of
digital heritage
'Exile/Nafy - Displacement and Repossession'
('Moving Objects' exhibition), 276–8
Existances, 20, 21

Farrell-Banks, David, 195
Fassin, Didier, 334–5
feeling, 356
feminist commemoration research. *See* Twitter,
Easter Rising feminist commemoration
research
fingerprints, 269
Flemish Government, Central Archaeological
Inventory, 252–5, 257
Florence, 158, 159, 162–6, 167–8, 357
food practices, Syrian refugees in
Lisbon, 51–2
conclusion, 62
food practices and integration, 59–62
services and facilities provided to asylum
seekers, 63
Syrian food practices overlooked by
Portuguese state, 53–8
footwear, 284
forgetting, 355
forgotten women of Easter Rising, 202–3
Fry, Tony, 128, 141
'futurability' of heritage, 8
future and past, 110–11, 127–8, 355, 356

gelukszoekers, 331
generations, 355–6
Genk, Belgium. *See* participatory design (PD)
and historical landscapes
Genova, Nicholas De, 343
geo-aesthetic research, megacity
landscapes, 91
city and landscape, 96–7
conceptual challenges, 91–3
geo-aesthetics, 93–6
material transformation, 99–101
mountain ecology, 101–3
sinkholes and erosion, 98–9
geografia, 179, 350, 352
geographical information systems (GISs),
214, 254
'geological turn', 93
geovisualisation, 214, 351
Ghaith, Khalil, 277
Glasgow Science Centre (GSC), 19–23
Glasgow Work Programme on Action for
Climate Empowerment, 27
Glick Schiller, Nina, 253
globes, 181, 184
Google Books and creation of
Europeana, 229–31
Google Maps, 185
Gorjão, Francisca, 59
Gotink, Dafne, 336, 337–8, 340
governmentality, 231–2, 236, 247, 254
GPS (global positioning system), 186–7
greenhouse gas emissions, 25–6, 27–8,
31, 34
embodied carbon in historic buildings, 40–5
Gregg, Josiah, 300
Gubbio Charter, 168, 169
Gutiérrez Rodríguez, Encarnación, 334, 336

Hafsteinsson, Sigurjon Baldur, 200
Hansen, Oskar, 354
Harrison, Rodney, 8, 111, 149, 200

INDEX   **359**

heritage
 definition of, 210
 dominant discourse of, 3
 perspectives on, 180–1
 role of, 2, 4
 use of term, 177
Heritage Counts, 43
heritage-development. *See* participatory
 design (PD) and historical landscapes
Heritage in Hospitals project, 79
heritage pharmacology, 352
 See also Palestinian asylum seekers and
 refugees, heritage pharmacology and
 'moving heritage'
heritage planning paradigm, 145, 146
Hermans, Klara, 134–5
Heylyn, Peter, 183
Higgins, Michael, 202–3
Hispanos and Hispanic people, 291, 293,
 300–1, 303–4, 305
 La Leyenda Negra, 298–300, 301
historic buildings
 conservation of, 45–6
 embodied carbon in, 40–5
 energy efficiency and usage, 37–40,
 41–3, 44
Historic England (HE). *See* climate change
 mitigation discourse, heritage as
 agent in
historic environment, 209–10
 background, 210–11
 and climate change, 36–7, 42–3
 conclusion, 220
 content creation, 217
 defining, 212–13
 recording, 213–16
 widening scope of, 217–20
Historic Environment Adaptation Working
 Group, 41
historic environment records (HERs), 210,
 211–12, 213–20
Hoge Kempen area, 128–9
'Home/Watan - Wholeness and
 Fragments of Place' ('Moving Objects'
 exhibition), 278–81
Horsti, Karina, 336–7
Howard, Peter, 210–11
Humboldt, Alexander von, 94, 101–2
Hunt Jackson, Helen, 302

illness narrative, 85
Illsley, William R., 213
immaterial and material, 179, 185
immigration officers, Netherlands, 343
Indigenous people. *See* contested monuments
 in United States (US)
infrastructures, digital, 245–7
 See also digital (heritage) platforms
integration and assimilation, refugees, 52, 53,
 54, 56, 58–62
Intergovernmental Panel on Climate Change
 (IPCC), 34–5
Italy. *See* overtourism and COVID-19
 pandemic

Joseph, Christina, 358

Kenyon, Kathleen, 278–9, 280
knowledge production/building, 111, 115
Know Your Place structure, 216
Kyoto Protocol (1997), 31

labour market, tourism industry, 164
La Jornada, 289, 293, 294
Lake Texcoco, 100, 110, 113
La Leyenda Negra, 298–300, 301, 303, 306
Lampedusa, 329, 343
Lampedusa Cruises (RL) project, 330–3,
 336–42
landscape archaeology, 211
landscapes
 and past violence, 351–2
 See also geo-aesthetic research, megacity
 landscapes; participatory design (PD) and
 historical landscapes
Lara's Kitchen, 60–1
Las Casas, Bartolomé de, 298–300
Latinos, 291, 298, 300, 302, 304–5
Latour, Bruno, 94, 217
Legacy Museum, 351
LGBTQI+ community, Brazil, 311, 312, 313
libraries. *See* Europeana and Europeanisation
 of digital heritage
Lisbon Project, 60
Lixinski, Lucas, 146–7
Lynching Memorial, 351

Maastricht Treaty (1992), 227
Macdonald, Sharon, 4, 5
Mackie, Vera, 193
Make Food Not War, 59–60
Mannheim, Karl, 355–6
mapped space, 217
maps and digital heritage, 177–8
 conclusion, 187–8
 datafication of heritage, 178–81
 digital mapping, 185–7
 maps as (datafied) heritage objects, 181–5
maps and mapping, 350–1
 definitions and classification, 181–2
 Palestine, 284–5
 See also water and urban heritage
Marhaba project, 60
Marighella, Carlos, 320–1, 325
Marshall, General George C., 184
Mascarenhas Álvares, Paulo Alexandre, 59–60
material and immaterial, 179, 185
meaning-making, 84
megacity landscapes. *See* geo-aesthetic
 research, megacity landscapes
memorials and monuments, 351–2, 354–5
 See also contested monuments in United
 States (US); plaques and memorials in
 São Paulo, Brazil
memory, 4, 319–20
 and European migration, 329–30, 336–7
 as resource, 333–6, 337
 and water, 110–11
Mercator projection, 184, 185, 187
Metalidis, Ina, 134–5
metaphors, mapping fluctuating articulations
 through, 112–14
methodological nationalism, 253–4

México, 291, 295, 300–2
   See also geo-aesthetic research, megacity
     landscapes; water and urban heritage
Mezze restaurant, Lisbon, 59
'migration-food nexus', 52
military dictatorship, Brazil
   (1964–1985), 311–14
Mission Myth, 302–3, 305
missions and missionaries, 295–6, 300, 302–3
Mission Style, 304
mitigation (climate change). *See* climate
   change mitigation discourse, heritage as
   agent in
Mobilising Museums for Climate Action,
   25–6, 27–8
monoculture, 144
monuments and memorials, 351–2, 354–5
   See also contested monuments in United
     States (US); plaques and memorials in
     São Paulo, Brazil
'Moving Objects: Stories of Displacement'
   exhibition. *See* Palestinian asylum seekers
   and refugees, heritage pharmacology and
   'moving heritage'
museum objects. *See* objects and wellbeing
   (cancer patients)
Museum of Open Windows, 20
museums, rethinking for climate
   emergency, 15–16
   conclusion, 29–30
   participatory thought experiment, 18–19
   reasons for, 16–18
   reflections on project and involvement in
     COP26, 26–9
   Reimagining Museums for Climate Action
     (RMCA) exhibition, 20–5
   'toolbox' of ideas, 25–6, 27–8
Muslim food requirements, 53–4, 55–6
Myth of Santa Fe, 303–4, 305

Nash, John, 187
Nasser, Noha, 147–9, 150
nationalism, European, and critical heritage
   studies, 2–6
National Lynching Memorial, 351
National Trust, 6
nation-state, 2, 3–4, 253
Native Americans, 291, 292, 295–6, 298,
   301, 302
Natural Future Museums, 21
Neimanis, Astrida, 111–12
New Mexico, 289, 291, 292–3, 300–2,
   303–4, 305
Nightingale, Andrea Joslyn, 35

object-relations, 271–3
objects
   maps as (datafied) heritage objects, 181–5
   perspectives and classification, 180–1
   See also Palestinian asylum seekers and
     refugees, heritage pharmacology and
     'moving heritage'
objects and wellbeing (cancer patients), 67–8
   art statement (participant), 81–3
   discussion and conclusion, 83–5
   engagement in clinic, 73–6

   first session, 69–73
   second session, 77–9
   setting, clinical presentation and referral
     process, 68–9, 70
   third session, 80–1
O'Farrell, Elizabeth, 201
Ogilby, John, 184–5
Olsson, Gunnar, 112–14
Oñate, Juan de, 289, 292–4, 305
On this Earth, 271
OpenStreetMap, 186–7
orientation, 114, 116
Ortelius, Abraham, 182, 183, 185
'Out of Place' ('Moving Objects'
   exhibition), 268–9
overtourism and COVID-19 pandemic,
   157, 357
   after pandemic, 166–9
   common features, 164–6
   definition and nature of overtourism, 158
   Florence, 158, 159, 162–6, 167–8
   growth of overtourism, 158–9
   Venice, 158, 159–62, 164–6, 167–8
(over)touristification of European historic
   cities, 143–5
   alternative future, 152–4
   rapid touristification, 150–1
   short-term rental market, 151–2
   theoretical framework, 145–7
   tourism phenomenon, 147–9

Palestinian asylum seekers and refugees,
   heritage pharmacology and 'moving
   heritage', 265–7, 352
   conclusion, 285–6
   heritage pharmacology, 270–1
   heritage work and/as object-
     relations, 271–3
   'Moving Objects' exhibition as journey and
     quest, 267–9
   'Talking Objects' (Palestinian heritage
     quests), 273–85
Paris Agreement (2015), 25, 26–7, 31
participatory design (PD), 350, 351
participatory design (PD) and historical
   landscapes, 125–6
   articulating design space of transition
     landscape, 137–40
   balancing preservation and
     development, 133–5
   conclusion, 140
   design space of historical landscapes, 127–8
   engaging with houses and trees, 135–7
   heritage-development as context, 126–7
   participatory atlas, 130–2
past and future, 8, 110–11, 127–8, 355, 356
path dependence, 144
persecution of 'undesirable' groups, during
   Brazilian military dictatorship
   (1964–1985), 311, 312, 313–14
Petrie, Sir Flinders, 278–80, 283
pharmacology. *See* Palestinian asylum seekers
   and refugees, heritage pharmacology and
   'moving heritage'
pharmakon, 270–1, 272, 280
Pineda, Baron L., 302

INDEX   **361**

Pitt-Rivers, Augustus Lane-Fox, 179
place, historical ideas of, 178–9
plaques and memorials in São Paulo,
  Brazil, 309–11
  contextualising military dictatorship
    (1964–85), 311–14
  creation of, and public policies, 317–20
  non-visible, 322–3
  pedagogy and elections, 323, 324
  plaques, monuments and visibility, 314–17
  reflections on, 323–5
  visible, 320–1
platforms, 246–7
  Central Archaeological Inventory of the
    Flemish Government (Belgium),
    252–5, 257
  'Enlightenment Architectures' project,
    248–52, 256–7
'poison-cure', 280
political iconography, 94
politically informed heritage, 219
politics of visibility, 194–5
  See also plaques and memorials in São
    Paulo, Brazil
populism, 1, 5, 195
'possibility', 8
'potency', 8
power and power structures, 8, 245
  digital infrastructure, 246, 247, 255
  discourse of heritage, 3
preservation
  and development, balancing, 133–5
  paradigm, 145, 146
'President's Globe', 184
printing, 182–3
projection (maps), 184, 185
'Promise/Wa'ad - Visions of Fulfilment'
  ('Moving Objects' exhibition), 281–5
'publicness', European, 218
public spaces, expropriation of, 165, 167
Pueblo Nations, 293

Quinta do Damasco, 60

racial system, United States (US), 302
racism, 291–2
Ramadan, 55–6
Rawls, James, 302, 304
Rechtman, Richard, 334–5
Reding, Viviane, 230
refugees
  Lampedusa Cruises (RL) project,
    330–3, 336–42
  memory as resource, 333–6
  See also food practices, Syrian refugees in
    Lisbon; Palestinian asylum seekers and
    refugees, heritage pharmacology and
    'moving heritage'
Refugio Cultural, 60
Reimagining Museums for Climate Action
  (RMCA) project. See museums, rethinking
  for climate emergency
Relations with Objects project. See objects and
  wellbeing (cancer patients)
rental market (short-term), and tourists, 143,
  144, 151–2, 153, 163–4, 167–8

Republic of Ireland. See Twitter, Easter Rising
  feminist commemoration research
restitution of cultural heritage, 6
Road, The, 354–5
Robinson, Arthur, 184
Rothberg, Michael, 337, 339
Roy, Ananya, 343

Said, Edward, 276–7
Sansour, Larissa, 283–4
Santa Cruz Map, 120, 121
Santa Fe Style, 304
São Paulo. See plaques and memorials in São
  Paulo, Brazil
Sarr, Felwine, 6
Savoy, Bénédicte, 6
'science' of the image (Bildwissenschaft), 91,
  93–4, 95, 101
'scientific archaeology', 179
Series of Collective, Non-Statistical
  Evidence, A, 23
Serra, Junípero, 294–8, 299, 303, 305
settler states, and authorised heritage
  discourse (AHD), 289–91
Sharrocks, Amy, 107
Shehadeh, Raja, 284
Sherif, Tommy Hatim, 331, 332, 338
short-term rental market, and tourists, 143,
  144, 151–2, 153, 163–4, 167–8
sinkholes, 98–9
Sloane, Sir Hans ('Enlightenment
  Architectures' project), 248–52, 256–7
Smith, Laurajane, 3, 127
'Snapshots from the Borders' project, 335
social media, 353–4
  See also Twitter, Easter Rising feminist
    commemoration research
Solemn Declaration on European Union
  (1983), 227
Space Exodus, A, 283
Spain, conquest and colonisation, 289, 291,
  292–3, 294–6, 298–300
statues, contested. See contested monuments
  in United States (US)
stewardship, 218, 219–20
Stichting Gelukszoekers, 331
Stiegler, Bernard, 270–2, 273
Story: Web, 22
sumud, 272–3, 277
surrogates, 232
Swyngedouw, Erik, 46
Syrian refugees. See food practices, Syrian
  refugees in Lisbon

'Talking Objects' ('Moving Objects' exhibition),
  270–1, 272–3
  'Exile/Nafy - Displacement and
    Repossession', 276–8
  'Home/Watan - Wholeness and Fragments
    of Place', 278–81
  'Promise/Wa'ad - Visions of
    Fulfilment', 281–5
  'Talking Turath/Heritage', 273–5
Tayybeh project, 60
technology, 243–5
Text Encoding Initiative (TEI), 249, 250, 251

tezontle, 100–1
Theatrum Orbis Terrarum, 182, 183, 185
There's No Place Like Old Homes, 43–5
This Morning, I Caught You in a Drop on My Finger, 120
tourism. *See* overtourism and COVID-19 pandemic; (over)touristification of European historic cities
transitional objects, 83, 84
Transition Landscape, 128
Transition Landscape Atlas, 130–2
traumatic heritage, 317
Treaty of Guadalupe Hidalgo, 300–1
Tsegaye, Sami, 337
Twitter, Easter Rising feminist commemoration research, 191–4
    'absence' (role of women), 200–3
    conclusion, 203–4
    data access and ethics, 197–8
    methods, 198–200
Twitter, for critical heritage studies, 194–7

Uffizi Museum, 163, 164
Understanding Carbon in the Historic Environment, 42–3
UNESCO, 4, 160–2, 166
United Nations Framework Convention on Climate Change (UNFCCC), 26–7, 31
United Nations Framework Convention on Climate Change (UNFCCC) Conference (COP26), 16, 19, 31
    Reimagining Museums for Climate Action (RMCA) exhibition at, 23–5
United States (US)
    authorised heritage discourse (AHD) and cultural appropriation, 302–6
    México and immigration, 300–2
    See also contested monuments in United States (US)

Valuing Carbon in pre-1919 Residential Buildings, 43
Venice, 158, 159–62, 164–6, 167–8, 357
visibility, 336–7
    politics of, 194–5
    See also plaques and memorials in São Paulo, Brazil
volcanoes, 99–101
Volkswagen, 309–10

Walker, Shawn, 197
Wall, The, 268–9
Warburg, Aby, 94
water and urban heritage, 107–10
    change and instability, 110–12
    discussion, 121–2
    mapping fluctuating articulations through metaphors, 112–14
    methodological framework and methods, 114–21
Waterschei, Belgium. *See* participatory design (PD) and historical landscapes
Weathering With Us, 21, 22
wellbeing. *See* objects and wellbeing (cancer patients)
Whitehead, Christopher, 4–5
Williams, Raymond, 355–6
'will to visibility', 317
Wimmer, Andreas, 253
Winnicott, Donald, 83
Winter, Tim, 111
women, during Brazilian military dictatorship (1964–1985), 312–13
#Womenof1916. *See* Twitter, Easter Rising feminist commemoration research

Yuhualixqui volcano, México, 99, 100, 101